Growing Pains

Transitioning from an Entrepreneurship to
a Professionally Managed Firm

Fourth Edition

Eric G. Flamholtz
Yvonne Randle

Foreword by Angelo R. Mozilo

JOSSEY-BASS
A Wiley Imprint
www.josseybass.com

Published by Jossey-Bass
A Wiley Imprint
989 Market Street, San Francisco, CA 94103-1741—www.josseybass.com

Wiley Bicentennial logo: Richard J. Pacifico

Jossey-Bass books and products are available through most bookstores. To contact Jossey-Bass directly call our Customer Care Department within the U.S. at 800-956-7739, outside the U.S. at 317-572-3986, or fax 317-572-4002.

Jossey-Bass also publishes its books in a variety of electronic formats. Some content that appears in print may not be available in electronic books.

Library of Congress Cataloging-in-Publication Data

Flamholtz, Eric.
   Growing pains : transitioning from an entrepreneurship to a professionally managed firm / Eric Flamholtz & Yvonne Randle.—4th ed.
          p. cm.
   Includes bibliographical references and index.
   ISBN-13: 978-0-7879-8616-2 (alk. paper)
   1.   New business enterprises–Management. 2.   Organizational change. I. Randle, Yvonne. II. Title.
   HD62.5.F535 2007
   658.4′063–dc22

                                                                        2006101795

Printed in the United States of America
FOURTH EDITION

HB Printing   10 9 8 7 6 5

CONTENTS

Foreword   vii

Preface   ix

PART ONE: A FRAMEWORK FOR DEVELOPING SUCCESSFUL ORGANIZATIONS   1

  1 How to Build Successful Companies   7

  2 Identifying and Surviving the First Four Stages of Organizational
     Growth   26

  3 Recognizing Growing Pains and Assessing the Need for Change   48

PART TWO: MANAGEMENT STRATEGIES FOR EACH STAGE OF ORGANIZATIONAL GROWTH   71

  4 The New Venture and Expansion Stages   73

  5 The Professionalizing Stage   93

  6 The Consolidation Stage   119

PART THREE: MASTERING THE TOOLS OF PROFESSIONAL MANAGEMENT 143

7 Strategic Planning   147

8 Organizational Structure   188

9 Management and Leadership Development   214

10 Organizational Control and Performance Management Systems   243

11 Effective Leadership   272

12 Corporate Culture Management   298

PART FOUR: ADVANCED ASPECTS OF ORGANIZATIONAL TRANSITIONS IN A GROWING AND CHANGING COMPANY 333

13 Advanced Strategic Planning   335

14 Managing the Advanced Stages of Growth   359

15 Making the Transition to a Public Company   379

PART FIVE: THE PERSONAL ASPECTS OF ORGANIZATIONAL TRANSITIONS IN A GROWING AND CHANGING COMPANY 399

16 The Special Case of Managing Family Business Transitions   401

17 The Transition CEOs Must Make to Survive Beyond the Entrepreneurial Stage   427

Notes   454

Index   463

This book is dedicated to all of the entrepreneurs, business owners, and managers with whom we've worked over the past twenty-plus years.

FOREWORD

In 1968 my partner, David Loeb, and I embarked on a journey to create the first "national" mortgage banking company in America and, therefore, selected the name Countrywide.

Our company was born in an era of a raging war in Vietnam, the Watergate scandal, and, subsequently, 18 percent mortgage rates and a 25 percent prime rate. At that time the order of the day was simply to survive to see another sunrise.

Since that time of turbulence and uncertainty, we have emerged from a period of relentless and continuous crisis; now we are one of the largest and most respected financial services companies in America.

The basic strength of Countrywide in the sixties and the seventies, as well as in the present, rests with the fact that we possess a culture of best-of-class execution and a core mission of facilitating home ownership for all who desire to experience the American dream of owning a home of their own.

Evolving from a start-up with two partners (namely, Dave and me) to 60,000 employees today, with operations on three continents, has required a continuous evolution from a company fighting for its survival to one that requires professional management and a culture of continuous improvement and proper controls, as well as a structured organization built on a strong foundation. All of this has been driven by a mandate to dominate the markets in which we serve.

Throughout this past decade, Countrywide has experienced its greatest period of growth and expansion, and I attribute much of our success not only to our management team and employees but also to the contributions made by Eric Flamholtz. Eric, with his unique approach, has taken Countrywide from a reactionary management team to one that focuses on mission, planning, execution, and a sound, durable organizational structure. Eric and his team have been an invaluable resource from both a business and a personal perspective.

Growing Pains: Transitioning from an Entrepreneurship to a Professionally Managed Firm (fourth edition), which Eric wrote with Yvonne Randle, is Eric's most recent book. It effectively surrounds the core issues that must be addressed when a company like Countrywide evolves from a de novo mono-line to a multifaceted, multinational financial enterprise.

Simply put, *Growing Pains* sets forth a road map that directs the reader down a path of enlightenment as to the challenges of growth but, more important, knowledge of how to effectively manage that growth.

In my opinion this book is a must-read for any management team, irrespective of size, whose company is experiencing long-term growth or who want to ensure that their efforts result in a successful outcome.

Angelo R. Mozilo, Founder and Chairman
Countrywide Financial Corporation

PREFACE

During the latter part of the twentieth century, as well as in the early years of the new millennium, we have witnessed an explosion in entrepreneurship. Companies in areas as diverse as bioengineering, pizza, computers, women's fashion, chocolate chip cookies, printing, publishing, distribution, real estate, and electronic commerce, to cite a relatively few, have flourished. Some entrepreneurships, including Microsoft, Starbucks, Wal-Mart, PowerBar, eBay, Dell Computers, Amazon.com, Countrywide Financial Corporation, and Southwest Airlines, have become spectacular successes and household names. Many more relatively unknown firms have also been very successful.

In some cases, entrepreneurial firms have led to the creation of entirely new industries; in other cases, they have achieved tremendous success because their founders were able to see their business a little differently. Entrepreneurs, in fact, are responsible for one of the most significant developments of the past forty years: the personal computer. It may seem difficult to imagine that less than thirty years ago, few people had access to computers and that those who did spent their time in large rooms located in laboratories, schools, and businesses. They worked at terminals connected to a mainframe or spent their time preparing punch cards that contained programs. Less than twenty years after they released the first Apple Computer, the vision of Steve Jobs and Steve Wozinak (the founders of Apple Computer) that each person would own a computer became a reality. Today, the average person *can* own a computer, which has the power not only to help the person be more productive but also can serve as a means through which to stay connected to others throughout the world. The power of the Internet provides personal-computer users with the ability to communicate with people throughout the world, obtain information on practically any topic, and buy and sell products—all from their homes or offices. The existence of e-commerce has served as a platform for the emergence of additional entrepreneurial companies all over the world.

While the efforts of some entrepreneurs have led to the development of entirely new industries, other entrepreneurships have achieved tremendous success in existing industries. Firms like Southwest Airlines, Starbucks, and Nike emerged in industries that already existed, but they became enormously successful, in part, by creating new ways of providing existing products or services, or both.

Now that we have entered the new millennium, the focus on entrepreneurship seems not only to be continuing but also expanding. Most leading business schools provide their MBA students with courses on this topic, and many have entire programs dedicated to entrepreneurship.

With all of this focus on entrepreneurship, however, a significant number of firms still experience problems and sometimes fail as they grow and develop beyond the initial "new venture stage." A key question, then, is this: Why do some entrepreneurial firms (like Starbucks, Nike, Southwest Airlines, and Microsoft) continue to be successful, while others (like Boston Market, LA Gear, People Express, and Osborne Computer) experience problems and even failure? Addressing this question has been the focus of our research and consulting over the past thirty years. This is also the question that we seek to address in this book.

In brief, our research and practical experience in working with entrepreneurial organizations over the past thirty years suggests that all organizations experience growing pains as a normal part of their development. Growing pains indicate that the company has outgrown its infrastructure and that it must develop new systems and processes, as well as a new structure, to support its size. When firms ignore growing pains, significant problems and even failure can result.

The purpose of this book, then, is to help present and potential managers and others understand what it takes to continue to grow successfully after a new venture or entrepreneurship has been started. It provides a lens, or framework, to help people understand how to manage organizational growth successfully in entrepreneurial organizations. It also presents and describes a set of tools that can be used to minimize growing pains, which are an inevitable part of successful organizational development.

This is the fourth edition of *Growing Pains*. The first edition was published in 1986, the second in 1990, and the third in 2000. We were pleased with the response to the book and the positive comments we have received over the years. The intent of this edition is to update the book with new ideas and concepts, which we have developed over the past few years, as well as with new examples and cases of companies. The basic structure and format of the book, which has proved valuable to entrepreneurs, managers in entrepreneurial organizations, students in MBA programs, venture capitalists, and bankers, remains the same. Our aim was to enhance and update the book to make it even more valuable for the new millennium, as it is based on our new research and experience.

ENTREPRENEURSHIP VERSUS PROFESSIONAL MANAGEMENT

The basic theme of the book, as indicated by its subtitle, is how to make the successful transition from an entrepreneurship to a professionally managed firm. Some people may conclude that because we suggest that entrepreneurships must make transitions and become something other than what they are, we are negative about entrepreneurship. This is hardly the case. We admire the entrepreneur, not only as an individual willing to bet his or her future on an idea but also as the critical element of our economy and the vanguard of the future. In addition, we believe that entrepreneurship *as a state of mind* is an essential component of an organization's culture and must be preserved. An organization must always continue to be "entrepreneurial" in the sense of seeking out new opportunities and innovating, both in terms of new products and processes. But we believe that at some stage of growth, entrepreneurship is not sufficient and that the nature of the organization must change, together with the people who run it.

The term *entrepreneurship* has, in current usage, taken on meanings that are somewhat different from its original meaning. In the classic sense, the *entrepreneur* is someone who creates a business, and an *entrepreneurship* is a business that has been created where none previously existed. In informal usage today, the term *entrepreneurship* seems to have the connotation of a certain way of managing a company. It appears to imply a very informal approach to management or, at the other extreme, the total lack of management of a firm. Because many initially successful entrepreneurships seem to be lacking in formal systems or procedures, or even a structure, many people incorrectly assume that these things are not required for successful organizations. The assumption, either explicit or implicit, is this: "We got started without formal systems and processes, and we are successful, so we clearly do not need them." In addition, some people point to giant companies like AT&T, General Motors, and U.S. Steel, to cite just a few, where formal systems and procedures have been carried to such an extreme that the company has become mired in bureaucracy. Therefore, it follows that having formal procedures can actually be a weakness for organizations. Both of these viewpoints, while undeniably attractive, are essentially simplistic.

Although it is true that having well-defined and formal processes for managing the business is often not a decisive factor in determining the success of a new venture, we believe (and will demonstrate throughout this book) that developing certain systems and processes is essential if a firm is to continue to grow successfully and profitably throughout its life cycle. In addition, although it is true that many firms choke on their own bureaucracy, it is not because these firms have formal systems; rather, it is because of the way these organizations use their systems. Moreover, some firms, such as Compaq Computers (which merged with Hewlett-Packard in 2002) and Federal Express, were, in fact, professionally managed entrepreneurships from their inception (as discussed in Chapter Five), and this led to their spectacular success.

For some people the term *professional management* has negative connotations. They see it as synonymous with *bureaucracy*. The fact that a firm is professionally managed does not mean that the entrepreneurship must inevitably become bureaucratic. In our view, a professionally managed firm has achieved the best of both worlds. It is entrepreneurial without entrepreneurship being its only strength; it is well managed without becoming choked on its own systems and procedures. An analogy might be a great sports team that has an excellent offense as well as a superb defense. Entrepreneurship is the essence of an organization's offense, while effective management is the essence of its defense. Just as a great defense can create opportunities for the offense, so can the systems, processes, and structure initiated by professional managers create opportunities for entrepreneurship.

The basic message we want to convey is this: *entrepreneurship, as a state of mind and a component of culture, must continue, regardless of the size of an enterprise.* However, the form of an entrepreneurial organization must change over time as it grows and increases both in size and complexity. It must evolve from a "pure" or early-stage entrepreneurship to what we have termed an *entrepreneurially oriented, professionally managed* firm. This is not a bureaucracy (an organization must never become bureaucratic), but it must inevitably change and develop more formal processes if it wants to maximize the likelihood of continuing to be successful. These make up, as we explain in Chapter One, the infrastructure required to facilitate future growth, just as a building's foundation provides the platform for its elevations. If an organization does this and it becomes an entrepreneurially oriented, professionally managed firm (or what we refer to throughout this book as simply a professionally managed firm), then it is likely to continue to grow and develop successfully, just as Starbucks, Countrywide Financial Corporation, and Microsoft have each done. If it does not do this at all or not sufficiently well, then it is likely to experience difficulties (for example, Sun Microsystems, Sybase, AOL), or even fail, just as Osborne Computer, Boston Market, and Maxicare did. We examine examples like these in this book and explain how firms like Starbucks have successfully made the transition from entrepreneurship to professional management while companies like Boston Market did not.

For many people the term *entrepreneurship* has the connotation of a small firm, but that is not how the term is being used here. There are many examples of large entrepreneurships, especially as we enter the electronic age, when firms such as eBay, Yahoo!, and Amazon.com can become very large almost overnight. There are also companies that are smaller in size (as measured by revenues or number of employees) that are merely small businesses and not entrepreneurial in any sense of the word.

When we use the terms *entrepreneurship* or *entrepreneurial company,* we are referring to the entrepreneurial ethos or mind-set and not to a particular size of firm. We are also referring to an organization that has not made the transition to a professionally managed firm. Similarly, when we use the term *professionally managed,* we are referring to a firm that has retained the entrepreneurial spirit, while at the same time developing the systems required to effectively manage the much larger firm it has become. In this sense, we use the terms *entrepreneurially oriented, professionally managed firm*, and *professionally managed firm* interchangeably.

INTENDED AUDIENCE

This book is addressed principally to the owners, managers, and employees of entrepreneurial companies (including not-for-profit companies), to investors, bankers, and venture capitalists, and to students and scholars of management who are interested in the success and failure of entrepreneurships. It focuses on the question, Why, after successful or even brilliant beginnings, do entrepreneurial companies often lose their way? More important, it explains what all companies, especially those at the entrepreneurial stage, must do to be successful as they grow and describes the transitions they must make to survive. Case studies of entrepreneurial companies at different stages of growth, drawn from a wide variety of industries, are included to illustrate different aspects of the transitions that must be made. The cases also show how the frameworks provided in this book can be used as conceptual maps of what needs to be done by an organization at each developmental stage. In addition, the book specifies the adjustments the founder or CEO of an entrepreneurial company needs to make so that he or she can grow with the organization, as did Howard Schultz at Starbucks, and not be left behind.

The book is also addressed to those interested not only in entrepreneurships but in established companies as well. Although it has been positioned primarily to help managers and scholars understand the problems and processes related to managing the transition from an entrepreneurship to a professionally managed firm, the underlying framework and content are applicable to all organizations, including large companies. (See, for example, the Foreword by Angelo Mozilo, founder and CEO of Countrywide Financial Corporation, about the relevance and application of the concepts and approach in his company.)

Specifically, the book is based on two different but related conceptual frameworks: (1) an organizational effectiveness model and (2) an organizational life-cycle model. The organizational effectiveness model, termed the Pyramid of Organizational Development (discussed in Chapter One) explains the variables that must be managed by companies to give them the optimal (most likely) chance of long-term success. The life-cycle model (discussed in Chapter Two and in Chapter Fourteen) identifies seven stages of growth from a new venture (corporate birth) to an established organization in decline and requiring revitalization. The book can, therefore, be viewed as providing a comprehensive framework for managing a company throughout its life cycle but especially as focusing on the stages of growth after its inception and until it reaches maturity as a professionally managed firm.

The book is also appropriate for companies that think of themselves as professionally managed but have begun to lose some of their momentum and may even have lost their entrepreneurial spirit. It can show them what has to be done to make the transition to an entrepreneurially oriented, professionally managed firm rather than a bureaucracy. Accordingly, we cite examples ranging from relatively small new ventures and medium-sized companies to very large organizations such as IBM.

OVERVIEW OF THE CONTENTS

This book is divided into five parts. Part One presents a conceptual framework for managers of entrepreneurial organizations to use in understanding what is happening to their firms and what they must do to reach the next stage successfully. The framework includes the six key factors for developing an effective, profitable organization and descriptions of the successive stages of growth at which transitions must be made. Part One also describes the organizational growing pains that are common in rapidly growing firms and presents a method for assessing the extent to which an organization suffers from them.

Part Two presents a series of organizational case studies as a vehicle for examining what an organization must do to develop successfully from one stage to the next. Specifically, Part Two presents examples of companies at each of the first four critical stages of growth, from new venture to organizational maturity. It describes the problems those companies faced and explains how such problems need to be dealt with as an organization grows.

Part Three presents the most significant managerial tools that entrepreneurial organizations must master if they are to grow and develop successfully and profitably: strategic planning, organizational structure, management development, organizational control, leadership, and corporate culture management. Although the tools of planning, structural design, and the like may be, at least superficially, familiar to some readers, our approach to these key components of a management system differs in some respects from other books; there is also an integrative aspect to the set of management systems components overall.

Part Four deals with some advanced issues and topics relating to organizational development and transitions. It includes a discussion of the advanced aspects of strategic planning. It also presents a preview of the problems to be faced by companies as they grow beyond the early entrepreneurial stages to the more advanced stages of organizational growth. In addition, it deals with the questions and issues involved for those entrepreneurial companies that decide to "go public." It is intended to be an introduction rather than a comprehensive treatment of these issues.

Part Five deals with the personal aspect of organizational transitions. It discusses the issues involved in managing and growing family businesses. It also deals with the issues facing the presidents or CEOs of entrepreneurial organizations; it is designed to help them focus on what needs to be done to successfully grow their firms and to help them grow personally along with their firms.

This fourth edition of *Growing Pains* differs from the third edition in several important respects. Although the overall direction and thrust of the book have been retained, all chapters have been revised to update material and references to companies, as appropriate. However, in some instances we have kept certain examples (such as Osborne Computers) and cases (Metro Realty and Tempo Products) because they are "classic," or prototypical, of the points we want to make, or because there are no better current examples, or because of their historical significance. Three new chapters have been added, dealing with the issues of advanced strategic planning, family business transitions, and going public. In addition, we have cited new empirical research that has been published during the past several years that supports the framework and ideas presented in the book.

Throughout the book, several new cases, examples, or "mini-cases" of companies dealing successfully or unsuccessfully with transitional issues have been added, including examples from companies such as Infogix (software), 99 Cents Only Stores (discount merchandise), PeopleSupport (outsourcing), and Countrywide Financial Corporation (mortgage and finance). New conceptual material has also been added to most of the existing chapters. New mini-cases and international examples of entrepreneurship have been added because of the widespread flourishing of entrepreneurship around the globe, including examples from Europe, Australia, and Asia. Chapter Thirteen includes a comprehensive example of an entrepreneur who was born in India and developed a very successful company in the United States. A number of cases (including Starbucks, Osborne Computer, Apple Computer, and Bell-Carter Foods) are used throughout the book to provide a consistent frame of reference for the perspective being developed. To a considerable extent, we have drawn on examples of companies where we have in-depth knowledge. In some cases, to protect the privacy of individuals and organizations, we have disguised the company's and individuals' names.

Entrepreneurship is a driving force in today's economy. Accordingly, entrepreneurial companies must be successful, not only for the good of the entrepreneurs and their employees but also because of the benefits to the general economy. Unfortunately, too many entrepreneurial companies flounder after promising or even brilliant beginnings. Companies such as Boston Market, People Express, Maxicare, and Osborne Computer were all once cited as great entrepreneurial successes, yet all have failed. In the face of these failures and difficulties, some cynical observers have even begun to define an entrepreneur as someone, such as Adam Osborne (who created the first portable computer) or Robert Campeau (a Canadian shopping center developer), who can start and build a company to a given level and then watch it fail.

Our experience in doing research and consulting with entrepreneurial companies has led us to write this book to help present and potential entrepreneurs, as well as their employees, advisers, and venture capitalists, understand the pitfalls typically faced by entrepreneurial organizations at different stages of growth and to explain how to make the successful transition to a professionally managed firm. It is also intended to help governmental policymakers understand the causes of the premature demise of entrepreneurial companies that are so vital to our economy. Although this book will not solve all the problems faced by entrepreneurial companies, our experience, as well as the positive feedback we received about the previous editions, indicates that if the ideas and methods described in this book are applied, organizations will have a significantly improved likelihood of continued success.

To enhance the value of the book, as well as to illustrate our ideas, we use numerous examples of both successful and unsuccessful—or at least relatively less successful—firms. We are not asserting that the successful companies will always continue to be successful. Indeed, if they do not continue to focus on developing their internal capabilities to meet the demands of their own development, their fortunes can be expected to change. For example, Compaq Computer, which was successful for a very long time, ultimately experienced difficulties and was purchased by Hewlett-Packard. Unfortunately, nothing is built to last forever. This is why Stage VII in our life-cycle model (see Chapter Fourteen) deals with decline and revitalization. However, there are things that can be done to increase the probability of organizational success at all stages of growth. That is the purpose of our book—to help people interested in building entrepreneurial organizations do so in ways that help increase the probability of organizational success and reduce the probability of failure.

ACKNOWLEDGMENTS

This work is a product of many years of action research and consultation with many different organizations. These range from new ventures to members of the Fortune 500. They were our research "laboratory." Simply stated, the most significant ideas that underlie this book were the products of observing, analyzing, and conceptualizing what actually happened in successful and unsuccessful organizations as they grew. The book could not have been written without having had access to those companies of various sizes, in different industries, with different degrees of success. Accordingly, we are greatly indebted to the CEOs, presidents, senior managers, and others who invited us to serve as researchers, consultants, or advisers for their organizations. (Many of these companies are not mentioned by name, to preserve their privacy. In some cases, fictitious names are used; in others, examples are cited without the company being named at all.)

First we want to thank Angelo Mozilo, cofounder, chairman, and CEO of Countrywide Financial Corporation, for his very gracious Foreword. We are honored by his comments and his willingness to write the Foreword to this edition.

We also want to thank Madhavan Nayar, founder and company leader of Infogix, for permitting us to prepare the case included in Chapter Thirteen on the transformation of his company.

We also want to thank Jeff Haines, founder and former CEO of Royce Medical Corporation, for allowing us to describe his firm's strategic planning process in Chapter Seven. We appreciate the time he took to review and provide feedback on the case.

Chapter Nine, dealing with the role of management development in the transition from entrepreneurship to professional management, describes the management development program that Bell-Carter Foods has used over the past ten-plus years to help develop its management team. We wish to thank Tim and Jud Carter, CEO and president of the company, for allowing us to describe this program and the results they have achieved. We also thank them for allowing us to share, in more depth, how they addressed the challenges of making the transition to professional management in a family business (Chapter Sixteen).

In Chapter Ten, we describe Southern California Presbyterian Homes' performance appraisal. We wish to thank Jerry Dingivan, CEO, and the members of his management team for letting us share the approach they used to develop a very effective, goal-driven approach to their appraisal process.

We want to thank 99 Cents Only Stores for permitting use to write a case about them in Chapter Fifteen. We also want to thank Lance Rosenzweig for permitting us to do a case about the process of going public at his company, PeopleSupport. Kathryn Schreiner assisted with the preparation of the PeopleSupport case.

Leslie Ray, then a Ph.D. candidate in UCLA's Anderson Graduate School of Management, did research that served as the basis for the descriptions of Compaq Computer, Mrs. Fields' Cookies, and Federal Express.

Quentin Fleming, then a consultant at Management Systems Consulting Corporation, assisted with several of the case studies that have been included in Chapter Eight on organizational structure.

The late Jason Richler, then a consultant with Management Systems, provided input on the Grange, Inc. case included in Chapter Three.

The Price Institute for Entrepreneurial Studies, under the direction of Alfred E. Osborne, provided financial support for research assistance to prepare some of the case studies presented in this book. We both have used this book as a text in a course we designed titled "Managing Entrepreneurial Organizations" in the Anderson School of Management at UCLA for many years.

The book has also been used in management development programs for our clients offered by our firm, Management Systems Consulting Corporation.

We want to thank Jennifer Han for help in preparation of the final manuscript formatting for this book at Management Systems Consulting Corporation. Laurie Flamholtz also assisted with this preparation. Special thanks go to Michel Tan, M.D., who saved days of work with a skillful computer data recovery at a critical time!

The data presented in Chapter Three are drawn from the organizational effectiveness database compiled by Management Systems Consulting Corporation. They are derived from a survey developed by Eric Flamholtz. Lily Arguello, then a junior consultant with Management Systems, assisted in the preparation and interpretation of the data (updated from the second edition) dealing with organizational growing pains (Chapter Three).

We are indebted to the Jossey-Bass staff for the highly professional and competent way in which this project was handled. They were enthusiastic about this book from its inception and supportive throughout its execution.

We also wish to acknowledge Diana Troik, executive vice president, Management Systems Consulting Corporation. She provided professional support throughout the development of this book, including the prior editions.

Although we acknowledge with gratitude the contributions of all those cited, we remain responsible for the book and its imperfections.

Eric G. Flamholtz
Yvonne Randle
Los Angeles
September, 2006

PART ONE

A FRAMEWORK FOR DEVELOPING SUCCESSFUL ORGANIZATIONS

T he first challenge entrepreneurs face is that of establishing a successful new venture. The basic skills necessary to meet this challenge are the ability to recognize a market need and the ability to develop (or to hire other people to develop) a product or service appropriate for satisfying that need.

If these two fundamental things are done well, a fledgling enterprise is likely to experience rapid growth. At this point, whether the entrepreneur recognizes it or not, the game begins to change. The firm's success creates its next set of problems and challenges to survival.

As a result of expanding sales, the firm's resources become stretched very thin. A seemingly perpetual and insatiable need arises for more inventory, space, equipment, people and funds. Day-to-day activities are greatly sped up and may even take on a frenzied quality.

The firm's operational systems (those needed to facilitate day-to-day activities), such as marketing, production or service delivery, accounting, credit, collections, and personnel, typically are overwhelmed by the sudden surge of activity. There is little time to think, and little or no planning takes place because most plans quickly become obsolete. People become high on their own adrenaline and merely react to the rush of activity.

At this point the firm usually begins to experience some, perhaps all, of the following organizational growing pains:

- People feel that there are not enough hours in the day.
- People spend too much time "putting out fires."

- Many people are not aware of what others are doing.

- People lack understanding of where the firm is headed.

- There are not enough good managers.

- People feel that "I have to do it myself if I want to get it done correctly."

- Most people feel that the firm's meetings are a waste of time.

- When plans are made there is very little follow-up, so things just don't get done.

- Some people feel insecure about their place in the firm.

- The firm has continued to grow in sales, but not in profits.

These growing pains are not merely problems in and of themselves; they are a symptom of an "organizational development gap" between the infrastructure required by the organization and the infrastructure it actually has. An organization's infrastructure consists of the operational support systems and management systems required to enable the organization to function profitably on a short- and long-term basis. As described more fully in Chapter One, a company's operational support systems consist of all the day-to-day systems required to produce a product or deliver a service and to function on a day-to-day basis. Management systems consist of the firm's planning system, organization structure, management development system, and control-performance management systems. These are the systems required to manage the overall enterprise on a long-term basis.

THE SECOND CHALLENGE FOR ENTREPRENEURS

Once a firm has identified a market and has begun to produce products or services to meet the needs of customers within that market, it will begin to grow. As the firm grows, it will be faced with the need to make a fundamental transformation or metamorphosis from the spontaneous, ad hoc, free-spirited enterprise that it has been to a more formally planned, organized, and disciplined entity. The firm must move from one in which

- There are only informal plans, and people simply react to events to one in which formal planning is a way of life.

- Jobs and responsibilities are undefined to one in which there is some degree of definition of responsibilities and mutually exclusive roles.

- There is no accountability and no control system to one in which there are objectives, goals, measures, and related rewards specified in advance, as well as formal performance appraisal systems.

- There is only on-the-job training to one in which there are formal management development programs.

- There is no budget to one in which there are budgets, reports, and variances.

- Profit simply happens to one in which there is an explicit profit goal to be achieved.

In brief, the firm must make the transition from an entrepreneurship to an entrepreneurially oriented, professionally managed organization.

As we see in Chapter Seventeen, this is a time when the very personality traits that made the founder-entrepreneur so successful initially can lead to organizational demise. Most entrepreneurs have either a sales or technical background, or they know a particular industry well. Entrepreneurs typically want things done in their own way. They may be more intelligent or have better intuition than their employees, who come to rely on their bosses' omnipotence. Typical entrepreneurs tend to be doers rather than managers, and most have not had formal management training, although they may have read the current management best-sellers. They like to be free of corporate restraints. They reject meetings, written plans, detailed organization of time, and budgets as the trappings of bureaucracy. Most insidiously, they think, "We got here without these things, so why do we need them?"

Unfortunately, at the stage of corporate development we are discussing, the nature of the organization has changed—and so must the firm's senior management. The owner-entrepreneur can deal with the situation in one of five different ways. He or she can

- Try to develop new skills and behavior patterns—difficult but quite possible.

- Retire, as Phil Knight did at Nike, and let others bring in a professional manager to run the organization.

- Move up to chairperson, as Howard Schultz did at Starbucks, and turn over operations to a professional manager while still staying involved.

- Continue to operate as before and ignore the problems, hoping they will evaporate.

- Sell out, as Steven Jobs did in 1985 at Apple Computer, and start another entrepreneurial company.

Founder-entrepreneurs typically experience great difficulty in relinquishing control of their businesses. Some try to change their skills and behavior but fail. Others merely give the illusion of turning the organization over to professional managers. For example, one successful entrepreneur brought two very highly paid and experienced managers into his firm, made a great flourish about the transition, and then proceeded to turn them into managerial eunuchs who lacked real power. After they had (predictably) failed, he was able to "reluctantly" resume control of the enterprise and plead that he had made every effort but the business obviously could not do without him.

There is no one pattern for a successful transition from an entrepreneurship to a professionally managed firm. Whatever path is followed, the key to a successful change is for the entrepreneur to recognize that a new stage in the organization's life cycle has been reached and that the former mode of operation will no longer be effective.

MAKING AN ORGANIZATIONAL TRANSITION

Once the entrepreneur has recognized that the company's mode of operation must be changed, the inevitable question arises: "What should we do to take the organization successfully to the next stage of growth?" To answer this question satisfactorily, it is necessary to understand that there are predictable stages of organizational growth, certain key developmental tasks that must be performed by the organization at each growth stage, and certain critical problems that organizations typically face as they grow. This understanding, in turn, requires a framework within which the determinants of successful organizational development may be placed. We present such a framework in Part One of this book.

Chapter One presents a holistic framework for successful organizational development. It deals with the issue of what makes an organization successful and profitable. Drawing on research and experience from consulting with many organizations, it presents a systematic approach to understanding the six critical variables in organizational effectiveness. It examines the six critical tasks of organizational development and describes what must be done to accomplish each task. These six variables or tasks are conceptualized as a Pyramid of Organizational Development.

Chapter Two identifies seven different stages of organizational growth, from the inception of a new venture through the early maturity of an entrepreneurial organization, and to the ultimate decline and revitalization of a company. The chapter then examines the first four stages of growth (the remaining three are discussed in Chapter Fourteen) and examines the relative emphasis that must be placed on each of the six critical developmental tasks at each stage of the organization's growth.

Chapter Three examines the growing pains that all developing organizations experience. It provides a method for assessing these growing pains and determining their severity. Senior managers need to be able to recognize such growing pains as symptoms of the need to make changes in their organizations.

Taken together, the ideas in Chapters One, Two, and Three provide a conceptual map of the tasks that must be focused on to successfully manage and develop an entrepreneurial organization. Part One also provides a guide for analyzing and planning the transitions that must be made in moving a company from one developmental stage to the next.

CHAPTER ONE

How to Build Successful Companies

The Pyramid of Organizational Development

The senior management of a rapidly growing entrepreneurial company must simultaneously cope with its endless day-to-day problems and keep an eye on its future direction. Furthermore, the managers of most such companies are going through the process of building a company for the first time. This is about as easy as navigating uncharted waters in a leaky rowboat with an inexperienced crew while surrounded by a school of sharks. The sea is unfamiliar, the boat is clumsy, the skills needed are not readily apparent or not fully developed, and there is a constant reminder of the high costs of an error in judgment.

Just as the crew of such a boat might wish urgently for a guide to help them with navigation, training, and ship repair, the senior managers of an entrepreneurial company may frequently wish for a guide to help them build their firm. The crew might also be glad to know that others before them have made the voyage successfully and to hear some of the lessons that the other voyagers learned in the process.

This chapter attempts to provide a guide for senior managers who are faced with the special challenge of building an entrepreneurial company. It gives a framework or lens for understanding and managing the critical tasks that an organization must perform at each stage of its growth. The framework presented in this chapter is an outgrowth of over three decades of research and consulting experience with organizations who have faced and dealt with the need to make a transition from one stage of growth to the next.

As we explain more fully in this chapter, as well as in Chapters Seven and Thirteen, which deal with strategic planning and organizational development, this framework can be used as a template to plan to build an organization such as a new venture. It can also be used as a strategic lens through which to evaluate the effectiveness of an existing organization in terms of its strengths and areas required for further organizational development.

THE NATURE OF ORGANIZATIONAL DEVELOPMENT

Organizational development is the process of planning and implementing changes in the overall capabilities of an enterprise in order to increase its operating effectiveness and profitability. It involves thinking about a business organization (or any organization, for that matter) as a whole and planning necessary changes in certain key areas in order to help a company progress successfully from one stage of growth to the next. The key areas that require focus include the firm's business foundation, on which the rest of the firm's systems and processes are built, as well as six key organizational development tasks.

The Foundation of a Business

All business or economic organizations are based on a conceptual foundation that is either explicitly or implicitly defined and consists of three components: (1) a *business definition* or *concept*, (2) a *strategic mission*, and (3) a *core strategy*. We deal with the development of a business foundation in depth in Chapters Seven and Thirteen, when we address strategic planning. However, at this point we introduce the key dimensions of the business foundation as a basis for understanding the process of building a successful organization over the long term.

Business Definition or Concept. The business concept defines what the purpose of the business is—what the organization is in business to do. For example, Coca-Cola is in the beverage business, Federal Express is in the package transportation business, Countrywide Financial Corporation is in the financial services (including mortgages) business, and Disney is in the entertainment business. In the nonprofit arena, Head Start agencies are in the business of providing comprehensive education, health, nutrition, and parent-involvement services to low-income children and their families, while Southern California Presbyterian Homes (whose performance management system is described in Chapter Eight), is in the business of meeting the service and housing needs of older adults.

Strategic Mission. The second component of the business foundation is the strategic mission, which defines what the company will try to achieve over a defined period of time (for example, five years or longer). For Countrywide Financial Corporation the long-term strategic mission was to dominate the mortgage business and become the number-one mortgage lender in the United States. For Starbucks the strategic mission articulated in 1995 was to become recognized as the leading brand of specialty retail coffee in the United States.

Core Strategy. The third component of the business foundation is the core strategy. This is the central theme around which the company plans to compete to achieve its strategic mission. For Countrywide Financial Corporation the core strategy was initially to be the low-cost provider and build a brand. For Starbucks the core strategy was "ubiquity"—to be everywhere.

In brief, identifying and clearly articulating a business definition, strategic mission, and core strategy provides the foundation on which all other aspects of the business are—and should be—built. The customers to be served, products offered, and day-to-day systems of the firm should all be built on the business foundation, as explained in the next section.

Six Key Organizational Development Tasks

Once a firm has identified its business foundation (either implicitly or explicitly), it begins the process of developing the organization that it will support. Our research[1] and consulting experience suggests that there are six organizational development areas or tasks that are critical in determining whether an organization will be successful at any particular stage of growth. Taken together, these six key tasks make up the Pyramid of Organizational Development, pictured in Figure 1.1.

As can be seen in this figure, the pyramid is built on the firm's business foundation. We first identify and describe each key organizational development task individually and then examine the Pyramid of Organizational Development as a whole.

Identify and Define a Market and, if Possible, Create a Niche. The most fundamental prerequisite for developing a successful organization is the identification and definition of a firm's market and, if feasible, the creation of a market niche. A market is made up of the present and potential buyers of the goods or services, or both, that a firm intends to produce and sell. A market segment is simply a place in the market differentiated by products offered (for example, compact cars, sedans, SUVs, trucks, and buses) or customers served (for example, businesses, schools, and homes). As used here, the term *market niche* is a place within a market where a firm has developed a sufficient

Figure 1.1. Pyramid of Organizational Development

number of sustainable competitive advantages so that it "controls" a market segment. Although this distinction is discussed more fully in Chapter Seven, which deals with strategic planning, it should be noted that, in contrast to popular usage and its implicit connotation, a market niche does not have to be small. A true market niche can be very large, as illustrated by Microsoft and its control over most of the operating system software in the personal computer (PC) market. Similarly, Amgen—a leading biotechnology-based pharmaceuticals company—has a niche in the market for kidney dialysis with its product Epogen, controlling over 90 percent of the market. In both Microsoft's and Amgen's case, part of their niche is derived from patent protection (the patent for Epogen, for example, will not expire until 2015). Another and more important contributing factor to the creation of the niche for both of these companies, however, is the focus they have placed on understanding and meeting their customers' needs.

The first challenge to organizational survival or success, then, is identifying a market need for a product or service to which the firm will seek to respond. This can be either a need that has not yet been recognized by other firms or a need not fully satisfied by existing firms. Many nonprofit foundations, for example, are created by individuals or groups who identify unmet or undermet needs of specific populations, raise funds, and then use these funds to meet these needs. The chances for organizational success are enhanced if a firm identifies a need that is not being adequately fulfilled or that has little competition for its fulfillment. This challenge is faced by all new ventures (whether for-profit or not-for-profit); indeed, it is the challenge for a new venture to overcome. It has also been the critical test of growing concerns and has even brought many once proud and great firms to near ruin or total demise.

Many firms have achieved great success merely because they were one of the first in a new market. For example, Apple Computer grew from a small entrepreneurship in a garage to a $1 billion firm in a few years because its founders identified the market for a "personal" computer. Similarly, Dreyers—a manufacturer of ice cream (now owned by Nestlé)—went from sales of $14.4 million to sales of $55.8 million in just five years because the company saw and cultivated a market segment between the "super premium ice creams" such as Haagen-Dazs and the generic (commodity) ice cream sold in most supermarkets. The retailer—99 Cents Only Stores—became a company of approximately $1 billion in revenues by selling manufacturers' excess products at deep discounts. PowerBar grew from a small basement operation in the mid-1980s to a Stage IV company in the late 1990s by focusing on providing products (including bars) to optimize performance of athletes and nonathletes alike. ("Stage IV" describes a firm that has attained organizational maturity. The stages are discussed more fully in Chapter Two.) Many Internet companies (like Amazon.com and eBay) have also achieved substantial size as a result of developing ways to sell products using this technology.

The reverse side of this happy picture is seen in firms that have experienced difficulties and even failed, either because they failed to clearly define their market or because they mistakenly abandoned their historical market for another. For example, a medium-sized national firm that manufactured and sold specialty clothing wished to upgrade its image and products and become a high-fashion boutique. However, it failed to recognize that its historical market was the "medium" market, and its efforts to rise out of this market were unsuccessful. Similarly, a $12 million printing company found itself in difficulty after trying to upgrade its position in the medium-priced market.

Attracted by the market segment where the highest-quality work was done (with accompanying high profit margins), the company purchased the best equipment available. It also hired a high-priced sales manager to recruit a salesforce that could compete in the new market segment. However, the company had underestimated the strength of existing companies in that market segment and found itself unable to break into this higher-priced market as easily as managers had hoped. Moreover, the additional investments it had made and the related increases in its overhead made the firm's cost structure higher than that of its former competitors, so it began losing business from its historical market. Thus the company found itself in a cost-price squeeze.

The first task in developing a successful organization, then, is the definition of the market in which a firm intends to compete and the development of a strategy to create a potential niche. This process involves the use of strategic market planning to identify potential customers, their needs, and so on. It also involves laying out the strategy through which the firm plans to compete with others for its share of the intended market. The nature and methods of strategic planning are described in Chapter Seven.

Develop Products and Services. The second task of an entrepreneurial organization is *productization*—the process of analyzing the needs of present and potential customers in order to design products or services that will satisfy their needs. For example, Brian and Jennifer Maxwell, who were both runners, saw the need for a nutritious, portable energy food that would assist athletes in achieving optimum performance. This led to the development of PowerBar and, in turn, the development of an entire new category—"energy bars." Similarly, Michael Dell saw a need to provide PCs directly to customers and began selling them out of his University of Texas dorm room.

Although many firms are able to correctly perceive a market need, they are not necessarily able to develop a product that is capable of satisfying that need adequately. For example, many dot-coms, such as Web Van, identified a potential market need but were unable to develop viable businesses. Many firms developed coffee bars or cafés, but Starbucks has grown to dominate this market. Clearly, being the first to recognize a need is not necessarily sufficient.

The productization process involves not only the ability to design a *product* (defined here to include services as well) but also the ability to produce the product. For a service firm, the ability to produce a product involves the firm's service delivery system—the mechanism through which services are provided to customers. For example, Domino's Pizza provides home-delivered pizza. Both the pizza and home delivery are aspects of the company's products. Similarly, although coffee is nominally the core product of Starbucks, the real product is the coffee experience provided by Starbucks' cafés. One service provided by Head Start agencies is education, which is provided to children in the agencies' centers (as is true of traditional preschools), as well as to children and their families at home. The service and the delivery mechanism, together, constitute Head Start's education product.

Productization is not simply a task for relatively new or small companies; it faces large, well-established firms as well. Indeed, it can even face whole industries. For example, in the 1970s U.S. automobile manufacturers were unsuccessful in productizing their products to meet the changing needs of their market, including the growing need for reliable, fuel-efficient, economical automobiles. The same problem was faced by Xerox in the photocopying industry, U.S. Steel in specialty steels, and all U.S. television manufacturers. As a result, Japan emerged as a powerful competitor in markets that the Americans had once dominated.

The success of productization depends, to a very great extent, on success in defining the firm's market (that is, its customers and their needs). The greater the degree to which a firm understands the market's needs, the more likely that its productization process will be effective in satisfying those needs. Productization is the second key development task in building a successful organization.

Acquire Resources. The third major task of a developing organization is acquiring and developing the additional resources it needs for its present and anticipated future growth. A firm may have identified a market and created products but not have sufficient resources to compete effectively. For example, small competitors in the soft drink industry need to be low-cost producers. This requires high-speed bottling lines, which, at a cost of $1 million-plus a line, the smaller firms simply cannot afford. In the nonprofit world, "capacity building" (having the funds needed to support ongoing operations) is a continuing challenge for many foundations, charities, and government-funded entities.

A firm's success in identifying a market and in productization creates increased demand for its products or services, or both. This, in turn, stretches the firm's resources very thin. The organization may suddenly find that it requires additional physical resources (space, equipment, and so on), financial resources, and human resources. The need for human resources, especially in management, will become particularly acute. At this stage of development, the firm's very success, ironically, creates a new set of problems.

The company must now become more adept at resource management, including the management of cash, inventories (if a manufacturing company), personnel, and so forth. It is at this stage that an entrepreneur must begin to think longer term about the company's future needs. Failure to do this can be costly. For example, one entrepreneur told how he kept purchasing equipment that became obsolete for the company's needs within six months because of the firm's rapid growth. Instead of purchasing a photocopying machine that would be adequate for the company's needs as it grew but was more than currently required, for example, he purchased a machine that was able to meet only current needs. The result was that he spent much more on equipment than he would have if he had purchased machinery that was adequate for potential future needs. Similarly, another entrepreneur found himself with insufficient space six months after moving into new offices that he had thought would be adequate for five years, because the company grew more rapidly than he had anticipated. Another entrepreneur described how he had had to unexpectedly move his offices every five years because, after five years it always seemed that he had run out of space.

Another resource-related dilemma facing entrepreneurial companies involves the people they can hire. Often, entrepreneurs facing the need to hire people believe that they cannot afford to hire those with long-range potential to help them build their businesses; rather, they settle for those with lesser skills and abilities. Unfortunately, this may be a false economy. A few entrepreneurial firms do invest for the future and hire people who can grow with them. For example, one of the secrets to Starbucks' success was that they hired people who could help them build a billion-dollar-plus business from a very early stage. Starbucks' CEO, Howard Schultz, realized that human resources would be as much a key to Starbucks' long-term success as its now-famous coffee. This insight helped Starbucks grow during a fifteen-year period from a small entrepreneurial company in Seattle with two retail stores to an institution with more than six thousand stores and approximately $6.4 billion in revenues by 2005.

Develop Operational Systems. To function effectively, a firm must not only produce a product or service but also administer basic day-to-day operations reasonably well. These operations include accounting, billing, collections, advertising, personnel recruiting and training, sales, research and development, production (or service delivery), information systems, transportation, and related systems.

The fourth task in building a successful organization is the development of the systems needed to facilitate these day-to-day operations—the operational systems. It is useful to think of a firm's operational systems as part of its ''organizational plumbing.'' Just as plumbing is necessary for a house or building to function effectively, organizational plumbing is necessary for a business to function well. Thus operational systems make up part of an organization's infrastructure and are necessary to facilitate growth.

Typically, firms that are busy focusing on their markets and products tend to neglect the development of their operational systems. As a firm increases in size, however, an increasing amount of strain is put on such systems because the company tends to outgrow the organizational plumbing available to operate it. Following are several examples of firms in that predicament:

- In one electrical components distribution firm with more than $200 million in annual revenues, salespeople were continually infuriated when they found that deliveries of products they had sold could not be made because the firm's inventory records were hopelessly incorrect.

- A medium-sized residential real estate firm with annual revenues of about $10 million found that it required almost one year of effort and embarrassment to correct its accounting records after the firm's bookkeeper retired.

- A $100 million consumer products manufacturer had to return certain materials to vendors because it had insufficient warehouse space to house the purchases (a fact no one noticed until the deliveries were at the door).

- A $15 million industrial abrasives distributor found itself facing constant problems in keeping track of customer orders and in knowing what was in its inventory. The firm's inventory control system, which was fine when annual sales were $3 to $5 million, had simply become overloaded at the higher sales volume. One manager remarked that "nothing is ever stored around here where any intelligent person could reasonably expect to find it."

- A $10 million service firm had no way of knowing whether the services it provided to customers were, in fact, profitable. Their financial management system did not provide this type of data, so they continued to offer their package of services and to hope for the best.

- A $2 million nonprofit that prided itself on providing "the best" client service had no way of knowing whether this was, in fact, true. Complaints (and there were more than a few) came in, but there was no comprehensive system in place to track and address them.

- A $100 million distributor of consumer products had a computer system that was so antiquated that few, if any, important reports were prepared accurately or on time. Whatever information was available had to be collected and analyzed manually.

These are just a few of the types of problems that firms encounter when they have not developed effective operational systems. The bottom line is that if these systems continue to remain underdeveloped, they can literally bring a business to a standstill. What is not well recognized by most entrepreneurs is that their company is competing not just in products and markets but in operational infrastructure as well. Wal-Mart is the classic example of how a small entrepreneurial company grew to be larger and more successful than its giant competitors. In the 1960s, Sears was the number-one retailer in the United States, and Kmart was the number-two retailer overall but the number-one discount retailer. Wal-Mart was a small company headquartered in Bentonville,

Arkansas. By analyzing his competition, Sam Walton understood that he could not compete head-to-head with Sears and Kmart, but he could develop some strengths for Wal-Mart (which might even become competitive advantages) by developing his company's logistics and information systems. Today, Wal-Mart has surpassed Sears and Kmart and has developed unsurpassed logistics and information systems, because Sam Walton understood that he was competing not just in products but in operational systems as well.

Develop Management Systems. The fifth task required to build a successful organization is developing the management systems needed for the long-term growth and development of the firm. There are four management systems: (1) planning, (2) organization structure, (3) management development, and (4) control or performance management systems. Management systems are another component of an organization's infrastructure, or organizational plumbing.

- *The planning system* consists of how the firm develops and implements its long-term plans for organizational development. It also includes operational planning, scheduling, budgeting, and contingency planning. A firm may do planning and have a strategy but still lack a planning system. The basic concepts and methods of strategic planning for entrepreneurially oriented, professionally managed firms are presented in Chapter Seven. Advanced concepts of strategic planning are described in Chapter Thirteen.

- *The organizational structure* of the firm determines how people are organized, who reports to whom, and how activities are coordinated. All firms have some organizational structure (formal or informal), but they do not necessarily have the correct structure for their needs. The concepts and methods for designing and evaluating organizational structure, required at different stages of growth, are presented in Chapter Eight.

- *The management development system* helps facilitate the planned development of the people needed to run the organization as it grows. Chapter Nine deals with management development and its role in making the transition from an entrepreneurship to a professionally managed firm.

- *Control or performance management systems* encompass the set of processes (budgeting, leadership, and goal setting) and mechanisms (performance appraisal) used to motivate employees to achieve organizational objectives. These systems include both formal control mechanisms, such as responsibility accounting, and informal processes, such as organizational leadership. Chapter Ten deals with organizational control systems.

Until the firm reaches a certain size (which tends to differ for each firm), it can typically operate without formal management systems. Planning tends to be done in the head of the entrepreneur, frequently on an ad hoc basis. The organizational structure, if it exists, tends to be informal, with ill-defined responsibilities that may well overlap several positions (or people). Management development tends to consist of on-the-job training, which basically means, "You're on your own." When control systems are used in such organizations, they tend to involve only the accounting system rather than a broader concept of management control.

The basic organizational "growing pain" that is a symptom of the need for more developed management systems is the decreasing ability of the original entrepreneur or senior executive to manage or control all that is happening. The organization simply becomes too large for senior managers to be personally involved in every aspect of it, and there is the gnawing feeling that things are out of control. This marks the need for developing or upgrading the firm's management systems.

Manage the Corporate Culture. Just as all people have personalities, all organizations have a corporate personality or culture—a set of shared values, beliefs, and norms that govern the way people are expected to behave on a day-to-day basis. *Values* are what the organization believes to be important with respect to product quality, customer service, treatment of people, and so on. *Beliefs* are assumptions that people in the corporation hold about themselves as individuals and about the firm as an entity. *Norms* are the unwritten rules that guide day-to-day interactions and behavior, including language, dress, and humor.

Organizational culture can have a profound impact on the behavior of people, for better or for worse. Many companies, such as Starbucks, IBM, Hewlett-Packard, McDonald's, Domino's Pizza, Countrywide Financial Corporation, Disney, and Southwest Airlines have achieved greatness at least in part because of a strong corporate culture. Culture, then, is a critical factor in an enterprise's successful development and performance. It functions as an informal control system, because it prescribes how people are supposed to behave.

Some managers believe that what is espoused as their corporate culture is actually the culture that affects people's behavior. Unfortunately, this is often an illusion. For example, one rapidly growing entrepreneurship in a high-tech industry stated that its culture involved the production of high-quality products, concern for the quality of the working life of its employees, and encouragement of innovation. In reality, the firm's culture was less positive. Its true concerns were to avoid conflict among its managers, set unrealistic performance expectations, avoid accountability, and overestimate its performance capabilities. Moreover, the company saw itself as hard-driving and profit-oriented, when its real culture was sales-oriented, regardless of profitability.

Sophisticated managers understand that their companies compete as much with culture as with specific products and services. The CEO of a major New York Stock Exchange company once said that he could predict a division's organizational problems as soon as he had identified its culture. The sixth and final challenge in building a successful organization, then, is to manage corporate culture so that it supports the achievement of the firm's long-term goals. The nature and management of corporate culture are examined in Chapter Twelve.

THE PYRAMID OF ORGANIZATIONAL DEVELOPMENT

The six tasks of organizational development just described are critical to a firm's successful functioning, not only individually but as an integrated system. They must harmonize and reinforce rather than conflict with one another. A firm's markets, products, resources, operational systems, management systems, and corporate culture must be an integrated whole. Further, the Pyramid of Organizational Development must support and be supported by the firm's business foundation. Stated differently, each variable in the pyramid affects and, in turn, is affected by each of the other variables (including the firm's business foundation). The management of an organization must learn to visualize this pyramid and evaluate their organization in terms of the extent to which its pyramid has been successfully designed and built.

Implications of the Pyramid of Organizational Development

There are several important implications of the pyramid for management. First, the business foundation and the six key organizational development tasks make up different phases of the "business game." Just as the American game of football (the "business foundation") is composed of six key phases (rushing offense, passing offense, rushing defense, passing defense, and kicking and receiving), there are six key phases of the game of business—markets, products, resources, operational systems, management systems, and culture management. If an organization is weak in any phase of its game, it will experience a variety of growth-related problems (discussed in Chapter Three).

Another implication is that all organizations compete with other enterprises at all levels of the pyramid. For example, Wal-Mart and Kmart do not compete only with products but with their operational and management systems and culture as well. Wal-Mart's logistics and information systems are a clear source of competitive advantage vis-à-vis Kmart and other discount retailers.

A third important implication is that, in the long term, the most sustainable competitive advantages are typically found at the top three levels of the pyramid (operational systems, management systems, and culture) rather than in products and markets. All markets can be entered by competitors, and all products can be copied or improved on over time (even pharmaceuticals can have generic versions), but the top three levels of the pyramid take time and money to develop and are difficult to copy. Even if an attempt is made by a competitor to emulate an enterprise's operational systems, management systems, and culture, their effort can be fruitless because of the unique aspects of each organization. We examine the strategic implications of the Pyramid of Organizational Development further in Chapters Seven and Thirteen.

Research Support for the Pyramid

During the past few years, a growing body of research has provided empirical support for the validity of the Pyramid of Organizational Development framework.[2] This research has consistently indicated that there is a statistically significant relationship between the variables contained in the pyramid and the financial performance of companies. The six variables are hypothesized to account for as much as 90 percent of financial performance, with the remaining 10 percent attributable to exogenous factors. See Figure 1.2 for a graphic representation of these variables as drivers of financial results. Empirical research[3] to date has, in fact, indicated that as much as 80 percent of gross margin and 55 percent of EBIT (earnings before interest and taxes) is explained by the

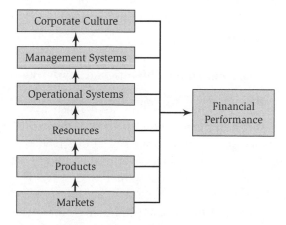

Figure 1.2. Six Key Drivers of Financial Results

variables in the model. Additional research has indicated that the pyramid has a statistically significant relationship to ROI (return on investment).[4]

The Pyramid as a Lens to Build and Evaluate Organizations

The pyramid framework can be used as a template for planning to build an organization and as a strategic lens through which to evaluate the strengths and limitations (or areas for improvement) of an existing enterprise. As such, it becomes the guide for planning to build a new business or to strengthen an existing business. This topic is addressed more fully in Chapters Seven and Thirteen, which deal with strategic planning and organizational development.

We must also recognize that although an organization should focus on the six levels in the pyramid, the emphasis on the components or subsystems of the pyramid must be somewhat different at different stages of organizational growth. Before we can explore this idea further, we must examine the different stages of growth through which entrepreneurial organizations develop. This topic is the focus of Chapter Two. First, however, we illustrate how the pyramid can be used to build a successful enterprise by describing the case of Starbucks Coffee Company.

Starbucks Coffee Company: Successful Use of the Pyramid

Starbucks Coffee Company (Starbucks) is one of the truly great entrepreneurial success stories of the past two decades. The scope and speed of its success are reminiscent of Apple Computer, Nike, Microsoft, and Amgen.

Starbucks is a classic example of an organization that has been successful because it was effective in building the entire Pyramid of Organizational Development. It has achieved success as an organization through its development of the six key tasks of organizational development, not only each task individually but the effective development of the pyramid as a whole, as described in the sections that follow.[5]

Identify the Business Foundation. The original Starbucks began as a local roaster of coffee. In 1972, the company had two retail stores that sold coffee beans: one opened in 1971 near Seattle's Pike Place Market; the other, in 1972, opened in a shopping center across from the University of Washington's campus. This original Starbucks did not sell coffee beverages. It sold fresh-roasted coffee beans, teas, and spices. However, sometimes the individual behind the counter would brew some coffee and serve it in Dixie cups as samples.

Howard Schultz was not the original founder of Starbucks. He joined the company as director of retail operations and marketing in 1982. About one year later, Schultz visited Milan, Italy, to attend a trade show. While strolling

Milan's streets, he was struck by the ubiquity of the Italian coffee bars. He was drawn into them and realized that the coffee bars were an extension of people's homes and a part of the Italian culture. He saw the opportunity to develop something like what he had seen in Milan back in the United States. In April of 1984, Starbucks tested Schultz's idea by opening a coffee bar inside a Starbucks retail store, and it was an instant success. Despite the experiment's success, the original founders of Starbucks decided not to adapt it to Schultz's vision—an American version of an Italian coffee bar. Schultz left to create his own company called Il Giornale, which was founded in 1985. In August of 1987, Schultz went back to Starbucks with a buyout offer and a vision of taking the company nationally. Il Giornale acquired the assets and name "Starbucks" and changed its name to Starbucks Corporation.

In brief, Schultz's business concept for Starbucks was of a "national specialty retailer and café," or, as noted earlier, an American version of an Italian coffee bar. His mission was to build a national chain of coffee bars, and his strategy was based on Starbucks being able to provide superior quality in all aspects of product and operations: stores, coffee, signage, packaging, and customer experience.[6]

Identify a Market and Develop a Product. In terms of the Pyramid of Organizational Development, Schultz perceived the market not for coffee per se but for a different kind of "retail and café experience." Thus the product was not just coffee but the atmosphere and experience of the Starbucks store. The store itself was part of the product experience for the customer, not just the place where the product was purchased. It was part of a coffee-related experience. Schultz also realized that customer service was part of the overall product or experience to be delivered in a Starbucks store. As a result, Starbucks emphasized its unique brand of customer service from the beginning.

Neither coffee nor cafés were new products, but Starbucks had redefined them in some magical way. Schultz had, indeed, solved the first two challenges of building a successful enterprise: he had (1) identified a market and (2) developed a product. This, in turn, led to the rapid growth of Starbucks and created the next set of challenges: resources and operational systems.

Acquire Resources and Develop Operational Systems. Unlike many entrepreneurial companies, Starbucks paid a great deal of attention to the acquisition of resources and the development of operational systems. From the beginning, Schultz believed that he had a big opportunity, and he thought that Starbucks had the potential to become an enterprise with $1 billion in sales.

He realized that if the company was going to fulfill its potential, he would need all the resources and systems required of a large company, including financial, physical (plant and equipment), technological, and human resources.

As he stated, "We could not have gotten where we are today if we had not had the commitment to build a national company with a national brand from the beginning. If you are going to build a 100-story building, you've got to build a foundation for 100 stories."[7]

The first step was to raise money, and this became a continuing challenge, as Starbucks grew rapidly. Schultz spent considerable time finding investors, and without the "bucks" there would have been no Starbucks! The financial resources were used to hire people capable of building Starbucks into a national brand and a national company. This was not only true of a strong senior management team but also the acquisition of people at the operating levels, such as real estate, finance, and retail operations. Funds were also used to upgrade the company's roasting plant, its logistics and manufacturing systems, and its overall day-to-day operating systems.

Starbucks' investment in a strong operating team, as well as the related aspects of infrastructure, paid off for the company in many ways. The strong real estate team led the company to choose solid locations and avoid the real estate problems of other, similar organizations such as Boston Market and Koo Koo Roo. The company's investment in developing strong financial systems led to a deeper understanding of store economics, and, in turn, a healthy business from a financial standpoint.

Develop Management Systems. In 1994, Howard Schultz and Orin Smith (then CFO and later COO of Starbucks) read the second edition of this book and invited Eric Flamholtz to visit Starbucks and assist the firm with its "growing pains."[8] This, in turn, led to the development of a more sophisticated set of management systems for Starbucks, including a strategic planning system similar to that described in Chapter Seven and a revised organizational structure. In 1995, Starbucks also developed its management development and performance management (control) systems. Before that, there was a strategy and a plan but not a formal, integrated planning system. There was training for customer service personnel but no management development. In addition, there was an incentive system for people but no well-developed performance management system.

Taken together, planning, structure, management development, and control systems made up the overall management systems for Starbucks and completed the development (at least for this stage of the company's growth) of the fifth level of the Pyramid of Organizational Development.

Manage the Corporate Culture. The highest level in the pyramid and the sixth task required to develop a successful enterprise involves culture management. From the beginning, Schultz and Starbucks had a clear idea that culture was important in building a successful enterprise. In addition, Howard Schultz had a well-defined concept of the kind of organization he wanted to build. Accordingly, Schultz articulated five guiding principles that were intended to serve as the foundation for Starbucks' culture. Subsequently, a sixth guiding principle was added: "Embrace diversity as an essential component in the way we do business." Following is a list of all six guiding principles that make up the core of Starbucks' stated culture.

Starbucks Corporation: Six Guiding Principles

- Provide a great work environment and treat each other with respect and dignity.
- Apply the highest standards of excellence to the purchasing, roasting, and fresh delivery of our coffee.
- Develop enthusiastically satisfied customers all of the time.
- Contribute positively to our communities and our environment.
- Recognize that profitability is essential to our future success.
- Embrace diversity as an essential component in the way we do business.

In addition to the stated guiding principles of Starbucks, other facets of its culture are important as well. Schultz believed that the kind of organization that Starbucks was, and, in turn, the way it did business would become a source of sustainable competitive advantage. In effect, Schultz understood the role of culture as a building block of organizational success. Although he was not then familiar with the concept of "corporate culture" per se, he understood it intuitively. This led Starbucks to be concerned about the treatment of people employed by the firm. Ideally, he wanted everyone employed by Starbucks to behave like "owners." The notion was this: the way we treat our people will influence the way they treat our customers, and, in turn, our overall success. This led Starbucks to a number of different personnel practices, including providing full benefits for all people working more than twenty hours each week and providing opportunities for stock ownership. In other words, the company developed ways to manage its culture so that it would be embraced by its employees.

Focus on the Pyramid as a Whole. Starbucks is an illustration of a very successful entrepreneurial organization. The earlier discussion shows that Starbucks understood the need to develop all aspects of the pyramid and not merely focus on products and markets. Prior to 1994, the company had done an excellent job of developing five of the levels of the pyramid—everything except management systems. As we see later in this book, this is the classic pattern of successful entrepreneurial companies. Beginning in 1994, at about $175 million in sales, Starbucks began to develop the management systems that were required to facilitate its continued successful development. This "completed" the developmental work prescribed by the Pyramid of Organizational Development.

What happened to Starbucks? By the end of its fiscal year 2005, Starbucks had grown to more than $6.4 billion in net revenues and more than 6,000 stores, including 4,200 company-owned stores. In addition, the company's stock price increased substantially. From September 1, 1994, to September 1, 2006, the stock price increased (adjusted for splits) from $1.78 to $31.76. An investment of $10,000 would have grown to $178,302, for an increase of 1,683 percent. Clearly, successful development of the Pyramid of Organizational Development pays off.

Boston Market: A Contrast with Starbucks

Boston Chicken (later renamed Boston Market) had people's mouths watering for more than just their food. The company was supposed to become "The McDonald's of the 90s." It never happened. Instead, Boston Market filed for Chapter 11 reorganization under the bankruptcy law.

While Starbucks was earning quite a few bucks for its investors, Boston Market was costing its investors and franchisees lots of money.

What was different about the two companies? Whereas Starbucks successfully focused on all of the six key aspects of the Pyramid of Organizational Development, Boston Market did not. Boston Market did identify a market and had developed a good product, but the emphasis was on selling area franchises rather than truly building a solid business. In other words, the focus was on the bottom two layers of the pyramid versus the pyramid as a whole. Whereas Starbucks' skilled real estate team identified good locations and negotiated sensible deals, Boston Market was perceived as overpaying for real estate. Whereas Starbucks' financial people were analyzing costs of store build-outs and operations, Boston Market never got the economics of their stores under control. Their stores were expensive to build and operate, and they were not profitable. Although the restaurants were losing money, Boston Market was showing a profit for a while because of the heavy franchise fees charged. But the firm's reported profitability was a mirage, which finally disappeared. In brief, Boston Market simply did not execute all of the six required tasks of organizational development effectively and ultimately paid the price.

This discussion is not intended to imply that Starbucks made no mistakes or was without problems—simply that it did a significantly better job in performing the required tasks to build a successful organization. Boston Market failed to focus on several of the key tasks of organizational development and went bankrupt.

SUMMARY

This chapter presents a framework for understanding what makes an organization successful, effective, and profitable. The foundation of this framework is the firm's business foundation—the nature of the business the firm is in, its strategic mission, and core strategy.

Building on the foundation, an organization must focus on six areas if it is to succeed over the long term. These are (1) markets, (2) products or services, (3) resources, (4) operational systems, (5) management systems, and (6) corporate culture. For organizations to be successful, they must first identify their business foundation. Then they must deal not only with each of these six areas individually and in sequence but also with the six as parts of a whole. We use the image of a Pyramid of Organizational Development to describe this holistic approach.

Starbucks illustrates the power of developing a company in a way that is consistent with the pyramid. In the next chapter, we examine the different stages of growth and the different emphasis on each part of the pyramid that is required at each stage for a firm to be successful over the long term.

CHAPTER TWO

Identifying and Surviving the First Four Stages of Organizational Growth

All organizations pass through various stages of development. These stages are, at least in part, determined by the organization's size, as measured by its annual revenues (or for nonprofits, in terms of annual budget). This chapter presents a framework for identifying and explaining the major stages through which all organizations grow and develop as they increase in size. It should be noted that this framework applies to a division of a large company, as well as to an independent organization.

First, we identify the various stages of organizational growth and examine the first four stages from the inception of a new venture to organizational maturity. Next, we examine the emphasis on each level in the Pyramid of Organizational Development that is required at each growth stage and explain the nature of the transitions to different stages. Then we discuss the differences between an entrepreneurship and a professionally managed firm and what must be done to make the transition between these growth stages. Finally, we discuss some implications of this framework for the management of entrepreneurial organizations.

STAGES OF ORGANIZATIONAL GROWTH

Seven stages of growth of a company's life cycle can be identified:

   I. New venture

  II. Expansion

III. Professionalization

IV. Consolidation

 V. Diversification

VI. Integration

VII. Decline and revitalization

The first four stages characterize the period from inception of a new venture to the attainment of organizational maturity. This period includes the development of an entrepreneurship through the stage when the firm becomes a professionally managed firm. Stages V through VII all deal with the period of a company's life cycle after the attainment of organizational maturity.

Because the principal focus of this book is on the development of companies from entrepreneurship to the stage of becoming a professionally managed firm, this chapter focuses on the first four stages of organizational growth. We return to the last three stages in Chapter Fourteen, which presents a preview of the challenges posed to continued organizational development success after an organization has reached maturity.

At each of these stages, one or more of the critical tasks of organizational development should receive special attention. The stages of organizational growth—the critical development areas for each stage and the approximate size (measured in millions of dollars of sales revenues for for-profit companies and in terms of annual operating budget for nonprofits)—at which an organization will typically pass through each stage are shown in Table 2.1.

Table 2.1. Stages of Organizational Growth

Stage	Description	Critical Development Areas	Approximate Organizational Size (millions of dollars in sales)	
			Manufacturing Firms	Service Firms
I.	New venture	Markets and products	Less than $1	Less than $0.3
II.	Expansion	Resources and operational systems	$1 to $10	$0.3 to $3.3
III.	Professionalization	Management systems	$10 to $100	$3.3 to $33
IV.	Consolidation	Corporate culture	$100 to $500	$33 to $167

A key word in this statement is *typically*. What this means is that for approximately 90 percent of manufacturing firms that have revenues in the range of $10 million to $100 million, they will typically have to encounter the critical issues of Stage III.

There are, however, certain firms that will have to face these problems at a smaller size in their development or much later in their development. For example, there may well be a $3 million manufacturing firm that is facing the need to professionalize its management systems. Or a few firms may well reach $1 billion in annual revenue without really having to face the need to professionalize their management systems. Accordingly, we need to view the relevant range as designated for the transition to occur at each stage of development as a "normal curve." In statistics, a normal curve designates the percentage of observations that fall under the area of the curve. This means that statistically 68 percent of the "cases" of firms will fall under one standard deviation of the normal curve, while 95 percent of the cases will fall under two standard deviations of the normal curve. There are, of course, always certain exceptions to this. Similarly, there are exceptions to the revenue parameters used to mark the various stages of growth.

It should also be noted that in Table 2.1 we use two different ranges of annual revenue to designate the various stages of growth. Our experience in working with a wide variety of organizations indicates that each stage of growth is reached somewhat earlier for service companies than for manufacturing firms. This occurs because of the greater complexity of a service company relative to a manufacturing company with the same annual revenues. This is, in turn, caused by the fact that manufacturing companies typically purchase materials that are semi-finished and use them in their manufacturing process. Accordingly, the manufacturing company's revenues include a return for the components of cost of goods sold that are derived from other organizations' work. This means that the manufacturing company's "value added" is less than the comparable value added for a service company at a given stage of annual revenues. This does not mean that the manufacturing company makes a lesser contribution than a service company; it merely means that the service company with more employees and no raw materials to be recouped as part of sales revenue has a relatively more complex operation than a comparably sized manufacturing company.

As a result of this phenomenon, we have found it useful to "convert" a service company's revenues into the comparable units of those of a manufacturing company. This process is similar to the conversion from the imperial system to the metric system or from dollars into any foreign currency. Thus to convert a service company's revenues into comparable units of a manufacturing company, we multiply the service company's revenues by a factor of 3 (as reflected in the figures shown in Table 2.1). This means that the typical service company is three times more complex to manage than a comparable manufacturing company. Alternatively, it means that a $5 million service company is the rough equivalent of a $15 million manufacturing company. It should be remembered that this is an experienced-based adjustment that we have found useful rather than a strict formula.

Most nonprofit organizations can be classified as service firms (providing services or funding for services to specific populations). Further, many nonprofits—particularly foundations, charities, and organizations that are government-funded—do not have any revenue per se. In these cases, the organization's annual operating budget can be used as a "surrogate" for revenues. The budget, in this case, represents the "size" and "complexity" of the business, in terms of clients served, projects funded, and so on.

In the subsequent discussion, we (for convenience) refer to a company at a given stage using the parameters for manufacturing companies as a base. The reader can adjust for service companies by using the service company adjustment factor of 3.0 or can simply refer to Table 2.1. Financial institutions, such as banks, savings and loans, and mutual funds, can be viewed as service companies under the framework. Distribution companies can be viewed as a hybrid manufacturing-service organization, and a multiple of 2 can be used as an adjustment factor. (In other words, a $5 million distribution company is the same as a $10 million manufacturing company and is, therefore, nearing Stage II of its development.)

Stage I: New Venture

Stage I of organizational growth involves the inception of a new venture. Stage I typically occurs from the time an organization has virtually no sales until it reaches approximately $1 million in annual sales for a manufacturing firm (or $.3 million for a service firm). During Stage I, the firm has to perform all the critical tasks necessary for organizational success, but the greatest emphasis is on the first two tasks: defining markets and developing products. This is represented schematically in the organizational development pyramid shown in Figure 2.1. These two tasks are critical to the survival of the firm because without customers and products or services to provide to them, a firm cannot exist. The ultimate purpose of this stage is to establish "proof of the business concept."

Many firms have succeeded in establishing new ventures because the entrepreneur was able to identify a viable market and product. Earl Scheib, the "king of the no-frills auto paint job," is one entrepreneur who met this challenge. When he began painting cars in his Los Angeles gas station in 1937, his original concept was to provide a no-frills face-lift for cars. Scheib built an entire business based on this concept. He had successfully identified a market that was not being served, and he proceeded to build a business to serve it.

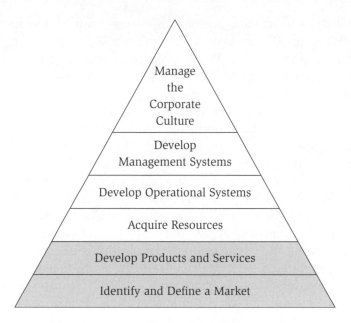

Figure 2.1. Developmental Emphasis in a Stage I Firm

The company is now publicly held and operates shops for paint and bodywork on cars throughout the United States. Moreover, his concept has been copied by a number of competitors.

Another example of an entrepreneur who established a successful new venture because he was able to identify an unserved market is Thomas S. Monaghan, who founded the company known today as Domino's Pizza. Monaghan's concept was to provide pizza for home delivery, which at the time he founded his business was not commonly available. As he has stated, "When Domino's began delivering pizza, the only pizza places that delivered were those that had to deliver to survive."[1] Monaghan believed that there was an unserved market need for high-quality, reasonably priced pizza to be delivered to the home. Today, his firm has eight thousand stores worldwide and serves approximately one-half of the home delivery pizza market—a market Domino's Pizza helped create.

Other examples of new ventures that came about when an entrepreneur perceived a market need to be served include PowerBar (a quick-energy product for athletes), Noah's Bagels (fresh bagels of the highest quality in the western United States), Federal Express (overnight delivery), eBay (the ability to buy or sell things over the Internet), and Amazon.com (the ability for anyone anywhere who has a PC and access to the Internet to purchase any book at any time).

Many other new ventures are reasonably successful and profitable but not as famous. They include businesses engaged in executive search, landscape design, printing, early childhood education, financial planning, restaurants, graphic design, repair services, weight loss, catering, equipment leasing, specialty retailing, and many more fields.

Entrepreneurs do not always have to be first to identify an unserved market segment. Often they can enter a market with a better product or service. The classic example of an entrepreneur who succeeded after others failed is Herb Kelleher, founder and former CEO of Southwest Airlines. Although others had identified the market for low-cost airfare, Kelleher was the first to find the successful formula for low-cost, no-frills airfare—a market segment that Southwest has grown to dominate. Coffee is certainly not a new product, but Starbucks has grown to dominate the retail coffee bar segment. Although girls have played with dolls throughout history, Isaac Larian, founder of MGA Entertainment, created Bratz Dolls to appeal to "tween girls" and grew his business to one of the largest toy companies in the world.

Stage II: Expansion

If an organization successfully completes the key developmental tasks of Stage I, it will reach Stage II, which involves the rapid expansion of the firm in terms of sales revenues, number of employees, and so on. For most manufacturing firms, Stage II begins at about the $1 million sales level and extends to the $10 million level. (For service firms, this stage typically begins at approximately $.3 million and continues through $3.3 million in revenues.)

Stage II presents a new set of developmental problems and challenges. Organizational resources are stretched to the limit when increasing sales require a seemingly endless increase in people, financing, equipment, and space. Similarly, the firm's day-to-day operational systems for recruiting, production or service delivery, purchasing, accounting, collections, information, and payables are nearly overwhelmed by the sheer amount of product or service being "pushed out the door."

The major purpose or challenge of Stage II is "organizational scale-up." This means that the business concept has been demonstrated to be valid (Stage I), and the organization must now acquire the resources and develop the systems required to facilitate growth.

The major problems that occur during Stage II are problems of growth rather than survival. It is during this stage that horror stories begin to accumulate:

- Salespeople sell a product they know is in inventory, only to learn that someone else has grabbed it for other customers.

- One vendor's invoices are paid two and three times, while another vendor has not been paid in six months.

- A precipitous drop in product quality occurs for unknown reasons.
- Turnover increases sharply just when the company needs more personnel.
- Missing letters, files, and reports cause confusion, loss of time, and embarrassment.
- Senior executives find themselves scheduled to be in two widely separated cities on the same day at the same time, or they arrive in a distant city only to learn that they are a day early.
- The computer system crashes frequently, leaving users without access to valuable information, basically shutting the company down for hours or sometimes days.

These are what we call growing pains.

Organizational growing pains that are typical of Stage II and later-stage companies are discussed in detail in Chapter Three. The relative emphasis on each key developmental task appropriate for Stage II is shown schematically in Figure 2.2.

Many companies experience a great deal of difficulty during Stage II and may even disappear. When this occurs, it is usually because the founding entrepreneur is unable to cope with the managerial problems that arise as the organization grows. A Stage II company needs an infrastructure of operational

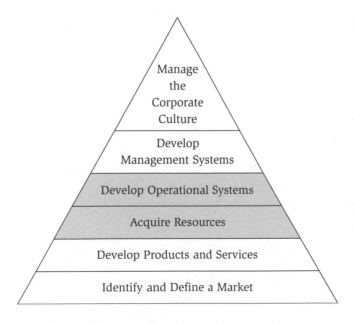

Figure 2.2. Developmental Emphasis in a Stage II Firm

systems that lets it operate efficiently and effectively on a day-to-day basis. Unfortunately, many entrepreneurs are not interested in such organizational plumbing.

Some firms that are fortunate enough to have discovered an especially rich market find themselves growing very rapidly. Although most development of a firm's resources and operational systems ought to occur during the period when the firm is growing from $1 million to $10 million in annual revenues, it is not unusual to find firms with $30, $40, $50—even more than $100 million in annual revenues—with the operational systems of a Stage II organization. This kind of discrepancy between a firm's size and the degree of development of its operational systems leads to serious problems, but these may be masked in the short term by the firm's rapidly rising revenues. This often proves to be the case in some of the most spectacular examples of organizational failure, such as Osborne Computer.

Adam Osborne was an entrepreneur who perceived the need for portable PCs, which are now known as laptops (even though his product weighed twenty-eight pounds and had a screen about six inches wide). He developed a company, which quickly grew to $100 million in revenues within two years, but then went bankrupt in its third year. It was a classic example of meteoric success followed by meteoric failure, brought about, at least in part, by underdeveloped operational systems. In an article on the rise and fall of Adam Osborne, Steve Coll states, "In retrospect, it seems clear that the company's accounting procedures were so slipshod that no one knew how things were."[2] Chapter Four presents several examples of companies that were successful at Stages I and II but experienced developmental problems during their transitions.

The lesson of what happened to Osborne and his fleetingly successful company needs to be learned by all entrepreneurs. Many companies continue to make the same mistakes, and the end results are similar. For example, system crashes experienced by several online brokerage firms are a warning that both the product and related infrastructure are not sufficiently developed to serve as a sound platform for future growth.

Taken together, Stages I and II—the new venture and expansion stages—constitute the entrepreneurial phase of organizational development. It is during these two stages of growth that the classic skills of entrepreneurship are most relevant. It is also during this phase that the need to make the transition from an entrepreneurship to an entrepreneurially oriented, professionally managed firm begins to occur.

Stage III: Professionalization

Somewhere during the period of explosive growth that characterizes Stage II, senior management realizes (or ought to realize) that a need for a qualitative change in the firm is arising. The company cannot merely add people, money, equipment, and space to cope with its growth; it must undergo a transition or metamorphosis and become a somewhat different type of organization.

Until this point, the firm has been totally entrepreneurial. It has operated with a considerable degree of informality. It may have lacked well-defined goals, responsibilities, plans, or controls but still prospered. However, once a critical size has been achieved, many of these practices and procedures must be increasingly formalized. The need for this transition typically occurs for manufacturing firms by the time they have reached approximately $10 million in sales. (For service firms, the need for this transition typically arises when they have reached $3.3 million in revenues.) At this level of revenues, the sheer size of the organization requires more formal planning, regularly scheduled meetings, defined organizational roles and responsibilities, a performance appraisal system, and control systems. The people who manage the firm must also change their skills and capabilities. Until this point, it was possible to be more of a doer or hands-on manager than a professional manager. At this stage, however, the organization increasingly requires people who are adept at formal administration, planning, organization, motivation, leadership, and control. In brief, the focus at this stage of development should be on developing the management systems required to take the firm to its next stage of development. Developing these systems, in turn, requires a planned program of organizational development, as described in Chapter Five and Chapter Seven.

It is at this stage that the organization must make a transition from an entrepreneurship to a professionally managed firm. This means that the organization, while still maintaining its entrepreneurial spirit, will also need to develop the infrastructure and professional management capabilities required to continue its growth successfully.

This is a delicate balancing act. An organization must *never* lose its entrepreneurial mind-set or spirit, but it must begin to develop the infrastructure and management systems required to facilitate its future growth. Although some people equate professional management with bureaucracy, we believe they are mistaken. It is true that if professional management exists without an entrepreneurial mind-set or culture, it can *become* bureaucracy. But it is also true that if entrepreneurship is carried to an extreme in large companies, it can result in chaos, and chaos ultimately leads to organizational difficulties and even bankruptcy.

As we discuss throughout the remainder of this book, making the successful transition from an entrepreneurship to a professionally managed firm requires some delicate surgery. At this point, the key thing we want to point out is that, based on our research and experience, this transition is not a choice but a requirement or imperative for continued organizational success and that it involves the development of management systems. We shall provide examples throughout this book of both organizations that have made this transition successfully and thrived, as well as others that have failed to make this transition and experienced great difficulties (such as Osborne Computers and Boston Market).

The relative emphasis on each key developmental task appropriate for Stage III is shown schematically in Figure 2.3. As the figure indicates, the most important task during this stage is the development of management systems.

Although the professionalization and related development of management systems of a firm ought to occur during the period when sales are growing from $10 million to approximately $100 million, the rate of corporate growth often outstrips the rate at which the enterprise's management systems are developed. This can lead to serious problems, which can either limit the potential development of a business or cause failure. This was the case at Starbucks Coffee Company in 1994.

At that time, Starbucks was essentially a Stage II company in the process of making the transition to Stage III (in terms of it organizational infrastructure),

Figure 2.3. Developmental Emphasis in a Stage III Firm

even though its corporate revenues were more than $100 million (Stage IV). As a result, the firm was beginning to experience significant growing pains, which could have hampered the company's development and ultimate success.

Similar problems occurred at the same stage of growth at Jamba Juice, Noah's Bagels, and PowerBar. Other examples include Apple Computer (revenues of more than $2 billion in 1985 but only Stage II in terms of infrastructure) and Maxicare (revenues of about $1.8 billion). Apple lost market share to IBM, and Maxicare had to downsize and ultimately file for bankruptcy. This company had grown rapidly through acquisitions but had not taken the time to develop an operational and management infrastructure that would support the much larger organization that it had become.

The entrepreneurial personality can be a barrier to success at Stage III. Making the transition from an entrepreneurship to professional management involves more than just the development of operational and management systems. It requires a profound mind-set change on the part of people, especially the founders—the entrepreneurs. For more than thirty years we have been working with companies to help them make this transition. One of the classic obstacles to this process is typically the entrepreneur; many fear becoming "bureaucratic" and then confuse bureaucracy with systems. Some of this is deeply rooted in their personalities; they do not want to be controlled by anyone or anything—not plans, not role descriptions, not policies, not procedures.

Because they have been successful in launching a new venture without these things, they assume (either explicitly or implicitly) that they are not necessary and that they are, in fact, barriers to success. What they fail to realize is that the "game" needs to be played differently at different stages of the organizational life cycle.

Without systems or plans or role definitions, the organization will definitely experience increasing confusion and quite possibly chaos. In spite of what one author has written, no one "thrives on chaos" indefinitely![3]

As noted in Chapter One, when Orin Smith (then CFO of Starbucks) invited one of the authors to work with Starbucks Coffee Company to assist them in making the transition to professional management, he stated that the biggest challenge would be getting Howard Schultz to buy in to the concept that a firm could be better managed without losing its entrepreneurial spirit. He cautioned that Schultz might not have the patience for much process and systems. In fact, Howard Schultz embraced these notions very quickly. They were consistent with his belief that if you are going to build a large building, you need a strong foundation.

This issue of the psychological acceptance of the need to transition from early-stage entrepreneurship to professional management is a traumatic one for many, if not most, entrepreneurs. It requires a leap of faith because their early experiences suggest that systems are not essential to success. Without making this leap, however, the entrepreneurs may put what they have built at risk of decline or even failure.

Chapter Five presents the detailed case history of one organization that made the transition from Stage II to Stage III successfully. It examines the process through which this transition was accomplished and the problems that were encountered along the way. It also discusses other examples of companies that were successful and unsuccessful at making this important transition.

Stage IV: Consolidation

Once an organization has made the transition to a professionally managed firm with workable systems for planning, organization, management development, and control, the firm must turn its attention to an intangible but nevertheless real and significant asset: corporate culture. Management of the corporate culture is the main task of Stage IV of organizational development.

Corporate culture can have a powerful effect, not only on day-to-day operations but on the bottom line of profitability as well.[4] During the growth that was necessary to reach Stage IV (which typically seems to begin at about $100 million in sales for manufacturing firms), the firm has brought in new waves of people. The first wave probably arrived when the firm was relatively small and informal, during Stage I. During this period, the firm's culture (values, beliefs, and norms) was transmitted by direct day-to-day contact between the founder and personnel. The diffusion or transmission of culture was a by-product of what the firm did. Virtually everybody knew everybody else. Everybody also knew what the firm wanted to achieve and how.

During Stage II, the rapid expansion of the firm most likely brought in a second wave of people. The first-wave personnel transmitted the corporate culture to this new generation. However, at an increased level of organizational size, especially once the firm develops geographically separate operations, this informal socialization process becomes more attenuated and less effective. The sheer number of new people simply overwhelms the socialization system.

By the time a firm reaches $100 million in revenues, a third wave of people usually has joined the organization, and the informal socialization is no longer adequate to do what it once did so well. At this stage, the firm must develop a more conscious and formal method of transmitting the corporate culture throughout the organization. This is the key challenge faced by Stage IV organizations. The relative emphasis on each key developmental task appropriate for Stage IV is pictured in Figure 2.4. Chapter Six presents the case history of the steps that one organization took to change its corporate culture as it made the transition to Stage IV, and Chapter Twelve examines in greater detail the management of corporate culture.

Figure 2.4. Developmental Emphasis in a Stage IV Firm

Another dimension of the culture-management challenge at Stage IV is to help consolidate or institutionalize the transformation from an entrepreneurship to a professionally managed organization. As the organization makes the transition required of Stage III and develops management systems, a cultural transition is also in progress. The company is going from a very loose, free-spirited organization to a more disciplined one; from a company with a strategy and perhaps a plan to one with a well-defined planning process; from one with vague goals to more specific, measurable goals; from one with loosely defined roles to one with more formal role descriptions, and from one with limited accountability to one with more accountability. Explicitly or implicitly, this involves a cultural change, and it is a change that must be managed if the transition is to be made successfully. We deal with this further in Chapters Six and Twelve.

Differences Between Entrepreneurial and Professional Management

Stages I and II, taken together, make up the entrepreneurial phase of organizational development, while Stages III and IV make up the professional management phase. As an organization passes from one of these phases of growth to the other, a variety of changes need to occur. There is a qualitative difference between an entrepreneurship and a professionally managed firm. The former tends to be characterized by informality, lack of systems, and a free-spirited nature. The latter tends to be more formal, to have well-developed systems, and to be proud of its disciplined, profit-oriented approach.

The most important differences between an entrepreneurship and a professionally managed organization involve nine "key result areas": (1) profit, (2) planning, (3) organization, (4) control, (5) management development, (6) budgeting, (7) innovation, (8) leadership, and (9) culture. Table 2.2 summarizes the principal characteristics of professional management, as compared with entrepreneurial management in each of these key result areas. We will now describe these differences in greater detail.

Profit. In a professionally managed firm, profit is an explicit goal; it is planned, rather than being a residual or whatever is left over at the end of the year. In an entrepreneurial firm, profit is sought, but it is not an explicit goal to be attained. The entrepreneur may be willing to invest and sacrifice current profits for a future big hit.

Planning. Unfortunately, in many entrepreneurial firms, the plan, if there is one, is in the entrepreneur's head. A professionally managed firm has a formal, written business plan. Planning becomes a way of life, and the firm begins to develop a strategic plan for what it wants to become, as well as operational plans at all levels of the company. In addition to strategic planning, operational plans and budgets are developed. Contingency plans also are developed. The practice of informal, superficial, ad hoc planning is replaced by a regular planning cycle.

Organization. An entrepreneurial firm has an informal organizational structure with overlapping and undefined responsibilities. People are expected to do whatever is necessary, without regard to job titles or positions. This is fine when a firm is small. But as it grows, chaos can set in, with people simply not knowing what they are supposed to do. A professionally managed firm has a set of written role descriptions that clearly state responsibilities. These descriptions are designed to be mutually exclusive and exhaustive. They are intended to help people understand what their roles are and to give focus to their efforts and use of time.

Control. In an entrepreneurship, control of operations tends to be lacking or at least is often piecemeal. The firm usually lacks formal measurement or performance appraisal systems. A professionally managed firm, by contrast, has a

Table 2.2. Comparison of Professional Management and Entrepreneurial Management

Key Result Areas	Professional Management	Entrepreneurial Management
Profit	Profit orientation; profit as explicit goal	Profit as a by-product
Planning	Formal, systematic planning: • Strategic planning • Operational planning • Contingency planning	Informal, ad hoc planning
Organization	Formal, explicit role descriptions that are mutually exclusive and exhaustive	Informal structure with overlapping and undefined responsibilities
Control	Formal, planned system of organizational control, including explicit objectives, targets, measures, evaluations, and rewards	Partial, ad hoc control, seldom with formal measurement
Management Development	Planned management development: • Identification of requirements • Design of programs	Ad hoc development, principally through on-the-job training
Budgeting	Management by standards and variances	Budget not explicit; no follow-up on variances
Innovation	Orientation to incremental innovations; willingness to take calculated risks	Orientation toward major innovations; willingness to take major risks
Leadership	Consultative or participative styles	Styles varying from very directive to laissez-faire
Culture	Well-defined culture	Loosely defined, ''family''-oriented culture

formal, planned system of organizational control or performance management. This system makes full use of explicit objectives and goals, measurements of performance, feedback, evaluation, and rewards.

Management Development. Management development is planned in a professionally managed firm. The firm makes a conscious effort to develop the managerial skills of individuals and to prepare a pool of managers that will help take the firm into the future. In an entrepreneurship, however, management development is unplanned and tends to occur, if at all, through on-the-job experience. Although the entrepreneurial firm may avoid the cost of management development programs, people may become victims of the Peter Principle (being promoted beyond their competence) and cost the company through inefficiency, mistakes, and replacement costs.

Budgeting. In an entrepreneurship, budgeting tends to lack detail. There is little follow-up on variances or deviations from the budget. A professionally managed firm's budget system focuses on standards and variances. Managers are held accountable for performance, compared against budget goals. Budgets are not cast in concrete but are there to guide performance.

Innovation. By definition, entrepreneurial companies are oriented toward innovation. Many are willing to make major innovations in products, services, or operating methods. Some entrepreneurs even "bet the company" on an innovation because of the possibility of a high payoff for success. They tend to need quick hits, or fast payoffs. Professionally managed organizations tend to be oriented more toward incremental innovations. They are less likely to bet the company, and they often spread their risk among a portfolio of different products or projects. They are willing to take calculated risks, but they may seem relatively averse to risks, at least in comparison to entrepreneurial companies. There are exceptions to this, and established professionally managed companies such as Boeing and IBM are famous for having bet the company on new technologies a number of times during their history. Many of the best-managed companies, however, are oriented to continuous, incremental improvements and long-term support of major innovations that do not require fast payoffs.

Leadership. In entrepreneurial companies, leadership typically ranges from very directive styles such as autocratic or benevolent autocratic to very nondirective styles such as laissez-faire (see Chapter Eleven for a discussion of different leadership styles). In a professionally managed organization, the tendency today is toward more interactive styles, such as consultative and participative management, or, in a few instances, to consensus or team-oriented styles. Entrepreneurial organizations are more likely to have charismatic leaders than are professionally managed companies because of the nature of the process of selection for promotion in large organizations.[5] A good example is Angelo Mozilo, cofounder of Countrywide Financial Corporation, who is without doubt the most charismatic leader we have encountered in more than thirty years.

Culture. Culture tends to be loosely defined in entrepreneurial organizations. Sometimes it is not explicitly managed by the firm. Often the culture of an entrepreneurial organization is oriented toward a family feeling, which is feasible because of the firm's relatively small size. Professionally managed organizations are more likely to treat organizational culture explicitly as a variable to be managed and transmitted throughout the organization. They tend to understand that culture is a source of sustainable competitive advantage.

Relevance of Differences. Our discussion of the differences between entrepreneurial and professionally managed firms is intended to be descriptive rather than evaluative. Both types of firms have strengths and limitations. The significant point is that different ways of operating are appropriate at different stages of organizational growth.

From an entrepreneurial organization's standpoint, it is clear that something inevitably will be lost as the organization makes the transition to professional management. However, something will also be gained. Just as a plant that has been successful in its pot must be transplanted if it is to continue to grow and develop properly, an organization that has outgrown its infrastructure and style of management must also make a transformation. Failure to do so will lead to a variety of problems.

Discrepancies Between Growth and Organizational Development

As we have seen, two independent dimensions are involved in each stage of organizational growth: (1) size and (2) the extent to which the enterprise has developed the systems required to support its size in each of the six critical development areas included in the Pyramid of Organizational Development. An organization can be at Stage III in terms of size, as measured in annual revenues, but only at Stage II in its internal organizational capabilities. In other words, its infrastructure is not developed to the extent that it needs to be to support the firm's size. For example, after only a very few years of existence, Osborne Computer was a Stage IV company in size, but it was only a Stage II company in terms of its infrastructure. The lack of infrastructure to support the firm contributed to significant problems, which ultimately resulted in the firm filing for bankruptcy.

An organization will face significant problems if its internal development is too far out of step with its size. As shown in Figure 2.5, the greater the

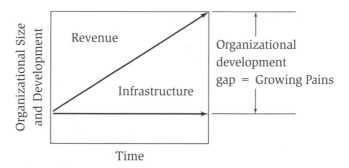

Figure 2.5. Causes of Organizational Growing Pains

degree of incongruity between an organization's size and the development of its infrastructure, the greater the probability that the firm will experience organizational growing pains (the topic of the next chapter). Such a firm is like a thirteen-year-old boy who is well over six feet tall: he has the body of a man but, most likely, the mind of a child. As a senior manager in one organization stated, "We are essentially a $30 million company that happened to have $350 million sales." The manager meant that the firm had the operating systems and developmental structure of a $30 million company, but its growth had given it more than ten times as much revenue. Predictably, the company was in trouble and was ultimately purchased by a competitor.

MANAGING THE TRANSITION BETWEEN GROWTH STAGES

What can management do to help make the transition required between growth stages? There are four steps by which the senior managers of a rapidly growing entrepreneurship can help their company make a smooth transition from one stage of growth to the next. They are as follows:

1. Perform an organizational evaluation or audit of the company's effectiveness at its current stage of development.
2. Formulate an organizational development plan.
3. Implement the plan through action plans and programs.
4. Monitor the programs for effectiveness.

We now examine each of these steps in detail.

Perform an Organizational Evaluation or Audit

An organizational evaluation or audit consists of systematic assessment, by means of data analysis and interviews with organization members, of the extent to which the company's organizational systems are adequate to meet the firm's current and anticipated future requirements. An organizational evaluation may be performed by the firm's management, but many firms prefer to have independent consultants conduct the audit in order to obtain greater objectivity or benefit from their experience with similar companies facing similar issues. The findings of the evaluation represent a diagnosis of the organization at its current stage of development.

Formulate an Organizational Development Plan

Once the organizational evaluation has been completed, management must develop a master plan or blueprint for building the capabilities needed for the organization to function successfully at its current or next stage of development. This is the strategic organizational development plan—a process described in Chapter Seven.

Implement the Organizational Development Plan and Monitor Its Progress

The third and fourth steps in helping an organization make the transition to a new growth stage are implementing the changes set forth in the organizational development plan and monitoring their effects. This includes both developing new organizational systems (planning, organization, and control) and developing management's capabilities through corporate education programs. Management development programs may focus on administrative skills (such as planning), leadership skills, or both. We examine the development of these management systems and capabilities in Part Three of this book. Once the development program has been implemented, management needs to monitor its progress in meeting the developmental needs of the firm. Such monitoring allows senior managers to make changes in the program whenever they determine that it no longer meets its intended goals.

These four steps—diagnosing, planning, implementing, and monitoring changes in the organizational capabilities of a company—are the keys to making a smooth transition from an entrepreneurship to a professionally managed firm. The steps are the same regardless of the size, industry, or current stage of development of a firm.

It should be noted that these steps may appear simple, but they are often quite complex in practice. The transition process typically requires one to two years for a Stage I firm; three years or more may well be required in a Stage IV firm. Some aspects of the change, such as changes in personnel (voluntary or otherwise), may be difficult to handle. However, where the process is suitably designed and well executed, the firm will almost always emerge from it stronger and more successful than ever.

Failure of senior management to take the necessary steps in negotiating transitions between each of the stages can have significant consequences. These range from stagnation and blocked growth to removal of the founders, as has happened at many companies, including Jamba Juice, Apria Healthcare, and Apple Computer. Or the company may experience bankruptcy or takeover, as happened with Osborne Computer and People Express. However, if the proper steps are taken, then organizations can experience a great deal of success. Starbucks and Microsoft are good examples of this.

Managing the Transition: Maxicare Versus PacifiCare

Maxicare and PacifiCare provide examples of two companies within the health care industry that had dramatically different experiences with growth. These differences can be attributed to the degree to which each was able to execute the four transition steps adequately, and, in turn, build the organizational infrastructure required by growth.

Maxicare's problems in executing the transition steps may account for the difficulties that ultimately led to the resignation of its founders and the firm's ultimate bankruptcy. Maxicare was founded in 1973. Originally called the Hawthorne Community Medical Group (HCMG), it was owned by nine physicians and entrepreneur Fred Wasserman. HCMG became the first company in California to qualify under the 1973 federal Health Maintenance Organization Act, which required that virtually all employers engaged in interstate commerce offer their workers a choice between traditional medical insurance coverage or membership in an HMO. The company changed its name to Maxicare, exploited its first-mover advantage, and began to grow rapidly.

Maxicare began an aggressive acquisition program in 1982. At this time, Wasserman was chairman and CEO, and Pam Anderson, his wife, was president. Although the company was growing rapidly, it had not built up its own internal infrastructure and was experiencing a variety of organizational growing pains. Two major acquisitions in 1986 nearly proved fatal, as the company, already dealing with growth-related problems, tried to integrate other businesses within its existing infrastructure. One of the acquisitions had more significant problems than had first been realized, and Maxicare was unable to integrate the company without significant damage to itself. Although it had reached more than $1.8 billion in revenues after the acquisitions, Maxicare was still dealing with problems common to much smaller Stage II firms. Moreover, the acquired companies also lacked an adequate infrastructure for their own operations. The net result was an organizational nightmare.[6] Following the 1986 acquisitions, Maxicare reported its first quarterly loss, and its stock declined from a peak of $28 in 1986 to a low of $3 in 1987. In 1987, Wasserman and Anderson left Maxicare and were replaced by Peter Radican, who had served on the firm's board. On March 16, 1989, Maxicare filed for Chapter 11 bankruptcy protection.

A lawsuit filed by shareholders before Maxicare declared bankruptcy stated that the firm "was suffering from significant management failures and shortcomings at the highest levels of its most important operations—financial reporting, accounting, and marketing—because they had been unable to manage and control the company's rapid growth, had been unable to solve Maxicare's operating problems, and had been unable to achieve the levels of earnings and revenue growth budgeted by the corporation . . . ."[7]

Maxicare again filed for Chapter 11 under the United States Bankruptcy Code on May 25, 2001. The company closed for business on December 31, 2001, and as of November 1, 2002, had ceased all operations except for final execution of its bankruptcy distribution and liquidation plan.

Maxicare's initial success was, to a great extent, attributable to growth by acquisition rather than to savvy market analysis. Maxicare's problems can be seen as the result of inadequate evaluation of its own and its acquisitions' strengths and weaknesses, as well as the lack of a plan that took these into account. This is a failure to adequately perform Steps 1 and 2 in the process of managing the transition from one stage of growth to the next.

PacifiCare Health Systems was also founded in the mid-1970s. Like Maxicare, PacifiCare also experienced rapid growth in the 1980s, including growth through acquisition. However, unlike Maxicare, PacifiCare had built up a strong organizational infrastructure, which enabled it to better deal with the problems caused by rapid growth. The firm was not just concerned about its growing market. The company's management also focused on developing the operational and management systems needed to support its growth. The company continued this focus on its infrastructure, even after it had met the initial challenges of growth. In the early 1990s, when PacifiCare was already a successful company with about $2 billion in revenue, the authors worked with the company to assist in long-range planning and structural (organization) design for the future.

While Maxicare was dealing with its problems, PacifiCare was well positioned to expand rapidly because it had created a better foundation for growth. As a result, PacifiCare became one of the five largest HMO companies in the United States, with a solid history of financial performance. By 1998, the company had grown to more than $9.5 billion in revenues.

In 2005, with the final stages of industry consolidation, PacifiCare was acquired by United Health Care and now operates as a unit of that company.

SUMMARY

This chapter presents a framework to help senior managers understand and guide organizations at different stages of growth and development. It describes the first four major stages of organizational growth, from the inception of a new venture (Stage I) to the consolidation of a professionally managed firm (Stage IV). It examines the degree of emphasis that must be placed on each level of the Pyramid of Organizational Development at each stage of growth. It also examines the differences between an entrepreneurial and a professionally managed organization and describes the steps that must be taken to make a successful transition from one stage of growth to the next. Finally, it describes a tale of two companies (Maxicare and PacifiCare) in the same industry but with dramatically different results.

In the next chapter we examine the nature of organizational growing pains and present a method for measuring and interpreting them. Recognition and identification of these growing pains is a necessary part of the organizational evaluation process, which is the first step of the transition from an entrepreneurship to a professionally managed firm.

CHAPTER THREE

Recognizing Growing Pains and Assessing the Need for Change

When an organization has not been fully successful in developing the internal systems it needs at a given stage of growth, it begins to experience growing pains. These growing pains are problems in and of themselves. However, they are also symptoms of a deeper, systemic problem: the need to transition to a different infrastructure to support the current and anticipated growth and size of the organization.

This chapter examines in detail the most common organizational growing pains, showing through examples how these growing pains emerge in real-life companies. It also presents a method of measuring organizational growing pains and interpreting the extent to which they signal the need for further organizational development. As part of this discussion we cite research showing that growing pains are statistically related to an organization's financial performance. The chapter then discusses the degree to which different sizes and types of businesses experience growing pains. Finally, it presents the case of Grange, Inc.—a company that faced many growing pains and worked to overcome them.

THE NATURE OF GROWING PAINS

Growing pains are problems that occur as a result of inadequate organizational development in relation to business size and complexity. They are symptoms that something has gone wrong in the process of organizational development.

As such, they are a signal or alert about the need to make the transition from one stage of organizational development to the next. They are, as discussed later in this chapter, a set of leading indicators of future financial performance.

Ironically, growing pains are problems resulting from organizational success rather than failure. Nevertheless, they are simultaneously problems in and of themselves and signs or symptoms of an underlying systemic problem in the organization. The underlying problem is the failure of the organization's infrastructure to match or keep up with the size and complexity of the business. This means that the organization's resources, operational systems, management systems, and culture (the top four variables of the Pyramid of Organizational Development) have not been developed to the extent necessary to support the size, complexity, and growth of the enterprise.[1]

A simple rule of thumb is that when an organization doubles in size (measured either in terms of revenues, production volume, annual budget, or number of employees), it requires a different infrastructure. When this adjustment in infrastructure does not happen, organizational growing pains will increase in number and severity.

If the root causes of the organizational growing pains are not dealt with appropriately, even organizations that are successful undoubtedly will experience difficulties and possibly failure. To deal with growing pains, we must first be able to identify them and assess their severity.

THE TEN MOST COMMON ORGANIZATIONAL GROWING PAINS

The ten most common (or classic) organizational growing pains are listed here:

1. People feel that there are not enough hours in the day.
2. People spend too much time "putting out fires."
3. People are not aware of what other people are doing.
4. People lack understanding about where the firm is headed.
5. There are not enough good managers.
6. People feel that "I have to do it myself if I want to get it done correctly."
7. Most people feel that meetings are a waste of time.
8. When plans are made, there is very little follow-up, so things just don't get done.
9. Some people feel insecure about their place in the firm.
10. The firm continues to grow in sales, but not in profits.

Each of these growing pains is described in the pages that follow.

People feel that there are not enough hours in the day. One of the most common organizational growing pains is the complaint that there is never enough time. Employees feel that they could work twenty-four hours per day, seven days a week, and still not have sufficient time to get everything done. They begin to complain about overload and excessive stress. Both individuals and departments feel that they are always trying to catch up but never succeeding. The more work they do, the more there seems to be, resulting in a never-ending cycle. People feel as if they are on a treadmill.

The effects of these feelings can be far-reaching. First, employees' belief that they are being needlessly overworked may bring on morale problems. Complaints may increase. Second, employees may begin to experience physical illnesses brought on by excessive stress. These psychological and physical problems may lead to increased absenteeism, which can decrease the company's productivity. Finally, employees may simply decide that they can no longer operate under these conditions and may leave the organization. This will result in significant turnover and replacement costs related to recruiting, selecting, and training new people.

When many employees feel that there is not enough time in the day, usually no one is suffering more from this feeling than the company's founding entrepreneur. The entrepreneur, feeling ultimately responsible for the firm's success, may work sixteen hours a day, seven days a week in an effort to keep the company operating effectively and help it grow. As the organization grows, the entrepreneur begins to notice that he or she no longer can exercise complete control over its functioning. This realization can result in a great deal of personal stress. We see examples of this in the cases of Metro Realty and Tempo Products in Chapters Five and Six.

The presence of this growing pain can suggest that the firm lacks or has an underdeveloped planning system, that there is a lack of a formal structure (in which roles and responsibilities are clearly defined), or that individuals do not understand how to effectively manage their time.

People spend too much time "putting out fires." A second common growing pain shows itself in excessive time spent dealing with short-term crises. This problem usually results from a lack of long-range planning, and, typically, the absence of a strategic plan. It can also result from the tendency to hold onto a culture that rewards fire fighters, rather than planners. Individual employees and the organization as a whole live from day to day, never knowing what to expect. The result may be a loss of organizational productivity, effectiveness, and efficiency.

Examples of the putting out fires problem are easy to find. In one $10 million service firm, a lack of planning caused orders to be needlessly rushed, resulting in excessive pressure on employees. Drivers had to be hired on weekends and evenings to deliver orders, some of which were already overdue. Similarly, at

Maxicare the "surprises" that were encountered after acquisitions led to an almost endless number of fires.

In other companies, which we discuss in more detail later, lack of planning produced other short-term crises. At Metro Realty, for example, it resulted in shortages of salespeople. Because of these shortages, Metro was forced to hire new people and put them to work almost immediately, sometimes without adequate training. This, in turn, contributed to short-term productivity problems because the new people did not possess the skills necessary to be good salespeople. Similarly, at Tempo Products the lack of personnel planning also created problems but for different reasons. There, personnel were hired to take up the slack when business was good. Once the crisis was over, the company found it had a number of people it simply did not know what to do with.

Fires were so prevalent at one $50 million manufacturing company that managers began to refer to themselves as fire fighters, and senior management rewarded middle management for their skill in handling crises. When it became apparent that managers who had been effective in "fire prevention" were being ignored, some of them became "arsonists" to get senior management's attention. The arsonists set fires that could be fought as a way of showing that they were contributing to the organization.

Many people are not aware of what others are doing. Another symptom of organizational growing pains is that many people are increasingly unaware of the exact nature of their jobs and how these jobs relate to those of others. This creates a situation in which people and departments do whatever they want to do and say that the remaining tasks are "not our responsibility." Constant bickering between people and departments over responsibility may ensue. The organization may become a group of isolated and sometimes warring factions.

These problems typically result from the lack of an organization chart and precise role and responsibility definitions, as well as effective team building. Relationships between people and between departments, as well as individual responsibilities, may be unclear. As becomes clear in the cases of Metro Realty and Tempo Products, people can become frustrated by this ambiguity and begin creating their own definitions of their roles, which may not always be in the best interests of the firm. The president of Metro Realty vividly described this phenomenon when he said, "We were a collection of little offices working toward our goals without consideration for the good of the company."

The isolation of departments from one another may result in duplication of effort or in tasks that remain incomplete because they are "someone else's responsibility." Constant arguments between departments may also occur over territory and organizational resources. We see in Chapter Six that Tempo Products suffered from the effects of the need to define and protect territory as well. This was also a problem at a large technology company where there were eighteen different divisions, each focusing on its own product line to the exclusion of the overall corporate goals. Even as product lines evolved and began to overlap, the salesforce continued to focus only on its own line to the exclusion of others. This resulted in some customers being called on by three or more salespeople, each representing a different product group and sometimes even offering similar services for different prices. In essence, the company competed against itself. Ultimately, the company lost control of its own destiny and was acquired by one of its competitors.

People lack understanding about where the firm is headed. Another typical growing pain is a widespread lack of understanding of where the firm is headed. Employees may complain that "the company has no identity" and either blame upper management for not providing enough information about the company's future direction or, worse, believe that not even upper management knows what that direction will be. This can result from the inability of senior management to agree about the company's future direction (as we see in the case study of Falk Corporation presented in Chapter Sixteen) or can be due to a communication breakdown.

When insufficient communication is combined with rapid changes, as is often the case in growing firms, employees may begin to feel anxious.[2] To relieve this anxiety, they may either create their own networks for obtaining the desired information or come to believe that they know the company's direction, even though management has not actually communicated this information. Both these strategies were used by Tempo Products' employees. Employees' speculations, as well as real information obtained from people who were close to senior management, circulated freely on the company's grapevine. Rumors were rampant, but in fact very few people really knew why certain changes were being made. Hence, employees experienced a significant amount of anxiety. If anxiety increases to the point where it becomes unbearable, employees may begin leaving the firm. It should be noted that turnover of this kind can be very costly to a firm.[3]

The primary factor underlying this growing pain tends to be inadequate strategic planning. Either the firm has an inadequate or underdeveloped planning process or plans that are made are not effectively communicated throughout the organization.

There are not enough good managers. Although a firm may have a significant number of people who hold the title of "manager," it may not have many good managers. Managers may complain that they have responsibility but no authority. Employees may complain about the lack of direction or feedback that their managers provide. The organization may notice that some of its divisions or departments have significantly higher or lower productivity than others. It may also be plagued by managers who constantly complain that they do not have time to complete their administrative responsibilities because they are too busy increasing business. When any or all of these events occur, something is wrong with the management function of the organization.

The problem may be that the company has promoted successful doers (salespeople, office workers, and so on) to the role of manager, assuming that they will also be successful in this role. These two roles require significantly different skills, however. Thus without proper training many doers fail in the manager's role. Their tendency to continue "doing" will show itself in poor delegation skills and poor coordination of the activities of others. Direct reports may complain that they do not know what they are supposed to do.

Problems like these suggest that the company has not adequately defined managers' roles or is not providing sufficient training to ensure that those in these roles have the skills needed to effectively fulfill them. If there are unclear role descriptions, those in management positions may not understand what they are expected to do. In an effort to "do something," these individuals may revert to re-creating their old roles—focusing too much attention on doing work, rather than managing work. If training exists, the firm may be relying too much on on-the-job training rather than on formal management development programs. In some companies, this on-the-job training is carried to such an extreme that companies literally or figuratively walk the new manager to his or her office and say, "Here's your department. Run it."

Management problems may also result from real or perceived organizational constraints that restrict a manager's authority. In the case of Tempo Products, we show how the perception that only top management could make decisions greatly affected lower-level managers' effectiveness. One person at this firm described the managers as "people with no real responsibility." The feeling that only upper management has decision-making responsibility is common in firms making the transition to professional management. It is a relic from the days when the founding entrepreneur made all the firm's decisions.

People feel that "I have to do it myself if I want to get it done correctly." Increasingly, as people become frustrated by the difficulty of getting things done in an organization, they come to feel that to get something done, they have to do it themselves. This symptom, like lack of coordination, is caused by a lack of clearly defined roles, responsibilities, and linkages between and among roles. It may also result from a lack of resources or the inability (or unwillingness) of managers to relinquish control over results to others.

As was discussed previously, when roles and responsibilities are not clearly defined, individuals or departments tend to act on their own because they do not know whose responsibility a given task is. They may also do the task themselves to avoid confrontation, because the person or department to whom they are trying to delegate a responsibility may refuse it.

Operating under this philosophy, departments become isolated from one another, and teamwork becomes minimal. Each part of the company "does its own thing" without considering the good of the whole. Communication between management and lower levels of the organization and between departments may be minimal because the organization has no formal system through which information can be channeled. We see how the lack of coordination between areas can lead to productivity problems and inefficiencies in the cases of Grange, Inc., Metro Realty, and Tempo Products.

Most people feel that meetings are a waste of time. Recognizing that there is a need for better coordination and communication, the growing organization may begin to hold meetings. Unfortunately, at many firms these meetings are, at best, nothing more than discussions among people. They have no planned agendas, and often they have no designated leader. Participants may be allowed to take cell phone calls, use their computers, check e-mail via computer or PDA, hold side conversations, and focus on many things other than the content of the meeting. Meetings become a free-for-all, tend to drag on interminably, and seldom result in decisions. The same agenda items appear again and again. As a result, people feel frustrated and conclude that "our meetings are a waste of time."

The impact of ineffective meetings can be significant. For example, after five full days of work, one high-tech company's senior management team had yet to finalize its strategic plan. Why? Each day of meetings was constantly interrupted by "today's crisis," which took one or more members of the team (including the CEO) out of the meeting for an extended period of time. Executives continually checked e-mail on their BlackBerries, resulting in a lack of focus on the discussions taking place. When each executive "tuned back in" to the discussion, the rest of the group had to spend time helping him or her catch up. Each executive had a specific agenda of items that needed to be discussed and, instead of listening to and staying focused on the topic that was on the table, decided to share whatever was on his or her mind. As a result, the discussion jumped from topic to topic, with only limited resolution of issues. After five days of meetings, over a period of three months, the team decided that the plan was good enough, simply because they didn't have the time to finish it.

Other complaints about meetings involve lack of follow-up on decisions that are made. Some companies schedule yearly or monthly planning meetings during which goals are set for individual employees, departments, and the company as a whole. These sessions are a waste of time if people ignore the goals that have been set or fail to monitor their progress toward these goals. As we see in Metro Realty's case, the budgeting process suffered from this condition. In a frustrating "yearly exercise," managers met and set goals, then met again the following year with no idea of whether they had achieved the previous year's goals.

Although the problems listed result from too many meetings or meetings that are poorly managed, at the other extreme are companies where meetings are seldom held. In these situations, there is limited communication and coordination. As a result, the company frequently suffers from productivity problems, including duplication of effort.

When plans are made, there is very little follow-up, so things just don't get done. Another sign of an entrepreneurship with growing pains is a lack of follow-up after plans are made. Recognizing that the need for planning is greater than in the past, an entrepreneur may introduce a planning process. People go through the motions of preparing business plans, but the things that were planned just do not get done. In one amazing case, there was no follow-up simply because the plan, after being prepared, sat in a drawer for the entire year until the next year's planning retreat. When asked about the plan, one senior manager stated: "Oh that. It's in my desk. I never look at it."

In some cases there is no follow-up because the company has not yet developed adequate systems (that is, control systems) to monitor progress against goals. For example, many firms desire to monitor financial goals but have not developed an accounting system that can provide the information needed to do so. Metro Realty suffered from this deficiency.

In other cases, follow-up does not occur because personnel have not received proper training in setting, monitoring, and evaluating goals. They set goals that cannot be achieved or cannot be measured, or they do not know how to evaluate and provide useful feedback on goal achievement. These problems tend to appear most often in the performance appraisal process, a topic discussed further in Chapters Five and Six. Chapter Ten deals with how to design and effectively use control and performance management systems.

Some people feel insecure about their place in the firm. As a consequence of other organizational growing pains, employees begin to feel insecure about their places in the firm. In some cases, the entrepreneur has become anxious about problems facing the organization and has therefore hired a "heavy-weight" manager from outside. This action may have been accompanied by the termination of one or more current managers. Employees feel anxious, partly because they do not understand the reasons for these and other changes. When anxiety becomes too high, it may result in morale problems or excessive turnover.

Employees may also become insecure because they are unable to see the value of their position to the firm. This occurs when roles and responsibilities are not clearly defined and terminations are also occurring. Employees begin to wonder whether they will be the next to get the axe. In an attempt to protect themselves, they keep their activities secret and do not make waves. This results in isolation and a decrease in teamwork.

Entire departments may come to suffer from the need to remain isolated in order to protect themselves from being eliminated. This can lead to a certain amount of schizophrenia among employees. They begin to ask, "Am I loyal to my department or to the organization at large?" This happened at Tempo Products, as we see in Chapter Six. In another Stage IV firm, one employee expressed her sense of anxiety this way: "This company could give me a trip around the world for free and I would think they were trying to get rid of me." In this same organization, people indicated that they were afraid they would be fired if they said anything controversial. However, when pressed about the extent to which people had been terminated, no one could identify a specific case. In effect, the culture of the organization had become one that promoted anxiety and fear. It also created a situation in which people spent more time covering their own vested interests than working toward achieving company goals.

The firm continues to grow in sales, but not in profits. If all the other growing pains are permitted to exist, one final symptom may emerge. In some instances, sales continue to increase while profits remain flat, so that the company is succeeding only in increasing its workload. In the worst cases, sales increase while overall profits actually decline. As we see in the chapters that follow, companies may begin to lose money without having any idea why. The business loss can be quite significant, even though sales are up. There are many examples of entrepreneurial companies that experienced this problem, including Apple Computer, Maxicare, People Express, and Osborne Computer.

In a significant number of companies, the decline in profits may be the result of an underlying philosophy that stresses sales. People in such companies may say, "If sales are good, then profit will also be good," or "Profit will take care of itself." Profit in these companies is not an explicit goal but merely whatever remains after expenses.

In sales-oriented companies, people often become accustomed to spending whatever they need to in order to make a sale or promote the organization. For example, at Tempo Products, employees believed that it was important to the company's image to always "go first class." They made no effort to control costs, because they believed that no matter what they did, the organization would always be profitable. Organizations may also suffer because of systems that reward employees for achieving sales goals rather than profit goals (examples of these problems are given in Chapters Five and Six).

For nonprofits, this growing pain can be restated as, "Our administrative costs have increased more rapidly than our funding (budget)." This growing pain can result from inadequate focus on fund acquisition (for example, in some nonprofits only a very few people are responsible for fundraising), from a belief that sources will continue to provide the same level of funding year after year, or from underdeveloped budgeting processes that do not provide the information needed to track administrative costs. The result is a lack of balance between "what we have" and "what we need" to support ongoing operations and can, at times, lead to the nonprofit's demise.

MEASURING ORGANIZATIONAL GROWING PAINS

Growing pains are not just binary, meaning they exist or not. There are degrees of severity of growing pains.

To assist the management of an entrepreneurial company in measuring the organization's growing pains, we have developed the Survey of Organizational Growing Pains, shown in Exhibit 3.1.[4]

This questionnaire instrument presents ten organizational growing pains that have been identified in a wide variety of entrepreneurial companies with annual sales revenues ranging from less than $1 million to over $1 billion. Responses to the survey are entered on a Likert-type five-point scale, with descriptions ranging from "to a very great extent" to "to a very slight extent."[5] By placing check marks in the appropriate columns, the respondent indicates the extent to which he or she feels each of the ten growing pains characterizes the company.

Scoring the Survey

Once the survey has been completed, the number of check marks in each column is totaled and recorded on line 11. Each item on line 11 is then multiplied by the corresponding weight on line 12, and the total is recorded on line 13. For example, Exhibit 3.1 shows four check marks in column B. Accordingly, we multiply 4 by the weight of 4 and record the result, 16, on line 13 of column B.

The next step is to determine the sum of the numbers on line 13. This total represents the organization's growing pains score. It can range from 10, which is the lowest possible or most favorable score, to 50, which is the highest possible or most unfavorable score.

Interpreting the Scores

Drawing on our research concerning the degree of seriousness of problems indicated by different growing pains scores, we have worked out the color-coding scheme shown in Table 3.1.

More detailed interpretation of score ranges is as follows:

- *A green score* represents a fairly healthy organization. It suggests that everything is probably functioning in a manner satisfactory for the organization at its current stage of development.

Exhibit 3.1. Survey of Organizational Growing Pains

Growing Pain	A To a very Great extent	B To a Great extent	C To some Extent	D To a slight Extent	E To a very Slight Extent
1. People feel that there are not enough hours in the day.		√			
2. People spend too much time "putting out fires."		√			
3. Many people are not aware of what others are doing.	√				
4. People lack an understanding of where the firm is headed.			√		
5. There are not enough good managers.		√			
6. People feel that "I have to do it myself if I want to get it done correctly."			√		
7. Most people feel that the firm's meetings are a waste of time.				√	
8. When plans are made there is very little follow-up, so things just don't get done.		√			
9. Some people feel insecure about their place in the firm.				√	
10. The firm has continued to grow in sales, but not in profits.	√				
Scoring					
11. Add the total number of responses in each column.	2	4	2	2	0
12. Multiply the number on line 11 by the number on line 12 and record the result on line 13.	5	4	3	2	1
13. Result of line 11 times line 12.	10	16	6	4	0
14. Add the numbers on line 13 in columns A–E and place the result on this line.	36				

Table 3.1. Interpretation of Organizational Growing Pains Survey Scores

Score Range	Color	Interpretation
10–14	Green	Everything OK
15–19	Yellow	Some things to watch
20–29	Orange	Some areas that need attention
30–39	Red	Some very significant problems
40–50	Purple	A potential crisis or turnaround situation

- *A yellow score* indicates that the organization is basically healthy, but there are some areas of concern. It is like hearing from your doctor, "Your cholesterol is in the normal range but on the high side. It's something to watch and be careful about but not an immediate concern."

- *An orange score* indicates that some organizational problems require attention. They may not be too serious yet, but corrective action should be taken before they become so.

- *A red score* is a clear warning of present or impending problems. Immediate corrective action is required.

- *A purple score* indicates that the organization is having very serious problems and is in crisis. The organization is in distress and may be on the verge of collapse. There may not be enough time to save it.

If a firm's score exceeds 20, a more in-depth analysis to identify problems and develop recommendations for future action is warranted. Such a score may be a signal that the firm has reached a new stage in its development and must make major, qualitative changes. Failure to pay attention to a score of this magnitude can produce very painful results.

Growing Pains Scores for Different Business Sizes and Industries

Table 3.2 presents average organizational growing pains scores of companies with different annual revenues, based on our extensive research over the past twenty-plus years. As can be seen, companies of every size experience some growing pains. As organizations grow, growing pains tend to increase until companies reach a significantly large size. Our data suggest that growing pains tend to increase in severity as firms increase in size from less than $1 million to $1 billion in revenues. However, firms that reach $1 billion have (on the average) reduced growing pains. This suggests that at revenue levels greater

Table 3.2. Organizational Growing Pains by Company Size

Size (Revenues)	Stage	Average Growing Pains Score
Less than $1 million	I	27.00 (Orange)
$1–$9 million	II	29.00 (Orange)
$10–$99 million	III	29.00 (Orange)
$100–$499 million	IV	32.00 (Red)
$500 million–$1 billion	V	34.00 (Red)
More than $1 billion	VI	27.00 (Orange)

than $1 billion, an organization has developed the "critical mass" sufficient to bring these problems under a greater degree of control.

Table 3.3 shows scores broken down by type of industry. Figure 3.1 graphically depicts these scores, showing the trends in growing pains as revenues increase. Clearly, timing of the occurrence of significant organizational growing pains differs across industries.

In the service industry, growing pains become severe when the firm reaches $5 to $9 million in revenues (Stage III for a service firm) and diminish slightly as the firm's revenues exceed $10 million. This dip in severity of growing pains may indicate that $10 to $24 million in revenue is an easier service company size to manage than those over $24 million and those between $1 and $9 million. Growing pains begin to increase in severity again as the firm's revenues exceed $25 million and remain significant until the firm's revenues exceed $1 billion.

High-tech companies appear to experience significant problems when they reach the $25 to $99 million range of revenues (Stage III). Problems then continue into the $500 million to $1 billion range, after which they begin to drop. Low-tech companies, in contrast, experience the most significant problems in the $5 to $9 million revenue range. Growing pains in low-tech companies also drop significantly at revenues over $1 billion. In fact, low-tech companies with revenues greater than $1 billion experience the least severe growing pains of firms in any industry at any size.

Companies in the financial industry begin experiencing significant growing pains when revenues reach $10 to $24 million (Stage III for financial firms), which continue through the $500 million to $1 billion revenue range. Financial companies with revenues exceeding $1 billion experience a significant drop in growing pains.

The information presented here suggests that entrepreneurs in different industries need to be concerned with growing pains at different periods of their

Table 3.3. Organizational Growing Pains in Different Industries

Size (Revenues)	Overall	Service	High-tech	Low-tech	Finance
Less than $1 million	26.52	26.98	25.95	26.27	24.30
	Orange	Orange	Orange	Orange	Orange
$1–$4 million	28.00	27.93	28.23	27.26	27.87
	Orange	Orange	Orange	Orange	Orange
$5–$9 million	29.47	29.30	28.38	31.31	28.74
	Orange	Orange	Orange	Red	Orange
$10–$24 million	29.32	27.78	28.09	29.24	31.57
	Orange	Orange	Orange	Orange	Red
$25–$99 million	29.22	29.88	30.11	26.79	30.21
	Orange	Orange	Red	Orange	Red
$100–$499 million	31.67	31.17	34.12	29.17	33.67
	Red	Red	Red	Orange	Red
$500 million–$1 billion	33.57	33.93	32.00	26.10	36.00
	Red	Red	Red	Orange	Red
More than $1 billion	27.43	28.42	27.53	17.00	25.75
	Orange	Orange	Orange	Yellow	Orange

organizations' lives. For organizations in the finance industry, critical periods occur when revenues begin to exceed $10 million. For high-tech companies, significant growing pains begin when revenues are at $25 to $99 million, while for service companies, they appear at $5 million in revenues and again when the firm's revenues begin to exceed $25 million. For low-tech companies, this critical point occurs when revenues are between $5 and $9 million. These data also indicate that large ($500 million to $1 billion in revenues) financial firms experience the most severe organizational growing pains, whereas large low-tech companies (in excess of $1 billion in revenues) experience the least severe growing pains.

Although the data presented in Table 3.3 and Figure 3.1 indicate that there are certain stages of growth in which organizational growing pains are likely to be severe, these growing pains at any stage can be alleviated. This is best done through early detection of problems and careful plans for handling them.

The data suggest that growing pains typically increase as an organization's size increases to approximately $1 billion in revenues. Although firms with more than $1 billion in revenues do encounter difficulties and even fail (for example, Compaq Computers and Maxicare), this appears to be a critical size for reduced growing pains. We can hypothesize that if a firm exceeds $1 billion in revenues, the organization may have achieved the critical mass

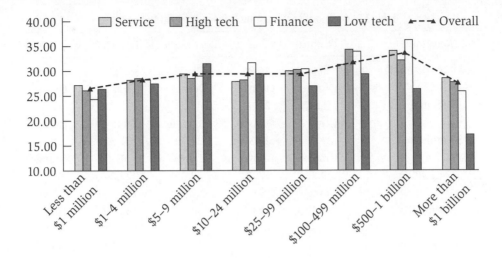

Figure 3.1. Organizational Growing Pains by Company Size (Revenue) in Different Industries

and resources necessary to deal with its problems and overcome its growing pains, and that the probability of continued survival is increased after $1 billion in revenues. In brief, most firms that achieve this size are likely to have become professionally managed firms and have a high probability of continued success.

Use of Growing Pains Measurements in Making the Transition

The Growing Pains Survey and related data presented here are important tools in helping organizations make the transition from entrepreneurship to professional management. They indicate the degree of distress being experienced by an organization and can function as an early warning of serious problems to be encountered by an organization, such as those ultimately experienced by Osborne Computer, People Express, and Maxicare.

We have been using the Growing Pains Survey since 1984 as part of our consulting practice to help firms identify the need to make the transition from an entrepreneurship to a professionally managed firm. Measures of growing pains are useful in creating the motivation for change. Without the measurements, there can be a vague awareness of organizational problems, but the growing pains measures identify the issues with clarity, and, we have found, are more likely to serve as a stimulus to action. This is consistent with the theory of "data-based change," developed by the University of Michigan's Institute for Social Research.

The survey can be used as part of the first step in the process of transition (described in Chapter Two). This is the evaluation of the company's effectiveness at its current stage of growth. This also serves to "benchmark" growing pains to assess developmental progress at a later stage. For example, Power-Bar, IndyMac Bank, Pardee Homes, Infogix (described in Chapter Thirteen), and Countrywide Financial Corporation have used measurements of growing pains over several years to assess their progress in organizational development. Progress is assessed not only with respect to the overall score but for each individual item as well.

Growing Pains Scores and Their Management at Grange, Inc.[6]

The use of growing pains scores as a tool in helping to facilitate organizational transitions and measure their effectiveness is illustrated in the case example of Grange, Inc. (a fictitious name for a real firm) presented next.

Company Background. Grange, Inc. is a general-purpose distributor of sundry products to over more than 2,500 customers in the western part of the United States. It specializes in providing good customer service to small retailers, helping them stock products in lot sizes that were too small for the manufacturers to handle. By 2003, the firm had grown to over $100 million in revenues. Although the firm had been extremely successful in growing its revenue base, profitability had been declining for some time. The firm's senior management team felt that they needed to better understand what was causing their profitability problems and hired a team of consultants to evaluate their firm's effectiveness.

Organizational Growing Pains. The consultants conducted an organizational audit, which included the administration of the Growing Pains Survey. Overall, Grange, Inc. was in the red zone, indicating some very significant problems. The consultant team also calculated the severity of *each* growing pain and found that seven of the ten growing pains were ranked purple or red. The complete scores are shown in Table 3.4.

The most severe growing pain at Grange, Inc., which ranked in the purple zone ("a potential crisis or turnaround situation"), was "People spend too much time 'putting out fires.'" This indicated that people were reacting to crises, many of which were caused by a lack of effective planning and by the decision-making processes in the firm. Qualitative information gathered through interviews with employees throughout the firm supported the conclusion that the company had a severely underdeveloped planning process (especially given that it was a Stage IV firm). Interview data also suggested

Table 3.4. Grange, Inc.'s Growing Pains Scores

Growing Pain	June 2003			April 2005		
	Rank	Score	Color	Rank	Score	Color
People spend too much time "putting out fires."	1	40.00	Purple	3	25.80	Orange
The firm has continued to grow in sales, but not in profits.	2	39.50	Red	7	16.70	Yellow
People lack understanding of where the firm is headed.	3	37.50	Red	4	23.30	Orange
Many people are not aware of what others are doing.	4	37.00	Red	1	29.30	Orange
People feel that "I have to do it myself if I want to get it done correctly."	5	36.50	Red	6	19.20	Yellow
People feel that there are not enough hours in the day.	6	34.50	Red	2	29.20	Orange
There are too few good managers.	7	33.50	Red	8	15.00	Yellow
When plans are made, there is very little follow-up and things just don't get done.	8	27.00	Orange	9	14.20	Green
Most people feel that meetings are a waste of time.	9	26.00	Orange	10	13.30	Green
Some people have begun to feel insecure about their place in the firm.	10	23.50	Orange	5	20.80	Orange
Overall		**33.50**	**Red**		**20.58**	**Orange**

that decision making (especially at the top levels of the firm) was reactive rather than proactive. Further, employees throughout the firm were expected to "jump" whenever such decisions were made by members of senior management, even if they disagreed with them. A final factor underlying the severity of this growing pain was the firm's severely underdeveloped computer systems. Although the company had been trying to upgrade its systems for a number of years, it had been unable to effectively execute its plans. This created a situation in which managers did not have the information needed to manage their businesses proactively and, therefore, were constantly fighting fires.

Six growing pains were ranked in the red zone. These included the following: *The firm has continued to grow in sales, but not in profits.* As stated previously, Grange, Inc.'s profits had been declining for a number of years.

Although the two owners of the firm—Fred and Lionel Black (two brothers)—suggested that this was due to increasing competition, other members of senior management believed the profits were being adversely affected by inefficiencies that existed within the company. Control systems (not holding people accountable, not rewarding outstanding performance) were ineffective, and there was a sense of complacency throughout the firm. The firm's owners believed that if they continued to provide good service, their customers would remain with them, regardless of what their competitors did. The problem was that the competition was offering the same product at lower prices, which customers found attractive. As a result, Grange, Inc. was beginning to lose market share. Internally, the sense of complacency was reflected in a culture in which employees felt a sense of entitlement. In addition, the lack of a strategic plan and budgets, as well as the firm's decision-making process, contributed to the lack of focus on profitability.

People lack understanding about where the firm is headed, and many people are not aware of what others are doing. As stated previously, the firm did not have a strategic plan and tended to make decisions in a reactive manner. People were never sure what would be done next. The standard way of operating was to wait for Lionel or Fred to make a decision and quickly respond to it. Although the company had formal job descriptions, they were not being used as tools to communicate the expectations of each individual's performance. Further, it wasn't always clear who individuals reported to. Some people thought they reported to one manager when, according to the organizational chart, they really reported to another. Changes in the organization's structure, although reflected on paper, had never been formally communicated to employees throughout the firm. The lack of understanding about the firm's direction and individual roles contributed to a number of productivity problems and certain inefficiencies (which, in turn, affected profitability).

People feel that "I have to do it myself if I want to get it done correctly." Grange, Inc.'s culture fostered the idea that being a doer versus a manager was most valued. This started at the very top of the organization, as Fred and Lionel took control of just about every situation and seldom delegated tasks that could reasonably have been performed by the managers who reported to them. Also, owing to the sense of complacency and poor accountability and training, most people did not trust others to complete tasks. They were worried that Fred and Lionel would be upset if something that they were asked to do was not handled directly and immediately.

People feel that there are not enough hours in the day. As several interviewees remarked, "the more hours in the day, the more of Fred's and Lionel's fires we have to put out." Without plans or budgets, people's priorities were determined by Fred and Lionel in an impromptu manner. Most people did not effectively plan and protect their time. Few people, in fact, had ever received any formal training in time management and, therefore, had only limited understanding of the importance of planning and scheduling their work.

There are too few good managers. Although many people held the title of manager, few were effective. Fred and Lionel did not effectively empower managers and often side-stepped them to deal directly with employees. All managers were "homegrown," and Grange, Inc. had never trained people in how to be effective managers. Most managers were promoted because of longevity or because of their "doer" skills (for example, a good, long-tenured salesman was made sales manager) not because of their management skills or aptitude.

The three remaining growing pains scored in the orange zone, indicating that issues required attention, as described next.

When plans are made, there is little follow-up and things don't get done. Whatever plans were made or goals that were set were seldom followed up on. People were seldom held accountable for their performance. In fact, Grange, Inc. gave all employees the same percentage salary increases every year. This created a situation in which people who were working hard and achieving decent results felt resentful that some people were "getting away with murder" and being rewarded for it. Over time, the high performers became de-motivated and began doing only what they needed to do to get by.

Most people feel that meetings are a waste of time. At Grange, Inc. there were very few formal meetings. If meetings occurred at all, they were called and conducted on an ad hoc basis. Under these conditions, it was impossible for people to prepare for those meetings, so they were ineffective. The lack of formal meetings contributed to communication and coordination problems.

Some people feel insecure about their place in the firm. Usually, when a firm's overall growing pains score is in the red zone, this growing pain tends to be ranked as more severe. The fact that it was the least severe at Grange, Inc. seemed to be an indication of the sense of complacency and entitlement that people had. Even though the firm was declining in profit, people did not feel that their position in the firm was threatened. Some of those interviewed could point to numerous cases of individuals who had not been performing at an acceptable level for years, yet they remained with the firm. The basic feeling was, "If there can be so much deadwood in the company, why should I worry?"

Overcoming the Growing Pains. The growing pains results and findings from the organizational audit served as the catalyst for Grange, Inc.'s senior management team to embark on a comprehensive program of organizational development. The team agreed to a twenty-four-month timeframe in which they would do the following:

- Implement a management development program in order to improve the skills of managers throughout the company, including those of the senior management team.

- Develop and implement a formal strategic plan that would be used to guide the company and help hold individuals accountable for results.

- Develop more formal and accurate role descriptions and an organizational chart and communicate how the structure would work to employees throughout the company.

- Redesign their performance appraisal and compensation processes so that they differentiated between high, average, and low performance.

- Develop a succession plan and provide training to the next generation of corporate leaders (Fred's and Lionel's sons).

All managers participated in the management development program, which consisted of twelve sessions, delivered one day per month over the course of a year. The program was designed so that managers could apply what they were learning in each session and then discuss the results of their efforts at the next session. In other words, it was designed to help hold managers accountable for changing their behavior and reporting on results.

Fred never agreed that the firm had no plan; after all, he knew exactly what he wanted for the firm. The key challenge, then, in developing an effective planning process was in leveraging what was in his head, supplementing his ideas with data, obtaining crucial input from key players, and documenting the results in a way that would be easy to implement at the company, departmental, and individual levels. Through a series of management team meetings, a written strategic plan was prepared. The plan outlined where Grange, Inc. wanted to go and how it was going to get there. The firm also implemented quarterly management review meetings to ensure that adequate progress was being made against goals.

The consulting team worked with Grange, Inc.'s management team to develop role descriptions for each position that were linked to the firm's strategic plan. Once developed, role descriptions were reviewed individually (for example, Is this role clear?) and as a group (for example, Do these positions work together to ensure that nothing is falling through the cracks and that efforts are not being duplicated?). Once approved, the role descriptions were used by each executive, manager, and supervisor to develop a personal plan that detailed results that they would be working to achieve within one year. The goals of the personal plans were linked to the goals of the corporate plan, ensuring that organizational priorities were aligned.

After personal plans were developed, Grange, Inc.'s management team worked with the consulting team to redesign their performance appraisal and compensation systems in order to hold people more accountable for results. Regular (twice annually) performance reviews were instituted, with each employee receiving objective feedback and coaching related to performance and results. Automatic salary increases were abolished. In their place, a bonus system based both on the firm's performance and on individual performance toward goals was instituted. A clear formula was developed and communicated, through which employees knew how the achievement of goals would result in increased bonuses, benefits, and advancement in the company. As a result of this process, a few long-time employees resigned or were asked to resign. At first, there was some shock. With proactive and positive communication, after a short while the remaining employees realized that they were chosen to remain with Grange, Inc. because of the positive contributions they could make.

Fred and Lionel were somewhat hesitant to let go of the company's management. However, they worked with the consultants and with their own sons to develop a succession plan and to develop strategies to ensure that the new generation of leaders would have the skills needed to effectively manage the firm. The two sons each grew through a process of one-on-one coaching. One became the head of marketing, while the other developed the skills that were needed to manage the entire company.

Results. Within two years of the organizational audit, Grange, Inc. had dramatically improved its management systems. More important, profits had tripled. Twenty-two months after first administering the Growing Pains Survey, it was re-administered to members of the firm. The results were dramatic: Grange, Inc.'s score had improved by more than a full color band, going from the red to the orange zone. Further, all individual growing pains had decreased in severity—some (like "continuing to grow in sales, but not in profits," "people feeling that they have to do it themselves," and "not enough good managers) had decreased quite dramatically. These changes in scores were also supported by interviews with managers, employees, customers, and vendors. It was universally felt that the company was better managed and well-positioned to address competitive challenges. The best praise came from Fred Black, who said, "Now Lionel and I can sleep well at nights, knowing our children and grandchildren will be financially secure. For the first time in my life, I can take a two-week vacation without calling into the office, knowing that we have built an excellent management team capable of running the firm."

ORGANIZATIONAL GROWING PAINS, GROWTH RATES, AND INFRASTRUCTURE

As we have noted in this and the previous chapter, when an organization's growth outstrips its infrastructure, organizational growing pains will result. The faster a firm is growing, the more difficult it will be for management to keep the organization's infrastructure at a level required to support the firm's rate of growth.

Based on our work with a wide variety of organizations, we have identified five different rates of growth that characterize different categories of growth. Growth at the rate of less than 15 percent a year can be thought of as normal growth. This is relatively unspectacular growth, but the firm will double in size in approximately five years if it is growing at a rate of 15 percent per year. A growth rate of between 15 and 25 percent per year can be thought of as rapid growth. A rate of growth from 25 to 50 percent per year can be considered very rapid growth. Growth at a rate of 50 to 100 percent per year can be thought of as "hypergrowth." If the firm is growing at a rate greater than 100 percent per year, it can perhaps be regarded as experiencing "light-speed growth."

Based on our experience, it is extremely difficult for firms to deal with growth rates greater than 50 percent per year. When the rate of growth of a firm equals or exceeds what we have characterized as hypergrowth, a firm can come very dangerously close to choking on its own growth. This has happened to a number of firms, including Osborne Computer, Maxicare, and People Express.[7]

GROWING PAINS AND FINANCIAL PERFORMANCE

Recent empirical research has found that there is a statistically significant relationship between growing pains and financial performance.[8] The data derived from this research also indicate that there are threshold levels of growing pains that are "unsafe" or "unhealthy" for future financial performance. The results also suggest that there appears to be a maximum level of growing pains beyond which organizational financial health is at risk. Specifically, the maximum healthy level of growing pains appears to be around 30. This means that to optimize the chances of being profitable, an organization ought to keep its growing pains score less than 30. In terms of the color-coding scheme used with the Growing Pains Survey, this means keeping the score below the red zone. These findings have significant implications for management theory and practice.

MINIMIZING ORGANIZATIONAL GROWING PAINS

Most entrepreneurs are concerned primarily with the risk of failure if revenues are insufficient to cover expenses. However, many ignore the equally damaging risks of choking on their own rapid growth. To avoid the problems accompanying hypergrowth, a company must have an infrastructure that will absorb that growth. If a company anticipates rapid growth, then management must invest in building the required infrastructure *before* it is actually necessary. It is very difficult, and sometimes impossible, to play catch-up with organizational infrastructure. Some companies, such as Compaq Computer, PacifiCare, and Starbucks, had their infrastructure in place prior to their explosive growth and reaped the benefits of this investment.

This strategy of building the infrastructure prior to growth is not merely appropriate for large companies but for relatively small entrepreneurships as well. For example, in 1992, one of the authors met with the president of a service firm specializing in insurance-based benefit programs for executives when the firm had approximately $3 million in annual revenues. At that time, the author advised the CEO that it was probably premature to build the infrastructure to the extent that was being contemplated. However, the CEO indicated that he wanted his firm to grow to $50 million in revenue by 1997. He then proceeded to invest in professionalizing his company before it was actually necessary. This was a wise move, because the company grew to more than $65 million in revenue by the late 1990s.

SUMMARY

Some people believe that the solution to the problems of growth is to avoid growth. Unfortunately, very soon after an organization is founded, it must grow or it will die. Managers can control the *rate* of growth, but it is unrealistic to try to remain at a given size or stage of development. This means we must learn how to manage growth and the inevitable transitions it requires.

This chapter presents an in-depth discussion of the most common organizational growing pains. It also presents a method for assessing the extent to which a company suffers from these growing pains. The company's score on the Organizational Growing Pains Survey can suggest both the extent of its problems and specific needs for action. Finally, the chapter provides information on the degree of organizational growing pains experienced by companies of different sizes and in different types of businesses. Variations exist here, but it is clear that organizations of all sizes and types experience some growing pains. As we have suggested, the severity of these problems can be affected by the rate of growth experienced by the organization. Managers of rapidly growing companies of any size or type must learn to recognize organizational growing pains and take steps to alleviate them so that their organizations can continue to operate successfully.

PART TWO

MANAGEMENT STRATEGIES
FOR EACH STAGE
OF ORGANIZATIONAL GROWTH

Part One of this book presented a framework for understanding the development of successful organizations. It explained the six key areas or tasks that make up the Pyramid of Organizational Development. It also identified and examined the first four stages of the growth of organizations and presented the four major steps involved in making the transition from one stage of growth to the next. Finally, it described the organizational growing pains that result when a firm has not been fully successful in its development and presented a way to measure and interpret them.

Part Two examines the issues involved in developing successful organizations at each stage of growth. It also studies the nature of the transitions that must be made in moving from Stage I to Stages II, III, and IV. It draws on a variety of case studies of organizations at different stages of growth.

Chapter Four begins by discussing the purpose and steps involved in developing a successful Stage I company. It gives several illustrations of firms that have been successful in accomplishing this stage of development and examines the problems faced by each company. Examples cited range from Jamba Juice, Compaq Computer, PowerBar, America Online, Dell Computer, eBay, Hotmail, and Yahoo! to Domino's Pizza, Mrs. Fields' Cookies, Federal Express, Liz Claiborne, Westfield, and Tse Cashmere.

Chapter Four also examines the key purpose, process, and problems involved in developing successful Stage II organizations. It describes some growing pains that may result when the process of organizational development has not been fully successful, especially when a firm has not developed the operational systems it needs to function well at Stage II.

Chapter Five describes the challenges of Stage III and the case of a company that made the transition from Stage II to Stage III. It describes the company's situation, the nature of its growing pains, and the actions it took to make a successful transition between these stages. This case study also illustrates the most common problems involved in making the transition from entrepreneurship to professional management, especially in developing management systems. We provide several other examples of companies that faced the challenges presented by this stage of development.

Chapter Six examines a firm that made the successful transition from Stage III to Stage IV and discusses the issues involved in managing corporate culture as a company grows.

CHAPTER FOUR

The New Venture and Expansion Stages

T his chapter deals with the issues involved in developing successful entrepreneurial organizations at Stages I and II of organizational growth. It examines the tasks that must be performed to establish a successful new venture (Stage I) and deals with the typical growing pains that arise during the expansion that takes place after a company has been successfully established (Stage II).

DEVELOPING SUCCESSFUL STAGE I ORGANIZATIONS

In the first stage of an organization's development or life cycle, the company is a new venture. This stage includes the period from an organization's birth to the point at which it begins to experience rapid growth (usually at about $1 million in annual revenues). The first section of this chapter identifies the key problems and challenges involved in building a successful new venture and provides several illustrations of actual firms that have successfully met these challenges. It examines why these firms have been successful.

KEY ISSUES AT STAGE I

The key challenge in developing a successful new venture is "proof of concept," which means that it is necessary to prove that the business concept or idea for the business venture is valid. Operationally defined, *proof of concept* means that there is a market for the product or service to be provided by the business venture and that the enterprise can ultimately make money by providing the product or service. This does not mean that the venture must be profitable during Stage I or even during Stage II but that it will ultimately *become* profitable. For many nonprofits (foundations, charities, government-funded entities, and membership-based organizations), creating proof of concept typically means showing that there is a market need for the service to be provided and that the organization can sustain its funding or its membership, or both, because it offers something that is truly differentiated from other nonprofits.

Although it might seem obvious that it is necessary to establish proof of concept, this was not done by many (if not most) of the dot-coms during the late 1990s and early years of the new millennium. The dot-coms operated on the principle that if they could establish a significant presence in the market, then it would ultimately be possible to create a way to make money. Clearly, this proved to be a great fallacy. If you are losing money on a per unit basis, it is not possible to make it up by increasing volume!

The key operational problems to be solved during Stage I are (1) to identify a market need and (2) to find a way to satisfy that need by providing a product or service. The skills required to solve these problems are essentially the classic entrepreneurial skills: the ability to see a market need, the willingness to make a risky investment to create a business that attempts to satisfy that need, and the ability to create an embryonic organization that is capable of providing the required products or services. The primary basis of entrepreneurship is an idea. The idea may be the product of long, tedious planning and research or of a brilliant, almost accidental insight.

Hotmail: A Classic Example of Entrepreneurial Success

On September 23, 1988, Sabeer Bhatia arrived at Los Angeles International Airport from Bangalore, India. He was nineteen years old, had $250 in cash, and knew nobody in the United States. He was to be a student at Caltech.

By August, 1995, Bhatia had decided he wanted to be an entrepreneur and build his own company. His idea for a "product" was free Web-based e-mail. After having his idea rejected by several venture capitalists, one finally agreed to provide start-up funding of $300,000, in return for 15 percent of the business.

In just under two and one-half years and with another round of financing, Bhatia built Hotmail's user base to more than eight million—faster than any other company in history, including America Online. The company also began to attract competitors, as well as interest by the six-hundred-pound gorilla itself—Microsoft.

In the fall of 1997, Microsoft began a bidding game for Hotmail. Ultimately, the game ended with the company being sold on New Year's Eve, 1997, for 2,769,148 shares of Microsoft stock, which was worth about $400 million at that time. Hotmail indeed!

Significant New Venture of the 1980s: Personal Computers

During the 1980s, there were a number of entrepreneurial successes in the computer industry, especially in personal computers (PCs). One of the most spectacular success stories is that of Apple Computer. Apple was founded by Steven Jobs and Steven Wozniak and was based on the perceived market for a "personal" computer—a small, relatively inexpensive computer that was user-friendly. Following this concept, the firm grew from being housed in a garage to having more than $1 billion in sales in 1983. Although Apple later experienced the classic symptoms of growing pains, it was clearly a successful new venture (a Stage I organization).

Adam Osborne, who founded Osborne Computer, had the concept of a relatively low-priced, easy-to-use computer that was also portable. His idea was a spin-off of the personal computer concept pioneered by Apple Computer, but Osborne identified a new market segment when he made his computers relatively easy to carry. For a few years, Osborne Computer was one of the fastest-growing companies in business history. In 1981, the firm's first full year of operation, its sales were $5.8 million; by 1982, sales had grown to $68.8 million. Similar to Apple, Osborne Computer also experienced severe growing pains and ultimately went bankrupt, but it was clearly a successful Stage I company.

Another company with the same idea as Osborne Computer was Compaq Computer Corporation (Compaq). It was formed by a group of former employees from Texas Instruments who also saw the opportunity to develop portable PCs. During its first year of business—1983—Compaq Computer Corporation's sales zoomed to $111.2 million. The firm's product was a portable version of the IBM personal computer. It was one of the first truly IBM-compatible PCs, but it was portable. As described next, Compaq had a different strategy and overall organizational development approach from Osborne's, and it became one of the leading computer companies in the world (even though it experienced some difficulties in both the late 1980s and late 1990s and was ultimately purchased by Hewlett-Packard).

In the early years of the PC, there was no standard operating system (what most of us take as a given today). When IBM developed its first PC in 1981, it originally looked to a company called Digital Research for a system called CPM. A variety of stories exist about what happened between IBM and Digital Research's founder, Gary Kildall, but the bottom line is that IBM could not reach agreement with him about "the deal." IBM went to Bill Gates (again, there are numerous stories about this event), who provided them with what would become the PC-DOS operating system. After Compaq became the first company to successfully "clone" the IBM computer, this system was renamed MS-DOS (Microsoft Disk Operating System). As a result of IBM becoming the industry standard, Microsoft became a major player (and perhaps the dominant) player in the software industry.

Another classic example of Stage I entrepreneurial success is Dell Computer. In 1984, Michael Dell founded Dell Computer with $1,000; he worked from his dorm room at the University of Texas. His concept was to sell PCs directly to customers. This simultaneously avoided the markup of retailers and allowed Dell to price his computers below those of competitors. This business concept has been very successful, not only for the growth of Dell Computer but also for shareholders. In the ten-year period from 1988 to 1998, Dell stock gained approximately 36,000 percent! As of 2006, Dell was one of the leading PC companies in the world, with revenues of $55.9 billion.

Significant New Ventures of the 1990s: Internet Firms

Beginning in the 1990s, and at least in part stimulated by the growth of PCs, the whole notion of "e-commerce" began to explode the opportunities for new ventures. Although this is still the beginning of the e-commerce era, a number of new ventures have already been established, geared to meet the needs of those who want to "shop" or "talk" online. These firms include Amazon.com (books, music, electronics, and a wide variety of products), Yahoo! (Internet portal), E*Trade (stock brokerage), America Online (Internet portal, advertising), Earthlink Network (network services), eBay (net auctioneer), and Google (Internet search and advertising).

Amazon.com was founded by Jeffrey Bezos. In the three-year period from 1996 to 1998, Amazon.com reached $148 million in sales revenue and became the third-largest bookseller in the world. In the late 1990s, the company began selling music and now offers customers a variety of products: electronics, computers, personal care, food, health and beauty, tools, and fashion. As of 2005, the company had grown to $8.5 billion in revenues.

Yahoo! was founded by Stanford University graduate students Jerry Chih-Yuan Yang and David Filo in 1994. Jerry and David both still hold the title "Chief Yahoo" at Yahoo!. Yahoo! is an Internet portal or "gateway" site, with a number of other services, including Yahoo! mail. Revenues, which exceeded $5 billion in 2005, are generated "by providing marketing services to businesses across the majority of 'our' properties and by establishing paying relationships with 'our' users for premium services."[1]

The story of the development of eBay approaches such classic fairy tales as Cinderella and the Pied Piper. As Internet legend has it, Pierre Omidyar was working at General Magic when his girlfriend remarked that it would be "neat" if there were a place on the Web where she and others could buy and sell Pez (the candy) dispensers. For his own amusement, Omidyar created a Web site. Then others who had things beyond Pez dispensers found the site and began using it as a place to trade.

As trading increased, maintaining the Web site became a time-consuming task. Omidyar began to charge a nominal fee ($0.25) to slow the use of the Web site. It did not happen. As envelopes piled up in his home, Omidyar realized that he had accidentally created a company. He hired someone to open all the envelopes, quit his job, and began his new venture in earnest.

By 1997, eBay was a growing, profitable company. At that point, the company acquired $3 million in venture capital and began to do some serious marketing. In September, 1998, eBay fulfilled the dream of many entrepreneurs and went public. The initial price was $18 per share, but the stock climbed very quickly to $47. By the beginning of 1999, the stock had climbed to more than $250 per share and doubled again from 2001 to 2006 (on a split, adjusted basis). This would enable Omidyar and Meg Whitman (the CEO and president since 1998) to buy quite a few Pez dispensers!

What is extraordinary about eBay, in comparison with many other Internet-based entrepreneurships, is that it became a profitable company at a very early stage. Sellers are eBay's source of revenue. The company charges a graduated fee for listing an item, and there is also a "final transaction fee" for items that have been sold. In a sense, the revenue model is similar to that of a residential or commercial real estate firm, with sellers being the source of revenue, not buyers. Later, eBay acquired the well-known auction house, Butterfield & Butterfield, in order to broaden its market base (while remaining in the same business of serving as a clearinghouse for those who wish to sell collectibles, antiques, and so on).

Although relatively few Internet firms have truly become established as successful organizations (in the sense that they have *profitable* operations like eBay), the promise of e-commerce is enormous, and it will undoubtedly continue to spawn many new ventures for a long, long time to come. Once they are spawned, they will face the challenges of developing into established companies like Microsoft, Yahoo!, or Google. In addition, countless "Internet entrepreneurs" of all types and persuasions are literally dreaming up new Internet-based business ventures on a daily, if not micro-second, basis.

Other Examples of New Venture Success

Although many of the examples just cited are in the computer industry or based on e-commerce, high technology is not a prerequisite for entrepreneurial success. There are many examples of successful new ventures where technology is relatively unimportant or of modest importance, as well as companies that provide services rather than products. These include Southwest Airlines (transportation), Federal Express (package delivery), 99 Cents Only Stores (a low-price retailer of "closeout" items), Mrs. Fields' Cookies (gourmet chocolate chip cookies), Domino's Pizza (home-delivered Pizza), Liz Claiborne (women's clothing), PowerBar (energy bars), Noah's Bagels (relatively healthy fast food), Jamba Juice (smoothies and meal replacement), and Tse Cashmere (high-quality cashmere clothing products).

Frederick W. Smith was the architect of Federal Express. At the time the company was founded, Emery Air Freight dominated the package-delivery business. Emery had built a successful business on the assumption that the major cost in air freight involved weight and, therefore, air carrier charges. This notion made sense for heavy items but not for small packages or letters. Federal Express built a different system, geared to the goal of minimizing handling costs rather than air carrier costs. It focused on a different market segment: small packages.

Dave Gold and his wife, Sherry, founded 99 Cents Only Stores with the idea that the firm could buy manufacturers' excess inventory cheaply and sell it at large discounts to customers for a single price point: 99 cents. The firm's merchandise constantly changes, as it purchases goods from a variety of suppliers. As described further in Chapter Fifteen, by 2006 the company had more than two hundred stores and more than $1 billion in annual revenues.

The success of both Debbi Fields of Mrs. Fields' Cookies and David Lieberman of David's Cookies not only shows that a new venture can be developed from a very old, familiar product, but it also shows that more than one company can operate successfully within the same market segment. Both entrepreneurs created successful new ventures by developing stores to make and market over-the-counter chocolate chip cookies. David's Cookies defined a market for consumers who prefer large chunks of chocolate in a thin, buttery cookie that is not sold until it cools. Mrs. Fields' Cookies, in contrast, defined a market for a more traditional chocolate chip cookie, with smaller chips in a larger-sized cookie that is served warm. Both firms have been quite successful.

Thomas Monaghan founded Domino's Pizza, based on the concept of providing free delivery of pizza that was priced lower than any of his competitors. Today, the company has eight thousand stores and revenues in excess of $1 billion. The keys to Domino's success were, first, the ability of its founder to identify a market need and, second, his ability to build a business to satisfy it. Monaghan's concept was the simple notion of pizza delivery. This may not seem like a brilliant or unique strategy today, but it was a novel idea when Monaghan pioneered it. Monaghan states, "Basically, any place that delivered, you really wouldn't want to buy a pizza from, because if they had a good product they wouldn't have to deliver. Nobody delivered unless they were crazy or stupid, and I was both."[2] Indeed, nobody wanted delivery except customers, so Monaghan focused on delivery as his competitive advantage.

The basic idea behind the success of Liz Claiborne, Inc. was also simple. The concept was to develop lines of fashionable, well-made sportswear that could be worn to the office. To keep distribution costs low, the firm focused on department stores, thereby minimizing the need for a salesforce. The Claiborne concept was successful, and the rest is history.

More recently, Brian and Jennifer Maxwell not only created a new business but an entire product category with the development of PowerBar. Both Maxwells were runners. The late Brian Maxwell was a world-class marathon runner, and his wife, Jennifer, was not only a runner but a nutritionist as well. The Maxwells, together with Bill Vaughan, a biochemist, created PowerBar—an energy bar—and launched the company in 1986.

The initial concept behind PowerBar was to develop a portable energy food that would help athletes compete more effectively. The Maxwells initially did this for themselves and their friends but, much like Pierre Omidyar at eBay, quickly found that they had the basis of a new business. In 1998, the company's revenues passed $100 million. The company also successfully launched its second new product line—Harvest Bar. The company was ultimately sold to Nestlé in the late 1990s.

Kirk Perron, founder of Jamba Juice, has always been committed to personal health. His mother introduced him to the benefits of "juicing." In addition, Kirk wanted to be an entrepreneur from an early age. Putting the two interests (juice and entrepreneurship) together, the result was a company first called the Juice Club and now known as Jamba Juice.

Jamba Juice is a San Francisco–based restaurant chain featuring smoothies, fresh-squeezed juices, a unique line of energy breads called Jambolas, and hot soups. From 1995 to 2006, the company grew to over $350 million in revenues and five hundred retail sites, including company-owned stores, franchised stores, airport sites, and sites within Whole Foods Markets.

Significant New Ventures of the New Millennium: International Firms

Although the United States is a bastion of entrepreneurial culture, there are an increasing number of companies all around the world where entrepreneurship is flourishing, including China, India, Australia, Latin America, and Europe. Entrepreneurs worldwide face most of the same issues as those involved in start-ups in the United States. Examples include Richard Branson, who built the Virgin Group of Companies in Great Britain; Frank Lowy, who built the Westfield Group of companies into a shopping center empire from his base in Australia; the Tata family in India, which has built a powerhouse group of entrepreneurial companies in industries such as steel and motors; and Anita Roddick, who built The Body Shop into a global franchise. In addition to these large enterprises, there are many emerging entrepreneurial companies around the world. One example is Cashmere House, the company built by Augustine Tse, described next.

For centuries China provided the bulk of high-quality cashmere to European companies that produced finished products. Storied brands such as Pringles (Scotland) and Loro Piana (Italy) produced expensive garments from the precious raw material. In the late 1970s, as China began moving toward becoming a market economy, its leaders were concerned about creating jobs. Officials from Xinjiang province approached one of Hong Kong's most powerful industrialists (Tang Hsiang Chien) about becoming a partner in a cashmere factory.[3] The Chinese government promised Tang that the factory would get a supply of high-quality cashmere and some of the quota it needed to export garments to the United States and Europe. The mission of Tang's company was to increase the quality of the garments exported so that they would ultimately compete with European and U.S.-made products.

Augustine Tse, who worked in one of Tang's companies in Hong Kong, was given the assignment to build a factory in Urumqi, the capital of Xinjiang province. In the mid-1980s, Tse moved to Los Angeles and established Cashmere House, in partnership with two of Tang's children. His strategic objective was to create a Chinese brand that could compete with the traditional luxury brands of Europe. Tse is CEO of Cashmere House, and he has succeeded in achieving his objective. His strategy was to produce different types of garments using raw cashmere. He hired designers and gave them the mandate to create the "unthinkable" with cashmere. The company's first big hit was a soft hooded sweater—a "hoodie"—that sold very quickly.[4] Tse's company redefined cashmere as a garment that could be worn to either a party, a grocery store, or a Starbucks café.

Entrepreneurs come from all backgrounds, and their visions are stimulated by a variety of things. In the early 1950s, John Saunders and Frank Lowy, both survivors of the Holocaust and immigrants to Australia, became partners in a new business venture. In March 1955, the two opened Blacktown Delicatessen in the western suburb of Sydney, offering foods unavailable elsewhere in the suburbs.

A year after the opening of Blacktown Delicatessen, Frank and John heard about the growing trend to purchase farmland, subdivide it, and then sell the new plots for residential use. They decided to try it on their own. They borrowed money from friends, bought land from a local farmer, and within six months had subdivided and sold the land to new immigrants for $1,000 a plot.

Based on the success of this initial venture, Frank and John continued buying, dividing, and selling larger and larger lots and, after becoming a private company bearing the name Westfield Investments Pty Ltd, eventually moved on to the development of small complexes of neighborhood stores. Later, Saunders and Lowy sold Blacktown Delicatessen in order to focus on land development full time, including their first shopping center. They created the small but innovative Westfield Place, as well as a number of progressively larger subdivisions and department stores across New South Wales, Australia.[5]

As of 2006, The Westfield Group was the largest retail property group in the world, as measured by equity market capitalization ($31.6 billion in Australian dollars). Westfield has 128 shopping centers located in four countries (the United States, Australia, New Zealand, and the United Kingdom). It has 22,500 retail outlets and 10.6 million square meters of space.[6] The company has offered investors incredible returns—$1,000 invested in 1960 would be worth more than $109 million in 2000—over the course of its history and has been at the forefront of many shopping center innovations. The path has not always been easy, though, and many lessons have been learned along the way.

On the other side of the world, Richard Branson has built an entrepreneurial powerhouse, based on his own unique personal vision and a sense of having fun. Branson's business career began when he founded *Student* magazine (the "voice of youth") while he was still in school. The core of Branson's vision was to make the magazine appeal to the baby boomers, who were moving through the early stages of their life cycle.

When the initial success of the magazine was not sustained, Branson saw opportunities in records. Branson lacked the financial resources to open stores, so he used the last issue of *Student* to advertise a set of records likely to appeal to young people at deep-discounted prices (about 15 percent below that of retail stores). Orders flooded in. Branson puckishly called his business Virgin, to the chagrin of registration authorities, who thought the name was in bad taste. Realizing that selling records requires more than just a vision, Branson recruited an old friend who was more disciplined than he was to help him run the business.

By the end of the 1970s, Virgin was made up of music retail outlets, a record label, recording studios, music and book publishing, night clubs, and movie theaters. Success was not consistent, and Branson faced a number of financial crises that could have scuttled the entire business. In the 1980s, Branson further leveraged the Virgin brand and purchased an airline. Nevertheless, Branson has succeeded in building an entrepreneurial empire on the concept of being an off-beat (unorthodox) source of products and services to a segment of the baby-boom generation, which he helped personify.[7]

KEYS TO A SUCCESSFUL
STAGE I FIRM

New ventures in computers, clothing, and cookies, not to mention package delivery, pizza, energy bars, juices and smoothies, e-commerce, sports nutrition, and rock records, would not seem to have much in common. Yet if we look closely, we will see that each of these diverse businesses demonstrates certain fundamental abilities. Possession of these abilities is the prerequisite for developing a successful new venture:

1. The ability to define a market need
2. The ability to develop, acquire, or provide a product or service that will satisfy the identified market need
3. The ability to build an organization that is capable of functioning on a day-to-day basis to provide the product or service

We discuss each of these critical factors next.

Ability to Define a Market Need

The most fundamental prerequisite for success as a new venture is the ability to identify and define a market need that is not currently being satisfied or that can be satisfied in a different way (higher quality, lower cost, and so on). Each of the firms we described was able to do this.

Apple Computer saw the need for a personal computer that the average person, not just the computer hobbyist, could use. The company followed the same strategy with its Macintosh, which was initially advertised as the computer "for the rest of us." Adam Osborne perceived the need for a portable computer, and Compaq saw the need for an IBM-compatible portable computer. David Liederman and Debbi Fields saw an unsatisfied need for gourmet chocolate chip cookies. Tom Monaghan saw the need for home delivery of good pizza. Frederick W. Smith saw the need for inexpensive, rapid delivery of small packages. Liz Claiborne saw the need for medium-priced fashionable clothing that could be worn to work. Brian and Jennifer Maxwell saw the need for a portable, healthy, energy bar that could enhance and sustain optimal athletic performance. Pierre Omidyar saw the need for a Web-based trading site.

It should be noted that the needs these entrepreneurs saw were not necessarily for a new product, although some of the products were new. Others, such as Mrs. Fields' and David's Cookies, were merely reconceptualizations of existing products or services.

Ability to Develop a Relevant Product or Service

The second major task in developing a successful Stage I firm is providing a product or service that satisfies the market need the company has identified. Apple Computer was not the first firm to perceive the need for a personal computer, but it was the first to develop an acceptable product and market it successfully. Similarly, Kirk Peron of Jamba Juice was not the first to develop a smoothie, but he was able to develop both a product and a service delivery platform that was appealing to a defined category of customers. Augustine Tse was not the first to provide garments made of cashmere, but he was able to establish a Chinese brand of luxury garments.

Some entrepreneurs do not succeed in developing successful new ventures because, although they are able to see the market for a product, they are not able to develop the required product or service.

Ability to Develop an Organization to Provide the Product or Service

The third requirement for a successful Stage I company is the ability to develop an organization capable of providing the chosen product or service to customers. This involves developing the basic systems for the day-to-day operation of the firm, as well as finding the people needed to staff the organization.

If the three things just described are done well, a company will pass the first test of survival. It will have established proof of concept.

Once proof of concept has been established, the company might begin to grow rapidly, and this growth will create a new set of problems to be solved. These problems are the subject of the next section of this chapter, which deals with the development of successful Stage II companies.

DEVELOPING SUCCESSFUL STAGE II ORGANIZATIONS

The second stage of organizational development is the rapid growth stage. This stage begins after a firm has solved the three critical problems involved in establishing a new venture and has demonstrated proof of concept. Stage II may start very quickly or only after many years.

The key challenge of Stage II is "scale-up." The company needs to build the organizational capabilities necessary to facilitate its growth and operations on a much larger scale than during the first stage when it was proving its concept. This involves acquiring the resources needed to facilitate growth, including the financial resources, human capital, technology, and space required. It also involves developing the day-to-day operational systems needed to run the business. These include all of the basic systems, such as the sales and operations (manufacturing or service delivery) systems, accounting systems, personnel management systems, and other day-to-day operational systems.

If this is done well, the company will grow and flourish. However, it is extremely difficult to accomplish scale-up without experiencing a variety of organizational growing pains.

Unfortunately, many firms that successfully meet the challenges of growth in Stage I ultimately flounder in Stage II. This happens because the problems of managing a rapidly growing organization are in many ways fundamentally different from those of setting up a new venture. A Stage II firm requires capabilities different from those of a Stage I firm, and the managers of such an organization must have different skills. Not all organizations and all entrepreneurs, even those who were brilliant in Stage I, can handle the required metamorphosis.

The Osborne Syndrome

One of the most spectacular and tragic examples of a firm that failed to make the transition from Stage I to Stage II successfully is Osborne Computer. Because Osborne's experience is such a classic example, we call the phenomenon it exemplifies the Osborne syndrome—the phenomenon in which an organization that has experienced rapid success as an entrepreneurial venture soon experiences equally rapid decline because it has failed to make the transition from an entrepreneurship to a professionally managed firm. As Adam Osborne himself stated, "When you become an entrepreneur you can go up awfully fast, but you can go down just as fast. It's so ephemeral, like actors who end up committing suicide. One day they're famous, the next nobody knows who the hell they are."[8]

Osborne Computer began when Adam Osborne recognized the market for a portable personal computer. Despite skepticism, Osborne produced and marketed his machines and, in doing so, created a new market. The firm experienced extraordinarily rapid growth, soon achieving more than $100 million in annual revenues and employing more than one thousand people.

Osborne's success was the classic entrepreneur's dream come true, but it turned into the classic entrepreneurial nightmare when the firm experienced its now-well-publicized difficulties. When some suppliers sued to collect $4.5 million, Osborne filed for bankruptcy under Chapter 11 of the federal bankruptcy code.

What caused the fall of Osborne Computer after its meteoric rise? Although the answer to this question is complex, a key to the basic problem was stated by Adam Osborne himself in reflecting on what had happened to his firm. As he said, the firm "had existed only eighteen months in terms of operation—hardly time to get my feet wet; all of a sudden the job was a whole different order of magnitude. I realized it was no longer an entrepreneurial operation in any conceivable way."[9] In spite of this recognition, Osborne was unable to make the required changes in himself or his company. His firm's infrastructure was severely underdeveloped, given his stage of growth. Among other things, he did not have adequate financial resources to support his growth, his operational systems (including his internal computer, accounting, and inventory control systems) were severely underdeveloped, and he did not have the management systems in place to assist him in sustaining a $100 million organization.

Unfortunately, there is a pattern in what happened to Adam Osborne. After the initial success of a new entrepreneurial venture, a rapidly growing firm will inevitably experience the kind of organizational growing pains we described in Chapter Three, just as Osborne Computer did. As we have stated, these pains are normal, but they are a warning—symptoms of a disease that can be fatal if left untreated. The fatality is the Osborne syndrome we have just described. The key to avoiding the Osborne syndrome is recognizing the warning inherent in an organization's growing pains and dealing with these symptoms before the condition becomes terminal. Unless entrepreneurs learn from this story, they may someday find themselves experiencing the Osborne syndrome.[10]

Other Examples of Problems at Stage II

Let us now look at several other companies that experienced organizational growing pains strong enough to put them in danger of suffering the Osborne syndrome.

- An industrial-products distributor had grown from $3 million in annual sales to $15 million, but profits had not increased proportionately. Indeed, they had actually begun to decline. The firm's accounting information system could not pinpoint the reasons for these profitability problems. Inventory had accumulated in the warehouse, but no one could say how much of each item there was or where it was located, because the firm's inventory control system was manual and not kept up-to-date. The firm hired an ever-increasing number of people to cope with day-to-day operational pressures, but many of these people worked without supervision because their managers were too busy putting out fires. The sales staff included some outstanding people, but others were simply not productive. The firm was beginning to lose accounts because of a series of embarrassing foul-ups such as missed delivery dates, incorrect merchandise shipments, and erroneous billings.

- A successful $35 million soft-goods manufacturer that had grown rapidly suddenly found itself constantly struggling to put out fires. Employees were unaware of what other employees were doing. The firm had the obvious goals of manufacturing and selling merchandise, but it had no concept of what it wanted to become. The firm did not have a profit plan or departmental budgets; it could determine profitability only at the end of the fiscal year, after the opportunity to correct problems had passed. It had no performance appraisal system, so people tended to do whatever they wanted to do. As long as the firm continued to grow in sales, these problems were "merely inefficiencies." When the economy suddenly turned sour, however, these growing pains almost became terminal, and the firm's venture capital group had the company's president replaced.

- A $75 million women's clothing manufacturer began to experience high turnover and low morale, with people complaining, "If I want to get anything done around here, I have to do it myself." The firm had no plans, no goals, no formal organizational structure, and no accountability; an almost incredible number of people were running around doing things without direction, and there were a dizzying array of operational problems. No one seemed to know who should report to whom. The firm was still profitable because it had identified a viable market segment, but it had spawned competitors during the last few years—some of them people who had left the original firm. These competitors were now growing rapidly and seemed to be passing the original firm in size and profits.

- A $100 million consumer products manufacturer found that parts of the organization were making decisions affecting other parts without informing people, leading to costly inefficiencies and duplication of effort. For example, materials delivered to a warehouse had to be returned to the vendor because of lack of space to store them. Fiefdoms had been built up at the senior executive level, and there was little communication except on a vertical basis. Because the firm was successful, people had gotten into the habit of going first class and operating with a country club mentality. Looming on the horizon, meanwhile, were some of the industry's bigger players, who had noticed the firm's success within its market and were planning their own entries.

- A $350 million industrial components distributor that had grown explosively found itself with extremely high personnel turnover. The firm was continuing to push products out the door, but sales personnel were constantly infuriated to find that products they had sold and believed were in inventory could not be delivered because the firm's control system was hopelessly incorrect. The company was ultimately purchased by a competitor.

- Maxicare was one of the first HMOs (health maintenance organizations). It was initially successful and grew to about $800 million. The company then decided to acquire two other HMOs and grew to $1.8 billion in revenues. The company's systems were not sufficient to support this rapid growth and new scale of operations, and the company experienced very severe growing pains.[11] The company ultimately experienced bankruptcy and no longer exists, even though it was an initially successful pioneer of its industry.

All the firms just described were initially successful. They experienced various problems, or growing pains, because of differences in size or market conditions. In some cases, they clearly recognized—or were at least told about—the growing pains being encountered. However, in some cases they simply ignored the growing pains. For example, one or both of the authors of this book had discussions with senior executives at some of these firms about the growing pains they were experiencing, but in some cases they chose to either do nothing or do the wrong thing; as a result, either organizational failure or an acquisition occurred.

Unfortunately, one of the costs of rapidly growing entrepreneurship is that all organizations have the *potential* for experiencing the Osborne syndrome: meteoric success followed by equally rapid failure. It is not, however, an inevitability, as we explain next.

KEYS TO A SUCCESSFUL STAGE II FIRM

All the firms we described in the last section were diverse in their products and markets, yet experienced difficulties because of their failure to meet the challenges presented by rapid growth. Specifically, they were unable to acquire the required resources and to develop the increasingly complex operational systems that became necessary as they grew. Thus two factors are involved in developing a successful Stage II firm:

1. The ability to acquire resources
2. The ability to develop complex operational systems

These two factors constitute a firm's "operational infrastructure"; we discuss each of these critical factors further.

Ability to Acquire Resources

The ability to acquire and manage resources effectively is an indispensable element in the successful growth of a company. Without sufficient physical, financial, technical, and human resources, a firm will be unable to meet the demands that growth places on organizations. For example, a $50 million furniture manufacturer with state-of-the-art production capability found itself at a competitive disadvantage because of a lack of adequate warehousing space and loading facilities. Customers complained about delivery delays and too much waiting time for their trucks.

People Express is an example of a firm that was able, despite failures in other areas, to acquire the physical and human resources necessary to support the growth of the company. It acquired remodeled planes from Lufthansa as its start-up fleet and made great effort to hire personnel who exemplified the "People type." (As we describe next, however, the process used to acquire these human resources was extremely cumbersome and eventually led to significant problems.)

The difficulties some entrepreneurs have in this area are related to acquiring resources for future needs, as well as to meet current needs. The other difficulty is related to the second task in this stage: developing the systems that allow the appropriate use of the resources.

Ability to Develop Complex Operational Systems

The second critical task in successfully meeting the growth challenges of Stage II is integrating new operating systems into the organization. Federal Express was able to do this with a sophisticated tracking system using bar codes. Mrs. Fields' Cookies developed an elaborate computer system that allowed the firm to maintain daily control over widely dispersed operations. Humana developed sophisticated information and control systems required for speeding the collection of receivables and for providing hospital managers with daily printouts of key variables to be monitored, such as patient satisfaction and drug inventory levels.

Osborne Computer required (but lacked) systems for control of inventories, cash management, and accounting information to facilitate the growth spurt that the company was experiencing. The industrial products distributor that had grown from $15 million to $43 million also had problems with its inventory management systems. A $35 million soft-goods manufacturer lacked proper budgeting and performance appraisal systems and consequently found its staff "out of control." Maxicare lacked the operational systems required by a $1.8 billion company. People Express, once hailed as a shining example of entrepreneurial success, suffered chronic understaffing and poor organization, and lacked other operational systems required to facilitate the growth it was undergoing. Its hiring process was so time consuming and cumbersome, at a time when the firm was experiencing rapid growth, that the company was frequently scrambling to find enough people to meet its staffing needs. A number of online stock brokerage firms have suffered system crashes, thus irritating their customers. The ultimate success of these companies will depend to a great extent on the reliability of their operational systems. The list could go on and on.

The basic problem all these companies faced was that the entrepreneurs who owned and managed them were more interested in the challenges presented at Stage I than in those of Stage II. Identification of a market and development of a product or service seem glamorous compared with the more mundane tasks involved in developing and refining the organizational plumbing or infrastructure. Unfortunately, although something like an accounting system may not be exciting, it is vital for a growing organization. The shipping dock may be a less elegant place than a well-appointed corporate headquarters, but if enough foul-ups occur at the shipping dock, they can render the headquarters an expensive albatross.

If entrepreneurs want to make the successful transition from Stage I to Stage II, they must force themselves to be concerned about the organizational plumbing or operational systems required for day-to-day performance. Their survival depends on it.

MANAGING THE NEW VENTURE AND EXPANSION STAGES: A COMPARISON OF OSBORNE AND COMPAQ

Osborne and Compaq—two companies that entered the PC market around the same time with products geared to similar users—had very different outcomes. The comparison of the differences in outcomes between these two companies is significant because they constitute what we can term a natural experiment: two organizations in the same market segment at about the same time with different approaches to organizational development and different ultimate outcomes. As we see next, a major part of the reason for Compaq's success and Osborne's decline can be seen in their respective approaches to the key developmental tasks at the first two stages of growth.[12]

Compaq successfully met the challenges of growth. It was what might be called a professionally managed entrepreneurship from the beginning. From the outset, the company operated like a mature organization. Attention was directed toward securing adequate resources and developing a tight infrastructure. Compaq's founders were able to see the pressures beyond market and product development and plan for their response. As Rod Canion, one of Compaq's founders and its former president, remarked, "If you're growing slowly, problems can sidle up on you almost unnoticed. With high growth, if you don't get out of the way first, they knock you down flat."[13]

Identifying a Market and Developing the Product

Osborne and Compaq chose the same arena—the portable PC market—in which to attempt to carve out a niche. Both of these new ventures were highly successful. Osborne saw a need for a portable, inexpensive computer for the naive, first-time user and brought the cost of personal computing within reach of the consumer. Osborne reached $1 million in sales within the first two months and was generating $10 million per month the next year. Keeping a focus on the market, Osborne launched a subsidiary in the United Kingdom a month after the first computers were shipped.

Osborne's early days were fully focused on market and product development (Stage I) tasks. The first computer was presented after just four months of development, and four months later the first units were shipped. This rush to market, however, resulted in over $140,000 of associated costs, because Osborne had to fix bugs that appeared in the field. Getting the product to the customer is an important part of productization, and Osborne acted to ensure availability to the customer. To guarantee adequate shelf space for its product, Osborne emphasized dealer relationships, offering dealerships attractive terms and not competing with a direct salesforce of its own.

Compaq also developed a portable computer that, in this case, was completely compatible with the IBM PC, which Compaq's management believed (in 1983) would become the industry standard. The firm correctly identified a market for a small, compact, relatively lightweight computer that could be carried almost anywhere. In addition, Compaq recognized that IBM could not (in the early years of its PC) meet the demand for its product. Hence, customers would purchase a Compaq computer as an alternative if they could not obtain an IBM machine (they could use the same software). Like Osborne, Compaq experienced phenomenal first-year growth and recorded sales of over $111 million in its first year (becoming one of the fastest-growing companies in history).

The need to get the product to the customer was met successfully by Compaq with a strategy similar to that of Osborne's. Compaq stressed the development and maintenance of good dealer relationships. Despite this similarity, Compaq dealt with the developmental task of productization in a fundamentally different way from Osborne. The product was not the sole concern at Compaq during its early days. Before production even began, attention was directed toward the infrastructure that would support the organization as it grew.

Acquiring Resources and Developing Operational Systems

Where the differences between Osborne and Compaq in handling key developmental tasks are most noticeable are in the two key issues to be faced in Stage II. Osborne hired personnel and developed systems on an "as needed" basis. The first financial person was not brought in until February 1981—a month after incorporation and just six months prior to the first shipment of the product. Market planning problems were the impetus for development of good financial reporting and control systems. Quality control problems a year after the company was founded led to the addition of a vice president for engineering. This was followed a short time later with a major restructuring in response to manufacturing problems. Rather than anticipating needs, Osborne Computer was caught responding to problems. Its resources and systems were inadequate to handle the fast-paced environment of the industry and explosive growth of the company.

Compaq took a longer view of its needs and invested in the operational infrastructure (resources and systems) that facilitated its future growth. It hired computer programmers who averaged fifteen years of experience and drafted the best sales and marketing professionals possible from IBM. In establishing operational systems, Compaq again demonstrated the importance of professional management. According to John Gribi, Compaq's vice president and CFO at the time, financial controls and forecasting systems were in place well before production began.

Both of these companies successfully negotiated the first stage of growth. They were able to establish a new venture that provided a product to a market previously untapped. Where Compaq had the comparative advantage was its ability to successfully acquire the resources and develop the operational systems necessary to support its growth. While Osborne ended up in bankruptcy, Compaq built a multi-billion-dollar company that was included in the Fortune 500 and achieved technological leadership in the PC market. Compaq also acquired DEC (Digital Equipment Corporation).

Compaq, too, faced challenges and organizational upheaval several times after its initial success, but the things it did during Stages I and II clearly provided the foundation for its future success for many years. Ultimately, Compaq merged with Hewlett-Packard in an effort to create a company capable of competing with IBM and Dell Computer. However, the development of Compaq provides a clear contrast with Osborne Computer about the process and the ultimate success when the correct things are done at Stages I and II of organizational growth.

ENTREPRENEURIAL VISION

How do entrepreneurs see opportunities for new ventures? How do they see an opportunity to create a multi-billion-dollar business out of coffee and cafés? How do they see the opportunity to sell computers directly to consumers, as Michael Dell did, when everyone else is selling them indirectly through distributors? This is one of the great mysteries. Somehow entrepreneurs see things differently from the way the rest of us do. Although some entrepreneurs recognize that they see things differently, they themselves cannot explain why and how. For example, Sam Zell, who is the founder of Equity Office Properties (an office REIT or real estate investment trust) and Equity Residential Properties (a residential property REIT), and reputed to have a net worth in excess of $2 billion, has stated, "Another way to put it is that I see things differently than anybody else does. I can't explain to you why.[14]" As Nike might have said, they just do it!

In order to create opportunities for new ventures, entrepreneurially oriented professional managers must learn to see thing differently from the way they see them now. They need to look at things differently. Although entrepreneurs have this as a natural advantage, this is a skill that can be learned by professional managers. We deal with some of the tools for doing this in Chapter Seven in a discussion of strategic planning.

SUMMARY

This chapter examines the development of successful Stage I and Stage II organizations. The primary challenge of Stage I is establishing a proof of business concept. The keys to success at Stage I are the ability to identify a viable market, provide a product or service that will meet the needs of customers in that market, and develop the basic organization required to run the infant business.

If a firm is successful in Stage I, it will begin to experience rapid growth. The primary challenge of Stage II is scale-up. The keys to success in Stage II are to acquire the resources and develop the operational systems to facilitate the growth and scale-up of operations.

It is extremely difficult to scale up in a way that will facilitate growth without experiencing difficulties. As a result, a company is likely to develop a variety of organizational growing pains. These growing pains are normal, but they must not be ignored. They are the signal that it is time to begin the transition from an entrepreneurial to a professionally managed firm. Failure to successfully make this transition can lead to severe problems and, ultimately, to the Osborne syndrome (meteoric success followed by meteoric failure).

In the next chapter, we describe the problems and challenges involved in developing a professionally managed firm at Stage III. We present a case study of a firm called Metro Realty and show how it made the transition from Stage II to Stage III successfully. We also cite other examples of companies that have made this transition successfully and identify the lessons that their experiences suggest.

CHAPTER FIVE

The Professionalizing Stage

Developing Management Systems

At Stage III the organization must begin the process of making a transformation from the relatively informal way of doing things to a more systematic, planned way of operating.[1] We call this transformation the process of going from an entrepreneurship to an entrepreneurially oriented, professionally managed firm.

Two different kinds of issues must be dealt with to make this transformation: (1) technical (the focus of Stage III) and (2) psychological or cultural (the focus of Stage IV). The technical requirements for an organization to be a professionally managed firm include the development of management systems of various kinds, as described in this chapter. Psychological requirements include shifting the entrepreneur's mind-set and, in turn, the company's culture so that they support operating as a professionally managed firm. Many, if not most, entrepreneurs resist the notion of transitioning to professional management for a variety of reasons and this, in turn, affects the company's culture. The core reason is that they believe that becoming a professionally managed firm is the equivalent of becoming a bureaucracy, and they fear the loss of entrepreneurial spirit. This is incorrect and not what we mean, either by "professional management" or by "entrepreneurially oriented, professionally managed firm."

It is possible to navigate between the two perils of "chaos" and "bureaucracy" and to become an entrepreneurially oriented, professionally managed firm. This has been accomplished by many companies, including Starbucks, Countrywide Financial Corporation, and American Century Investors.

Because there are both psychological and technical dimensions to the transformation to professional management, two stages are required to complete it. At Stage III the technical aspects of the transformation are accomplished. Then at Stage IV the transformation must be completed by changing the organization's culture from one rooted in the entrepreneurial spirit to one that embraces the notion of an entrepreneurially oriented, professionally managed firm.

This chapter focuses primarily on the technical aspects of the transition to professional management at Stage III. Then in Chapter Six we deal with the cultural dimensions of change required to complete the transformation. The first section of this chapter identifies the key problems or challenges facing the organization as it changes from an entrepreneurship to a professionally managed company. The next section describes, in depth, the case of Metro Realty—an organization that was successful in transforming itself from an entrepreneurship to a professionally managed firm. This is a classic case study, which has been retained from previous editions because it illustrates in a very comprehensive manner the challenges encountered by firms in need of making the transition to professional management. The final section provides several other illustrations of actual firms, including Federal Express, Starbucks Coffee Company, and American Century Investors, that have successfully met these challenges. It examines why these firms have been effective.

DEVELOPING A SUCCESSFUL STAGE III ORGANIZATION

During the entrepreneurial stages of growth (Stages I and II), planning, control, and management development are done on an ad hoc basis in many firms, and a formal organization structure is practically nonexistent. Individuals and departments operate on a day-to-day basis, making adjustments in various systems to meet the demands of the environment in which the company operates. This may actually contribute to the success of entrepreneurial firms, but it can be quite detrimental once an organization reaches Stage III. As organizational growing pains resulting from the rapid growth that characterizes Stage II increase in severity, senior management begins to realize (or should realize) that a qualitative change in the nature of their firm is needed. The firm has reached the threshold of Stage III.

The key challenge for a Stage III firm is to develop or formalize the management systems that are needed in a professionally managed firm. As described in Chapter One, there are four management systems: planning, organization structure, management development, and control or performance management systems. These systems help the company coordinate the functions of its personnel and departments, provide direction to its employees, and motivate employees to achieve organizational goals. Basically, management systems formalize many of the activities that earlier, when the organization was small and growing, were performed through face-to-face interaction with the entrepreneur.

The following sections focus on a case study of Metro Realty—an organization that was successful in transforming itself from an entrepreneurship to a professionally managed firm. We describe the company's history, as well as the growing pains it experienced as it rapidly increased in size, personnel, and revenues. We also discuss the program its management designed to help the company overcome its problems and make the transition to a Stage III firm. Although the case is about a real estate company, we have chosen it because the problems experienced at Metro are typical of those encountered at Stage III. Specifically, it provides an example of the problems experienced by a rapidly growing company and the kinds of programs that can help an organization formalize its management systems and overcome its growing pains.

The company described actually existed, although its name has been changed and certain facts about its situation have been slightly modified in order to preserve confidentiality; the basic situation described here really occurred in this company. This case is included in this edition of this book because it represents a classic and detailed example of the challenges faced by a Stage II firm that is making the transition to Stage III. Over the past twenty-plus years, we have encountered numerous "Metro Realities" in a variety of industries. All have experienced the types of problems (at one level or another) as those described in the case presented here.

DEVELOPING A SUCCESSFUL STAGE III ORGANIZATION: THE CASE OF METRO REALTY

Harvey and Dolores Brown opened the first office of Metro Realty on July 5, 1938, in Center City, the heart of the metropolitan area. The company prospered and grew as a result of both the personal creativity and dedication of the founders and their ability to recruit people who could contribute to the success of the firm. Harvey Brown died in 1963, and a group of seven investors acquired Metro Realty. The company was, at this time, still a small entrepreneurial enterprise emphasizing residential real estate. It had three offices and thirty employees.

By 1970, little had changed since the company's founding. Metro Realty remained small in terms of employees, office space, and revenue and operated under a "family-style" management system. Its staff still consisted of twenty-eight to thirty people occupying three offices. The president of the company,

Bob Mitchell, was expected to supervise the entire company's functioning, much as Harvey Brown had done from the company's inception until his death.

Metro still operated very effectively as an entrepreneurial firm, as evidenced by its growth. Between 1970 and 1978, the total number of branch offices grew from three to eleven, and the total number of employees increased from 30 to 250. Revenues increased from $1 million to nearly $10 million in this same period. According to management, this prosperity resulted from the firm's ability to do certain things very well. These included knowing how to select locations, how to time moves, and how to recruit and train salespeople.

Growing Pains

Between 1970 and 1978, Metro Realty grew very rapidly in terms of sales, size, and personnel—and it was continuing to grow. By 1978, Metro included a management and leasing department, a loan and investment department, a referral department, an administrative department, and eleven branch sales offices, all seemingly operating successfully. Plans were even being made to acquire another realty firm, which would increase the company's size to twenty offices and about five hundred employees.

Unfortunately, the organization's original infrastructure could no longer support the enterprise that Metro had become. Everyone from the president to the sales associates could feel the impact of the problems that the company's rapid growth was creating. As one branch manager put it, "The attitude that now exists is that the company wants to be larger than it is and is moving faster in this direction than can be accommodated by its organization structure, leadership, and personnel." Lack of coordination in functions and activities was leading to increasing frustration among employees. Certain aspects of the company needed to be changed if it was to continue to be successful.

Culture. According to the president of Metro, "Part of the real estate culture is to tolerate poor performers," and Metro was no exception. At Metro, poor performers were tolerated, partly because the culture emphasized being "part of a family," and one could not very easily dismiss a family member. Managers also retained poor performers in order to avoid conflict. The culture promoted the notion that it was better to keep such people than to disrupt the system by dismissing them.

A third factor that contributed to the problem of poor performance was the concept of productivity that was promoted at Metro. "Productivity" was considered to include anything from sending out fliers and making phone calls to actually completing a sale. Only the last-named activity directly contributed to the firm's revenues, but all three activities were regarded as "productive" in and of themselves. One cultural belief of the firm seemed to be, "If a person looks busy, he or she is productive." With an increased number of personnel, this loose definition of productivity was becoming quite costly.

A final component of the firm's culture that may have contributed to retaining poor performers was an apparent lack of concern with the costs related to retaining these individuals. Traditionally, Metro had been concerned only with revenue production. Profit was not an explicit goal; it was simply the amount of money that remained after commissions and other costs had been paid. Cost control, therefore, was not an important consideration, as the company was not explicitly concerned with retaining income for future use. As the firm grew, however, a critical need arose to change the culture toward one that emphasized profit and considered both costs and revenues. This new culture would not be able to tolerate poor performers.

Roles and Responsibilities. The roles and responsibilities of different management positions had not been clearly defined at Metro. The organization functioned on an ad hoc basis, with responsibilities often overlapping. This lack of role definitions had not detracted from the functioning of the entrepreneurial firm, but it became a source of frustration as the company expanded. One manager, perhaps speaking for many, said that he was "fed up with the role confusion."

The ambiguity of role definitions also contributed to an unwillingness to accept responsibility. At Metro, it was relatively easy for managers to blame problems on other people or levels in the organization. There was no way to hold specific managers responsible for specific tasks, given that responsibilities had not been clearly defined.

Planning. Like many activities, corporate planning at Metro was done on an ad hoc basis. Metro never had a written plan that outlined the financial and nonfinancial goals, objectives, and targets of the organization; the size and success of the company had led its members to believe that such an effort was not warranted. As the organization grew, however, the need to plan for the company's future became apparent. The personnel at Metro began to desire some direction to guide their actions. It seemed that the company could no longer function effectively without goals.

Budgets and Accounting System. An important component of a company's planning process is a yearly budget that states financial goals. Unfortunately, the administrative systems necessary to help Metro know how it was performing financially and plan for its future were not formalized.

The budgeting process at Metro had traditionally been only a yearly exercise, because managers had no systems by which to monitor costs and revenue. They received little feedback from the organization concerning the amount they had spent or the profit they had earned. Most of the available financial statements provided information only on the performance of the organization as a whole, not on that of individual branch offices. The small amount of information on branch office performance that was available was often incomplete or inaccurate. Further, one branch manager suggested that he did not believe the accounting information that was being provided to him; he said he "couldn't understand where the numbers were coming from."

Metro clearly needed a more formalized budgeting process, but its underdeveloped accounting system did not support such an effort. Metro's system of accounting was described by an independent accounting firm as having "no thoroughly designed master plan." This system clearly needed to be revised.

Difficulties arising from the lack of an effective system to monitor costs and revenues began to surface in 1978. At this time the company experienced a significant decrease in its profitability, although, according to the firm's president, profits for the industry were at an all-time high. In 1977, profits were $190,000, but in 1978 they fell to $130,000.

Control. Traditionally, Metro had operated with a top-down management style in which the president oversaw the entire company's operations. By 1978, however, it was clear that Metro had grown too large for this style to be effective. At this time, the president described Metro as a "collection of little offices and divisions, each working toward its own goals without considering the good of the company." It was becoming evident that because of the expansion of the company in terms of profit as well as size, the president could no longer be the sole controller of its fate.

Performance Appraisal. Metro's performance appraisal system (or lack of such a system) contributed to its retention of poor performers. Performance appraisals, when they did occur, consisted of discussions in which only positive feedback was given. There was no system for evaluating progress in terms of meeting goals, because there was no goal-setting process. Negative feedback and suggestions for improving performance were rarely given, reflecting a culture that stressed conflict avoidance.

Decision Making and Leadership. Partly because of the lack of clearly defined roles and responsibilities and partly because of the traditional style of management, decisions were deferred to top management. Day-to-day decisions like those relating to the purchase of office equipment, which should have been made by department heads or branch managers, were all presented to the president for approval. This resulted in a slow and ineffective decision-making process.

The tendency for upper management to make all decisions decreased the participation of other managers and employees in the decision-making process. This contributed to a lack of responsibility for actions taken and a lack of commitment to the decisions that were made. Management from the top down had been a successful way to make decisions when Metro was an entrepreneurial organization, but it had clearly become inappropriate for a firm that was ready to make a transition to professional management.

Communication. One branch manager remarked that while communication within each region was good, total company communication was poor. Communication between individual branch offices and the firm's upper management was especially ineffective. Branch managers seemed to feel that upper management was not giving them enough information for them to operate effectively. As one branch manager put it, "Upper management assumed we knew what was wanted or needed when we, in reality, didn't know."

Upper management was equally frustrated by its inability to communicate with the branch offices. As one manager put it, the lack of communication made it "too easy for a branch or region to run its shop its own way."

Recruiting. Metro Realty did not have a formal recruiting plan, because the company had traditionally been able to attract top job candidates without expending much effort and had never experienced staffing problems. As the firm continued to grow, however, it found it needed to formalize recruiting plans in order to ensure that all branch offices had an adequate number of personnel to meet the company's future goals.

In terms of recruiting, 1979 was a particularly critical year. Due to a downturn in the economy, fewer people were entering the real estate profession. It became evident that a recruiting plan was a necessary component of Metro's continued success.

Training and Development. Metro's major problem in the area of training and development was a lack of management development programs. Without proper training, most potential managers were not prepared to assume managerial roles. The lack of qualified managers indirectly affected the functioning of the firm.

Metro also lacked a standardized training program for sales associates. All sales associates were required to possess a state license as evidence that they had minimal competence in real estate sales, but additional training was usually needed. At Metro, each branch had traditionally offered its own on-the-job program. There was little standardization of the programs' contents, so the quality of the programs was potentially different at different branches.

Compensation. Metro's compensation system was designed to promote increased revenue at the branch level rather than profitability for the firm as a whole. The organization rewarded managers and sales associates for revenue production rather than the ability to meet financial and nonfinancial goals.

Branch managers were rewarded for the ability of their offices to generate revenue. This created certain inequities because their different locations meant that some branches automatically produced more revenue than others, regardless of the quality of the staff they employed. This compensation system led to a situation in 1978 in which two managers who possessed only marginal skills and had caused some difficulties for the organization were among the highest-paid managers in the firm.

Making the Transition

In 1978, Metro's executive committee, composed of the company's president, heads of the regional offices, and department heads, began to realize that the company was experiencing problems that required changes in its traditional operating systems. The committee felt that managers and brokers were too close to the situation to work adequately to resolve these problems, so it hired an independent consultant to help the firm identify and alleviate its growing pains.

In 1978, Metro began a program designed to help it make the transition to a professionally managed firm. The consultant and the company president worked together to design the program, which would be implemented over a period of four years in order to reduce employees' resistance to change. This program was designed to be evolutionary rather than revolutionary. The purpose of the effort was not to "Clean the house and throw out the garbage" but rather, "Repair what we can and throw out what we find to be irreparable after we have tried to fix it."

1978. After identifying the problems described in the last section, the consultant and president began planning an organizational development program for the company. The planning process included establishing goals for the firm's transition, designing programs intended to achieve these goals, and planning how and when these programs would be implemented.

The consultant began working with the organization's members to determine what sort of company Metro would become—that is, what the goals of the transition process would be. The group decided that the "new" organization would do the following:

1. Have a decentralized system of responsibility, with strong managers

2. Be managed under a participative style of leadership

3. Promote increased accountability

4. Be profit-oriented rather than strictly revenue-oriented

In order to achieve these goals, the organizational development program would focus on three major, interrelated areas: (1) organization and business planning, (2) management development, and (3) design and formalization of organization structure. Training programs in these areas would consist of lectures, group discussions, exercises, and individual counseling sessions. As the members of the organization began to put into practice what they had learned from their training, the consultant would be available to provide feedback.

The consultant and president established yearly priorities for the organizational development program. A long-term schedule was created, outlining yearly objectives and presenting suggested completion dates for various aspects of the program. This schedule is presented in Table 5.1.

Table 5.1. Metro Realty Organizational Development Program: Contents and Schedule

1978: Plan organizational development program.

    Identify problems.

    Set goals.

    Design programs.

    Set schedule.

  Begin program implementation.

    Organizational planning

      • Provide training in design and use of goals.

      • Provide training in creation and use of budgets.

      • Develop business plan for 1979.

    Management development

      • Work with president to develop skills necessary to make personal transition.

      • Work with upper management to help them develop skills necessary to make the transition to professional managers.

    Organizational structure

      • Present exercises aimed at facilitating discussion of roles and responsibilities.

      • Begin working toward consensus on definition of roles

(continued)

Table 5.1. *(continued)*

1979: Review, revise, expand, and formalize programs.

Organizational planning

- Provide feedback on goals.

- Increase ability to meet goals.

- Develop more professional planning process.

Management development

- Continue work with president.

- Expand group program to include branch managers and potential managers.

Organizational structure

- Formalize roles and responsibilities.

- Provide written descriptions of roles to all employees.

1980–81: Continue to review, revise, expand, and formalize programs.

Organizational planning

- Make planning an integral part of the organization.

Management development

- Continue work with president.

- Formalize program for present and potential managers.

Organizational structure

- Put formalized structure into operation.

Having outlined the goals and designed an organizational development program to meet these goals, the group devoted the latter part of 1978 to program implementation. In that year, members of the organization completed a business plan that outlined the mission, goals, objectives, and targets for the coming year (1979). This process was facilitated by giving the executive team members training in how to develop and use goals. Managers were encouraged to create goals for their individual areas of responsibility (branches, departments, or regions), as well as to contribute to the formal plan for the organization as a whole. Managers were also shown how to create and use a realistic budget.

Training in creating and using goals was but one part of a management development program that began to take shape in 1978. This program was intended to provide present and future managers with the skills necessary to become more effective in their positions. These skills included planning, budgeting, recruiting, performance evaluation, and decision making. The consultant provided seminars in each of these areas, with practical exercises in which the new skills could be applied. He also provided feedback on performance, once the skills became a part of the managers' everyday work lives. During 1978, management development efforts were concentrated on members of upper management, though the committee planned eventually to expand the program to include all present and potential managers at Metro. The president was a member of this first group of participants, and he also worked with the consultant on an individual basis. This close working relationship was intended to help the president make his personal transition from being the leader of an entrepreneurial firm to being the CEO of a professionally managed organization. This personal transition was a key element in the success of the overall organization transition process.

The management development program initiated in 1978 served as a forum in which role ambiguities could be discussed. Exercises were used to facilitate discussion of roles and responsibilities. The consultant provided information on the need to clearly define roles and helped group members resolve ambiguities.

1979. During this year, the programs begun in 1978 were reviewed, revised, expanded, and formalized. The planning process was refined and systematized. Regularly scheduled branch, departmental, and executive committee meetings were established to facilitate the setting of goals, objectives, and targets for the coming year. Through such meetings, goal setting became a participative process in which all organization members contributed to the formulation of the company plan. These meetings also served as a means of monitoring performance and providing feedback to the various segments of the organization.

During 1979, emphasis was placed on setting realistic financial and nonfinancial goals and working to attain these goals. The consultant provided feedback to managers on the strength of the goals they had set for their departments or branches and offered suggestions for improving their goal-setting skills.

During 1979, the firm began to incorporate goal setting into its performance evaluation system. Evaluations were to be based on the extent to which employees met or exceeded the goals they had set for themselves. Compensation was to be contingent on the ability of people to meet their goals.

Management development programs were expanded during 1979 to include existing branch managers and potential managers. The program provided managers with the skills they needed to be more effective in their present positions and also prepared selected branch managers for promotion to upper-management positions. Selected sales associates were included in the program to ensure that the organization would have a pool of qualified potential branch managers to fill positions when needed.

By the end of the second year of the organizational development program, Metro had, for the most part, reached a consensus on role definitions. Written role descriptions were distributed to the organization's members so there would no longer be any confusion about responsibilities.

1980–81. Review and revision of the programs began in 1978 and 1979, and continued through 1981. By 1981, people were actively participating in the planning process, which was now an integral part of the company's operating systems. Management development programs had been formalized at all levels, and role ambiguity had been minimized.

Problems Encountered

As Metro began its transition from an entrepreneurial firm to a professionally managed organization, it encountered three critical problems. One of these problems—resistance to change on the part of the organization's members—was expected. The other two problems—a severe downturn in the economy and the departure of key personnel from the organization—could not have been planned for. We now provide further discussion of these problems and their effects.

Loss of Personnel. In December 1978, one of the most successful managers at Metro left the company to form his own firm. This was a critical loss in a company that was just beginning to make the transition to a professionally managed firm, because at this point strong managers and a complete salesforce are particularly important. There is also a need for everyone to pull together, and individuals who leave a firm at this time may discourage others from supporting the change effort.

The reason for the manager's departure was not clear. He may have simply "outgrown" the organization, so that Metro was no longer meeting his need for personal development and self-fulfillment. He may also have recognized that the organization was experiencing problems that he did not want to help it solve.

The manager made matters worse by taking quite a few salespeople with him when he left. As a result, at least two of the eleven branch offices became severely short staffed. Upper management at Metro had received little warning that this would occur. The net effect of the manager's actions was that while Metro was engaged in the already difficult task of working to overcome its growing pains, it also faced a short-term staffing crisis and a possible accompanying drop in morale.

The president of Metro responded quickly to the situation by rehiring Doug Perry, an experienced manager who had left the company only a year before.

Perry was given the job of revitalizing the branch offices that had been devastated by staff departures. To accomplish this, Perry took over as manager in one of the affected offices and, with the president's approval, promoted a company sales associate to the position of manager of the other affected branch. Both managers began an aggressive recruiting campaign, and within only six months the two branch offices were again fully staffed and functioning well. Because it was able to recruit quality people, Metro survived this crisis with relatively little adverse impact on its efforts to become a professionally managed firm.

Declining Economy. Having survived this staffing crisis, Metro suffered another blow in 1979 when the economy experienced a severe downturn. Real estate sales dropped suddenly and unexpectedly because of unprecedented high interest rates, vanishing mortgage funds, and uncertainty about the future.

The president of Metro suggested that this downturn was merely part of a cycle that occurs every few years. He pointed out, "This cycle begins with a period of prosperity like that which occurred in the late 1970s. Assuming that real estate is one of the best hedges against inflation, many people begin to buy houses left and right with the expectation that they can make profits without running any risks. This type of speculation cannot continue indefinitely. It eventually results in a declining market like that of 1979–80." At such times, he noted, weaker firms begin to fail, as salespeople leave not only the firms but the industry itself and new people fail to enter the profession.

Nonetheless, the shift in the economy that occurred in 1979–80 was one of the most severe downturns the real estate market had experienced. The economic shift was especially threatening to Metro because it occurred when the company was just beginning to make the transition to a professionally managed firm. In response to this threat, the president took the stance that Metro could either be a victim or it could take advantage of the market. He chose the latter course of action and adopted a strategy that was intended to play on the strengths of Metro and to concentrate on the long term, making the most of opportunities. This strategy would allow Metro to respond when the market changed.

Metro Realty was fortunate in that it had a strong image in its community and also in that its management had prepared itself for possible economic downturns by designing contingency plans. The plan that the company adopted in 1979–80 promoted both cost containment and production. It also emphasized maintaining the salesforce; in such periods fewer people enter the industry, and qualified people are at a premium.

All managers were asked to contribute ideas about specific expenses to cut, but the president had the final say in this effort. He decided that advertising budgets would be fixed, charitable contributions would be suspended, greater control of expense reimbursement to sales associates would be instituted, a freeze would be placed on the hiring of management and salaried personnel, and closing of nonproductive branch offices would be considered.

The company's strategy apparently paid off. Despite market conditions, the company's performance in 1980 was one of the best in its forty-two-year history.

Resistance to Change. Even after people realized that there were problems with the old operating systems at Metro, some individuals refused to take part in the changes necessary to solve these problems. They seemed to have a great desire to cling to old values and operating procedures. They showed their resistance to change in a variety of ways, including excuses for not adapting to procedures, justifications for using old practices, complaints that the changes were taking away the "family atmosphere" that people treasured, and, ultimately, outright refusal to adopt the new values and practices.

Some managers complained, "I just can't do it that way." The consultant replied, "Yes, you can, if you try," and the president added, "You will do it that way." People who absolutely would not change were finally asked to leave because they were detracting from the transition process. By 1981, after a certain amount of struggle, most employee resistance had been reduced through adoption of the new strategy or through termination (both voluntary and involuntary) of the chief resisters. It now appeared that Metro Realty had, for the most part, successfully made the transition to a professionally managed firm.

Program Outcomes

Metro Realty's organizational development program was successful in helping the company make the transition from an entrepreneurship to a professionally managed firm, even in the face of the problems that were encountered. Fundamental changes in the organization, shown in Table 5.2, eliminated most of its growing pains.

Culture. One of the most difficult changes Metro had to make was to replace its "family atmosphere" with an atmosphere that was more conducive to accomplishing the tasks of a professionally managed firm. This meant that managers had to learn how to confront conflict and eliminate poor performers. It did not necessarily mean that a family feeling could no longer exist. However, the dysfunctional aspects of this part of the firm's culture had to be eliminated.

Another component of the culture—the definition of productivity—also had to be changed. Individual productivity in the "new" organization was to be assessed in terms of profit contributed to the firm. This meant that people not

Table 5.2. The "Old" and the "New" Metro

	Old	New
Culture	Poor performers are tolerated.	Poor performers are not tolerated.
	The company is a "family."	The notion of "family" remains but is modified.
	Managers avoid conflict.	Managers are able to deal with conflict.
	Productivity is loosely defined.	Productivity is closely related to profitability.
	The company concentrates on revenue production.	The company concentrates on profit production.
Roles and responsibilities	Roles and responsibilities are not clearly defined.	Roles and responsibilities are clearly defined.
	Responsibilities often overlap.	Responsibilities are agreed on and do not overlap.
	Role confusion causes frustration.	Written definitions distributed to all employees eliminate confusion.
Planning	No formal business plan exists.	Formal planning becomes an integral part of the organization.
	Company has no formalized goals, objectives, or mission.	Managers are taught how to design and use goals, and regularly scheduled meetings are used to evaluate progress toward goals.
	Little direction is given to personnel.	Personnel are asked to participate in planning a course of action for the company.
Budgets and accounting system	No formalized budget exists; budget process is only an "exercise."	Managers design and use realistic budgets.
	Financial information is available to only certain levels of the company. Information is often inaccurate or incomplete. The accounting system is underdeveloped.	A new accounting system provides information for all levels of the company in a timely manner.

(continued)

Table 5.2. *(continued)*

	Old	*New*
Organization	Top-down management style is used.	Participative management style is used.
Control	Control is often ineffective.	Regularly scheduled meetings monitor performance and provide feedback.
Performance appraisal	Appraisal consists of discussion between managers and direct reports. Only positive feedback is given; little effort is made to improve performance.	Supervisors provide both positive and negative feedback and ways to improve performance.
Decision making and leadership	Most decisions are made by top management; decision making is slow and often ineffective.	Decision-making responsibility is distributed throughout the organization.
	Lack of participation in decisions leads to lack of commitment to decisions made.	The planning process encourages maximum participation by all employees.
Communication	Total company communication is poor; communication between upper management and branch managers is most ineffective.	Clearly defined roles and responsibilities contribute to better communication.
	Poor communication contributes to branch managers' role confusion and control by upper management.	Regularly scheduled meetings increase communication between various levels of the organization.
Recruiting	No formal recruiting plan exists.	Recruiting is a planned activity.
	With a growing number of branches, staffing is becoming a problem.	Managers are evaluated partly on their ability to set and meet recruiting goals.
Training and development	No management development program exists.	A management development program is in place.
	No standardized training for sales associates exists.	The training department is responsible for training of sales associates.
Compensation	Compensation is based on ability of branch to generate revenue.	Compensation is based on ability of personnel to meet financial and nonfinancial goals.

only had to increase revenues; they also had to control costs. Something like mailing fliers could no longer be considered productive work in and of itself, but only as it contributed to the overall profitability of the branch and firm. If any activity was judged too costly in terms of the revenue it was expected to generate, it would be eliminated.

Profitability was also important in the evaluation of branch productivity. The executive committee decided that in the "new" organization, each branch would be regarded as a profit center instead of simply a revenue center. The goal of each branch manager thus was to have a profitable branch, which meant continuing to produce high revenues while controlling and being responsible for expenses. Profitability would become a measure of managerial success, and the management development program would help managers achieve this success by providing them with the skills they needed to be effective professional managers.

Roles and Responsibilities. Through the lectures, discussions, and exercises used in the management development program, the organizational structure of Metro was defined. Roles and responsibilities of position holders and formal links between various positions were identified, formalized, and distributed in written form to all employees so that there would no longer be any confusion about who was responsible for what.

Planning. Systems for planning were formalized. The organization developed an ongoing means of setting, monitoring, and evaluating goals. This included a series of branch, departmental, and executive committee meetings that facilitated the setting of goals, objectives, and targets for the coming year. The meetings also helped in evaluating progress toward goals. An important part of the planning process was the use of contingency plans, whereby the firm attempted to determine what strategy to adopt in an optimistic or pessimistic market. Such planning helped the company weather the severe economic environment of 1979–80, when many less-prepared companies failed.

Budgets and Accounting System. Organization members' ability to design and use budgets was developed through seminars presented by the consultant. In the first year or two that managers attempted to use the techniques described in these seminars, nearly all the branch managers failed to meet their budgets because of either unrealistic goals or inadequate monitoring of goals. By 1981, however, managers had become better able to meet their financial, as well as nonfinancial, goals.

To further promote this process, Metro implemented a new accounting system. In the new system, information was available on each level of the organization, from the organization as a whole to each region to the individual branch offices. There was initially a problem with the timeliness of the reports: Information was not being received at a rate conducive to effective monitoring of financial goals. In 1980, however, this problem was reduced when a computerized accounting system was installed. The new system increased the speed with which financial reports could be generated and distributed.

Control. A series of regularly scheduled meetings replaced the top-down management style as a means of control. These meetings helped to monitor performance and provide feedback to various segments of the organization, thus also serving to increase communication.

Executive committee meetings were held monthly. Members of this group, along with branch managers, formed the "planning committee," which met quarterly to prepare priorities and nonfinancial objectives, and to review plans and status reports. Department and branch meetings were also to be held monthly to review the status of goal achievement. Annual planning meetings, in which all the branch managers, department heads, regional managers, and administrative personnel were involved, were to be held in June and July of each year.

Performance Appraisal. A performance review system based on goal achievement was created. Evaluation sessions were designed to provide feedback (both positive and negative) to each employee on his or her performance and to provide specific direction for improvement in the coming year. Managers' performance was assessed according to how well they met their goals in profit, recruiting, training, planning, control, turnover, and reliability. Sales associates' performance was assessed in terms of performance toward goals in sales, number of contracts, open houses, and other areas deemed important by the individual manager and sales associate. Goals for all employees were established through mutual agreement between employee and supervisor and were to be congruent with the overall company goals.

Decision Making and Leadership. One purpose of defining roles and responsibilities was to distribute decision-making responsibility to various levels throughout the organization, that is, to decentralize responsibility. The president would no longer be responsible for all company decisions. Instead, managers would make the day-to-day decisions for their individual branches, regions, or departments.

The formal planning process developed at Metro allowed an even greater number of people to have a voice in the decisions that affected the company. The process was designed to encourage maximum participation by the organization's members. All those involved were to have input into decisions that would directly affect them.

Communication. Clarification of roles and responsibilities, along with the establishment of regular meetings, eliminated the communication problems that Metro had experienced. The company now had a clearly defined "chain of command" through which information could filter both down and up.

Recruiting. As part of the yearly plan, each branch manager was to set goals for the number of individuals he or she would recruit in the coming year. Each manager was also to devise an action plan for meeting these goals. Managers were encouraged to seek new employees at local junior colleges, through business contacts, or even at other firms. Part of each manager's performance appraisal was an evaluation of success in meeting recruiting goals.

Training and Development. In an effort to provide continuing education, Metro established a training department that was responsible for all programs presented to Metro employees. The head of this department was to work with each branch to design programs that would meet the needs of the individual branch offices and the organization at large. The training department was therefore able to control the quality of the programs offered to employees and to ensure that all employees received sufficient training. As described previously, Metro also developed a formal management development program to help individuals become professional managers and to create a pool of potential managers.

Compensation. The objective of the new compensation system was to reduce the emphasis on increasing the revenues of individual branches and replace this with an emphasis on increasing the profit of the organization as a whole. To achieve this end, managers were to be rewarded for meeting or exceeding financial and nonfinancial goals. Common costs were to be allocated to branches and departments in proportion to their ability to generate revenues, thus reducing inequities in revenue generation between various branch locations.

Under the new system, each manager would receive a base salary plus a certain percentage of the company's profit, based on the extent to which that manager's branch had met or exceeded its financial goals. Such a system encouraged managers to exercise care in establishing budgets. It offered managers an incentive to meet or exceed budgets, thus increasing the profit of the firm as a whole.

Overall Results. The results of Metro Realty's organizational development program suggest that the company was successful at meeting the goals it had set for its transition.

1. The company now had a decentralized system of responsibility: branch, department, and regional managers were responsible for setting and meeting their own goals.

2. Participative leadership was becoming a reality: all managers took part in a yearly planning process for their individual areas of responsibility and for the company as a whole. The president no longer had the ultimate decision-making responsibility.

3. Accountability had been increased: all employees were held accountable for meeting the goals they had set for themselves, and compensation was based on their ability to do so.

4. The organization had become more profit-oriented: the culture had been changed to emphasize profit rather than revenue. Rewards were based on ability to generate profit for the company rather than simply revenue for the branch.

In the late 1980s, after Metro Realty had made the successful transition to professional management, the owner was approached by a large national financial service company that was engaged in purchasing residential real estate companies throughout the United States. Metro Realty had been developed as a valuable property, and it was attractive to the company we call here Diversified Financial Products, Inc. (DFP).

DFP made several offers for Metro Realty and was turned down each time. Metro was attractive to DFP because the latter's strategic plan for diversification called for acquisition of one of the three leading residential real estate firms in each major population center. Finally, Metro accepted an offer from DFP. The owner of Metro joined DFP as a senior executive.

In a sense, the attractiveness of Metro to DFP was external recognition of the success of the professionalization strategy.

OTHER EXAMPLES OF SUCCESS WITH PROFESSIONALIZATION

Many other firms provide examples of the successful transition to professional management. We discuss some of these companies in order to emphasize the skills and processes that are necessary to the development of a successful Stage III company. Some are highly visible success stories—stories about companies that have become very large; others are about smaller and medium-sized firms with significant growth potential.

Professionalization of Federal Express

In April 1973, Federal Express began transporting the first packages in its overnight delivery service. What Frederick W. Smith developed into the number-one air freight service was initially an idea presented in a college paper in 1965. Convinced of the significance of a delivery service dedicated to small, time-sensitive packages, Smith weathered $27 million losses in the first two years. He set up a system and waited for the market to develop, struggling to obtain the necessary financing. From the 16 packages transported on its first night, Federal Express grew to 500,000 packages per night in 1985.[2]

The attention to planning and control necessary to develop a successful Stage III company are seen in many of Smith's actions. Early on, while attempting to attract investors, he commissioned two feasibility studies, using 10 percent of the company's net worth.[3] In anticipation of a new two-hour delivery service, a recruitment strategy designed to identify a different type of employee was formulated. Control and planning were further facilitated by an advanced decision-support system that allowed flexible budgeting and by computerized optical scanners that sorted packages as they came into each of Federal Express's hubs. These scanners, along with handheld devices carried by the truck drivers and mainframe-linked terminals in each truck, permitted packages to be tracked as they moved through the system.

An underlying ingredient in the development of professional management systems is a professional perspective. This was present at Federal Express and was exemplified by its chief executive. Smith, who the general public hails as the classic entrepreneur, sees himself "primarily as a professional manager. The fact that I am also someone who saw an opportunity was coincident to that."[4] He recognized that the qualitative differences between a $1.2 million and a $1.2 billion company require different management styles.

Federal Express solved many of the challenges facing a Stage III company. Despite this professionalization, however, industry observers have commented on the company's unique enthusiasm and entrepreneurial spirit, seen in bold and innovative product development and expansion into new territories. Within a strong professional management structure, this spirit can provide the foundation for the next phase of organizational growth, that of consolidation.

Professionalization of Starbucks Coffee

Howard Schultz is the consummate entrepreneur. Together with his partners (as he calls his employees), he has built Starbucks from a small local roaster to an international company with more than $6 billion in revenues. Although Schultz understood the need to build Starbucks on a strong foundation, he was, like most entrepreneurs, not a fan of "process." Nevertheless, one of Schultz's strong suits is his willingness to listen and change his mind *if he is convinced* of an alternative viewpoint.

A number of people worked hard to convince Schultz that "it's hard to execute entrepreneurially!" This means that while a ready-fire-aim approach may work in making bold decisions, execution requires much more of a disciplined ready-aim-fire approach. Ultimately, Howard Schultz had to decide for himself that, to become a truly great company and realize its full potential,

Starbucks needed a blend of both the entrepreneurial spirit that had created it and the professional management disciplines that provided the infrastructure to facilitate its growth.

Once that decision was made, Starbucks developed the management systems necessary to make the transition to a professionally managed firm, as described in Chapter One. These systems included a comprehensive corporate planning process, an organizational restructuring from a "functional structure" to a "divisionalized matrix structure" (as explained in Chapter Eight), and development of planning processes for each strategic business unit (retail, specialty sales, mail order, and international). The professionalization process at Starbucks also included advanced management development for selected senior managers, team building, and culture management programs. The concepts and tools of planning, structure, management development, leadership, and culture management (many of which were applied at Starbucks) are discussed in Chapters Seven through Twelve.

Professionalization of American Century Investors

Founded as Twentieth Century Investors in 1958, American Century is a highly successful, rapidly growing investment management company. American Century's founder, Jim Stowers Jr., started his first fund in 1958 with $100,000 in assets and twenty-four shareholders. Today, the company manages a family of mutual funds (both equity and fixed income), employs more than two thousand people, and has more than $50 billion in assets under management.

The company began the process of professionalization in 1988. By that time it had grown to more than $6 billion in assets under management. Because the firm charged a 1 percent management fee, its revenues were in the range of $60 million. The company had excellent people, products, and day-to-day operational systems. It also had a strong culture that emphasized "doing the right thing." However, the company lacked well-developed management systems. It did not have a formal strategic planning process. There was no budgeting process. In addition, although there were several individuals with strong managerial skills, there was no process for management development.

During 1988, Stowers and the senior management team recognized that the firm had outgrown its informal management systems, and they embarked on a process of making the transition to a professionally managed firm. An outside consultant was engaged to facilitate the process of organizational development and help the firm (and its management team) make the transition to professional management.

The first step was the introduction of a strategic planning process. This process focused not only on the firm's competitive strategy but on goals for the development of American Century's organizational infrastructure as well. In this sense, the planning process was designed to facilitate strategic organizational development—not simply traditional strategic planning. This type of planning process is described in detail in Chapter Seven.

At first, planning meetings were difficult. There were some contentious issues to be resolved (such as whether the firm's funds would continue their no-minimum-investment policy). In addition, there were problems in the decision-making and meeting-management processes of the firm. The senior management group was accustomed to meetings where virtually anything might be discussed: major issues, personnel problems, how much to spend on holiday decorations. In addition, these discussions tended not to remain focused, as one issue led to another.

The new strategic planning process focused on some of the core strategic planning issues (see Chapter Seven) like, What business are we in? and What do we want to become in the long term? Planning was also done for specific objectives and goals in each area of the Pyramid of Organizational Development (markets, products, resources, operational systems, management systems, and culture) and financial results. In addition, the firm's management team met on a quarterly basis to review performance against goals and to refine the plan to better reflect changing market and organizational conditions.

Another aspect of the professionalization process was the introduction of a management development program. The mission of the program was to help managers develop the advanced management capabilities required to take the firm to the next level successfully. The management development program used at American Century is very similar to the approach described in Chapter Nine.

American Century's management team remained committed to the changes in the systems that they had begun making in 1988. By 1996, the results of their efforts were evident. The management team had improved their capabilities with respect to managing the much larger firm that American Century had become. Over this time, in fact, the company had grown to managing more than $50 billion in assets. The ultimate test of a company is its ability to enhance shareholder value. In 1996, J. P. Morgan acquired a 45 percent interest in American Century for $800 million. This implies a market value of $2 billion for the firm.

KEYS TO A SUCCESSFUL STAGE III FIRM

Each of the companies discussed in this chapter met the challenges posed by professionalization and were able to successfully grow beyond the new venture and expansion stages. Several factors are involved in making the transition to Stage III. These are as follows:

1. The ability to plan and develop strategy
2. The ability to develop an appropriate organizational structure and controls

3. The ability to provide management development

4. Willingness to transform to professional management.

Chapters Seven through Ten deal with each of the factors on a more in-depth basis.

Ability to Plan and Develop Strategy

A primary factor in successful professionalization is the ability to plan for the future and develop appropriate strategies for maximizing market opportunities. Each of the companies cited in this chapter was able to do this. At Metro Realty, the organizational planning process taught employees how to formulate financial and nonfinancial goals and help the company develop systems for setting, monitoring, and evaluating these goals. As a result, Metro Realty was better able to meet the challenges presented by its environment.

Federal Express employed a complex decision support system and assumed developmental risks that required some time to show profit. It saw this as essential to company success. Domino's Pizza—a company described in Chapter Four—examined its traditional market and added drive-through service. It also provided a structure and mechanism for its franchisees to give input into planned organizational actions with the initiation of the position of national director of franchisee concerns. Similarly, Starbucks invested in sophisticated operational and management systems long before they were actually needed.

Ability to Develop an Appropriate Organization Structure and Controls

A second major factor in developing a successful Stage III company is developing an organizational structure and controls that will coordinate efforts and provide information and motivation to employees.

Metro Realty developed a formal organization structure that allowed people to understand their roles, responsibilities, and reporting relationships. Through developing monitoring systems (such as performance appraisals and a budgeting system), Metro also created a control system.

Federal Express's Frederick W. Smith is a legend in employee motivation. He structured his firm to allow employees access to him and provided for an employee panel to hear grievances.

Ability to Provide Management and Leadership Development

The third major factor for success at Stage III is the ability to design and implement programs to provide present and potential managers with the skills needed to perform their roles effectively. At Metro Realty, a formalized management development program helped present and potential managers be more effective in their roles. American Century and Starbucks Coffee developed and implemented management development programs that were designed to help build the capabilities of the management team. In particular, these programs were intended to help managers develop the skills that would be needed during the firm's next stage of growth.

Developing management systems can take a number of years, and there can be many obstacles to overcome, as happened at Metro Realty. However, if an organization is to continue to be successful as it grows, its management must recognize that problems exist and begin taking steps toward reducing them, no matter how painful the process may be.

Willingness to Transform to Professional Management

The final major factor for success at Stage III is the willingness to let go of the "old" way of doing things and embrace the notion of the need to transform to an entrepreneurially oriented, professionally managed firm. This is a key psychological Rubicon—one that many entrepreneurs do not cross.

It is a difficult transformation to make. There are powerful forces resisting the change. First, the old (current) way has worked successfully in Stages I and II, and it is difficult to let go of a winning formula. Second, there is a comfort with the idea that informality is the secret to early success. This was a key issue for Howard Schultz at Starbucks. However, as Starbucks has demonstrated, it is possible to be entrepreneurial and professionally managed at the same time.

SUMMARY

Metro Realty's transition from Stage II to Stage III is typical of many companies in a variety of industries. As companies expand and begin to experience growing pains, farsighted managers like those at Metro Realty, Federal Express, Starbucks Coffee, and American Century Investors recognize the need for a change and begin to develop and formalize management systems needed to overcome these problems.

This chapter—the Metro Realty case, in particular—teaches a number of lessons about making the transition from an entrepreneurship (Stage I or II) to a professionally managed firm (Stage III). The first lesson is that growing pains like those experienced by Metro are unavoidable. Entrepreneurial firms that are successful and therefore grow rapidly can expect to experience certain problems related to the fact that they have not had time to develop effective management systems. Other areas of the company have, justifiably, required more attention.

The second lesson is that management must recognize the symptoms of organizational growing pains and realize that it is time for a change. Management and others may prefer to ignore the problems or blame them on some fluke because no one wants to admit that the company's success is threatened. Some people may believe that the problems will disappear if the company keeps operating in the manner that has proved effective in the past. But this belief, as we saw in Chapter Four, can cause the organization to fall victim to the Osborne syndrome.

The third lesson is that the needed changes can be quite painful for those involved. People desire to cling to familiar, traditional ways of operating. Formalization of roles, responsibilities, planning, and control suggests to many people that the warm atmosphere of the entrepreneurial firm is being replaced by cold professionalism. Whether or not this actually occurs, management must remain steadfast in its efforts to transform the organization.

The final lesson to be learned from Metro Realty is that the transition process cannot be accomplished overnight; indeed, it may take years. This need for slowness is, in fact, an asset. Introducing change slowly can help to reduce employee resistance and anxiety. It is also important to help employees understand why changes are being made so they do not feel threatened and will know what to expect in the future.

This chapter attempts to show how an organization can recognize the need for management systems and set about developing them. This critical challenge must be met if the organization is to make a successful transition from an entrepreneurship to a professionally managed firm.

CHAPTER SIX

The Consolidation Stage

Managing the Corporate Culture

This chapter deals with the issues facing companies at Stage IV, using a case history to show the impact of corporate culture on the development of a successful Stage IV firm. The history of this company demonstrates how culture changes in unintended ways as a company grows, what problems arise as a result of those changes, and how an organization can manage cultural change in a way that lets it become a successful Stage IV company. Chapter Twelve presents additional examples of firms that have faced the challenge presented in making the transition from a Stage III to a Stage IV company.

DEVELOPING SUCCESSFUL STAGE IV ORGANIZATIONS

After a company has successfully professionalized its management systems, it must meet a further developmental challenge that involves making very different types of changes. At this point the organization has reached Stage IV, and its main task becomes the management of its corporate culture. Although every company, from its inception, possesses a culture, culture does not become a critical concern until the company is faced with making the transition to Stage IV. At this stage of development, companies must become concerned with culture management if they are to continue to be successful. Otherwise, individual members of the company are likely to interpret cultural elements in ways that meet their needs but not those of the company. Sometimes, as in the case presented in this chapter, a company reaches Stage IV and has to simultaneously focus on the development of its management systems and the management of its corporate culture.

The key challenge faced by a Stage IV firm is creating and implementing a system for explicitly managing the corporate culture so that it supports the development of a professionally managed firm. As we explained in Chapter One, corporate culture consists of the values, beliefs, and norms that govern the behavior of people in an organization. The culture reflects what the organization stands for in its products or services, the management of its people, and the way it conducts business. Culture can have a profound impact on an organization's success or failure. It can determine the degree of employee commitment to a firm and affect the way customers perceive the enterprise.

During a firm's early stages of growth, culture is transmitted informally through employees' day-to-day interactions with the entrepreneur. As the firm grows, however, the entrepreneur tends to have less time for contact with an ever-increasing number of people. Accordingly, unless a formal mechanism is substituted for the process of cultural transmission by osmosis, the firm will find that its people no longer have a shared vision of what the company is or where it is going. (The creation of a shared vision for a company is part of the managerial function of strategic leadership, which is examined in Chapter Eleven.)

A number of companies have become quite sophisticated in managing their culture and transmitting the organization's vision and values. Indeed, this is a key task or core competency that must be developed by any firm that is truly an entrepreneurially oriented, professionally managed firm. Organizations that have done this well include Southwest Airlines, Amgen, Countrywide Financial Corporation, Neutrogena, PowerBar, IndyMac Bank, Starbucks, Mrs. Fields' Cookies, The Body Shop, and Wal-Mart, as well as many smaller and less-well-known firms. For example, Starbucks has articulated six guiding principles that are the foundation for the firm's way of operating (presented in Chapter One). In addition, the company manages its culture in a variety of ways, including its personnel practices, its stock option program, and its training programs. Southwest Airlines is another company that is recognized for its unique culture and methods of managing it.

The next section of this chapter examines a case study of an organization at Stage IV. It illustrates how culture changes in unintended ways as a company grows and why the management of culture is critical, especially during Stage IV. We present the tools of culture management in Chapter Twelve.

As with Metro Realty, our example company actually exists (although it is now part of a larger organization), but we have changed its name and certain facts about its situation to preserve its confidentiality. In addition, we have retained this case as a part of the new edition of this book because it represents a classic case study of the types of problems organizations encounter as they make the transition from Stage III to Stage IV.

BACKGROUND OF TEMPO PRODUCTS

From very modest beginnings, Tempo Products grew into a large, successful consumer products corporation, with revenues exceeding $150 million.[1] Much of the firm's initial success could be attributed to its owner, Ronald Harrison, who was willing to take certain risks that allowed his company to grow and prosper.

The first few years of Ron's ownership involved constant struggle. Sales were not bad, but they could have been better. The company was not growing, though it seemed to be maintaining its market share. The turning point for Tempo Products came when Ron and his small staff decided to implement some new product ideas and marketing strategies. These changes were very effective at increasing sales, and within five years, the company had revenues totaling $5 million and included about sixty people on its staff.

In the company's eighth year of operations, Ron concluded that it was time for his company to expand further. Because he had had great success with the new product line, he decided to invest in other products that might appeal to his target audience. He added two new products to the existing ones, and both met with great success. Ron and his company seemed to be doing everything right.

In the ensuing years, Ron invested in a few other products, selected for their appeal to his target audience. By its tenth year in business, Tempo Products had revenues of more than $150 million and employed 650 people. This rapid growth was very much the result of the entrepreneurial skills Ron Harrison possessed: the ability to identify a market, the ability to create and produce a product appropriate for that market, the willingness to take risks, and the ability to attract talented people to help him build his enterprise. In short, Ron was a classic entrepreneur.

ELEMENTS OF TEMPO PRODUCTS' CULTURE
AND THEIR ATTENUATION

Tempo Products had been successful at creating most of the operating systems it needed to remain profitable as it grew. The firm's accounting system and control systems were reasonably well developed and were operating effectively. The company had implemented a planning system and was continuing to formalize it. However, the firm's management realized that problems unrelated to operating systems were arising. These problems proved to be the result of unintended reinterpretations of the values, norms, and beliefs that had served the company well during its growth. Tempo Product's original culture, management realized, was in the process of attenuating.

When Tempo Products was small, Ron was the source of its corporate culture. He relied on close interaction with employees to disseminate his beliefs and his vision for the company's future. As the company grew, however, such interaction was no longer possible, and the company's culture became increasingly unclear to new generations of employees. Some of these employees, therefore, began to create their own values, beliefs, and norms. At times, this new culture was at odds with Tempo Products' original culture.

As differing and sometimes opposing values, beliefs, and norms were translated into action, conflicts arose. People lacked a shared perception of what the company was and where it was going. As one manager said, "We don't know what business we're in. We have many employees who don't know what type of products we make." This form of growing pains typically occurs at about the time a company is ready to make the transition from a Stage III to a Stage IV firm.

Changes in certain elements of Tempo Products' culture were particularly important. Let us examine these elements as they existed in the original company culture and then see how they were becoming attenuated.

Tempo Products Is a Family

The culture at Tempo Products had traditionally emphasized a family atmosphere. In the company's early years, everyone knew everyone else, and everyone pulled together for a common cause: the success of the firm. This corporatewide family feeling was easy to maintain because most employees interacted with one another on a regular basis and were able to interact directly with Ron, who provided the guidance needed to keep people working together effectively. However, as the firm began its rapid growth, the "family" became less cohesive, because the size of the company made it impossible to have the number of interactions necessary to sustain it. This dissolution of a family feeling is a common occurrence in rapidly growing, entrepreneurial firms.

At Tempo Products an employee's organizational family became redefined as either those who were of the same generation or those with whom the employee worked most closely. There were two generations of employees at Tempo Products. The older one entered the firm in the years prior to its period of rapid growth, while the new generation entered after growth had slowed down.

The older generation of employees came to believe that they were the *true* family members—the ones who had really built the company. They considered the new generation to be outsiders. Consequently, members of the older generation, many of whom occupied middle- and senior-management positions, believed that they were entitled to certain privileges that the new generation of employees should not receive. These privileges included access to people, information, and other resources.

This belief was supported, at least in part, by the emphasis that Tempo Products' management placed on the use of confidential information. Only family members (management) were entitled to such information, and members of the new generation who were denied access to it came to resent not being in on company activities and decisions. They responded by creating their own "family grapevine" through which they could circulate information. Management, in turn, came to resent the fact that there really was no confidential information; everything was readily available to most employees through this informal system of corporate communication.

An individual's work group also became a family. This made sense because interaction among individuals in a work group is usually high, so people have a good chance to create satisfying relationships. This definition of *family* was also influenced by the structure that evolved as Tempo Products grew.

During the company's early development, its structure had been loose. As more products and personnel were added, however, a more formal structure developed, with its basis in the various functions of the company. Each area, such as production or sales, came to see itself in isolation from all other areas. This "separate islands syndrome" led to duplication of services and inefficiencies within the organization. It also replaced the total family feeling with a feeling of identification mainly with the work group. As a result, employees began to experience conflicting loyalties. "Do I work for my group or for the corporation?" became a prevalent question. It was often answered with, "I work only for my group."

Decision Makers Are Few and Invincible

Ron Harrison, as founder and owner, had obviously been responsible for providing the vision of what Tempo Products was to become. In Tempo Products' early years, this involved making most of the company's decisions and providing direction to employees. Employees accepted the fact that it was Ron's responsibility to make decisions involving his investment, and they supported him in whatever course of action he chose. The belief was that, as one manager put it, "Ron will decide. He knows what he wants the company to be. I don't worry about it because it's all in his head."

People wanted Ron to make the decisions because they thought he had the uncanny ability to always make the right one. This ability created the belief that Ron was somehow invincible—a superman that no one could surpass. The company's spectacular success reinforced this belief.

As Tempo Products grew, the decision-making ability and presumed invincibility that Ron alone had originally been thought to possess became attributed, through a halo effect, to anyone who occupied a senior management position. Thus the belief became, "Senior management will decide; they know what's right."

Because of this belief, it became an accepted practice to defer most decisions to senior management, even when the decisions could have been made at a lower level in the company. Inefficiencies resulted from this practice for three reasons. First, senior managers were no longer able to make rational decisions on some matters because they were too far removed from the daily activities that their decisions would affect. Their decisions were, therefore, sometimes inappropriate and sometimes made too slowly to be of value.

The second reason that inefficiencies arose was that deferring decisions to the upper levels of the company allowed lower-level managers to avoid responsibility for decisions that affected them or their work units. If lower-level managers failed to reach a goal set for them by senior management, they could claim that they were not accountable because "it was not my decision."

A final reason for inefficiencies was an excessive dependence on outside consultants, which was costly in terms of both time and money. Consultants seemed to be used in instances where decisions should have been made by the managers themselves. According to some people in the company, consultants were used so often because upper management did not want to take responsibility for their own decisions.

In fact, senior managers came to deny that they had sole decision-making responsibility. They created policies suggesting that lower-level personnel should be involved in decision making. In practice, however, lower-level managers were still controlled and restrained by upper management's decisions. For example, one person said of Tempo Products' budget process, "It lacks credibility because budget cuts are issued from the top after the budget is approved. This is seen as a mockery of the system, since people aren't given decision-making responsibility."

The lack of decision-making responsibilities made some managers feel powerless; therefore, they did nothing at all. As one person pointed out, "There are too many managers who have no real authority because someone else can overrule them." This situation frustrated managers who were supposed to be invested with authority, but complaints seldom reached upper management because the notion of upper management's invincibility had come to mean that people should not challenge their superiors. Doing so was likely to result in adverse personal consequences.

This fear of reprisals for making waves contributed to the adoption of a top-down communication system that provided little opportunity for lower-level employees to communicate their ideas to upper management. In fact, it almost prohibited such communication. One employee said, "Employees tell managers what they want to hear, not necessarily what they believe."

Afraid to voice opposition, most lower-level managers simply accepted the need to seek direction for future activities from senior management and to do as they were told. One person described the situation this way: "Always being on the outside, doing just what you're told without explanations or understanding of long-range goals, gives employees the idea that they are a commodity and not a resource."

"Get it Done with Excellence"

One of the beliefs on which Tempo Products was founded was that its products should be of the highest quality. People believed that Ron was willing to devote whatever resources were necessary to reach this goal. Cost was less important than the desire to produce excellent products. An implicit motto at Tempo Products was, "Whatever it takes, get it done with excellence."

It appeared to both employees and outsiders that Ron believed that to create excellent products, one must employ excellent people. This, in turn, fostered the belief that Ron was willing to spend more than his competitors to attract and keep such people. Tempo Products employees believed that they were paid above the industry average. At least one person suggested, in fact, that Tempo Products employees were spoiled by excessive rewards.

Ron's stressing of excellence in products and people had created a positive image of Tempo Products in the eyes of both employees and outsiders and had made a major contribution to the company's success. As Tempo Products grew, however, these positive values came to be misinterpreted. The goal of product excellence came to mean, "We are a first-class organization." This, in turn, was interpreted to mean, "We always go first class." The implicit corollary of this was, "Cost does not matter."

The goal of excellence in people was also misinterpreted. People came to believe that they could not help performing well, and they expected rewards, regardless of what their actual performance was. The standard of employee excellence was redefined to mean, "Whatever a Tempo Products employee does is excellent."

Our Company Is Unique

Tempo Products employees believed that their company was unique in both its good and its bad attributes. This belief was supported by policies and practices that Ron had created to help employees feel special and thus increase pride and motivation.

Unfortunately, as the company grew, this belief led to problems at the organization level. Tempo Products employees came to feel that the company's excellence rested on its supposed uniqueness and that treating it like any other company would jeopardize its survival. They believed that Tempo Products was so unusual and special, in fact, that it could not learn from the lessons of others. They complained about the proposed use of organizational development methods that had proved successful elsewhere because "they won't work at a company like ours" and "we can figure out our own problems." The belief in excellence through uniqueness thus came to be used as a way to protect people against change and to excuse their resistance to modification attempts.

We Play It by Ear

Tempo Products' early success was partly due to its ability to change to meet environmental requirements—to play it by ear. Formal roles and responsibilities, a planning system, and well-defined operating systems did not exist in the early years, nor were they necessary for the company's success. Tempo Products and its employees operated on a day-to-day basis, making whatever adjustments they needed to in order to carve out a market. This was a very effective approach in an entrepreneurial firm, because it allowed for rapid change.

As the company grew, however, the practice of playing by ear became dysfunctional. Tempo Products' management realized that the company could no longer successfully operate on an informal basis and began taking steps toward formalizing its management and operating systems. Specifically, the firm became concerned with three levels of problems resulting from the play-it-by-ear belief.

At the individual level, this approach meant that some employees did not have clearly defined roles and responsibilities. As the firm grew, role definitions were made for some positions but not others. Many of the positions that remained ill-defined had been created when the company needed additional employees to cope with its rapid growth. Because Tempo Products' management was relatively young and inexperienced, it had tended to add people without trying to reconceptualize the functions being performed or the organizational structure required to perform them. Ambiguous role definitions contributed to productivity problems when employees unknowingly worked at odds with corporate goals. Furthermore, individuals in these positions sometimes believed that they could not be held accountable for their actions because their roles had not been defined.

At the management level, informality contributed to problems in communication. When Tempo Products was a small company, informal communication met both employee and company needs. As the firm grew, however, the need for a formal communication system became apparent, but one was not created because of the desire to cling to the old value of playing it by ear. The lack of a formal system contributed to inefficiencies in production, duplication of effort, and misunderstanding between and among divisions.

At the organization level, it became clear that the lack of a formal planning process and a clearly articulated culture were causing problems. Each division within the company was allowed to design its own strategic plans, but these plans were often formulated without considering the needs of other departments. Similarly, each department or work unit had its own financial and nonfinancial goals, and these sometimes conflicted with the goals of other areas. An integrated strategic plan was needed so that employees could understand and focus on company goals rather than just the goals of their particular unit.

We Have Fun

Although Tempo Products' culture stressed working to achieve excellence, it also emphasized that people should enjoy their work. This element of the company's culture was based on Ron's desire to create a pleasant work environment to balance the uncertainty that is unavoidable in a growing, entrepreneurial firm. As Ron said, "I've tried to establish a spirit that we shouldn't take ourselves too seriously; we should have fun. You need to relieve the pressure of not knowing what the future holds."

Unfortunately, as the company grew, Ron's belief that people should have fun became transformed into a mandate that all employees "will have fun." In practice, this meant avoidance of conflict; people believed that conflict was disruptive and not good for the company or its personnel. Avoiding conflict with senior managers became particularly important, because they could punish those who challenged them. It was also important, however, to avoid conflict with one's peers and direct reports—not to make waves. According to one manager, it was generally accepted that "the best way to get fired is to talk too much" and that "80 percent of the terminations are of people who made waves across organizational lines."

Managers believed that it was better to avoid conflict with their direct reports than to disrupt the system by providing negative feedback or dismissing poor performers. One manager remarked that when direct reports were criticized, they either cried or made excuses. Many managers, therefore, came to believe that it was better to say nothing at all. This contributed to the retention of poor performers.

We Do Our Own Thing

One belief that had existed at Tempo Products from its inception was that people should be allowed to find their own levels of performance and that if excellence in products and work environment was emphasized, every employee's standard would be high. In the company's early years, "Do your own thing and do it well" was carried out in practice, as employees devoted a great deal of energy to making the company a success. Employees were motivated to achieve the standard of excellence implicit in "do it well" because they were encouraged by others and, most important, by Ron to "do your best." A high degree of interaction between Ron and his employees increased motivation, and inadequate performers could easily be identified and dealt with. The high degree of interaction also created a feeling of togetherness, so people's "own thing" usually fit in with the goals of the company. As the organization grew, however, people grew apart both physically and psychologically, and "do your own thing" became distorted at three levels.

At the individual level, employees came to interpret "do your own thing" as "do what is best for yourself." This sometimes meant doing nothing at all, as suggested by one manager: "People don't work around here anymore. They loaf, visit, chat, or wander the halls." This distortion grew partly out of the lack of a clearly articulated culture, partly out of the lack of formally defined roles and responsibilities, and partly out of the belief that conflict should be avoided at all costs. Without a well-defined and clearly communicated culture, it became acceptable to interpret "do your own thing" in many ways. Ambiguous roles led some employees to believe that they could create their own positions without considering the goals of the company. Furthermore, some employees became so frustrated by the lack of formal responsibilities or the overlap between their roles and those of others that they just gave up and did nothing at all. Such behavior was allowed to continue because challenging it might result in conflict, and the culture stressed conflict avoidance.

At the managerial level, "do your own thing" came to mean that managers could choose the leadership style that best met their personal—but not necessarily the company's—needs. Managers differed in their ability to delegate and make decisions, and those with well-developed leadership skills were sometimes dependent on those who did not have such skills. Effective managers thus often became frustrated because they were unable to attain their goals. One person noted, "There are many different leadership and management styles among Tempo Products' managers, and this has tended to create uneven delegation of responsibility and unclear decision making." The culture was not strong enough to support the adoption of effective styles of management, nor was there an institutionalized management development program in which managers could learn the skills they needed to be effective in their jobs.

At the organization level, one interpretation of "do your own thing" gave support to the "separate islands syndrome." Each work unit came to believe that in order to fulfill its own needs, it had to compete with other units for resources. This led individual work units to become highly protective of their territories. As an example, unit managers often believed that if "outsiders" (such as consultants) were able to audit their operations, they might lose resources and even their jobs. The cultural belief became, "Do your own thing, but stay out of my territory."

In response to this fear, communication between areas became minimal. Some employees, in fact, said that horizontal communication at Tempo Products was practically nonexistent. Lack of communication resulted in duplication of effort between divisions and departments, as well as a reduction in the ability of different work units to work together effectively. For example, on one occasion production manufactured more of a product than the service center could store. The product had to be stored elsewhere, resulting in unanticipated costs. Production had failed to communicate its needs to the service center because the company's culture discouraged horizontal communication in the interest of "protecting one's territory."

REDEFINING A CULTURE

Tempo Products' senior management began to realize that certain aspects of the company's culture needed to be changed if the company was to continue to be successful. Ron Harrison, therefore, worked with others to create an organizational development program to help Tempo Products redefine its culture. The program was to emphasize four broad areas: (1) organizational design, (2) strategic planning, (3) management development, and (4) culture management.

Organizational Design

As Tempo Products grew, its structure remained relatively unchanged. This lack of structural change, combined with certain cultural elements, resulted in a number of growing pains. For example, when combined with the cultural element of "Do your own thing," the company's obsolete structure led to the separate islands syndrome.

Tempo Products' managers recognized the need for organization redesign. They realized that the design process should not only aim to alleviate current problems but should also focus on the company's next stage of development in order to avoid future problems.

It became evident to Ron Harrison that the company's redesign should include some changes in leadership. During Tempo Products' first stages of development, Ron's unique skills as a risk taker, investor, and market identifier had contributed greatly to the company's success. This type of leadership is termed *strategic leadership* (see Chapter Eleven). Ron realized, however, that the $150 million company that Tempo Products had become required different leadership skills for its continued success. At this stage of development, Tempo Products needed a leader who was skilled at maintaining its day-to-day operations. This type of leadership is termed *operational leadership*. As is explained in Chapter Eleven, Ron had two alternatives in meeting this need: (1) develop the required skills himself or (2) hire someone who had the skills that he had not adequately developed.

After much discussion with experts and consideration of the matter, Ron decided that his company's and his own needs would best be met if someone else were appointed to run Tempo Products on a day-to-day basis. Ron could then assume the role of chief executive and remain responsible for strategic planning, new ventures, and organizational development. Ron appointed Stewart Page, who had been an adviser to Tempo Products for a number of years, to the office of president. Stewart was selected because he was familiar with the business and because Ron believed he could get the type of results that the company needed.

The change in leadership was communicated to employees through both word and action. The word consisted of a formal announcement of Page's appointment, and the action consisted of a number of changes in policy and practice that symbolized a change in the company's culture, as well as a change in leadership.

Stewart Page made his presence felt almost immediately by reducing the company's deadwood in two ways. First, he asked people who had been doing their own thing without regard for the company's benefit to leave. Second, he analyzed positions for their contributions to the overall functioning of the firm. Positions that appeared to have no clear responsibilities and did not serve a critical function for the company were eliminated. Employees who occupied these positions were either terminated or relocated. During this period, as they say, heads rolled.

After the deadwood had been eliminated, a new and more formalized organization chart that clearly depicted how different positions related to one another was developed. Job descriptions were reviewed and revised (or created) to accommodate the changes made in the organization's structure. These new definitions of roles and responsibilities were communicated to employees both formally and informally so that everyone would clearly understand the way their jobs related to the company's total functioning.

Stewart Page also promoted cost control. He made it clear that the company would no longer tolerate excessive spending and that managers would be held accountable for their budgets.

Stewart set about reducing the separate islands syndrome by increasing communication across organization lines. He did this by creating a company-wide operating committee that brought together middle managers from various divisions and departments within the company. This group also increased communication between middle and upper management by acting as the liaison between senior management and the rest of the organization.

Eventually, Stewart hoped to create operating committees for each product division. These committees would be responsible for setting, monitoring, and evaluating the division's goals. The creation of these committees was intended to move the organization's structure toward a focus on "profit centers," with functional general managers.

Through these actions and others, the change in leadership and the change in culture that it represented were communicated to Tempo Products' employees. It became clear that several aspects of the old culture, including playing it by ear, doing your own thing, and operating in isolation from other areas of the company, were gone forever. The company was going to develop the culture of a professional firm, which included more formalized operating systems, making "your own thing" conform to the company's interests, and working together in an integrated, cooperative fashion.

Strategic Planning

Tempo Products had made an attempt to implement a corporate planning process, but this process had not been institutionalized and was not functioning effectively. Senior management became aware that a more formal corporate plan was needed and set about creating one. (For a complete discussion of strategic planning, see Chapter Seven.)

The initial challenge the company faced was to decide what business it was in. Creating a corporate identity is the first step in defining a corporate culture and designing a strategic plan. Tempo Products had grown into a company with five divisions related to different products, and it lacked focus. Upper management, therefore, worked to clarify the company's identity through meetings and discussions outlining its present and future growth opportunities. Corporate leaders eventually decided that Tempo Products was in the business of producing small consumer items designed for the tastes of a special market segment.

Once managers had reached agreement on the firm's business definition, or concept, they began to create a strategic plan and to formalize the strategic planning process. Stewart Page established a planning department to concentrate on the long-term growth and goals of Tempo Products and integrate the plans of various divisions.

Management Development

Tempo Products had traditionally offered management development opportunities to its employees, but it had never had a formalized training program. Thus the quality of management training varied from year to year, depending on its frequency, content, and instructors.

Stewart Page and his senior managers recognized the need for formalized and continuing training programs. A belief in such programs was consistent with Ron Harrison's view that the key resource of Tempo Products was people and that training could help to increase the value of this resource. Stewart, however, saw that these programs could also serve as a means of redefining and communicating the company's culture.

Both Ron and Stewart believed that it was important for members of upper management to understand and be able to perform their responsibilities effectively. Because the company's existing management training programs appeared to be insufficient, Tempo Products' leaders asked an independent consultant to help them design new training programs for senior management. These programs consisted of counseling and skill-building sessions overseen by a professional trainer.

Stewart also recognized the need to improve the training programs offered to middle managers. Traditionally, these programs were not formal, and attendance at them was not required. Thus the quality of managers' training varied greatly. Stewart decided that the company needed a more formalized management development program that was precisely tailored to Tempo Products' unique qualities and problems.

Working with an independent consultant, Stewart and other members of upper management developed a program that both provided training to present and potential managers and helped the company redefine and communicate its culture. The program consisted of lectures, readings, structured exercises, and group discussions, all focusing on the unique aspects and skill requirements of being a manager at Tempo Products. (An in-depth example of the use of a management development program in a company facing issues similar to those at Tempo Products is presented in Chapter Nine.)

Initially, only selected middle managers participated in these programs, although the programs were intended to eventually include all present and potential managers. This gradual implementation allowed the programs to be tested for their ability to meet the company's needs. It also helped to reduce participants' potential resistance to change.

Stewart hoped for three important outcomes from the management development programs. First, they should create a pool of skilled managers, who would become the next generation of senior managers to run the firm. Second, because participants were drawn from different areas of the company, he hoped that the shared experience of taking part in the programs would create lasting relationships that could serve as linking pins between areas of the company. Finally, he hoped that program participants would bring back to their areas both new skills and the new definition of the company's culture, which would then spread throughout the rest of the organization.

Culture Management

Stewart Page, Ron Harrison, and Catherine Forest Harrison (a senior vice president and Ron's wife) began to focus on the management of Tempo Products' culture. They both realized that culture can be managed; it is not just "there."

One of their first tasks was to define what Tempo Products' culture was. They began with an informal culture survey that was distributed to a sample of employees. The survey asked respondents, who remained anonymous, a series of questions about their satisfaction with various aspects of their jobs and with the company in general. The goal was to have respondents answer the underlying question, "What do you see as the company's personality?" The information obtained was analyzed to determine what employees thought the current culture was. Interviews were then conducted with selected middle managers, asking them for their perceptions of the company's culture.

Stewart, Ron, Cathy, and other members of upper management then worked to develop a definition of what Tempo Products' culture should be. Once this statement was developed, they turned to identifying ways of effectively communicating the elements of this culture throughout the firm. To support this effort, the firm established a corporate communications department to articulate, design, and reinforce elements of the new culture. This department, headed by Mary Ryan, reported to Cathy Forest Harrison.

Another important ingredient in the process of cultural change and management at Tempo Products involved the formal and informal influence of Cathy Forest Harrison. As senior vice president in the firm, she was responsible for one of the major functional areas of the firm. She was also, however, a co-owner of the firm and a member of its board of directors.

Cathy's role in her company's development to a Stage IV company and in the redesign and management of its corporate culture was both direct and subtle. As a member of the board of directors, she had a senior management perspective on what was happening in the company, but she also had the ability to think about the firm in a very different way from the way Ron and Stewart did. Ron was the classic entrepreneur. His skills have already been described, and he was the one who contributed the brilliant strategic vision to create the company. Stewart was the day-to-day administrator. One of his primary skills was problem solving. He was emotionally and intellectually prepared to make the difficult decisions involving people and resource allocation required at this stage of the firm's development. But successful development to Stage IV also required a third type of thinking skill: the ability to think holistically about this organization and its developmental processes. Although both Stewart and Ron certainly possessed this third kind of skill to a considerable extent, of the three, Cathy Forest Harrison had the greatest talent for this type of thinking.

Based on her own analysis of the transformation taking place at Tempo Products, as well as on selected inputs from a consultant working with the firm, Cathy formulated her views and expressed them at board meetings, thus helping to shape the corporate culture. She championed the corporate communications department and served as senior management's representative to the organization by hosting a series of working lunches to meet employees, answer their questions about the firm's future direction, and, by her very presence, communicate the company's interest in people and their concerns. She was also a major player in the decision-making process involving all the other aspects of the organizational development program just described, including the new corporate structure, the management development program, and strategic planning.

THE NEW TEMPO PRODUCTS CULTURE AND ITS IMPLEMENTATION

This section considers how the elements of the professional culture at Tempo Products evolved from the entrepreneurial elements described in the first section of this case study. In some instances, the new culture promoted a belief, value, or norm that reflected a cultural element on which the company was originally founded. In other cases, where going back to traditional elements would have been dysfunctional, new values, beliefs, or norms were created and communicated. Each element of the new culture that Tempo Products' management created and the method used to reinforce it is described in the pages that follow.

Tempo Products is One Family, Not a Collection of Separate Families

Tempo Products wanted to communicate to its employees the belief in a need to pull together as a company: "We can no longer operate as a group of separate entities, concerned only with ourselves."

The adoption of this belief was symbolized, in part, by the creation of the operating committee. This group increased communication among work units, although there was initially some resistance to the idea that the company could pull together. Individual divisions and departments feared that they would lose resources (power, people, and materials) if they submitted to the new culture. People also wanted to remain loyal to their work groups, because they found the most support there.

To reduce such resistance to whole-company loyalty, Tempo Products began promoting companywide activities such as picnics, parties, and luncheons. These gatherings encouraged individuals from different areas to talk with one another informally and thus established lines of communication. The result was that people felt more comfortable phoning an acquaintance in another work unit to find the answer to a problem or question.

Another effort to reunite the company was the creation of a newsletter and a formal corporate communications department (mentioned earlier), which provided information on corporate activities and on the people who made up the company. In the biweekly newsletter, individuals were honored for company service, recognized for their participation in company-sponsored management development programs, congratulated on promotions, and even given best wishes on birthdays and anniversaries. This publication became a symbol that Tempo Products cared about its personnel. More important, from management's perspective, it also reduced employees' need to rely on the grapevine for information. There were many key performers in the company, in addition to senior management. The addition of the company newsletter and a new corporate awards program provided the firm with the ability to recognize employees throughout the firm.

Decisions Will Be Made at All Levels of the Company, and People Will Be Held Accountable for Their Decisions

Tempo Products' management recognized the need to develop effective decision makers at all levels of the company and to eliminate the notion that upper management must never be challenged. To accomplish these goals, Tempo Products began training individuals in effective decision-making techniques and encouraging them to apply these skills.

Participants in Tempo Products' management development program were formally taught how to make effective decisions. They also learned that they were responsible for certain decisions and that these decisions should not be bumped up to senior management. As program participants returned to their jobs, the hope was that they would pass these skills on to others through example and, wherever possible, through actual training of their own direct reports.

Formalization of the strategic planning process also helped distribute decision-making responsibility throughout the organization. Individuals were encouraged to participate in decisions affecting them by setting goals for themselves, for their work groups, and for the organization at large. Management also stressed that employees would be evaluated on their success at meeting these goals. If employees did not understand or were unhappy with goals that had been set, it was their responsibility to clarify them.

A third way of promoting decision-making skills and reducing the practice of deferring decisions to upper management involved the refinement of role and responsibility descriptions. These new descriptions, in many cases, helped individuals at lower levels of the organization to understand that they would be held accountable for making certain decisions—that this was now part of their job.

The new culture also stressed that no one was invincible. Everyone would be held accountable for decisions made, including senior management. The notion that senior management was invincible was reduced not only by policy but also by example. Certain members of senior management who were not performing their jobs well were terminated.

Get It Done With Excellence

The emphasis that Tempo Products traditionally placed on excellence in products, people, and the company at large was maintained in the new culture. However, excellence in people was no longer defined as "whatever Tempo Products employees do." Rather, excellence was redefined in terms of quality work and desire to "do something extra" for the good of the company. A new bonus system was created that supported this definition. This system rewarded only those who performed above standard.

The management development program and the strategic planning process also reinforced this revised definition of excellence. Both of these efforts stressed that individuals would be held accountable for achieving the goals they had set for themselves and that rewards would be contingent on meeting these goals. Participants in the management development program were taught how to recognize and reward excellence in order to increase employee motivation.

Another change in the definition of excellence was that the company no longer tolerated excessive expenditures. The motto became "whatever it takes to get it done with excellence and in a cost-effective manner." Managers were held accountable for meeting their budgets, and the notion of always going first class was eliminated.

Our Company Can Learn from Others

Although Tempo Products continued to promote the notion that it was a unique company, it also wanted employees to understand that they could learn from the experience of others. This belief was promoted through the management development program, which was designed to meet Tempo Products' specific needs and at the same time demonstrate techniques that had proved successful for other companies and other managers. These techniques included a performance review system that evaluated individuals based on observed performance; a strategic planning system in which goals are set, monitored, and evaluated; and an organization design that is functional for the kind of company Tempo Products had become.

We Can No Longer Play It by Ear

Tempo Products recognized that some of its growing pains resulted from a lack of formalized management and operating systems. It focused on replacing the play-it-by-ear cultural element with one that emphasized the planning, procedures, and policies of a professional firm.

At the individual level, the company carefully reviewed the roles and responsibilities of its employees. It got rid of most of its deadwood in the form of both nonfunctioning people and nonfunctional positions. This painful but necessary process not only improved the bottom line but also affected people in a positive sense. There was now little ambiguity about job roles, and employees were aware that each had a valuable contribution to make to the company.

The communication problems that the company experienced at the management level were difficult to resolve, but Tempo Products' managers came to view the new management development program as an important step toward improving horizontal communications. Many groups of program participants developed a team spirit that continued after they returned to their individual areas, allowing them to feel comfortable in calling one another about problems. More than a few of these relationships were maintained as the individuals were promoted to higher levels within the company.

Just as participants in the management development program continued to help reintegrate areas on an informal basis, the strategic planning process—which emphasized corporate rather than divisional planning—helped reintegrate the company on a formal basis. Each division and department was now responsible for its own financial and nonfinancial goals, but these were formulated with consideration for other work units, not in isolation from them. The planning department helped coordinate this effort so that company interests would remain of paramount concern.

Even more significant than the steps just described was the firm's decision to improve horizontal communications through the creation of three separate product operating committees. Because of the nature of the company's products, the operating committee, consisting of representatives from different functional areas (production, sales, and so forth), became a highly effective tool for facilitating interdepartmental communication and decision making.

Have Fun, But Not All the Time

The new culture stressed that conflict cannot and should not be avoided. Rather, conflict should be confronted and resolved.

The first step in this process was to help individuals admit that conflict existed. Tempo Products' employees had operated for many years in what seemed, on the surface, to be a very smooth-running and peaceful atmosphere.

However, like all organizations, Tempo Products had underlying conflicts between people and areas. Traditionally, these conflicts had been ignored. However, when Stewart Page was made president, and major changes began, a great deal of conflict came to the surface and could no longer be denied.

The culture survey also brought conflicts to the surface. The survey itself was evidence that management believed that not everyone was having fun and that some problems existed. It was intended to reinforce the belief that it's all right to criticize, to be unhappy about certain things—and get them out in the open so we can resolve our problems.

The next step was to train employees to confront conflict. This was accomplished, in part, through the management development program. Participants were shown how to deal with conflict, particularly how to give and receive criticism. Again, management hoped that participants would take both these skills and the new culture that they represented back to their jobs and start them filtering both up and down throughout the organization. As Cathy Forest Harrison pointed out, conflict is not necessarily bad. Senior management fostered a new culture of accountability, and this led to conflict. Moreover, the increasing sophistication of the finance department led to its ability, mandated by senior management, to ask the hard questions, which leads to conflict. In brief, healthy conflict became a part of the company's culture.

"Do Your Own Thing and Do It Well"

This element of the organization's culture was positively redefined, in part, by the organizational development program. The program helped redefine this value on three levels.

At the individual employee level, the new definition was, "When you do your own thing, it should be congruent with the goals of the organization." To put this belief into practice, the company created procedures and policies that stressed real excellence in performance and emphasized that those who do not perform at the expected level will be dismissed. Employees came to recognize that those who worked toward excellence would be rewarded, while those who did not would be forced to leave the company. Better definitions of roles and responsibilities acted as guides to help employees determine what constituted excellent performance. People would no longer be allowed to merely wander the halls.

At the managerial level, managers were encouraged to use leadership styles that would help the company be more effective. (Chapter Eleven discusses the basic concepts and methods of increasing leadership effectiveness.) Tempo Products' senior management hoped that, through the training that participants in the management development program received, they would gain the skills necessary to be effective delegators and decision makers.

At the organization level, the company focused on reducing the do-your-own-thing-but-stay-out-of-my-territory element of its culture. This was accomplished, partly by the formation of the operating committee and partly by the management development program. The team feeling that was created among program participants helped decrease the need for territoriality—for protecting turf.

Postscript

For several years Tempo Products competed successfully with a much larger player in its space. In spite of spending many millions of dollars to upgrade its products, operations, and marketing, the larger competitor (more than twenty times larger than Tempo Products) was unable to take away market share from Tempo Products, which had built a defensible market niche. Finally, the large competitor company made overtures at an acquisition. Ron Harrison turned down two offers from his competitor, who finally made the proverbial offer that cannot be refused. Ron decided to sell the firm. Although Tempo Products as a separate entity is gone, its product continues to be a success within its marketplace, and the internal capabilities that Ron and his senior management team put in place continue to support its success.

Ron and his wife, Cathy, retired from the business and are involved in charitable and other activities.

KEYS TO A SUCCESSFUL STAGE IV FIRM

By the time a firm like Tempo Products reaches Stage IV, the lack of a shared culture can produce a number of problems. Individuals are left to create their own cultures, which may not always be in the best interest of the company as a whole. Thus the key factor involved in making the transition to Stage IV is the ability to develop a formal program of auditing the corporate culture and transmitting it to peer groups of employees.

To begin this process, management must first determine what the culture is. This can be a difficult process, as members are not always able to articulate values, beliefs, and norms. It is much like asking a U.S. citizen what it is like to be an American. However, interviews with organization members in which they are asked to relate stories about their lives in the company may provide some clues. Careful thought and analysis—including feedback to the organization for confirmation, refinement, or redefinition—is also important.

From the information provided by this cultural diagnosis, management can determine where it is in terms of culture. Then it can focus on redefining the company's culture and begin communicating the new culture to employees through changes in policies and practices like those described in the case provided in this chapter. A more in-depth examination of the culture management process is presented in Chapter Twelve.

SUMMARY

The events we describe for Tempo Products are typical of those that occur as companies attempt to make the transition from Stage III to Stage IV.

Several lessons can be learned from Tempo Products' experience. The first is that the need to manage a firm's corporate culture is just as real and important as the need to manage cash or inventory. Culture can have significant positive or negative effects on operations and, ultimately, on the corporate bottom line.[2]

A second lesson is that cultural change is inevitable as an organization grows. Senior managers may think they know what the firm's culture is because they have a close association with the owner or founder, who directly communicates his or her vision to them. Unfortunately, as more and more new people enter the organization, the culture of the owner or founder is increasingly likely to become distorted because there is no longer much direct communication with him or her. The changes that occur are not necessarily malicious; they may simply arise from "noise" picked up through the process of cultural transmission.

A third lesson is that cultural change can reinforce and be reinforced by the broader process of organizational development that a firm must go through as it moves from Stage III to Stage IV. The culture that management wants to reinforce or introduce can be manifested in the firm's leadership style, its management development programs, its structure, and its strategic planning process. Indeed, the firm's culture must be consistent throughout all management systems if it is to become fully effective.

Another lesson concerns the process of cultural change. The change process must begin with an audit or assessment of what the firm's present culture is. This can be accomplished with a variety of tools, including questionnaires, interviews, and analysis of stories and internal corporate materials. Once the present culture has been identified, the organization must decide on the form of culture it desires and compare this ideal with the present situation. This comparison leads to identification of cultural gaps or desired cultural changes. The last step in bringing about cultural change is designing the strategy and action plan for introducing the desired changes.

A final lesson concerns the different kinds of management thinking required to develop an enterprise to a successful Stage IV company. From our analysis of Tempo Products it should be clear that organizational success at Stage IV is more than merely a matter of products and markets, though they are an essential prerequisite. It is a matter of different modes of thinking as well. Classic entrepreneurial thinking is required for success at Stages I and II. However, the successful transition from Stage II to Stages III and IV requires two additional modes of thought: (1) the problem-solving mode and (2) the holistic organizational development perspective.

At Tempo Products, all three of the senior managers (Ron, Cathy, and Stewart) possessed each of these different modes of thinking to some extent. However, each also possessed a considerable advantage in at least one mode. As a management team, they possessed all of the three key ways of thinking about their company.

Cultural change can be accomplished through a variety of methods. As seen at Tempo Products, several different ingredients were used, including a formal corporate communications program, informal family-style gatherings, changes in senior management attitudes and skills, a culture survey, the use of a committee structure to increase interdepartmental communication, and management development. It should also be noted that the successful organizational development program at Tempo Products was not without its problems. Moreover, although the roles of certain people are highlighted in this chapter, many other individuals played significant roles as well.

As this chapter shows, cultural change in a corporation is complex and difficult—but necessary. It is the critical developmental task involved in building a successful Stage IV organization and making the last part of the transition from an entrepreneurship to a professionally managed firm.

PART THREE

MASTERING THE TOOLS OF PROFESSIONAL MANAGEMENT

P arts One and Two of this book presented a framework for understanding and managing the transitions of an entrepreneurial organization from one stage of growth and development to the next. Part Three focuses on the basic tools for managing organizations professionally. Specifically, we discuss some of the major elements of a firm's management infrastructure, its management systems, and corporate culture. Management systems and corporate culture were described briefly in Chapter One; their places on the Pyramid of Organizational Development appear in Figure 1.1.

An organization's management system consists of (1) the planning system, including the strategic planning process, (2) the organization structure, (3) its system for management development, and (4) the company's control or performance management systems. Management systems have a critical influence on an organization's performance and profitability.

A firm's planning system includes its processes for strategic planning, operational planning, budgeting, and contingency planning. In entrepreneurial companies these processes tend to be relatively informal, while in professionally managed firms they tend to be more developed.

The strategic planning process is a critical resource or tool for managing organizational growth and development. Chapter Seven presents concepts and methods of strategic planning. It also explains the role of strategic planning in making the transition from an entrepreneurship to a professionally managed firm by using the example of one organization's strategic planning process.

Finally, it examines an organization's requirements for strategic planning at different stages of growth.

The way people are organized in a business enterprise can have a critical impact on overall operating effectiveness, efficiency, and, in turn, bottom-line profitability. Chapter Eight discusses the nature of an organization's structure and examines the alternative forms of structure. It also identifies criteria for the design and evaluation of organizational structure and presents case studies of structural issues at different stages of growth.

Management and leadership development is another major tool for organizational development in entrepreneurial firms. As we saw in the case study presented in Chapter Six, the management development process can be used not only to train managers but also to shape or reshape the corporate culture. Chapter Nine examines the tools and functions of management and leadership development and presents a case study that shows how one company used the management development process in making its transition from an entrepreneurship to a professionally managed organization.

The organizational control or performance management system is another critical component of the firm's management systems. Chapter Ten discusses organizational control and its role in making the transition to a professionally managed firm. It explains the need for control and the nature and role of organizational control and performance management systems. It also presents a model of the key components of a control system and explains how they function to motivate and control behavior. Finally, it examines organizations' need for control at different stages of growth.

Another critical factor in helping organizations make the transition from an entrepreneurship to a professionally managed firm is leadership. Leadership is involved both in the day-to-day operations of firms and in their long-term organizational development. Chapter Eleven presents basic concepts and research findings concerning leadership effectiveness. It examines the leadership styles available to managers and presents the results of some research concerning the extent to which each style has been observed in organizations of different sizes and at different stages of growth. It also examines the key tasks that managers must perform if they are to be effective leaders and presents some research on the extent to which these tasks are actually performed by managers in organizations of different sizes.

The nature and management of a company's culture also have a significant impact on an organization's success. Culture influences a firm's ability to develop the systems needed to support its growth. Like other variables in the Pyramid of Organizational Development, culture must be effectively managed if a firm is to make the transition to professional management. Chapter Twelve describes the nature of corporate culture and how it is manifested in organizations. It also presents techniques for managing this variable effectively and describes the nature of corporate culture at different stages of organizational growth.

Part Three, then, gives a basic description of some of the most important concepts and tools that can help entrepreneurs successfully manage their firms' transition from one stage of growth to the next. These tools provide an essential foundation for the successful management of entrepreneurial organizations at all stages of growth, but especially at Stages III and beyond.

Figure III.1 summarizes schematically the relations among the key components of an organization's management system. As seen in the figure, the management process begins with the planning system, which articulates a firm's business concept, strategic mission, core strategy, objectives, and goals. Strategic leadership is involved throughout the planning process. The firm's plan and leadership should determine how it is organized (organizational structure). This, in turn, enhances the organization's operational systems and leads to the firm's results, which are measured by the performance measurement system.

The performance measurement system is a component of the company's control system, which also includes objectives and goals from the planning

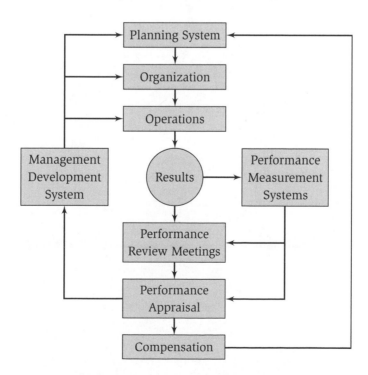

Figure III.1. The Management System

system as well as performance appraisal and rewards (compensation). Performance review meetings, as well as formal information, are the mechanisms through which these components of the overall management system operate. The management and leadership development system supports the other components of the management system by training managers in the skills required to do planning, to use the various forms of organizational structure, and to manage day-to-day operations (operational leadership). Input about the skills that need to be built through management development is received from the performance appraisal process.

Leadership—a key component of the management system—is not shown explicitly in Figure III.1, but it should be viewed as a part of the various components such as strategic planning (strategic leadership), operations, performance review meetings, and performance appraisal (operational leadership). Similarly, corporate culture is not explicitly shown in Figure III.1, but it must be recognized that corporate culture affects and is affected by all of the components of the management system.

CHAPTER SEVEN

Strategic Planning

Previous chapters have provided an overview of the things an organization must do to make a successful transition from an entrepreneurship to a professionally managed organization. This chapter focuses on one of the major tools available to help senior managers make this transition: strategic planning.

The strategic planning process is one of the management systems that an organization must develop if it desires to function effectively. Strategic planning plays a dual role. It is not only an important tool for managing organizations; it is also part of the process through which organizations make the transition from one stage of growth to the next.

Strategic planning is one of the major tools by which management can create a shared vision of what a company (whether for-profit or not-for-profit) wants to become. The strategic planning process can also help to shape the corporate culture. The very act of instituting such a process, when one was not used in the past, signals to the organization's members that things are changing. It warns that planning must now become a way of life and that the firm has embarked on a program to professionalize itself. Strategic planning can also provide a sense of direction for a company and its employees, as well as specific goals to motivate and guide behavior.

This is the first of two chapters dealing with strategic planning; it provides a framework to help managers understand the strategic planning process, as well as a step-by-step approach to strategic planning in organizations. We first introduce and define the basic concepts of the strategic planning process. We then describe the steps involved in developing a strategic plan. To illustrate the nature of strategic planning, we then examine the planning process at an entrepreneurial company, Royce Medical Corporation. Finally, we describe the strategic planning process at each stage of growth. Chapter Thirteen deals with advanced aspects of strategic planning, including the use of the Pyramid of Organizational Development as a lens to focus on strategy.

The framework and approach to strategic planning presented in this chapter include some familiar concepts, but there are subtle differences, which we point out.[1] There is a great deal of semantic confusion in the language of strategic planning. We are careful to clearly define our concepts and terms, then tie them together as a true planning system. Although some people are critical of the concept of strategic planning, the approach presented here has actually been used by many organizations, and it works!

STRATEGY DEFINED

Although the term *strategy* is widely used, it is frequently either undefined or loosely defined. Everyone "knows" what it is when they see it, but they can't define it. The first challenge, then, that managers face in trying to implement a strategic plan is to define what is meant by the word *strategy*.

Strategy can be defined as "the different, yet integrated courses of actions that will be taken by a firm or business unit to compete effectively in its chosen markets in order to obtain desired results." Thus strategy implies both competition and intended achievement. Taking this definition a step further, strategy consists of (1) *where* (in what markets) a firm chooses to compete and (2) *how* the firm will compete in its chosen markets in order to achieve the best results. We come back to this definition a little later in this chapter.

THE NATURE OF STRATEGIC PLANNING

An organization can have a strategy and not have a strategic planning process or plan. The process of strategic planning involves deciding about the future direction and the capabilities that will be needed to achieve the organization's goals. It involves analyzing the organization's environment to assess future opportunities and threats, assessing the organization's capabilities, and formulating the mission, objectives, and specific goals to be achieved, as well as developing action plans to attain them. An effective strategic planning process also includes a system for monitoring performance against the strategic plan.

A strategic plan is a written document that details where and how the firm will compete. An effective strategic plan serves as a guide for the behavior of people within the firm. In a sense, it is the firm's "play book." We believe that an effective strategic plan must deal not only with a company's markets and external business opportunities but also with the internal organizational capabilities required for future growth. In this sense, the term *strategic planning* is more appropriately viewed as a process of "strategic organizational development." It simultaneously deals with both the strategic aspects of markets and competition and the organizational infrastructure—its capabilities required for long-term organizational success, as described in Chapter One. This notion is developed further in Chapter Thirteen.

There are three critical aspects of a firm's strategic planning process: (1) strategic issues to be addressed, (2) the "flow" of the process itself, and (3) the components of the strategic plan. We discuss each in turn.

STRATEGIC ISSUES

Although many people think of strategic planning as a number-crunching exercise, its primary focus should be on identifying and resolving strategic and related organizational development issues. To articulate its future direction and strategy, it is necessary for the firm to address a wide variety of issues that are relevant to its market, competition, environmental trends, and organizational development.

Each organization will have a number of strategic issues that are specific to its market, how it will compete, and the internal systems that it needs to have to support its development. There are, however, seven generic questions that *must* be addressed by all organizations, regardless of their size and their industry:

1. What business are we in?
2. What are our competitive strengths and limitations?
3. Do we have or can we develop a true market niche?
4. What do we want to become in the long term?
5. What is our strategy for competing effectively in our chosen markets and for achieving our long-term mission?
6. What are the critical factors that will make us successful or unsuccessful in achieving this long-term mission?
7. What goals shall we set to improve our competitive effectiveness and organizational capabilities in each of these critical success areas?

The answers to these questions result in the development of key components of the firm's strategic plan. For example, by answering the first question, the firm develops a statement of its *business concept;* addressing the fourth question leads to the development of the firm's *strategic mission statement.*

We examine how these questions are addressed in the discussion of the steps or flow of the strategic planning process. We also illustrate how these questions must be addressed in the context of a case study later in this chapter.

THE STRATEGIC PLANNING PROCESS

Even though all firms need to address certain key issues, there is no such thing as the ideal strategic planning process for any organization. The nature of the process will differ, depending on its stage of growth. There are, however, six phases or steps that must be included in any strategic planning process. As shown in Figure 7.1, these six key steps are (1) the environmental scan, (2) the organizational assessment (or audit), (3) the analysis and resolution of key strategic issues, (4) the (strategic) business plan, (5) the budget, and (6) the management review.

The first two steps of this process involve collecting information on the environment in which the firm has chosen to compete and on its internal capabilities. Using the information collected in the first two steps as input, the third step involves identifying and working to resolve key strategic issues (including those identified earlier). In the fourth step, the management team is actually producing the firm's plan. A budget to support the plan developed in Step 4 is created in Step 5. The final step in this process is what makes the planning process really work. This step involves periodic monitoring of performance against the plan. It provides a firm's management with the opportunity to make adjustments, as needed, so that it can continue to achieve the best results.

Step 1: The Environmental Scan

As seen in Figure 7.1, the first step in the planning process is the environmental scan. This step involves collecting information on (1) the market in which the firm competes, (2) the firm's competition, and (3) key environmental trends that may affect the firm (positively or negatively) in the future.

Market Analysis. The first step in the environmental scan is to collect and analyze information on the firm's current and potential market. In brief, this step involves collecting information on the nature of the firm's customers, their needs, how they buy, and the potential of different market segments. The output of this analysis should be a very clear picture of what the firm's current market consists of—who its customers really are. In addition, the

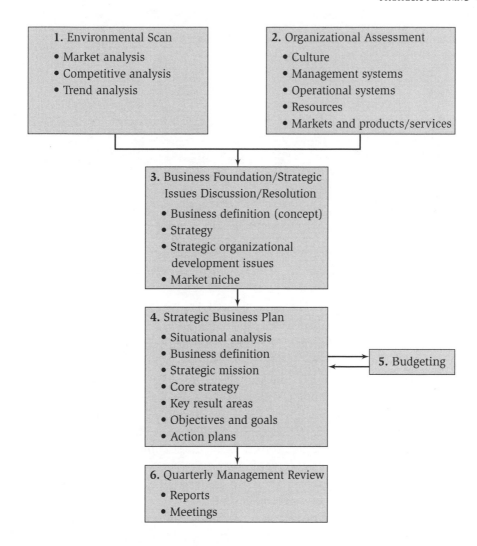

Figure 7.1. Flow Diagram of the Strategic Planning Process

market analysis should identify the threats and opportunities that exist within the firm's present and potential markets.

Competitive Analysis. The next step in an environmental scan is to assess the competition. The first step in this process is to identify who the firm's present and potential competitors are. Then the strengths and limitations of each competitor need to be identified. It is important that in identifying these strengths and limitations, a firm be as objective as possible. In addition, the firm should examine how customers perceive each of their competitors.

Horizontal Segments	Vertical Segments				
	Sedans	Sports Cars	SUVs	Light Trucks	Minivans
I	• Rolls-Royce • Lexus • BMW • Jaguar	• Porsche • Ferrari • Lamborghini	• Hummer • Mercedes • Lexus • Range Rover • Escalade		
II	• Honda Accord • Toyota Camry • Ford Taurus	• Toyota Celica • Volkswagen Jetta	• Ford Explorer • GMC Blazer • Jeep Cherokee	• Toyota Tacoma • Ford Ranger	• Toyota Sienna • Ford Windstar
III	• Toyota Corolla	• Cooper "Mini"	• Toyota RAV4 • Suzuki Samurai		

Figure 7.2. Where You Play "The Game": Analysis of the Strategic Board

Identifying a Firm's Market Segment: One Output of the Market and Competitive Analysis. The information collected through the market and competitive analyses can be used to help a firm better understand where it is competing or might compete within its marketplace—its market segments. A market segment is defined in terms of the product-service categories a firm will offer, as well as the tier of the marketplace in which the organization will compete. These two dimensions of the market come together in what we call the *strategic board,* which identifies the segments that are included in the market in which a firm is competing. An example of a strategic board for the automobile industry is presented in Figure 7.2.

The market for any product or service typically exists in terms of three different tiers or levels of the market (shown on the vertical axis of Figure 7.2). In order to position themselves effectively, companies must understand that customer wants differ at each tier.

The typical buyer in the Tier I market is affluent enough to afford whatever he or she wants. Accordingly, the primary concern is for the overall quality, service, and prestige of the product or service received rather than for the price per se. At the margin there may well be some buyers in the Tier 1 category who have a significant concern with price. However, buyers in this price category typically are less concerned with price or even price differentials than they are with the other factors. For example, an individual who is purchasing an automobile in the Tier I category may consider a Mercedes, a Jaguar, or some other luxury automobile and may very well not be concerned with a major differential in price between these particular products.

Viewed figuratively, the products and services in this tier can be thought of as ranging from a Lincoln to a Rolls-Royce. This is true not only for automobiles per se but for all products and services that fit this particular categorization by quality. The same kind of demarcation can be true for legal services, personal care, or products provided by aerospace firms.

The second tier of the marketplace is usually significantly larger than Tier I in terms of the number of customers in this segment. As for quality, the products in this category figuratively range from Volvo down to a Chevrolet. In Tier II, the buyer is concerned with a combination of quality, service, prestige, and price. Typically, the buyer is making tradeoffs between two or more of these variables. As before, this tier of the marketplace is not just applicable to automobiles but to a full range of products and services.

In Tier III, the typical buyer is concerned primarily with price. Quality, service, and prestige are relatively unimportant. This particular segment is generally the largest of all three tiers of the marketplace. The buyer in this segment of the marketplace is looking for a "serviceable" product or service. It may well be a commodity or a generic brand. This tier can be symbolically represented by looking from Chevrolet down through Hyundai or Yugo automobiles.

To illustrate the fact that the three tiers of the marketplace do not merely apply to tangible products such as automobiles but to all other products and services as well, consider some examples, such as legal services, medical services, aerospace, and retailing. In Los Angeles there is a well-known law firm by the name of O'Melveny & Meyers. This firm operates in the Tier I segment, and to paraphrase a well-known saying, "If you have to ask the price, you probably cannot afford it." In Tier III we have a firm that specializes in being a legal service supermarket: Jacoby & Meyers. And in Los Angeles, there are certainly many Tier II law firms—probably several with a "Meyers." With respect to medical services, community or public clinics occupy Tier III of the marketplace. PPOs occupy Tier II, and HMOs occupy the lower portions of Tier II and upper Tier III; many private physicians are in various levels of Tiers I and II. The upper end of Tier I tends to be occupied by some of the elite private hospitals, as well as by certain private physicians. In the aerospace sector, Hughes Aircraft had traditionally occupied Tier I of the marketplace. It specialized in being able to do whatever was required by its "customers," which were subunits of the U.S. Department of Defense. Quality, rather than cost, was the primary consideration. Today, most aerospace firms occupy Tier II, because the customer is concerned with the tradeoff between price, quality, and service; a few aerospace firms operate in Tier III. In the retailing sector, Saks Fifth Avenue and Neiman-Marcus occupy Tier I. Stores such as JCPenney and Macy's occupy Tier II, while Tier III is served by Wal-Mart, Kmart, and 99 Cents Only Stores.

It is typically very difficult for firms to compete in all three segments of the marketplace simultaneously. Only some of the largest firms have traditionally been able to accomplish this feat. For example, General Motors begins with its lower-priced Chevrolets and moves its customers all the way through its product ladder to the Tier I version of its Cadillac. However, in the lower reaches of Tier III, General Motors does not compete with some of the less expensive foreign imports, and it does not compete in the highest levels of Tier I with products offered by Mercedes and Rolls-Royce.

Developing and analyzing the strategic board can help a firm understand where it currently competes and with whom it competes. This can then help a firm focus on the strengths and limitations of its most significant competitors rather than assume that it competes with "everyone." For example, if a firm competes in Tier II of the retail market, it should be most concerned with understanding the strengths and limitations of firms in this segment. Firms competing in Tier I or Tier III of this market should be of less concern *unless* there is the possibility that these firms might move into Tier II. Analyzing the strategic board can also help a firm identify "open segments" in which it might compete because no other firms have yet entered them.

Trend Analysis. The final step in the environmental scan is to survey the larger economic, social, political, legal, and cultural environment for emerging trends that may affect the firm in the future. The organization needs to try to answer such questions as this: What will our industry be like in five years? What emerging trends in demographics, workforce values, the economic and political environment, technology, and so on might affect our organization? What potential opportunities and threats are implicit in those trends? What actions can or must we take to deal with them?

One trend that is affecting practically every business in the new millennium is the rapidity with which information system technology is evolving. Firms of all sizes need to find ways to meet the demands of an increasingly greater reliance on information technology, not only for supplying information within their own organizations but also for communicating with others (customers, suppliers) and doing business (e-commerce). Organizations need to be planning for this impact *now*. For example, retailers operating out of malls need to consider the impact of changed shopping patterns, and so do mall developers such as Simon Properties, General Growth, and Westfield's.

Step 2: The Organizational Assessment

The second step in the strategic planning process is to conduct an organizational assessment. This consists of identifying the strengths and limitations of a firm at each level in the Pyramid of Organizational Development, described in

Chapter One: markets, products and services, resources, operational systems, management systems, and corporate culture.

The organizational assessment may be done in several ways. It may involve a self-assessment of strengths and limitations in each area. It may also involve the use of questionnaires to be completed by a sample of people in the organization or by all of its personnel. Some firms use independent consultants to perform an organizational assessment; the consultants interview personnel and analyze operational data. This process, also called an organizational audit, is described further in Chapter Seventeen.

Output of the First Two Steps

The output of the environmental scan and organizational assessment should be a summary of the information collected, along with an analysis of what this information suggests about areas that the firm needs to focus on in order to continue its success into the future. By analyzing the information collected through the environmental scan and organizational assessment, a firm may also identify specific strategic issues that should be addressed in Step 3 of the strategic planning process.

Step 3: Analysis and Resolution of Key Strategic Issues

Once the environmental scan and the organizational assessment have been completed, the next—very critical—step in the strategic planning process is to identify and work to resolve key strategic issues facing the firm. It is important that during this step, the firm address the seven issues previously identified. Each of these seven issues is described in more depth.

What Business Are We In? One of the most fundamental and important strategic issues that a firm needs to address is, What business are we in? This is a deceptively simple question, and it is one of the most critical strategic decisions an organization must make, because it defines the platform or scope of the business. If the business definition (business concept) is too broad or too narrow, it is of no real strategic value. Many organizations fail or at least do not prosper because they do not really understand the nature of their business or because they view it too narrowly. For example, during the nineteenth century and the early part of the twentieth century, the railroads were successful and powerful. However, they viewed the answer to the question, What business are we in? as obvious: we are in the railroad business. Unfortunately for them, the obvious answer was not correct. They ought to have viewed themselves as being in the *transportation* business—the business of transporting people and goods. By defining their business as being railroads, they completely missed the significance of the development of air transportation, which ultimately eroded their strength.

Similarly, Curtis Publishing Company was a great success during the early part of the last century. Cyrus Curtis, a great entrepreneur, built a publishing empire with major properties such as the *Saturday Evening Post* and the *Ladies' Home Journal.* Unfortunately, the company eventually failed because it had defined its business as the "publishing business." It failed to realize that in consumer media, advertising follows consumers, and one of its principal revenue streams was from advertisers. The managers of Curtis did not appreciate the implications of the new medium—television—and its impact on advertising revenues. Thus they chose to purchase a printing plant to vertically integrate the firm's operations, turning down opportunities to acquire NBC and CBS—a disastrous decision.

Examples of changes in business concept or definition that have worked well include (1) Nike, which transformed from a foot-wear company to an athletic-wear company and is moving toward becoming a "sports" company, and (2) Disney, which transformed from an animated motion picture company to a global entertainment enterprise. More subtle examples of broadening business concept include Intel, the world's largest semi-conductor company, which acquired Level One Communications—a leading maker of microprocessors for high-speed communications—as part of a strategy of moving toward the Internet and its use as a communications network. Similarly, Microsoft has moved from a concept of software for microcomputers to a broader notion of software for e-commerce.

An organization that is trying to decide what business it is in must understand what its present and potential markets are and what the customers in those markets need. It must answer these major questions: (1) Who are our present and potential customers? (2) What are their needs? (3) How do they acquire our products or services? and (4) What do they consider to be of value in a product or service? To effectively address these questions, a firm's management should use the information collected and analyzed in Steps 1 and 2 of the strategic planning process. The analysis of the strategic board, along with the information collected on the firm's internal capabilities (through the organizational assessment), can assist in identifying what a firm's business definition or concept should be. For example, if the railroads had thoroughly analyzed the trends in their marketplace (for example, the advent of new technology to move people and products from one location to another), they might have recognized the need to broaden their business definition. A magazine publishing company such as Curtis must recognize that it serves two related but distinct groups of customers: subscribers, who read its publications, and advertisers, who wish to reach particular groups of people in order to market their own products or services. An organization must understand the needs of all its different segments of customers, especially when those needs differ significantly.

The resolution of this issue results in a business definition (or concept) statement, which is incorporated into the firm's strategic plan. The creation of this statement is a complex and subtle exercise, requiring time and skill. Management teams may spend several days—over a period of weeks or months—discussing and debating this issue until they get it right. This is discussed further in Step 4 of the strategic planning process.

What Are Our Competitive Strengths and Limitations? The competitive analysis, along with the organizational assessment, provides the information needed to address this question. A firm needs to objectively identify those areas where it has a relative strength, as well as those areas where it is faced with a competitive disadvantage. In addition, the firm needs to identify what truly distinguishes it from its competition. It is not sufficient to identify "strengths," because competitors also have strengths. This is an essential step even for successful firms, because in order to continue its success an organization must understand what caused it. Xerox, for example, inappropriately believed its success was because "we are good managers," rather than the real reason: ownership of the proprietary process that was the basis for photocopying (the Haloid Process). In contrast, a $75 million industrial products company was unafraid of Japanese competition because it understood that customer service was the competitive key to its market. Similarly, a relatively small producer of disposable medical products was able to compete among giants in its field because of its ability to create new products for well-defined market segments.

The resolution of this issue typically results in a list of areas on which the firm needs to focus in order to maintain its key strengths and minimize its limitations. The resolution of this issue feeds into the development of the firm's strategy.

Do We Have or Can We Develop a True Market Niche? The concept of a market niche must be distinguished from that of a market segment. Although many people use the terms *niche* and *segment* interchangeably, in our opinion they are not equivalent. A market segment is any subdivision of the marketplace defined by the tier of the market in which the firm competes and products-services it offers (as discussed previously).

A market niche is a place within a market segment where an organization has developed a sufficient number of sustainable competitive advantages to "control" a portion of the market. A competitive advantage is "something" (tangible or intangible) that gives an organization a superior opportunity (however marginal) to compete in the marketplace. It can range from a proprietary product (such as a drug under patent) to a well-known brand. Potentially, anything can be a source of competitive advantage: greater resources, speed in execution, a new technology, better customer service, superior management systems, greater skill in strategic planning, or a firm's culture.

We view a competitive advantage as sustainable if it will last for at least two years. This is analogous to a "fixed asset" under generally accepted accounting principles. Just as a current asset is something that will last or be consumed within one year, and a fixed asset is something that will last for more than one year, a sustainable advantage is essentially an organizational resource that will provide the enterprise benefits for at least two years. It can be tangible or intangible, reflected in financial statements or not, but it is still real. Accordingly, just by being the first company into a market does not mean the firm will establish a sustainable competitive advantage.

At times, the source of sustainable advantage can be the business model (or way the company does business) adopted by an organization. An interesting example of this type of sustainable competitive advantage is found at Grocery Outlets. This firm is in the business of selling excess inventory for name-brand vendors, such as Coca-Cola, Gillette, and Johnson & Johnson. Grocery Outlets has developed a business model as the source of their competitive advantage. The firm has established a network of stores that are owned by families under an agreement with Grocery Outlets, which typically funds the store development. The stores purchase their products only from Grocery Outlets, and the margins are "shared." This results in some unique advantages, including having store owners rather than employees focusing on the sale of goods, because owners are typically more motivated than employees.

Another example of a business model being the source of sustainable advantage is found at PHH Mortgage (formerly Cendant Mortgage). As its name implies, PHH Mortgage is in the mortgage loan business. Its primary sustainable advantage is derived from its use of a "telephone platform," together with "affinity marketing," for doing its business. Its mortgages are executed over the telephone. This means that the firm does not have to invest in the bricks and mortar of traditional mortgage companies. In addition, much of its business comes from affinity marketing programs, which involve special offers to people in defined groups, such as professional organizations, single employers, and the like.

The concept of a market niche and, in turn, the notion of a sustainable competitive advantage is important for two strategic reasons. From an "offensive" standpoint, the primary advantage of a niche in a marketplace is typically that the price (and, in turn, the gross margin) of products is superior to that of competitors. This results in greater profitability and in the opportunity to reinvest those profits in a variety of ways. From a "defensive" standpoint, during periods of economic decline, holders of a market niche tend to suffer less than their competitors. Their products tend to sell to a greater extent than those of more generic or less established products and services.

A niche is also important "defensively," if a competitor wishes to "invade" the firm's market segment. For example, when IBM chose to invade the PC marketplace, Apple was unable to defend the entire market. However, Apple had established a niche in a smaller segment of the PC marketplace. Specifically, Apple had established a niche in the educational segment of the PC marketplace. By providing its computers at a lower cost to educational institutions and to teachers, Apple had familiarized instructors and students with their products and services. Accordingly, Apple had established a sustainable competitive advantage in that segment of the marketplace.

A key point to keep in mind in identifying or working to create a market niche is that the most sustainable advantages are those that exist in the upper levels of the Pyramid of Organizational Development. If a firm has a competitive advantage based on its culture, this will be extremely difficult to copy. For example, Southwest Airlines may have initially had an advantage in terms of the product it offered (low-cost airfare). However, it also had an advantage that was and has been extremely sustainable—a well-managed culture that stresses customer service and fun. No other airline has been able to copy this aspect of Southwest's operations, although others now offer comparably priced airfare.

A firm whose only competitive advantage rests with the products it offers leaves itself extremely vulnerable to competition. Any product or service can be copied, thus taking away the firm's advantage. Although we have used Compaq as an example of a firm that was successful in making the initial transition from an entrepreneurship to a professionally managed firm, Compaq failed to recognize that its most sustainable advantages were in the areas of markets and products. When companies like Dell Computers began producing similar products at lower cost, Compaq lost its advantage and its stock went into a downward spiral. This ultimately led to its merger with Hewlett-Packard.

Viewed in this way, a market niche does not have to be small, as conventional usage implies; it can be very large. For example, Microsoft has a true market niche in personal computers because of its dominance in operating systems, and this niche is very large.

What Do We Want to Become in the Long Term? The next key issue a firm needs to address is what it wants to become over the long term. We define *long term* as three to five years out. The identification of what a firm wants to become should be grounded in the analysis of data from the environmental scan and the organizational assessment. In brief, the answer to this question helps the firm define where it is going. The output of this discussion is what we call a Strategic Mission Statement, which will be included in the firm's plan. We discuss this later in this chapter.

In 1994, when Starbucks was still a relatively small company, it established a strategic mission to become the leading brand of specialty coffee in North

America by the year 2000. This was strategic because it was intended to allow Starbucks to achieve a size and critical mass that would be defensible against potential competitors. The debate within management in 1994 centered around whether this could be accomplished if Starbucks achieved $1 billion in revenue and approximately 1,000 stores, or whether a larger number of stores and more revenue were required. The final decision was to target $2 billion in revenue and 2,000 stores by the year 2000. The strategic intent was to prevent a large company like Nestlé or McDonald's from copying the Starbucks "formula" and controlling the market before this could be achieved by Starbucks itself.

What Is Our Strategy for Competing Effectively in Our Chosen Markets and for Achieving Our Long-Term Mission? Once a firm has identified the market in which it will compete (its business concept or definition), its competitive strengths and limitations, and what it wants to become (its strategic mission), the next question involves determining *how* it will compete in order to achieve the desired results. This involves identifying three levels of strategy that will

Figure 7.3. How You Play "The Game": Three Levels of Strategy

guide the behavior of the team toward desired results within the chosen market. These three levels constitute a strategy "wheel" that is shown in Figure 7.3.

The first level of strategy is what we call core strategy, which defines the overall concept of how the firm or business unit will compete. In developing its core strategy, a firm should consider the results of its environmental scan and organizational assessment. This information will help a firm determine how realistic its strategy is.

For example, Starbucks' initial core strategy was something like "to redefine the coffee café and blanket the U.S." With the exception of small, local roasters, there was really no competition in Starbucks' initial market. In other words, there were no national chains of coffee cafés. Southwest Airlines' initial core strategy (now somewhat changed) was to provide "no-frills, short-haul, high-frequency discount air travel in relatively noncompetitive markets." When Southwest began to expand its operations from its base in Texas (where it had perfected the short-haul, no-frills concept), most airlines were losing money. Southwest's strategy was not to go head-to-head with the majors but to stay in noncompetitive markets, offering potential customers low-cost air travel. The strategy has been successful; Southwest has remained profitable as it has grown to serve markets throughout the United States. Wal-Mart's core strategy is to be the price leader ("Always Low Prices").

The second level of strategy is called *supporting strategies,* which describe what a firm or business unit needs to do in each level of the Pyramid of Organizational Development to support its core strategy. The supporting strategies a firm will pursue at each level in the pyramid tend to be defined in one or two sentences. They are "big picture" strategies, not a list of to-dos.

Examples of supporting strategies for Southwest Airlines (based on its initial core strategy) are shown in Table 7.1.

Operational strategies identify how a firm will implement its core strategy. Operational strategies might be thought of as the to-dos. However, they should focus on the most critical to-dos versus everything that a firm needs to focus on to make its core strategy a reality. Examples of operational strategies for Wal-Mart are presented in Table 7.2.

What Are the Critical Factors That Will Make Us Successful or Unsuccessful in Achieving This Long-Term Mission? Once the firm has identified its strategy, it then needs to identify where it should focus to maximize results over the long term. This typically involves clearly identifying those factors that will support or detract from the firm's ability to execute its strategy. These factors might include aspects of the firm's internal operations or environmental factors that are presenting threats or opportunities. Again, the answers to this question are typically derived from the results of the environmental scan and organizational assessment.

Table 7.1. Sample Supporting Strategies for Southwest Airlines

Markets-Products and Services
- Enter only noncompetitive markets.
- Keep fares competitive with, or lower than, other airlines' prices.
- Offer high customer service but few amenities (for example, offer only drinks and snacks on board rather than full meals).
- Stick to short routes.

Resources
- Use only Boeing 737 jets (one type of plane means easy turns, fuel efficiency, mechanics' ease to service).
- Hire people who fit culturally.

Operational Systems
- Do own ticketing.
- Do not engage in "interline baggage" (transfer of baggage directly to other airlines).
- Ensure speedy aircraft "turns."
- Focus on cost-control operations.
- Use HR selection devices and rigorous interviewing that help identify attitudes rather than skills, producing new employees that fit well into the organization.
- Focus on customer service.

Management Systems
- Focus on recognition to motivate employees and to manage and guide employee behavior.
- Establish a profit-sharing program for all employees.
- Pursue a strategy of controlled growth consistent with Southwest's core strategy.

Culture
- Create a family-like, fun culture that governs day-to-day life, as well as how employees relate to customers.

What Goals Shall We Set to Improve Our Competitive Effectiveness and Organizational Capabilities in Each of These Critical Success Areas? The output of addressing this final strategic question is a list of goals that the firm will focus on to continue its success into the future. These goals will become part of the firm's strategic plan (which is discussed in the next section).

Step 4: The Strategic Business Plan

The fourth step in the strategic planning process involves preparing a strategic business plan. A strategic business plan (also known as a strategic organizational development plan) is a written statement of the future direction of an enterprise based on the environmental scan and the organizational assessment.

Table 7.2. Sample Operational Strategies for Wal-Mart

Wal-Mart

- Purchasing through central computer, based on in-store data input
- Stores open 9 A.M. to 9 P.M., seven days a week
- Thirty-six departments in each store
- Approximately 95 percent of merchandise branded
- "No questions asked" policy on returns
- Employees polled for their views on what merchandise to include and how to display it

Based on our work with organizations over more than a twenty-year period, we believe that an effective business plan must include eight basic components:

1. The situational analysis
2. The business definition
3. The strategic mission of the organization
4. The core strategy or strategies
5. Key result areas for planning
6. Objectives in each result area
7. Goals for each objective
8. Action plans to attain each goal

These eight components of the business plan are presented in Table 7.3 and described in the sections that follow.

Situational Analysis. The intent of the situational analysis is to provide background that will help the reader understand why the firm is pursuing the courses of action defined in the remainder of the strategic business plan. The situational analysis should include a brief overview of key findings from the environmental scan and organizational assessment, along with a summary of what these findings suggest about where the firm needs to focus to continue its success into the future. If needed, more detailed information can be presented in an appendix to the plan.

Business Definition or Concept. The output of addressing the first strategic issue will be a statement that answers the question, What business is the firm in? Ideally, the business definition (concept) statement should consist of no more than one or two sentences.

A good example of a concise business definition statement is that developed by a rapidly growing health care products manufacturer: "We are in the

Table 7.3. Elements of a Business Plan

1. Situational Analysis	Brief overview of the key threats and opportunities presented by the firm's current environment and the firm's internal strengths and limitations. Should also include a brief summary of the implications this information has for the firm.
2. Business Definition	Statement of what business the organization is in.
3. Strategic Mission	Broad statement of what the organization wants to achieve during the planning period. Should be dated (three to five years out) and measurable.
4. Strategy	How the organization is going to compete. Includes core strategy, supporting strategies, and operational strategies.
5. Key Result Areas	Performance areas that are critical to achieving the organization's mission.
6. Objectives	What the organization wants to achieve in the long run in each key result area.
7. Goals	Specific things that the organization seeks to attain by a specified time to support each objective.
8. Action Plans	Activities that must be performed to achieve a specific goal.

business of solving nurses' problems." To implement this concept, the company stayed in close contact with nurses to learn about their problems and develop products that were actually "solutions" to these problems. For example, the company developed a "light glove" to solve the problem of handling hot light bulbs in the operating room. Based on this business concept, the company grew from $6 million in revenues in 1984 to more than $75 million in 1996, when it was purchased.

Strategic Mission. A strategic mission statement is a broad statement of what an organization or subunit wants to achieve during a planning period and is the output of addressing the fourth strategic issue. The strategic mission provides an overall sense of direction for decisions and actions.

Our notion of a strategic mission is that it must specify something that the organization wants to *achieve,* and it should include a date (typically three to five years from the current time) by which the firm wants to achieve these results. For example, Starbucks might state: "We want to become recognized as the leading brand of specialty coffee in the world by 2010." Or they might state: "Our strategic mission is to grow to $10 billion in revenue and have

10,000 points of distribution by the year 2010." These are both strategic missions in the sense of the framework presented here.

The strategic mission must be measurable, at least in a broad sense. It is potentially feasible to measure whether Starbucks has become recognized as the leading brand of specialty coffee in the world by using brand-recognition surveys. It is also clearly feasible to determine whether Starbucks achieves $10 billion in revenue and has 10,000 points of distribution.

By including the date by which the mission will be achieved, as well as a measurable big-picture target to aim for, the firm is providing employees with a sense of direction, which is important from the standpoint of motivating people. The firm will be able to measure whether or not it attained its strategic mission and, hence, its success. Mission statements that are vague, by their very nature, are not as motivational.

The type of strategic mission statement developed for an organization will, at least to some extent, depend on its size and the scope of its operations. For example, a mission statement for Industrial Abrasives, Inc.—a regional industrial abrasives distributor—for a five-year planning period might be: "To develop into the leading full-service distributor of industrial abrasives in the Western United States by 2010." Similarly, a mission statement for a medium-sized residential real estate firm located in a single city might read: "To develop into a full-service residential real estate company, providing services throughout the northern part of the state." In the nonprofit arena, the mission statement for a child development agency might read: "To serve a minimum of 900 children and their families and be recognized in the communities we serve as an expert in early education."

The term *mission* is sometimes used in a different sense from the way we define it here. It is sometimes used to refer to the purpose or philosophical mission of the organization. An example of this more abstract type of mission statement is this one, developed by a large national certified public accounting (CPA) firm:

> Our mission is to develop a profitable, professional international accounting firm with a dynamic environment that will retain and motivate outstanding people who will provide high-quality services to business, government, and not-for-profit clients.

Although there is nothing wrong with this type of mission for philosophical or culture management purposes, it is not a strategic mission in the sense described here. Throughout the rest of this book, we use the terms *strategic mission* and *mission* interchangeably, but we mean them in the sense of an achievement-oriented, strategic mission rather than a cultural mission.

Mission statements can be developed not only for an organization as a whole but for specific subunits as well. For example, the mission statement for the human resource department of a $1 billion high-tech company is as follows:

By December 31, 2011, the HR team will:

- Fill 90% of open headcount annually by becoming a magnet attracting the best talent in our field.

- Reduce turnover to 3% to 5% or less.

- Be nationally recognized for our world-class HR practices.

- Provide our employees and managers with HR tools to improve efficiency.

- Partner with the company's leadership to sustain and enrich the company's culture.

Strategy. As defined earlier in this chapter, *strategy* refers to how the organization is going to compete, and there are three levels of strategy: core, supporting, and operational. Defining strategy in this way helps a firm focus on those aspects of its business that will provide it with the biggest payoff.

When a core strategy is unique, it can be sufficiently powerful not only to fuel a company's growth but also to force competitors to change the way they do business. For example, Michael Dell's core strategy in founding Dell Computer was to sell personal computers that were built to order directly to customers and avoid the markup of retailers. As his fast-growing firm has succeeded, it has forced huge competitors such as IBM, Hewlett-Packard, Apple Computer, and Compaq to change the way they do business.

Many organizations do not have a core strategy, or at least cannot clearly identify one. When this happens, an organization can become somewhat chaotic as it reacts to the challenges of its competition rather than proactively determines how it will defend or attack. These firms can also miss major opportunities and run the risk that a competitor will take their market from them (because they have not developed a clear understanding of how they should compete). A firm that lacks a clearly defined strategy for competing in its chosen market is analogous to a major college or professional football team entering a game without a scouting report on the rival team. In the absence of a great deal of luck, these teams are destined to lose the game. This is true in business, as well.

In one family-run $75 million consumer-products company, for example, senior management spent years trying to determine not only what business the company should be in but what its strategy should be. Even though this firm saw a major competitor rising within its market and major opportunities being created within its existing market, senior management developed no concrete strategy to "attack" the rival firm or defend its position. Over a period of five years, the competitor grew to national dominance of its market, while the other company continued to lose market share and to argue about whether they could or should take advantage of new market opportunities.

An organization's core strategy should be supported by strategies (we call them supporting strategies) at each level in the Pyramid of Organizational Development. Most strategies are built around markets and products, but powerful strategic advantages can be derived from other levels of the pyramid as well. For example, part of Dell Computer's strategic advantage comes from its core strategy of a consumer-direct business model, but additional advantages come from its related supporting strategies. Dell has extremely high inventory efficiency in comparison to its major competitors, such as Hewlett-Packard and IBM. Similarly, as discussed in Chapter One, Wal-Mart has competed with Kmart and other discount retailers, not just in products and market selection but at all levels of the pyramid, including operational systems, management systems, and culture.

Organizational culture can be an important component of strategy — even core strategy. For example, Starbucks believes that it is competing not just with its coffee but its customer service as well, and its customer service depends, to a great extent, on how the company treats its people.

Key Result Areas. Key result areas are the areas of an organization's operation in which performance has a critical impact on the achievement of the overall mission. Unsatisfactory performance in a key result will inhibit the organization from achieving its mission.

One of the critical differences in the approach to strategic planning presented in this book relates to the concept of key result areas. A second important difference is our recommendation that all firms use the six levels in the Pyramid of Organizational Development, plus financial results, as *their* seven primary key result areas. Based on our research, the research of others, and our experience as consultants, we believe that all organizations ought to build their strategic plan around seven key result areas: markets, products (including services as explained in Chapter One), resources, operational systems, management systems, culture, and financial results.

The rationale is that the six key aspects making up the Pyramid of Organizational Development are all critical phases of the "business game" and must, therefore, all be the focus of management attention. We believe that, whether they realize it or not, all organizations are competing at *all* levels of the pyramid. Competition is not only in products and technology; it is in management systems and culture as well. Our research and work with organizations suggest that if a firm successfully manages these seven areas, it will dramatically increase the probability of success over the long term.[2] If the company ignores any of these key result areas, it leaves itself vulnerable to the competition. We also recognize that there may be some specific key result areas appropriate to a given organization, and a few others can be added to the seven core areas.

Although divisions may adopt the seven key result areas listed, the key result areas for a particular department or other subunit of a firm will tend to be more specific in nature. They tend to define, using a few categories, what the department is responsible for. For example, the key result areas for the human resources department of the $1 billion high-tech company were the following:

1. Recruiting and Selection
2. Staff Development
3. Compensation and Benefits Administration
4. Human Resource Information Systems Management
5. Staff Retention
6. Employee Relations
7. Regulatory Compliance
8. Corporate Culture and Organizational Development Support
9. Staff Planning

Objectives and Goals. Objectives are broad statements of what an organization or subunit wants to achieve in the long run (during the planning period) in each key result area. Goals, by contrast, are specific and measurable—results that the organization wants to attain by a specified time in order to achieve its objectives. The responsibility for each goal should be assigned to a specific individual on the planning team. It is his or her responsibility to ensure that adequate progress is being made in achieving the goal. In developing a strategic plan, goals tend to be set within a twelve- to eighteen-month time horizon; objectives tell a firm what it wants to accomplish during its planning period (three to five years out). In a sense, objectives might be viewed as a strategic component of the plan, whereas goals are the tactics for helping the firm make progress in achieving its overall mission.

For example, an objective for a medium-sized manufacturer of electronic components might be "to increase our annual sales volume," while a specific goal might be "to increase sales volume from current level of $150 million in 2011 to $180 million in 2012." Similarly, an objective in the area of facilities and equipment might be "to increase our capability for inventory storage," while a specific goal might be "to handle 150 percent more inventory than existing facilities by 2014." In the area of profit, an objective might be "to earn a satisfactory return on investment." A specific goal might be "to earn a minimum of 18 percent ROI before taxes in each operating division by fiscal year-end."

Both objectives and goals are necessary. Objectives should not change very frequently during a planning period; goals are subject to frequent change. For example, the objective of a marketing department for a large, Fortune 500 manufacturer of electronic equipment is "to effectively support the launch and marketing of new products." A goal for 2015 is "to develop and implement a campaign to introduce electronic toys into the market for the winter season."

Action Plans. Action plans specify the particular activities or steps that must be performed to achieve a goal. Although action plans are not necessary for all goals, they are useful for achieving relatively complex projects or tasks. In brief, action plans detail what must be done, who must do it, and by when to achieve a particular goal. Action plans can be thought of as sets of to-do lists. The steps in these plans appear in chronological order, and no step in an action plan should extend beyond the date at which the goal is due.

In most cases, we recommend that companies avoid putting detailed action plans in their corporate strategic plans. Instead, we recommend that only major milestones from these plans (for example, a major step that should be completed by the end of the quarter) be included. The more detailed action plan should be developed and retained by the person whose name appears on the goal. If a problem arises with respect to achieving a particular goal, the more detailed action plan can be reviewed by the team and adjusted, as needed.

Step 5: Budgeting

Once the overall strategy of a business has been developed, the next step is budgeting. Budgeting involves translating the overall strategic business plan into financial terms. It should be noted that the development of a strategic business plan and budget is an iterative process—that is, it may be that a firm will need to adjust its strategic business plan if it finds that there are inadequate financial resources to support it. Similarly, if the firm finds that it has more financial resources than anticipated, it may need to adjust the plan.

Once developed, the budget then constitutes a performance standard against which actual performance can be assessed. As used here, budgeting includes capital expenditure as well as operating budgets.

Step 6: Management Review

The final, but very important, step in the strategic planning process is management review—the process by which management evaluates organizational performance against the plan and makes adjustments as required. This step is also part of the control and performance management system discussed in Chapter Ten.

To effectively implement this step in the process, we recommend that managers hold quarterly plan implementation and review meetings. The purpose of these meetings is twofold: (1) to review and discuss progress against the plan and (2) to discuss and resolve specific strategic issues as they arise. At these meetings, managers should present results of operations and discuss performance against the plan. Where actual results differ from plans, managers should explain the reasons for the differences and develop strategies to address current or anticipated problems in achieving goals.

In addition to plan review, agendas for these meetings should also include one or two specific strategic issues that the management team needs to resolve in order to make progress in achieving its mission, minimize long-term organizational problems, or reduce environmental threats. These issues should be identified and, to the extent possible, researched in advance of the meeting. Meeting discussion time should focus on resolving the issues. The resolution of each issue will become new objectives or goals that will be included in the firm's strategic plan.

The use of quarterly meetings helps to reinforce the idea that strategic planning is a way of life in a company and makes it part of the organization's culture. It also helps hold individual managers accountable for results that will support the achievement of the firm's strategic mission.

ROYCE MEDICAL CORPORATION: DEVELOPMENT OF A STRATEGIC PLAN

To illustrate the process and output of a strategic organizational development planning process, let us examine the planning process adopted by Royce Medical Corporation, which was, at the time, a Stage III medical products manufacturing company. This case demonstrates the dual use of strategic planning as a management tool per se and as a vehicle for making the transition to professional management.

Company Background

The company that was to become Royce Medical Corporation was founded by a podiatrist, Dr. Daniel Haines, in the late 1960s. Dr. Haines saw an opportunity to import and sell "post-op shoes" and "cast shoes" through distributors. He developed a very small mail-order business, while at the same time continuing his medical practice.

Dr. Haines's eldest son, Jeff, entered the business in 1981 as his father's partner. At that time, the company had approximately $250,000 to $300,000 in annual sales. Even though Jeff Haines was relatively young (twenty-three at the time), he had had a great deal of experience in telemarketing and believed that he could use these skills to help grow the business. Jeff established a telemarketing entity called Royce Medical and began selling the inventory that his father had accumulated.

Jeff's telemarketing efforts began to pay off, as the firm experienced rapid increases in sales. By 1986, the firm had annual sales of over $5 million and was profitable. In 1986, Jeff began to realize that even though his firm had been successful, it could not continue to grow simply be selling other people's products. Although Royce Medical's salespeople were a tremendous asset, the company's products were not unique. The firm was still selling products that it imported from overseas, while its competitors had patented products that gave them an advantage. Jeff decided that developing a unique line of products would be the next area for the firm to focus on.

The first product that the firm produced, as a joint venture with another company, was pink and blue casting tape—a product that customers were asking for but that was not being produced by any other company at the time. Shortly after this product was introduced, however, 3M entered the market with thirteen different colors of tape. Jeff began to realize that to continue growing the firm, it needed to become an innovator.

At about this time, the firm that Royce had partnered with on its first product was sold, and one of its engineers, Tracy Grim, decided to consult for Royce. Tracy is the type of person who is continually looking for and developing concepts for new products. He also understands the medical community. Jeff showed Tracy a product offered by a competitor and asked if Royce could make a better product. Tracy designed a product, and the R&D function at Royce was off and running. Royce Medical's first internally developed product was a Gel Cast Ankle Support, released in the summer of 1987. It was a success, and the development of unique, innovative products at the lowest possible cost has continued to be a focus for the firm ever since.

In 1989, Royce Medical experienced its first year of flat sales and barely broke even. Jeff realized that he needed to change the way the company was managed. People at Royce Medical had become accustomed to Jeff making all of the firm's major decisions. This was comfortable for Jeff, who described the dominant style of management at the firm at this time as a "traditional, old-version dictatorship." When the company began to experience problems, Jeff decided that he needed to focus on the firm's management and culture, as well as other aspects of its internal operations. The company had become so large—now employing about eighty people—that it was impossible to manage it effectively without better-developed systems and a well-managed structure. So in the early 1990s, Jeff began to professionalize his business. It was also about this time (in the early 1990s) that Jeff became the sole owner of the firm.

One of the first things Jeff did was to change his style. He said of this time, "I decided I was a bad manager and that some things needed to change." He implemented a variety of control systems, including a budgeting process in which managers were held accountable for financial goals. He also helped his management team focus on more clearly articulating and beginning to manage the business in accordance with a set of stated values. People were held accountable for adhering to these values, and everyone in the company knew what they were. Another component of the system that Jeff created included more regular meetings of the management team. Although these meetings helped the organization become more focused, they still weren't enough. There wasn't anything structured on paper with respect to where the firm was headed. Planning was still very much ad hoc.

In the summer of 1995, even though his company was very much a success, Jeff decided that it was time to develop and implement a more sophisticated approach to planning. Annual revenues at the time were approximately $17 million. The steps that Jeff and his management team took to implement this process and the results he achieved are described next.

Developing the Strategic Plan: The Environmental Scan and Organizational Assessment

In 1995, Jeff Haines and many members of his management team had a very good understanding of the market in which their firm was competing. Although they had not completed an extensive, formal market research study, they knew their competitors well and understood their strengths and limitations. They also knew and understood their customers and their customers' needs. They had not yet, however, developed a formal system for "scanning the environment" to identify trends in the health care industry and develop strategies for minimizing potential threats and taking advantage of opportunities. Like many entrepreneurial firms, then, they based their initial plan on the information that they had collected (through informal mechanisms) by staying in close contact with customers (podiatrists, orthopedic surgeons, and hospitals, for example) and by attending various trade shows.

In August 1995, Jeff decided that he wanted an independent assessment of his firm's effectiveness. He engaged a consulting firm to complete an assessment of his firm's internal operations. To collect information on the firm's internal capabilities, the consulting team conducted a series of interviews with managers and associates at Royce Medical and administered the Survey of Organizational Growing Pains (described in Chapter Three) and another organizational effectiveness survey to all those interviewed.

Using the Pyramid of Organizational Development as a lens for assessing organizational effectiveness, results suggested the following:

Markets and products-services. The company understood its market and had developed unique, patented products to meet customer needs. In addition, Royce Medical had a reputation for providing exceptional customer service. It was, in fact, suggested that Royce Medical's R&D team's ability to develop unique, patented products, using customer suggestions and input, was becoming a competitive advantage. A number of new market opportunities were presenting themselves, but the company had yet to develop a comprehensive marketing strategy that detailed which of these opportunities (if any) it would pursue.

Resources and operational systems. For the most part, Royce Medical had the resources needed to support its current and future growth. It had attracted people who were extremely committed to the company and its success and who were, for the most part, well qualified for the positions they held. The firm had the financial resources needed to take it into the future.

One of Royce Medical's greatest strengths was telemarketing. This function had contributed greatly to the company's initial success and remained an area in which the firm had developed a competitive advantage. The firm had also developed a fairly sophisticated approach to product development, which emphasized the need to develop high-quality products at a reasonable price that would meet customer needs.

One of the most problematic areas for the company in 1995 was its computer and information systems. A number of critical functions (for example, tracking of individual accounts) were still being done manually. In addition, computer resources (for example, PCs) were fairly limited, leading to inefficiencies, as people performed tasks manually that could have been performed using a computer.

There was some concern that certain R&D resources were being spread thin, as they worked not only to develop new products but were also involved in ensuring that the production of new products met specifications and quality standards. There was also some concern that the process for new product development and introduction needed to become more formalized.

Many people felt that the firm could improve its overall production planning system, especially with respect to sales forecasting and interdepartmental communication, as it related to inventory management. At the same time, however, the manufacturing unit was working on implementing systems that would provide continual feedback to associates on performance against key goals (for example, scrap, built-to-spec, quality). This was viewed as strength.

Another area that was underdeveloped was the firm's marketing system. At the time the assessment was completed, there was no formal marketing function and no formal marketing plan. The company was advertising its products and had developed and used promotions, but there was no overall strategy guiding these efforts.

Management systems and corporate culture. Although Jeff recognized the need for a more formal and systematic approach to strategic planning, Royce Medical (as a whole) was already a very goal-oriented company. Performance-based goals were set by each associate, working with her or his manager. The performance management system recognized people based on their performance against these goals.

However, the structure of the company had not been formally defined. Although role descriptions existed in some departments, others learned about their jobs through discussions with their managers. In addition, many senior managers had had little managerial experience. Although there was no formal system to ensure that those in management positions had the skills needed to take the company to its next stage of growth, the firm did have some informal training taking place. Jeff made it a practice of working both one-on-one and in small groups with members of his management team to develop their skills.

As stated previously, the company had developed a written statement of its values—a statement that emphasized empowerment, excellent customer service, and continuous learning and improvement. Most associates and managers embraced these values, and the company had developed many ways to reinforce them on a daily basis. Further, people were held accountable for behaving in ways consistent with these values.

The overall findings of the organizational assessment suggested that Royce Medical had done a good job building the infrastructure needed to support a $17 million firm but that it needed to develop additional systems, structures, and processes to support the much larger organization it was going to become.

After completing the organizational assessment, Royce Medical's management team decided to use a strategic planning survey to collect additional information on the firm's environment, internal capabilities, and thoughts about the firm's future direction. Each member of the Royce Medical management team was asked to complete this survey. The information collected in this survey was analyzed and summarized into a report that, along with the results of the organizational assessment, was used as input into the development of Royce Medical's first comprehensive strategic plan.

Developing the Strategic Plan: The Retreat

Royce Medical's formal strategic planning process began with a two-day retreat, held in October, 1995, that was facilitated by one of the authors. Jeff and all his key functional managers, including the managers of his sales units (telemarketing, direct sales, retail), information systems, finance, human resources, R&D, manufacturing, and customer service, attended. Prior to the retreat, each manager was sent a summary of the information collected through the survey and the organizational assessment, along with an agenda for the retreat. They were asked to review the information contained in these documents and think about their own vision for what they felt the firm should become.

During this retreat, the firm's management team was first trained in the methodology of strategic planning (presented in this chapter). Next, the team focused on addressing key strategic issues facing the firm, including deciding what business the firm was in. Finally, the management team began the development of the firm's written strategic plan. The team agreed that their plan should focus on the next three years of the firm's development. It was felt that the environment was changing so rapidly that planning out three years (rather than five) seemed most reasonable.

Developing the Strategic Plan: Addressing Key Strategic Issues

The outcome of the team's discussion of strategic issues is briefly described below.

What Business Are We In? Royce Medical's planning team spent a significant amount of time discussing and attempting to reach agreement on the nature of the firm's business. Several different alternatives were initially identified in the planning survey. These were discussed during the retreat and are presented next.

We are a customer-oriented developer and supplier of innovative products that treat or prevent injury. This concept reflected the emphasis that Royce placed on being customer-oriented, as well as its focus on innovation. This definition of the firm's business was fairly broad, suggesting that the company might provide any product that would treat or prevent injury. At some level, the team felt that this was *too* broad.

We sell high-quality orthopedic products at low-to-competitive prices. This concept narrowed the firm's focus to orthopedic products. It also provided a focus on costs. However, this definition did not mention the strengths that the firm had built in terms of being innovative and emphasizing service.

We design innovative orthopedic products in the orthopedic disposable products market, focusing on high-volume sales of a few core products rather than being a total source of all orthopedic soft-goods needs. This definition of Royce Medical's business was intended to help put boundaries around the type of orthopedic products that the firm would offer. However, it did not include any reference to price, customer service, or innovation—three concepts that the management team felt were extremely important with respect to defining the business the firm was and should be in.

After much discussion, the management team finally developed the following definition of the company's business, which would serve as the driving force for the rest of its planning efforts:

> Royce Medical Company develops and distributes competitively priced, highly functional customer-driven products, tailored to fit specific portions of the anatomy which are used to treat or prevent medical/orthopedic conditions. We combine exceptional (way beyond the call of duty) customer service with our unsurpassed, innovative product line. To maintain and improve our position, the company creates an extremely productive environment, with a constant focus on the company's "values," which support individuals in achieving great results.

It should be noted that although the team developed a statement of the firm's business in October, it wasn't until April of 1996 that they finally reached closure on addressing this important issue. Royce Medical's team recognized that it was important to address the question, What business are we in? and took the time to do so.

What Are Our Competitive Strengths and Limitations? Managers were asked to identify the strengths and limitations of each of their major competitors as a part of the strategic planning survey. This information was used as input in developing the firm's strategic mission statement, objectives, and goals.

Do We Have or Can We Develop a True Market Niche? During the retreat, managers devoted some time to discussing whether Royce Medical had or could develop a market niche. Managers felt that the company had developed a niche based on the following factors:

- A corporate culture that supported achieving excellence in customer service, innovation, and empowerment

- Significant expertise in telemarketing (which either competitors did not engage in or did poorly)

- The ability to patent innovative customer-driven products

As the management team developed Royce Medical's plan, they wanted to ensure that these competitive advantages were retained.

What Do We Want to Become in the Long Term? To address this question, the firm's management team drew on information provided from the strategic planning surveys, their knowledge of the environment in which the firm was competing, and their knowledge of the firm's internal capabilities. Survey respondents differed in their opinions as to what the firm might be or become by FY 1999. Some thought revenues might grow to $35 million, while others had a more conservative estimate of $22 million. Some felt that the firm would enter a number of new markets, while others believed that expansion would come through providing new products to existing customers or through growing the number of customers served in existing markets. All participants agreed that the company would continue to grow, that it would continue to develop and offer innovative products, and that its culture would continue to be a source of competitive advantage. (We present a statement of the firm's mission later.)

What Is Our Strategy for Competing Effectively in Our Chosen Markets and for Reaching Our Long-Term Goals? Royce Medical's management team did not directly address this question during its initial planning retreat. Instead, the team worked to develop objectives that would focus the firm on what it needed to do in each of its key result areas to maintain its competitive strengths, grow its business, and minimize limitations.

The method for developing the firm's strategy initially adopted by Royce Medical tends to be appropriate for an early-Stage III firm: instead of explicitly stating the strategy in the written plan, it is implied by the firm's objectives. However, at the firm's first formal quarterly review and implementation meeting (held in April, 1996), it was decided that this strategy should become more explicit. At this meeting, Royce Medical developed the following Strategic Statement:

> Royce Medical Company will continue to be an extremely customer- and values-driven company and a leading developer and provider of innovative, competitively priced products, tailored to fit specific portions of the anatomy, which contribute to either the treatment or prevention of medical conditions.
>
> We will continually improve our position by using the most efficient manufacturing strategies combined with the utilization of leading technologies to achieve a competitive advantage. Our products will be protected by patents whenever possible.
>
> We will continually improve our productivity by using technologically advanced information systems and by continually developing the skills of our people.
>
> We will adapt to our environment by remaining constantly open to capitalizing on the opportunities created through our business and development efforts to enter new or existing markets by way of licensing agreements, joint ventures, or direct distribution.

This statement provides information on the firm's core strategy: "to be a customer-driven developer of innovative, competitively priced orthopedic products." It also provides information on supporting strategies; that is, what the firm will do at each level in the Pyramid of Organizational Development to support the core strategy (for example, focus on manufacturing, protect products with patents, develop skills of people, and increase efficiency of systems). Although this strategy statement is not necessarily in the format described earlier in this chapter, it does provide information on how the firm will compete.

What Are the Critical Factors That Will Make Us Successful or Unsuccessful in Achieving This Long-Term Mission? In organizing its strategic plan, Royce Medical decided to use the six levels in the Pyramid of Organizational Development, plus financial results, as its seven key result areas. In addition, during the second year of its planning process, the firm decided to identify what it called its Key Strategic Priorities, in order to ensure that it was making progress on its most important strategic objectives or initiatives. The list of strategic priorities was composed of five to nine key initiatives, taken directly from the firm's strategic plan.

What Goals Shall We Set to Improve Our Competitive Effectiveness and Organizational Capabilities in Each of These Critical Success Areas? A sample of the goals that Royce Medical's management team set in each of its key result areas is presented in the next section.

Developing the Strategic Plan: The Written Strategic Business Plan

The resolution of the key strategic issues formed the foundation of Royce Medical's strategic plan. Based on these discussions (which took place during the two-day retreat), the management team developed a draft of the company's business definition statement, mission statement, and some objectives. Following the two-day retreat, small groups of managers worked together to develop additional objectives and specific, time-dated, measurable goals to support these objectives and to help the firm make progress in achieving its mission. The results of these small group discussions were submitted and consolidated into a written plan, which was reviewed and finalized by the management team in January of 1996.

At Royce Medical, a decision was made from the very beginning that the development of detailed action plans would be "delegated" to the individual responsible for a given goal. The company strategic plan would contain very few, if any, specific action steps. Royce Medical's management team felt that the most important part of their process was to stay focused on the results, as specified by the goals. Action plans were available for review when (and if) a manager was experiencing problems in achieving a specified goal.

Excerpts of Royce Medical's first strategic plan are presented in Table 7.4. Please note: The information presented in this table does not contain the Situational Analysis but focuses instead on the other key elements of the business plan, beginning with the Business Definition Statement. It also does not include the strategy statement, which was presented earlier in this chapter.

Developing the Strategic Plan: The Budgeting Process

From the very beginning, Royce Medical's management team was conscious of the budget expectations under which they were to operate. Royce Medical's CFO, Kent Webster, had worked with management to develop a fairly sophisticated budgeting process and was able to provide managers with monthly updates on how they were tracking against revenue and expense targets. The budget process, then, was designed to support the firm's strategic planning process.

Table 7.4. Excerpts from Royce Medical's 1996–1999 Strategic Plan

Business Definition Statement

Royce Medical Company develops and distributes competitively priced, highly functional customer-driven products, tailored to fit specific portions of the anatomy which are used to treat or prevent medical/orthopedic conditions. We combine exceptional (way beyond the call of duty) customer service with our unsurpassed, innovative product line. To maintain and improve our position, the company creates an extremely productive environment, with a constant focus on the company's "values," which support individuals in achieving great results.

Strategic Mission Statement[3]

By June 30, 1999, we will be recognized as an industry leader, achieving minimum revenues of $27 to $33 million, while maintaining our expense and margin targets.

Each year we will grow a minimum of 15% in revenues.

The above targets will be achieved without compromising our values.

Sample Objectives and Goals Organized by Key Result Area

Key Result Area 1.0: Markets
Objective 1.1: Explore and take advantage of opportunities in the managed care market.
Objective 1.2: Continue developing current markets so that they provide us with acceptable returns.
  Goal 1.2.1: Achieve $17 million in sales by 6/30/96 (Sales Managers).
  Goal 1.2.5: Maintain sales division expense budgets as a percentage of sales by 6/30/96 (Sales Managers).

Key Result Area 2.0: Products/Services
Objective 2.2: Manufacture quality products (i.e., built to specifications) at the lowest possible prices.
  Goal 2.2.1: Achieve quality levels (built to spec) of 95% or better on product X by 5/25/96 (Manufacturing Manager).
Objective 2.3: Patent products and processes.

Key Result Area 3.0: Resources
Objective 3.1: Increase the skills, effectiveness, and quantity of our salesforces to meet the revenue objectives set forth in our mission statement, within budget.
  Goal 3.1.1: Implement the best methods to successfully train new and existing sales reps to achieve desired revenue objectives by 7/1/96. (Sales Managers).

(continued)

Table 7.4. *(continued)*

Objective 3.3: Ensure that we have the optimum space and environment to achieve our mission, within budget.

Goal 3.3.1: Develop a short-term space plan by 6/30/96 (CEO and CFO).

Key Result Area 4.0: Operational Systems

Objective 4.1: Increase the efficiency of our inventory management systems.

Objective 4.2: Develop better, more accurate forecasting systems and improve our ability to react to actual sales trends.

Goal 4.2.1: Achieve a 95% unit accuracy rate on existing product forecasts by 9/30/96 (Purchasing Manager).

Objective 4.5: Continually improve our manufacturing efficiency, quality, and cost.

Goal 4.5.1: Achieve a minimum of 94% line efficiency by 12/31/96 (Manufacturing Manager).

Goal 4.5.4: Reduce machine downtime from 125 hours to 85 hours per year by 12/19/96 (Manufacturing Manager).

Key Result Area 5.0: Management Systems

Objective 5.1: Develop and manage an organizational structure that will help us meet our mission.

Objective 5.3: Improve the skills of our management team.

Goal 5.3.1: Formalize the company's definition of what training skills for managers are by 4/15/96 (CEO).

Goal 5.3.2: Have 50% of the managers attend time management classes by 6/30/96 (HR Manager).

Key Result Area 6.0: Corporate Culture

Objective 6.1: Develop systems to stay focused on values.

Goal 6.1.1: Receive input on a regular basis from associates on current values system (CEO).

Goal 6.1.4: Conduct at least 20 interviews with non-managers to determine if the company is living up to values by 11/30/96 (CEO).

Objective 6.7: Continually review and develop communication alternatives to make sure associates have appropriate ways of communicating their point of view concerning our values.

Goal 6.7.1: Survey managers and associates every 6 months as to whether the current communication options are effective (HR Manager).

Key Result Area 7.0: Financial Results

Objective 7.1: Achieve revenue goals.

Objective 7.2: Achieve budgeted margin goals.

Implementing the Strategic Plan: Quarterly Management Review and Implementation Meetings

As stated previously, the team spent additional time in its first strategic planning review and implementation meeting (held in April, 1996) reviewing the plan and making additional changes. From the very beginning, then, Royce Medical's management team treated its strategic plan as a living document.

By the time the firm held its second quarterly review and implementation meeting in July, 1996, the team was ready to begin devoting more time to the discussion of key strategic issues and less time to plan review. At the July meeting, in fact, the team decided that the written plan would be updated prior to each meeting so that more meeting time could be devoted to strategic issue discussion versus plan review. The process the team decided to use was as follows:

1. Each manager would submit his or her changes, additions, or status updates in writing approximately four weeks in advance of the scheduled quarterly review and implementation meeting to a designated manager who was responsible for helping to manage the plan.

2. These changes and updates would be incorporated into the written strategic plan. The status updates appeared next to each goal and were intended to let all managers know about the progress being made in achieving that goal. For example, if the goal was to achieve "97% customer satisfaction by FYE," the status column next to this goal would provide information on how the company was doing year-to-date.

3. Once the written plan had been updated, a copy was given to each member of the planning team at least two weeks prior to the scheduled quarterly review and implementation meeting, along with the agenda for that meeting. Managers were responsible for reviewing the plan and noting any questions, comments, or concerns that they had regarding the changes made or the status of goals.

4. Managers were also asked to think about and submit their ideas for strategic issues that might be discussed by the team. These were to be submitted to Jeff at least four weeks prior to the scheduled meeting.

Using this process, an even greater percentage of meeting time could be devoted to the discussion of strategic issues. In fact, by 1998, very little time was being devoted in these quarterly review and implementation meetings to discussing the plan. The majority of the team's time was being devoted to discussing and working to resolve key strategic issues.

Taking the Planning Process to the Next Levels: Departmental and Individual Planning

While most firms do not embark on departmental planning until the second or third year after beginning their corporate strategic planning process, Royce Medical's managers felt that it was important and consistent with their culture that they take the planning process to the department level as soon as possible. Therefore, the firm began developing departmental plans in July of 1996. Each department was asked to develop a Business Definition-Purpose Statement, a Mission Statement, a list of Key Result Areas, and Objectives and Goals that would support the achievement of the corporate plan. Once developed, these plans were presented and discussed during one of the firm's quarterly review and implementation meetings in order to ensure that all departmental plans supported one another.

Once departmental plans were developed, managers next decided that it would be important to have personal strategic plans that defined what each individual on the team was expected to do to help achieve the department's—and, in turn, the company's—mission. The foundation of these plans was formed by the key-result-area-based job descriptions, which will be discussed in the next chapter. In brief, Royce Medical made planning a way of life at all levels of the firm.

Results of the Planning Effort at Royce Medical

Over the next eight years, Royce Medical's management team continued utilizing and refining its planning process at all levels of the firm to best meet its ever-changing needs. The management team held annual corporate planning retreats to plan for the firm's long-term development, updated their plan on a quarterly basis, and met every three months to discuss progress in achieving the plan and to resolve key strategic issues.

Although the process was time consuming for Royce Medical's management, Jeff and the rest of the management team felt that it paid off. With respect to the planning process, Jeff has said that " . . . it helped get control of everything that was occurring in the firm and allowed us to manage the firm more effectively. We were fine where we were [in 1995], but we weren't going to be able to maintain control because we were growing too fast. We couldn't keep up. The plan and planning process helped us focus [not just on markets and products], but on developing more effective systems." By FYE 1999, revenues had grown to over $28 million. Royce had, indeed, achieved its mission (in terms of revenues) while, at the same time, maintaining its profitability.

As Royce entered its fifth year of having a formal strategic planning process, Jeff offered managers considering this process the following advice: "While this process can be extremely valuable, it requires a commitment and patience to make it work. Initially, there may be resistance to the process, but this needs to be managed. This is an extremely valuable process [from the standpoint of managing your business], which will evolve over time. However, if you never get started with the process, you will never receive the benefits."

Postscript

On July 28, 2005, Ossur, a leading global supplier of prosthetic and orthotic devices, announced that it had acquired Royce Medical for $216 million. In the press release, Royce Medical was described as "a well established manufacturer and distributor of orthotic products (which) has shown high growth and solid profitability in recent years."[4] Clearly, the time that Jeff and his management team had devoted to developing, implementing, and monitoring the company's strategic plan had paid off!

ONGOING FUNCTIONS OF STRATEGIC PLANNING

We have described planning as an independent system. However, some of the outputs of planning are also key components of a firm's control-performance management system, as we discuss in Chapter Ten. The plan specifies what the organization seeks to accomplish. Stating the organization's mission or general direction provides a focus for its efforts. This in itself is a form of organizational control. The more specific statement of key result areas, objectives, and goals increases the degree and effectiveness of the control. A written plan, such as the one illustrated for Royce Medical, facilitates the planning aspect of the control process by providing criteria against which performance can be measured and evaluated.

STRATEGIC PLANNING AT DIFFERENT STAGES OF ORGANIZATIONAL GROWTH

Previous sections of this chapter presented the basic concepts and methods of strategic planning for entrepreneurial organizations. They also illustrated the strategic planning process in the context of an example company. This section discusses how strategic planning should differ at each of the first four stages of organizational growth.

Stage I

During Stage I, strategic planning is probably a very informal, even intuitive process done mostly or entirely by the entrepreneur. Our research has suggested that very few entrepreneurs do formal strategic planning in the sense described in this chapter.

As we saw in Chapter Four, new entrepreneurial ventures arise mostly from personal—sometimes almost accidental—insights. For example, the idea for Domino's Pizza grew out of a university student's need for income.

Many times the entrepreneur is consciously or unconsciously following an informal strategic planning process at this stage. The entrepreneur often knows a particular business or industry, such as advertising, printing, publishing, ship repair, garment manufacturing, electronics, landscaping, insurance, or financial planning. Steeped in this knowledge, he or she perceives some market opportunity that is either not currently being served or not being served very well. For example, Thomas S. Monaghan, who founded Domino's Pizza, perceived that there might be a market for high-quality, delivered pizza. Similarly, another entrepreneur, Fritzi Benesch (cofounder of Fritzi of California) perceived that there was a market for budget-priced blouses among teenagers and as a result created a business with more than $80 million in annual revenues. Her concept was that the blouse ought to be priced at what a teenager could earn during one evening of baby-sitting. Still another entrepreneur (a university professor of accounting who had been successful with his own real estate investments) perceived the market for a financial planning and counseling firm aimed at relatively affluent investors.

Stage II

During Stage II, the informal strategic planning process of an entrepreneurial company may begin to change in certain ways. The rapid growth of the organization places considerable demands on the entrepreneur's time and energy, and his or her focus is increasingly on day-to-day operations. This leaves less time and, most important, less emotional energy to do the strategic planning required for the future development of the company. Entrepreneurs in charge of Stage II companies often work sixteen hours or more per day simply handling short-term problems and trying to keep up with the momentum of business. The entrepreneur may thus become a "one-minute decision maker," not by choice but by necessity. Unfortunately, the failure to do strategic planning is itself a kind of strategic plan, for the company that does not plan its future has implicitly chosen to allow the future to happen to the organization. As the great coach of UCLA's national champion basketball teams, John Wooden, used to say: "The failure to prepare is to prepare for failure." Similarly, to paraphrase Wooden, we believe that the failure to plan is to plan for failure.

At Stage II a company does not need a very formal planning system, but it does need some strategic planning. Because the entrepreneur is likely to be more absorbed in other activities than was the case at Stage I, it becomes necessary to substitute a system for what was initially a personal activity.

In essence, a formal strategic planning process is analogous to a "zone defense" in sports. If, for example, a college basketball team has a seven-foot center, the team is likely to have a comparative advantage in rebounding. If the team's center is only six-foot-six, the team is likely to be at a disadvantage in rebounding, but it may be able to compensate for this by using a zone defense. The zone defense is essentially a system in which people are positioned to perform certain tasks; in this example, they will be placed where they are most likely to give the defensive team a comparative advantage at rebounding. In effect, a seven-foot center is a one-person zone defense.

Similarly, if an organization has an entrepreneur who is brilliant at explicit or intuitive strategic planning, it may not need a formal strategic planning process. However, this presumes that the entrepreneur has the time and energy to perform strategic planning. When this ceases to be the case, the company must use a formal strategic planning process as a kind of zone defense to ensure that some strategic planning is accomplished.

During Stage II, a company's strategic planning process can be reasonably simple. In a company with between $1 and $10 million in annual revenues, the process may consist merely of a one- or two-day meeting devoted to developing the corporate strategic plan, followed by departmental meetings to develop plans for each functional area in support of the overall corporate plan. Every company, even a relatively small one, ought to be able to devote one week a year to strategic planning at Stage II. If this modest amount of time and effort is not spent, there is an increasing chance that external events that may profoundly affect the company will go either unnoticed or without response.

Stage III

By the time an organization reaches Stage III, it needs to establish a formal process of strategic planning. This is the professionalizing stage of organizational development, and strategic planning is one of the key management systems of a professional firm.

From approximately $10 million to $25 million in annual revenues, the major focus can be on the overall corporate strategic planning process, with departmental or functional plans done more informally. By the time an organization has reached $25 million in annual revenues, however, it needs a more extensive strategic planning process. The corporate plan should be accompanied by formal departmental plans, and the overall amount of planning time and effort should increase.

By the time a company reaches the size of $50 to $100 million in annual revenues, the strategic planning process ought to be well in place. It should be beginning to be a "way of life" in the company. Generally speaking, a minimum of two to three years are needed to institutionalize a strategic planning process in firms of this size. The first year simply involves the process of learning the planning system's mechanics. During the second and third years, people should increase their planning skills.

How much time should management invest in strategic planning? A reasonable guideline is that management should invest the equivalent of at least one week per year on planning and perhaps up to 10 percent of its time. If less than one week per year is devoted to planning, management is planning to fail.

Stage IV

By the time a company has reached Stage IV, the planning process ought to be well institutionalized. Strategic planning ought to be a topic in the company's management development programs.

During Stage IV there can be a wide variety of refinements to the strategic planning process. At this point, for example, the company has the resources to do more extensive market research analysis and environmental scanning studies.

CONSULTANTS AND STRATEGIC PLANNING DEPARTMENTS

A final issue involved in strategic planning concerns the role of external consultants and internal corporate planning departments in the planning process. We believe that the strategic plan ought to be based on line management's decisions rather than those of consultants or a planning department. Unless the plan is "owned" by line managers, it will tend to get ignored. Consultants or planning departments can, however, play a significant role as facilitators of the planning process. They can help to plan the overall process and serve as catalysts to its completion.

An internal planning department can serve as the source of market research and other competitive information. It can also aid in the logistical aspects of the planning process. External consultants can perform these facilitative roles, too. Moreover, because of their experience with other organizations, they can provide an independent, relatively objective perspective and raise questions that can be very useful for a company. For example, this simple inquiry can be a catalyst for a fresh look at some practice: "Other companies seem to be doing it this way. What is the rationale for your company doing it that way?"

Our experience as educators and consultants has indicated that strategic planning can be effective, that it can be learned, and that it is not necessary for a single leader to have a vision from the mist. A management team can develop a strategy and a strategic plan. In this regard, consultants can play another role. One CEO of a rapidly growing entrepreneurial company with more than $350 million in revenues engaged us to facilitate a strategic planning process, and after a few months expressed pleasure with the results of the process. He stated: "I had the vision for what we wanted to become five years ago, but I was unable to convince people that I was correct. The process you have used, even though you did not know what my vision was, has led to the place where I wanted to go all along. The value to me is that now others have 'bought in' to the vision, because they created it, and that is invaluable!"

A FINAL NOTE

The approach to strategic planning described in this chapter has been applied at a wide range of companies over the past twenty-plus years. These companies include Starbucks Coffee Company, PacifiCare Health Systems, Pardee Homes, Infogix, PowerBar, Royce Medical, and Countrywide Financial Corporation. It was also used by advisory boards in Los Angeles and Santa Clara counties to develop each county's "Master Plan" for implementing California's Universal Preschool Initiative.[5]

The approach has been applied at Countrywide since 1999. The foreword by Angelo Mozilo, founder and CEO of Countrywide, speaks to the benefits perceived from this application. In addition, in 2004, Countrywide's Strategic Planning Department was honored by the Association for Strategic Planning with the 2004 Richard Goodman Strategic Planning Award for large for-profit enterprises. The award honors organizations at the leading edge of strategic planning practice. This provides independent verification of the value of the system developed at Countrywide.

SUMMARY

This chapter examines the nature of strategic planning for entrepreneurial organizations. It describes strategic planning as a tool for organizational management and (as in the case of Royce Medical) as a vehicle for making the transition to professional management.[6] The chapter presents a framework of the strategic planning process, describes the components of a business plan, and presents a step-by-step approach for developing a written business plan. The chapter also illustrates the steps in developing a strategic business plan by showing how one company implemented them. Finally, the chapter discusses how strategic planning should differ at each of the first four stages of organizational growth. This framework ought to be useful to entrepreneurial companies in designing or revising their own strategic planning processes.

CHAPTER EIGHT

Organizational Structure

This chapter deals with one of the critical management systems of a firm: its organizational structure. An enterprise's organizational structure relates to the way people are organized to perform productive work and help achieve the firm's strategic business plan. The way people are organized, then, can have a critical impact on the overall success or failure of the firm. However, in many firms the way people are organized comes not as a result of planning but as the cumulative result of a series of ad hoc decisions. In addition, based on our research and consulting experience with many organizations, we have found that organizations require different structures to be effective at different stages of growth. Although a firm may have been adequately organized at a former stage of development, the company's success will facilitate its growth, which, in turn, will make it likely that a new structure will be required.

This chapter provides a framework to help managers understand how to design and use organizational structure as a managerial tool. It is also intended to assist managers in understanding what must be done to change an enterprise's structure as it grows and is faced with the need to make a transition from one stage of development to the next. First, we define the nature and purpose of organizational structure. Second, we examine the different types of organizational structures that exist in companies. Third, we present some guidelines for the design and evaluation of organizational structure. Next, we examine a few case studies of structural problems faced by companies at different stages of growth. Finally, we examine the nature of organizational structure changes that are required at different stages of growth.

NATURE OF ORGANIZATIONAL STRUCTURE

An organization does not merely consist of people; it consists of the set of jobs or roles that have been patterned into certain specified relationships to achieve a purpose. An organization, then, can be viewed as a patterned arrangement of specified roles to be performed by people. It is something that management designs to help the organization achieve its mission, objectives, and goals.

A *role* is a set of expectations about how an individual will behave in a given job. The role consists of a group of *responsibilities* that the role incumbent is expected to perform. If properly designed, each individual role provides a unique contribution to the achievement of the organization's goals. Further, effective *role descriptions* help people understand who is responsible for what. This minimizes duplication of effort and the possibility that things will fall through the cracks because they are no one's responsibility.

The guiding principle underlying the organization of all the various roles that constitute the structure of a firm is that form should follow function. This means that the form of the structure of the organization should be designed in such a way as to maximize the likelihood of achieving the overall functions that that structure is intended to perform. For example, if the function of an organization is to develop new products and services, then the structure (or form) of the set of roles that combine to make up the organization should be organized in such a way as to maximize the likelihood that this function will be attained. Similarly, if the function of an organization is to design and produce a product, then manufacture it as efficiently as possible, the organization should be designed in such a way as to maximize the likelihood of that happening. This principle also implies that there is no one best structure. In fact, any structure can work if it is properly designed and managed in a way that helps the firm achieve its goals.

THREE LEVELS OF ORGANIZATIONAL STRUCTURE

Although some people view structure simply as the boxes on an organization chart, we believe that there are really three distinct, yet related, levels of structure that must be designed and managed.

The first level is what we call the *macro structure*. This consists of the boxes on an organizational chart and how they are arranged. The second level is what we call the *micro structure*. This level consists of how the roles and responsibilities of each position-holder are defined and the methodology for defining these roles. For firms beyond Stage II, all roles should be articulated in formal, written role descriptions. These role descriptions should be used as guides for the behavior of people within the firm, not simply used by the human resource function.

The final level of structure is what we call *supporting systems*, which include the operational systems of the organization, its management development process, its performance management systems, and its corporate culture. A structure will not function effectively if these systems are not adequately designed to support it.

In evaluating an existing structure or designing a new structure, all three of these levels need to be considered. If any level is poorly designed or doesn't support the others, the structure will not function effectively and, in turn, the likelihood of achieving desired results will be decreased.

ALTERNATIVE FORMS OF ORGANIZATIONAL STRUCTURE

There are basically three pure forms that are available to management when designing an organizational structure. In addition to these three pure forms, there are an almost infinite number of hybrid forms or variations that are also available. Any organizational form carries with it certain strengths and limitations that must be managed in order for the structure to function properly.

The three basic forms of organization structure may be described as follows: (1) the functional structure, (2) the divisional structure, and (3) the matrix structure. Each of these is described next, along with its strengths and limitations. We also provide information on the nature of the situations in which each type of structure tends to be the best fit.

Functional Organizational Structure

As the name implies, roles in the *functional organizational structure* are organized according to the various functions that must be performed to achieve the entity's overall mission. In a small manufacturing firm, for example, the following functions are typically found: (1) engineering, (2) manufacturing, (3) sales, (4) human resources, and (5) finance. In addition to these basic functions, there may be a variety of other functions found in the structure, depending on the size of the organization. The functional structure is illustrated in Figure 8.1.

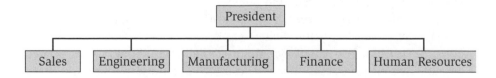

Figure 8.1. Functional Organizational Structure

As can be seen in Figure 8.1, the functional type of organization is basically a system in which managers of specific functional areas (for example, manufacturing or sales) report to a senior executive who is responsible for coordinating the overall operations of the company. The senior executive has the ultimate responsibility for the entire firm.

A variation of the functional structure that is typically found in small entrepreneurial organizations can be termed a *prefunctional organizational structure.* This structure is most prevalent in the earliest entrepreneurial stages of development where there are relatively few people, and the firm has not yet differentiated and specialized into various functions; rather, the same individual may perform a number of functions or parts of functions. Accordingly, if we were to try to diagram an entrepreneurial organization at Stage I as a functional organization, we might find the same individual occupying several functions in the organization, as illustrated in Figure 8.2. For example, the president, Mark Booth, occupies three positions at Plastic Molding Corporation. He performs both the marketing and R&D functions, while simultaneously functioning as president.

The primary strength of a functional structure is that it provides for greater specialization of function, allowing people to develop very specialized skills in each area. It also allows for the recruitment of people with predeveloped specialized skills in given functional areas. Accordingly, rather than have an individual with only a general familiarity with manufacturing as its head, an organization can recruit an executive who is highly experienced and specialized in that area.

Many large organizations continue to operate under a functional structure. However, as the size of an organization increases, the many advantages of a functional structure tend to be offset by certain critical disadvantages. One primary disadvantage is that as the operation increases in size and number of

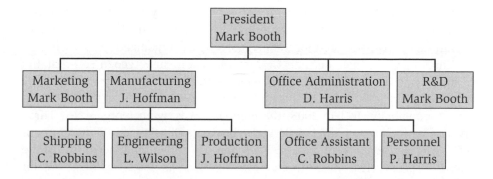

Figure 8.2. Prefunctional Organizational Structure: Plastic Molding Corporation

products, the focus of its most senior executives (who are responsible for the entire enterprise) is spread so thin that certain products receive considerable attention while others receive significantly less. A related problem is that as the size of the organization increases, the primary concern is with the overall efficiency of each functional area (such as manufacturing or sales), rather than with a particular product segment and its related customer groups. The functions may be efficiently producing products that are out of touch with the marketplace. Large companies, ranging from Kodak to Microsoft (prior to 2000) to homebuilders like Pardee Homes (whose structure management process is described later in this chapter) have experienced these problems to such a degree that they have changed from functional structures to different forms in recent years. Because of the problems, a different type of organizational structure has developed that strives to take advantage of key aspects of the functional system while also dealing with the problems of reduced focus and lack of in-depth concern for a particular product and customer grouping. This is known as the *divisional structure* and is described in the next section.

Divisional Organizational Structure

As suggested earlier, the divisional organizational structure tends to group together related clusters of products and customers. A division may be set up to focus on a particular customer segment and to produce and market products that are designed for that group. Divisions can also be structured around different technologies. A classic example of divisional structure was the one built by General Motors under the leadership of Alfred P. Sloan. Sloan, who was an MIT-trained engineer, guided General Motors to supremacy in the automobile industry, replacing Ford as the number-one automobile producer in the mid-twentieth century.[1] The basic structural concept that Sloan used was to organize General Motors into several related divisions—Chevrolet, Pontiac, Buick, Cadillac, and so on—with each division focusing on a different customer market segment. The idea was to grow customers from one General Motors product to the next, up to the ultimate, which was produced by the Cadillac division. Each division had some of its own functional aspects, but there were certain overall functions performed for the divisions by the organization as a whole.

When Steve Ballmer became CEO at Microsoft, he "recognized that the company had become unwieldy and over-centralized."[2] To help the company continue moving forward, he created seven divisions, each with profit-and-loss responsibility. In late 2005, the company was again reorganized. Three divisions—Platform Products & Services, Business Division, and Entertainment & Devices Division—were created. Each had a president and, according to the Microsoft press release, the structural change was intended to "drive greater agility in the execution of (the company's) software and services strategy"[3] (a clear reflection of the need to align strategy with structure).

As illustrated by these examples, the basic concept of the divisionalized structure is to create divisions that focus on particular customer segments to drive results. In most cases, divisions are provided certain "common" services at the corporate level. Typically, these include capital allocation, finance, legal, and administrative services, among others. An example of a classic divisional structure is presented in Figure 8.3. As shown in the figure, InfoEnterprise is a producer of computer hardware and software and provides consulting services to its customers. A general manager heads each division, and each division uses its own functional structure. The corporate services group also reports to the president.

There is wide variation in the way organizations implement the divisional concept. Some organizations have large corporate staffs that are very involved in the affairs of the divisions, including helping to set the strategic direction for the division and reviewing its performance. This may be termed the *M-type divisional structure* because of the active management from the corporate staff. This model is used by many large enterprises, such as Johnson & Johnson, Bristol-Myers Squibb, Allied Lyons, and GE.

At the other end of the spectrum, the corporation operates as a holding company, or in a certain sense as a "vertical bank." By this we mean that the larger corporation is essentially an investor, in that it buys businesses and allows them to operate in a very independent manner. In return, the businesses must meet certain performance standards, such as return on investment or cash generation. A classic model of this style is Berkshire Hathaway—a company that prides itself on having a relatively lean corporate staff. It accomplishes this because Berkshire Hathaway is essentially an "investor-type" corporate structure (I-type divisional structure), in which the various divisions are essentially part of a portfolio of investments. Similarly, Teledyne is an investor in many small entrepreneurially oriented companies, and the basic criterion for their maintenance is the ability to generate cash for the overall holding company.

Both of these divisional structure models (the M-type or the I-type) may be used, and both can be made workable and effective.

The primary strength of the divisional form is that it creates a focus on specific market or product segments. The primary disadvantage is that it

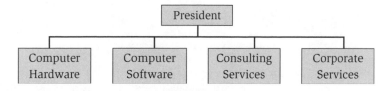

Figure 8.3. Divisional Organizational Structure: InfoEnterprise

results in duplication of functions in different divisions and creates the need for coordination among divisions. This is what leads to additional corporate staff. The divisional structure can also lead to intense competition among the general managers of each division. Therefore, it is important that if an organization decides to adopt a divisional structure, it must invest in growing true general managers who understand not only how to run a "business within a business" but also how to be an effective member of the overall corporate management team.

Matrix Organizational Structure

The final "pure" type of organizational structure has been termed the *matrix*. This structure was originally developed in the aerospace industry, although similar forms might have existed elsewhere for quite some time. In concept, the matrix approach is an attempt to achieve the best of both the functional and the divisional structures. As shown in Figure 8.4, the matrix organizational structure lists the various programs, projects, or products in the far left column of the matrix organizational chart.

Each of these programs has a program manager. Where the organization is large enough, there is a manager who is responsible for coordinating all of the programs. On the other side of the matrix, over the vertical columns, we have the various functional areas. Each of these functional areas, such as engineering design, manufacturing, and so on, is headed by an executive who is responsible for the functional specialization. The matrix operates by having the program managers "borrow" people from the various functional areas to work on their programs. When the program is finished, the people are returned to the functional pool. For example, a large aerospace company

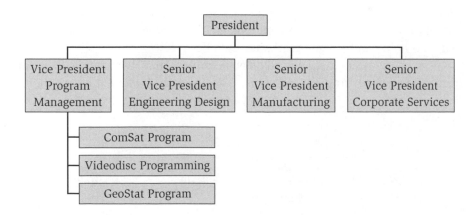

Figure 8.4. Matrix Organizational Structure: Ultraspace Corporation

that is involved with the design of a new aircraft for the U.S. Department of Defense will borrow engineers and assign them to that particular project. When the responsibilities of those engineers are completed, they will return to the overall engineering pool to be reassigned. In this structure, an engineer might be simultaneously involved in more than one project.

The basic strength of the matrix structure is that it permits a focus on the customer and the product, and also allows functional specialization. The major disadvantage or limitation of the matrix structure is that it requires a high degree of coordination to be effective. The keys to successfully operating a matrix structure are conducting regularly scheduled meetings to review the status of work and having the ability to deal with the inevitable conflict that arises when employees are accountable to more than one supervisor (a program supervisor and a functional supervisor) and possibly involved in more than one program (where they are now responsible to multiple supervisors). Accordingly, the matrix structure requires a considerable amount of training in work-related interpersonal skills to ensure its smooth operation.

While having many advantages, a matrix structure is quite difficult to execute effectively in practice. It is a very complex structure that requires a great deal of coordination and communication to make it function properly. Therefore, an organization that believes that a version of the matrix structure will be best for its long-term development will need to be willing to invest in helping people, both managers and other employees, in order to develop the skills (for example, meeting management and team decision making) needed to help the structure function properly.

One company that has done this well as it transformed from an entrepreneurship to a professionally managed firm is Pardee Homes. Initially, Pardee was organized in a functional structure, with "departments" such as land development, purchasing, construction, marketing and sales, and finance reporting to a CEO and COO, who functioned as "super project managers." However, as the company grew in size the CEO and COO found themselves spread too thin. The solution was to change the organization's structure. Over a period of about ten years the company evolved toward a matrix structure, as described in the section on cases in organizational structure.

CRITERIA FOR EVALUATION AND DESIGN OF ORGANIZATIONAL STRUCTURE

In many firms where organizational structure has not been well designed, problems arise that can have a significant impact on the organization's ability to achieve its goals. As organizations grow, they tend to add jobs and levels in a piecemeal manner to meet current needs. If this process continues, the entire organization develops an ad hoc character. Indeed, the result can be an "organizational Frankenstein." At this point, it is necessary to review the entire organizational structure in light of these overall changes in the level and scope of business activities.

Eight criteria can be used to evaluate an organization's existing structure or to design a new structure to better meet a firm's needs as it makes the transition from an entrepreneurship to a professionally managed firm. These eight criteria are as follows:

To what extent does the current (or proposed) structure support the organization's strategy? As stated previously, this is the most basic principle on which an organization's structure should be based; that is, form should follow function. Addressing this question involves developing an understanding of what the firm's mission and key objectives are. Then the existing structure (including the macro structure, micro structure, and supporting systems) should be evaluated for the extent to which it will help the firm achieve these goals. For example, if a firm wants to move beyond being a one-product company and is functionally organized, it might want to consider moving toward a divisional structure. Another alternative, however, is to redesign its planning process and control systems (supporting systems) in order to ensure that adequate attention is being focused on developing the new product line.

To what extent does each function add value, or what new functions will we need to better support our goals? A firm should next examine the roles and responsibilities of the different functions that make up its macro structure. The outcome of this analysis is to determine the contribution that each function is making to the goals of the organization. Based on this analysis, some firms may find that certain functions have become obsolete. In one company, for example, a functional unit had been created, the sole role of which was to ensure that the data input by another department was correct. As technology had evolved over time, there was no longer the need for such a control mechanism (that is, the probability that mistakes would be made in data input had become practically zero). Therefore, this unit was providing no true value to the organization. The decision was made to eliminate it and re-deploy personnel to other areas.

In other cases, organizations will find that, as they grow, they need to develop new functions to better meet their needs. By the time a firm reaches Stage III, for example, it will typically find that it needs some type of formal marketing function (if it has not already developed one). Many Stage III and Stage IV firms also find that they need to develop a formal human resource function that has responsibilities beyond payroll, recruiting, and hiring.

To evaluate whether a firm has developed all of the functional units needed to support its goals or whether certain units are no longer making the contribution that they should involves determining the extent to which all key result areas are reflected within existing organizational units. For example, one key result area may be customer service. This does not necessarily mean that the organization must have a customer service unit; however, the organization must in some way have an individual or group of people who are directly responsible for the performance of customer service.

Unless key result areas are somehow incorporated into organizational units, there is a tendency for organizations to ignore these critical responsibilities. These key result areas tend to be neglected in favor of other tasks that may seem more pressing. Examples of this phenomenon have occurred in the key result area of product development, which has led to the divisionalization of many organizations. For example, Medco Enterprises, a $20 million medical manufacturing firm discussed in Chapter Seventeen, experienced difficulty using the functional form of organizational structure because coordination problems emerged with respect to new product development. Rather than having a unit focused on a particular market segment, Medco had separate functional units for engineering, sales, and manufacturing, which created a variety of problems with respect to the timeliness and appropriateness of new products. The company ultimately shifted to an organizational structure in which one key organizational unit was responsible for the combined functions of design, manufacturing, and sales. This change shifted the focus of product development and sales to a single organization unit rather than require the coordination of three separate units with differing responsibilities for a much wider range of products.

To what extent do individual roles support the achievement of the firm's goals? Are there any changes that need to be made in existing roles or new roles that need to be created to assist us in more effectively meeting our goals? To address these questions, there must first be a clear understanding of what people's roles are. Formal, written job or role descriptions are typically used for this purpose. In some organizations, the first problem is that there *are* no written job descriptions. In other cases, there may be job descriptions, but they are so out of date that they no longer adequately reflect what the incumbent is expected to do. In still other cases, there are written job descriptions, but they are only used by the human resource function as tools for hiring and evaluation. They are not used as guides for individual behavior. Finally, there are cases where job descriptions are developed, based on the capabilities of the people who are currently on the team instead of being developed to reflect what the company needs to effectively achieve its goals. As is true of other aspects of organizational structure, the structure should be designed to support the company's strategy.

Effective job or role descriptions should provide those occupying a particular position with the information they need to understand what is expected of them. Therefore, each position-holder should have a copy of his or her job or role description and use it as a guide for behavior. Traditional job descriptions, however, are not necessarily designed to promote effective goal-directed behavior. Most traditional job descriptions provide the position-holder with sometimes very lengthy lists of key responsibilities. These key responsibilities appear as sentences in the job description, and sometimes there are several pages full of this type of information, with no or limited organization. In one small entrepreneurial firm (under $1 million in revenues), the office manager had an eight-page job description! The problem with developing job descriptions in this format is that important information and key responsibilities can be too easily lost as the incumbent struggles to determine what he or she should be doing.

We believe that effective job or role descriptions should focus people on their position's key responsibilities but that to be effective, these key responsibilities need to be presented in a somewhat nontraditional manner. We suggest that individual job or role descriptions be designed to mirror the format used in corporate or departmental planning (discussed in Chapter Seven). In brief, they should identify the mission, key result areas, and objectives for each position. (Goals are not included in the role description but are, instead, developed for each person who occupies each role in the context of the performance management system, which is described in more detail in Chapter Ten.)

In the context of a role description, the mission answers the question, Why does this position exist? For example, the mission for the role of president might be stated something like, ''To manage and profitably grow the overall business.'' Key result areas for individual positions define the categories of activities that the position-holder needs to focus on to be successful in his or her role. As was true at the corporate and departmental levels of the company, key result areas are stated in one, two, or three words. Further, each position should have between five and nine key result areas for which the incumbent is held accountable. The rationale for having between five and nine key result areas is that research suggests that most people can remember only five to nine things at any one time.[4] Therefore, to maximize the probability that people will be focused on those areas that will maximize results, we want to present this information in a manner that it can be remembered—hence, the ''5 to 9'' guideline. Key result areas for the role of president might include strategic planning, profitability management, new business development, supervision, external relations, and organizational development.

Clearly defining key result areas, however, is only part of what effective job descriptions should do. They should also provide information on how people should be allocating their time among these key result areas in order to maximize results (measured in terms of the ability of the firm to achieve its goals). Finally, role descriptions should provide a description, in the form of objectives or ongoing responsibilities, of what the position holder should be spending his or her time on in each key result area. Examples of objectives or ongoing responsibilities for the key result area of supervision might include the following:

- Recruits and selects direct reports.
- Works with direct reports to create annual goals and regularly monitors performance against these goals.
- Coaches direct reports.
- Provides annual performance appraisals to direct reports.

The first aspect of evaluating structure with respect to roles involves

- Determining the extent to which there are existing written role descriptions
- Evaluating the effectiveness of these written role descriptions in terms of the methodology used and in terms of the extent to which they actually reflect what incumbents do
- Evaluating the extent to which the organization uses its role or job descriptions as guides for employee behavior

The next step in evaluating roles is to look at the components of an individual's role, both separately and in relation to other roles in the organization. This is done to determine the "value-added" of each individual role to the organization. In essence, then, this analysis focuses on the contribution made by individual roles, as well as the relationship between these roles. As an organization grows, the roles that people occupy will undoubtedly change. Most of this change occurs in an ad hoc fashion. Accordingly, it is periodically necessary to do a systematic analysis of each role, both individually and in relation to the other roles that make up the organizational structure. When we have conducted such analyses, we have frequently found superfluous positions and levels within an organization, which leads to reduced efficiency and profitability.

Finally, the analysis should turn to determining whether new roles will be needed to support the long-term goals of the firm. As a firm grows, for example, it will need to move from a prefunctional to a functional structure. This will mean the creation of new roles.

To what extent are reporting relationships clearly defined, and does each position holder have the authority needed to effectively execute his or her role? How should reporting relationships be defined, and what authority do position-holders need to support our long-term goals? The organization chart should clearly define reporting relationships. As stated previously, however, some organizations have no organizational charts. In this case, reporting relationships need to be identified through discussions with key personnel.

Even if an organization chart exists, there can be a problem with using it as the primary mechanism for understanding reporting relationships: it may not accurately reflect how the company really works. In a $100 million distribution firm, for example, while the structure on paper suggested that each middle manager reported to a specific vice president, in reality, everyone reported to the two owners of the firm. Whatever the owners asked a person to do, regardless of level within the firm, was the priority.

A further analysis of reporting relationships involves identifying the underlying rationale behind them and how they support the effective achievement of the company's goals. Reporting relationships should be clearly defined in individual role descriptions and should be designed in a way that creates a highly functional organization. When these relationships are poorly designed or defined, problems can arise. In a $500 million manufacturing firm, for example, there were a number of new product development teams that had been created by bringing in people from different functions within the company. One of the company's primary goals was to develop and launch new products, so the product teams made sense. However, each new product team reported to a different senior manager. In other words, there was no single product champion among the senior management team (which was functionally organized). Reporting relationships, in this case, were detracting from the company's ability to effectively design and release new products.

As a general rule, decision-making authority should be distributed to the lowest possible management level within a company in order to maximize its efficiency. The "lowest possible" level depends on the nature of the company and the skill levels of the management team. If, however, a company has reached Stage III and all major decisions are still being made by the president of the firm, chances are that there are opportunities to improve in this area.

In designing a new structure, both reporting relationships and the decision-making authority of each position should be carefully considered. The objective is to create an organization structure in which everyone knows what they are responsible for and understands to whom they report.

What is the appropriate span of control and number of levels that should exist within the company to facilitate the effective and efficient achievement of its goals? Span of control relates to the number of people who report directly to a given manager. The greater the manager's span of control, the lower the cost of supervision of individual employees. The cost of supervision (per employee) decreases as the span of control increases, because supervisory costs are allocated over a greater "base" of employees. However, in the absence of an extremely well-developed control system (the subject of Chapter Ten), a manager is limited in the number of employees that can be supervised before he or she begins to do an inefficient job. Conversely, it is expensive to employ more managers than is necessary. An effective span of control balances the decreasing per-employee supervisory costs against the increasing costs of managerial inefficiency.

Traditional management thought suggests that if a position has fewer than three direct reports, it is likely to be unnecessary; if it has more than nine direct reports, effective supervision is not likely to occur unless the manager is very experienced and uses sophisticated leadership methods (see Chapter Eleven). There are, however, exceptions to this rule of thumb. If an organization or functional unit employs highly skilled and highly motivated individuals and if there is a well-developed planning process and comprehensive control system, the number of people who can be supervised effectively by an individual manager might exceed nine. There are cases where managers operate effectively and achieve acceptable results while supervising twenty or more individuals. Again, however, these tend to be the exception, rather than the rule.

Span of control and the number of layers that exist within a company tend to be inversely related: the larger the span of control, the fewer the number of layers; the smaller the span of control, the greater the number of layers.

Any organization structure can also be viewed in terms of the number of levels of roles that have been aggregated to make up the structure. An organizational level consists of a group of positions that are comparable in terms of the nature of the work done. There are basically five pure (or distinct) types of levels of work in organizations, shown in Figure 8.5, and these create an organizational hierarchy. Each of these organizational levels is described briefly.

The first or *entry level* in the organizational hierarchy is the level at which technical or individual contributor work is performed. People who occupy this

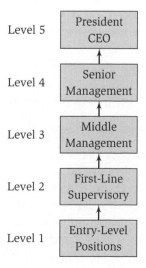

Figure 8.5. Organizational Hierarchy

level of the organizational hierarchy are typically involved in doing a wide variety of technical work like computer programming, sales, production, or clerical work.

The next level may be termed the *first-line supervisory level.* People at this level may still be doing a certain amount of technical work, but they also have more responsibility for the supervision of technicians or other individual contributors within the organization. Individuals who are first-line supervisors have no other managerial employees reporting to them, only technical or individual contributors.

The third level in the organizational hierarchy can be termed the *middle-management level.* The function of middle management is to supervise one or more levels of other managers, which may include first-line supervisors or other middle levels of managers. Organizations can ultimately have a number of middle levels of management. However, regardless of the number, the primary function for the middle managers is a supervisory and coordinating function, and a liaison between first-line supervision and senior management.

The fourth, relatively distinct level of an organizational hierarchy is the *senior-management level.* This level tends to have two major responsibilities: (1) managing a major function within the company and (2) assisting the CEO or COO with the overall planning and management of the company as a whole.

The fifth level that can be distinguished is the *chief executive* (CEO) or *chief operating officer* (COO) *level* of the enterprise. The CEO has ultimate responsibility for the overall planning and direction of the enterprise; the COO has primary responsibility for the execution of the overall strategic planning implementation in terms of day-to-day operations. These two positions can be treated as a single "level" of the organization to which senior managers report.

Organizations are not required to have all five of these levels to be effective. Small (under $10 million in revenues) firms may have only three levels. Larger organizations may have more than five levels.

In analyzing span of control and number of levels, the key is to determine what the optimal balance is between the two in order for the firm to achieve its goals. In general, however, if a manager has fewer than three or more than nine people reporting to him or her, further analysis should be done to determine why. If it is the case that the organization anticipates growing a particular function, then a small span of control may be appropriate. If the organization has sophisticated planning and control systems in place, a span of control greater than nine may be acceptable. Generally speaking, however, organizations that operate at either extreme can have problems with respect to accomplishing their goals efficiently and effectively.

With respect to number of levels, the farther removed senior management is from the customer, the higher the probability that problems will arise. If there are nine or ten levels between senior management and the firm's customers, it may be only by chance that senior management adequately understands and incorporates customer needs into their planning process. It is not impossible to stay in touch with customers when there are a large number of levels present in a company. When this is the case, however, the firm needs to develop supporting systems that allow its management team access to this and other types of information or it runs the risk of making poor strategic decisions.

To what extent do those in management and technical positions possess the skills needed to be effective in their roles? What types of skills need to be developed at each level of our company to help us effectively and efficiently achieve our goals? Answering these questions involves first determining the skill set that each position-holder should possess to effectively accomplish his or her responsibilities. Next, an assessment should be made of the extent to which existing position-holders actually possess these skills. If it is found that certain position-holders lack the skills required to be effective in their roles, then the organization may decide to provide them with training, or they may decide to move these individuals into roles that are more suited to their capabilities. The organization will then fill the open positions with people from outside the company.

It is important in examining skills that the company identify not just what it will need in the next year but what it will need over the next three to five years. Further, it is important that there be an assessment of management skills (which are different from technical skills) possessed by all levels of management. Assessment and development of management skills is the subject of the next chapter.

To what extent do interdependent departments and functions effectively coordinate with each other? What types of coordination will be required to help us effectively achieve our goals? This, again, is a supporting system component of the company's structure that can be promoted through well-designed job descriptions, the planning process, or organizational control systems. In brief, analyzing this dimension of structure involves identifying which units within the company need to coordinate on a regular basis and then assessing the extent to which this coordination is working effectively. In some cases, functional units can work at cross-purposes with one another, either because of poor planning or a culture (as in the Tempo Products case) that promotes the separate islands syndrome. This can create problems for the company in terms of its ability to effectively achieve its goals.

In designing a new organizational structure, a firm's management should determine what types of coordination need to take place and the timing of these events. Effective coordination mechanisms are particularly important (as explained earlier) if a firm is going to adopt a matrix structure.

What supporting systems do we need to have in place to ensure that our chosen structure will function effectively? If a firm is evaluating the effectiveness of its structure, it needs to examine how its planning process, control systems, management development process, operational systems, and corporate culture support its structure. For example, if the corporate culture promotes the idea that "we are an organization of separate functional teams that all do their own thing," a functional structure in which everyone needs to pull together toward the same common goals will be ineffective. The culture, in this case, might need to be changed (see Chapter Twelve) to better support the structure. If an organization adopts a divisional structure but does not have a management development process in place to grow true general managers, the structure will not function properly because the management of the divisions will be ineffective.

In designing a new structure, a key principle to keep in mind is that any structure will work as long as it has the appropriate supporting systems in place. Therefore, it is important that management take the time to consider what systems, structures, and processes will be needed to support whatever structure is adopted.

Answering the questions listed here involves performing several related analyses as part of an organizational structure assessment or audit. These questions, as stated previously, can also be used to help design a more effective structure. The bottom line is that through addressing these questions, a firm can identify the strengths and limitations of its current structure or any other structures it is considering adopting.

CASE STUDIES OF ORGANIZATIONAL STRUCTURE

The next section of this chapter looks at organizational structure issues from a different perspective. Specifically, we examine cases of organizational design in order to identify some of the strengths and limitations affecting organizations at different stages of growth. We focus on Stage II and Stage IV companies because at these stages organizational structure becomes a critical variable. However, because organizations of all sizes must focus on designing and managing structure so as to allow the firm to continue growing from one stage to the next, we examine cases at different size (revenue) levels, including larger firms that have faced organizational structure issues.

Design Corporation

Figure 8.6 shows the organizational structure of Design Corporation—a Stage II company. This firm specializes in interior design for industrial and commercial enterprises. As can be seen in the figure, the organization has three divisional units: downtown and suburban units that specialize in interior design, and a subsidiary organization that specializes in purchasing furnishings required

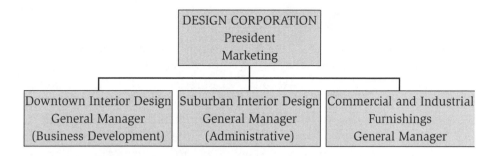

Figure 8.6. Organizational Structure of Design Corporation

for commercial and industrial organizations. At the time this organizational structure was being used, Design Corporation had approximately $3 million in annual revenues, which made it a Stage II company.

The basic problem facing Design Corporation was not in the design of its macro structure but in the difficulties caused by the lack of managerial and other capabilities of various people occupying key positions in the organizational structure (supporting systems). Specifically, the basic marketing strength of the organization was in the entrepreneurial founder who occupied the role of president. The manager of the downtown office had reasonable business development capabilities but was lacking in administrative capabilities, as was the president. The manager of the suburban office was lacking in business development capabilities but was an effective administrator. The operation of the third division was reasonably successful as a stand-alone entity and is not considered further here. The net result of the various skill gaps on the part of the three key managers (the two general managers and the president) meant that each individual was trying to compensate for the inadequacies of other individuals in a different part of the organization.

For example, the president was doing a great deal of marketing for the suburban division because of the lack of business development capability on the part of that division's general manager, while the manager of the suburban division was increasingly responsible for some of the administrative work of the firm as a whole. Because the president was deeply involved in the business development of one of the divisions, he did not have sufficient time to devote to the organizational development needs of a rapidly growing company.

Although none of this could be seen from looking at the organization structure on a sheet of paper, when evaluating the appropriateness of an organizational structure for an entrepreneurial organization, we must consider the skills of the players who occupy key positions in order to determine whether the structure truly makes sense. In other words, looking at the structure on paper alone would seem to indicate that it made sense, but when we examine the skills of the various managers in the firm, this structure is one that is clearly inappropriate for this organization.

There are several solutions to the problems described in this situation. One would be to add the role of executive vice president to the firm (a macro and micro structure solution). The executive vice president would be responsible for the day-to-day administration of the organization, which would free up the president to devote time to long-range planning, organizational development, and business development, as well as to train the general managers to do business development. This solution would add to the cost of operating the organization. Another approach might be to work with each division general manager to help develop the missing skills (a supporting system issue). This might involve bringing in an outside resource to work with these individuals or sending them to training. If it was then found that they could not perform effectively in their roles, the president might decide to fill these positions with individuals possessing more appropriate skills.

Hitek Manufacturing

Hitek Manufacturing Company was a rapidly growing, Stage III manufacturer of high-tech products. The firm had recently achieved revenues of approximately $75 million. Up until that time the firm's revenues were approximately $50 million, and it was organized in a functional fashion. The firm had developed a number of products but was experiencing certain difficulties in the coordination of new product development and with the successful introduction of these new products into the marketplace. This was due, in part, to the fact that the existing functional structure emphasized the more successful existing products. The firm realized that it needed to have a steady stream of new products and that one way to enhance the development of new products was to have them developed in a division that was focused on a particular product market segment. Accordingly, when Hitek reached approximately $50 million in annual revenue, the firm made the decision to take steps to transition itself from a functional structure to a divisional structure.

Except for the president of Hitek, all the senior managers were functional specialists in areas such as sales, marketing, manufacturing, and product development. Hitek realized that to ensure the successful transition to a divisional structure, it had to develop senior managers who were capable of operating as general managers. Accordingly, part of the company's organizational development plan was focused on the development of some of its functional managers as potential general managers. By the time the firm had reached $75 million in revenue, it had two people who were thought to be very likely candidates as general managers, and a third individual who was thought to possess the capabilities of being the general manager of a smaller division. Hitek was able to successfully introduce the divisional management structure.

GoodEats, Inc.

GoodEats was a $100 million consumer-products firm, nominally organized into two divisions. One division focused on sales within the United States, while the other division sold the same product internationally. General managers headed each of the two major divisions and had profit-and-loss responsibility for their geographic territories.

As can be seen in their organizational chart presented in Figure 8.7, reporting to the general manager of the U.S. Operations was production, R&D, sales, marketing, purchasing, and distribution. The general manager of the International Operations had only sales, marketing, and distribution reporting to him. The general manager of International Operations needed to rely on obtaining product from the manufacturing entity that reported directly to the U.S. general manager. In addition, the general manager of the international division had to rely on the R&D function that reported to the U.S. division for assistance in developing new products. In other words, while the U.S. division was a *true* division, the international division did not control all of the functional units that would contribute to its results.

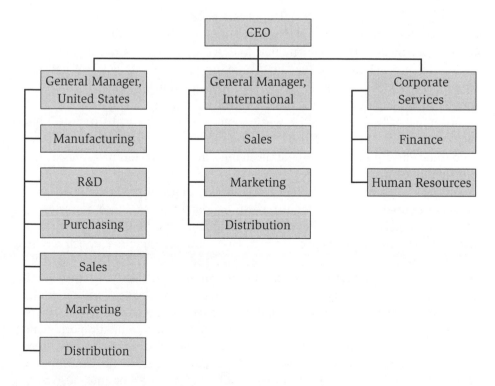

Figure 8.7. Organizational Structure of GoodEats, Inc.

Although this is not an optimal situation, it could have been managed by using a comprehensive planning process in which both general managers, the CEO, and the head of finance and administration participated. The plan developed by this team would clearly articulate how functional areas that were shared by the two divisions should invest their time and resources for the good of the company as a whole. Unfortunately, the planning process at GoodEats was done in divisional silos: the U.S. general manager developed his plan, and the international general manager developed his plan, both in isolation from the other. This led to a situation in which the heads of manufacturing, purchasing, and R&D constantly felt that they were being pulled in different directions by two very strong horses. The problem was that when these managers needed to make a decision about whose directives to follow, they would, of course, follow those of their manager—the general manager of the U.S. operations. This contributed to a situation in which the company, as a whole, was not achieving the results that it might have achieved and in which the international division (even though it was viewed as a strong source of company growth) was treated like a second-class citizen.

Pardee Homes

Pardee Homes is a multiregional real estate development company with a focus on developing master-planned communities and building single- and multifamily homes. The company was founded by George Pardee in 1921 as a builder of custom homes. In 1969, the company was acquired by Weyerhaeuser Company—a global leader in the forest products industry—and became the largest subsidiary of Weyerhaeuser Real Estate Company.

For much of its history Pardee was organized in a functional structure,[5] but as a result of growth its CEO and COO found themselves stretched too thin and embarked on a process of structural change that would ultimately lead to a divisionalized matrix structure.

In the first phase (1996–1999) of structural change, home-building projects were structured around regional cross-functional teams. These teams were led by a project manager, who functioned like a coordinator more than a manager. Team members were specialists from architecture, construction, engineering, finance, marketing, purchasing, and sales. These team members had a direct reporting relationship to the department heads and a "dotted–line" (coordinating relationship) to the project manager (team leader). Although this structure worked reasonably well and contributed to the company's ability to achieve its growth goals, there were times when certain coordination problems arose. Specifically, sometimes a project team member was pulled in different directions by the project manager and the department head (to whom he or she had a direct reporting relationship). Managers were, for the most part, able to identify and address these problems. However, there was recognition that some supporting systems, like planning and performance management, needed to be refined to support the "new" matrix structure.

The next phase of change (2000–2004) was stimulated by the desire to grow, facilitated by a favorable housing market. One of the key differences between this phase and the prior phase was the delegation of increasing authority to regional team leaders who were informally referred to as regional managers but formally held the title vice president of community development. This was a first step toward divisionalizing the company. The company also continued formalizing the matrix component of its structure—creating systems to better support its effective and efficient operation.

The final phase of the evolution from a functional structure to a division-alized matrix structure began in 2005–06. In 2005, the company established a pilot project in one region to treat it as a full division (with profit and loss responsibility) and determine best practices for a full roll-out in other geographic areas. Project managers retained responsibility for managing spe-cific projects, with team members being matrixed in from functions, but now project managers would report directly to the head of the division versus to the company's CEO.

As can be seen, the proper implementation of this concept takes time. It also requires a variety of supporting management systems to facilitate the structural change, including well-developed planning and performance management systems.

Starbucks Coffee

In the mid-1990s, when Starbucks' revenues were in the range of $350 million, the company decided to revise its structure as a result of planning being done for its future business. Until that point, the company was essentially organized in a functional structure. However, it also had some components (mail order and specialty sales) that were divisional in nature but not treated as true divisions because they were so small. For example, mail order reported to Howard Behar, who ran retail operations. Howard Schultz was CEO, and his direct reports included several functional areas, including retail operations, real estate, marketing, logistics and manufacturing, finance, human resources, and legal.

As the company began its planning for the future, it became clear that two things needed to happen: (1) the company was at the point where it needed a COO, and (2) the company was moving in the direction of leveraging its brand name and creating additional businesses. In addition, the company had just experienced a growth spurt and had hired several new executives.

In revising its structure, Starbucks switched from a functional structure to a matrix. Four business units were created: (1) retail operations, (2) specialty sales, (3) mail order, and (4) international. Retail operations included all of the functions involved in setting up and managing Starbucks' retail stores. Specialty sales involved sales of Starbucks' products and distribution arrangements outside the retail system. This included Starbucks' deals with Barnes & Noble, Inc. for the distribution of coffee in their stores, with UAL (United Airlines) for distribution of Starbucks coffee on all UAL flights, with PepsiCo for joint ventures involving ready-to-drink coffee-based beverages, and with Dreyers for a joint venture involving coffee-flavored ice cream. Mail order (also known as direct response) was responsible for coffee and other products being marketed and distributed via mail. The international unit was formed to spearhead an effort by Starbucks to expand internationally. This was to be done via joint ventures. The functional components of the matrix included the same units identified earlier.

As part of this organizational restructuring, Orin Smith who had been CFO became COO. Howard Behar who had headed retail operations became the president of the international division, and Diedre Wager who had assisted Behar became head of retail.

This structure was designed to facilitate and support Starbucks' growth from approximately $350 million in revenue and 350 stores to at least $2 billion in revenue and 2,000 stores. By 1998, Starbucks had grown to almost $1.4 billion in revenue and more than 1,800 stores. In 2006, Starbucks revenue exceeded $5 billion, with more than 5,000 stores throughout the United States and internationally.

ORGANIZATIONAL STRUCTURE AT DIFFERENT STAGES OF GROWTH

This section examines the organizational structure requirements of various kinds of firms at different stages of growth. It provides guidelines for the design and selection of organizational structure, rather than offering a precise formula for selecting a particular organizational structure.

Stage I

A Stage I organization usually has what we have termed a prefunctional organizational structure. This means that the typical organization at Stage I has a number of individuals who simultaneously perform a wide variety of duties. The same individual may be performing marketing and administrative tasks because the organization is not yet large enough that it can define its structure in terms of specialized functions.

Although the situation described is probably typical of most Stage I organizations, it is possible that a Stage I organization has made the transition to a functional structure. This can only be determined on a case-by-case basis, without any precise rules being given.

Stage II

A Stage II organization typically has annual revenues from $1 million to $10 million if it is a manufacturing company or from approximately $330,000 to about $3.3 million if it is a service company. Stage II organizations are usually organized according to functional specialties. They have made the transition from a prefunctional stage but are probably not yet ready for a divisionalized form of structure.

Stage III

Organizations at Stage III, ranging from $10 million to $100 million in annual revenues for manufacturing companies and one-third of these values for service organizations, can be viewed in terms of three substage groupings: Stage III (A) from $10 million to $25 million, Stage III (B) from $25 million to $50 million, and Stage III (C) from $50 million to $100 million.

During Stage III (A) the organization typically has a functional organizational structure. As the firm grows in size, there is an increasing need for coordination in the development of new products and services, as well as in their manufacture and distribution. At some point, the firm begins to neglect some of its products and services. The "more important" products and services receive primary attention, while newer products, or those that are less significant in terms of current sales revenue, will be somewhat neglected. This could become a serious problem, because some of the newer products have not yet achieved significant sales revenue but may be vital to the firm's long-term development. Accordingly, sometime during this period of development the organization may wish to consider moving toward a divisionalized structure. The primary advantage of a divisionalized structure is that it allows a group of people to focus on the development, marketing, and distribution of a common set of products and services.

For many companies, the transition from a functional structure to a divisionalized structure begins to occur during Stage III (B). This transition involves the development of managers who will become general managers of the various divisions. Because most managers prior to this time have been technical or functional specialists in an area such as engineering, sales, or production, they now need development that will enable them to coordinate all the various functional areas. This is a task of management development, which is examined further in Chapter Nine.

Another organizational problem that increasingly becomes apparent during Stage III (B) is the need for greater coordination of overall operations than is probably feasible when a single individual serves as president. Sometime during this period, the president of the organization becomes stretched very thin. This means that the individual is simultaneously involved in so many aspects of both day-to-day and long-term operations that he or she begins to feel increasingly torn apart.

What has happened is that the size of the organization and the corresponding complexity of its operations have combined to make it extremely difficult for a single individual to hold everything together. At this point the president of the organization needs to think seriously about bringing in an executive vice president or COO.

Two major transitions need to be made at this time. The first requires a role change for the president, who will give up this position to become the CEO. This involves the transition from a role focusing on both the day-to-day operational issues and the long-term development of the organization to a role in which the CEO is concerned about the organization's long-term development, strategic planning, and organizational development. The introduction of a COO who is now responsible for coordinating the day-to-day operations is the second transition. The changes in the CEO's role are examined further in Chapter Seventeen.

By the time the organization reaches Stage III (C) these two transitions should be completed. This means that a COO will be in place and that the organization probably will have a number of divisions. It should be noted, however, that there are exceptions to this pattern. Many organizations reach $100 million without a COO or any divisions. There are examples of billion-dollar organizations that still have a functional organizational structure. This is not to say that these organizations operate without problems; rather, it is merely to say that they have maintained their functional organizational structure and that some of their operational problems are being caused by this structure.

Stage IV

By the time a firm reaches Stage IV, it has either made the transition to a divisionalized structure or is in the process of doing so. The challenge at Stage IV is for a divisionalized organization to consolidate the cultures in the various operating divisions, making them reasonably consistent with the overall corporate culture. These issues are further discussed in Chapter Twelve, which deals with the management of corporate culture.

SUMMARY

Organizational structure is the patterned arrangement of specified roles to be performed by people to achieve a purpose. When properly used, it is a tool that helps management increase productivity and makes it more likely that people will perform the tasks required of them to help the organization achieve its mission.

Three levels of structure must be considered when designing or redesigning an organization: macro, micro, and supporting systems. In designing structure, there are also three primary forms: functional, divisional, and matrix. Each form has its particular strengths and weaknesses, and the limitations of each can be controlled through the proper attention of management. Each of these forms of structure becomes more appropriate to use as a firm progresses through the organizational life cycle. It is therefore important that management match the organization's stage in its life cycle with the appropriate organizational structure. Further, there are eight criteria outlined in this chapter that managers can use in selecting the best structure to meet their needs.

Structure, as can be seen in the case examples presented in this chapter, can be a critical contributor to organizational effectiveness and success. It is, therefore, essential that managers understand how to effectively use this key management system to support their company's growth.

CHAPTER NINE

Management and Leadership Development

M anagement and leadership development is another major tool available to the senior management of an entrepreneurial organization that is trying to make the transition to a professionally managed company. It can help to meet one of the greatest ongoing needs of rapidly growing entrepreneurships: the need for managerial talent and for the next generation of managers. Many CEOs of such firms are familiar with the cry, "We just don't have enough good managers!"

Management development can provide people with the skills they need to effectively manage a firm. But sophisticated companies such as GE, IBM, Hewlett-Packard, Motorola, and Countrywide Financial Corporation recognize that management development is more than a tool for training people in new skills. It is also a tool for educating managers in the company's corporate culture: its values, beliefs, and norms.

This chapter begins by discussing the general role of management and leadership development in organizational development and transitions. It then examines this topic further by describing how one company—Bell-Carter Foods, Inc.—used its management development program to help it make the transition to a professionally managed organization.

THE NATURE OF MANAGEMENT AND LEADERSHIP DEVELOPMENT

Broadly defined, management and leadership development is the process of building the present and potential performance capabilities of an organization's managers. *Management development* focuses on helping individuals develop the capabilities to manage the day-to-day operations of the business (the company or their business unit). *Leadership development* focuses on helping individuals develop the capabilities needed to strategically manage the business, their unit, or their team. Throughout this chapter, the term *management development* is used to refer to activities and programs that focus on helping participants develop both management and leadership capabilities.

To maximize its effectiveness, a management development program should focus not just on skill development but also on helping participants understand how to behave and think in their roles as managers and leaders. The overall results of a management development program should be measured in terms of the behavioral change of managers and their direct reports and, ultimately, in terms of increased productivity of the entire team.

As has been noted, one of the growing pains in entrepreneurial organizations is the lack of enough good managers. To overcome this deficiency, a firm can hire experienced managers from outside the organization, develop them from within, or do both. Most successful firms use both external recruitment and internal development.

Management development is just as real an investment as the investment in plant and equipment. It is an investment in the human capital of an organization—the skills, knowledge, and experience of people.[1] It is an investment in the infrastructure of an organization.

Companies in a wide variety of industries and of varying sizes, such as Royce Medical Corporation (the company described in Chapter Seven), Navistar, Windham Hill Productions, American Century Investors, and Countrywide Financial Corporation, have all created management development programs. In addition, a number of not-for-profit entities, like Head Start, are working to develop the skills and capabilities needed to manage their entities as true businesses in order to continue their success into the future. The entrepreneurs and leaders of these organizations recognize that one of the critical factors in their company's ability to continue to grow successfully will be the presence of sufficient managerial talent. As the owner of one firm that had grown in about seven years to more than $100 million in revenues stated, "We have plenty of product and expansion ideas, and I can borrow money for expansion from a bank, but my critical need is for people who will be capable of managing what we plan to become."

In response to this kind of need, Melvin Simon & Associates (now Simon Properties)—one of the largest shopping center developers in the United States—established The Simon Institute, an in-house management development program for senior executives designed to provide advanced leadership and organizational development skills. Similarly, the Westfield Group—an international shopping center development and management company headquartered in Australia and with malls in the United States, Australia, and Europe—engaged the Anderson School of Management at UCLA and The Australian Graduate School of Management to design and deliver a leadership development program for its entire senior management team. They considered the program of sufficient importance to cite it in its Corporate Annual Report.[2]

On the not-for-profit side, since 1991 Johnson & Johnson has sponsored (through the Price Institute for Entrepreneurial Studies) a two-week program each summer at UCLA, during which Head Start directors (the CEOs of their organizations) are trained in the methodology of effective management. Competition to attend the program is intense, but program results suggest that directors who have attended this program achieve significantly better results (measured in terms of meeting certain national standards of performance) in their organizations than directors who have yet to attend the program.

Although management development can play a positive role in building managers, it is not a panacea. It cannot be expected to turn people into managerial wonders overnight. The development of managers takes time. Consequently, it is useful to regard management development as a process of *building* managers. It requires a commitment on the part of the individual who participates in the programs, as well as on the part of the organization. In the absence of such a commitment, the investment in management development will not realize a return with respect to creating better managers and, in turn, improving the company's overall effectiveness.

FUNCTIONS OF MANAGEMENT DEVELOPMENT

Management development has several functions, all of which are especially relevant in organizations making transitions from one stage of growth to the next. The most obvious is to enhance the skills of the firm's managers. Management development can also be used to (1) help define or redefine the corporate culture, (2) help promote the style of leadership that the organization desires, and (3) serve as a reward to or recognition of good managers. Let us discuss each of these uses further.

Enhancing Management Skills

The focus of most management development programs is on skill development. However, as we discuss further in this chapter, the ability of individuals to *apply* these skills in practice is influenced by their attitude and mind-set. Management development programs that focus only on skills may not produce desired results, as skills are only part of the equation for creating effective managers.

The true test of whether a management development program has been successful is evidenced in an individual's ability to apply these skills in practice and to achieve desired results. In other words, the desired outcome from any management development program is behavioral change.

Shaping the Corporate Culture

One of the most powerful uses of management development programs is to help articulate and communicate the corporate culture. Programs may communicate culture by various means, such as by using example cases to describe "the GE way" or "the H-P" way and identifying "heroes" who personify corporate values and serve as models to be emulated.

The very act of implementing a management development program communicates that the company values training and that it expects the management team to work to continuously improve its skills. These are both values that can greatly assist a firm as it continues to grow and develop.

At Domino's, "hustle" is the predominant attitude, and its management development programs inspire it. One manager-in-training requirement—skills in pizza making—is one of the most celebrated events in a national competition held annually. This reinforces the training program, which, in turn, instills the Domino's style and culture.

Promoting Leadership Style

Another major function of management development is to communicate the leadership style that is acceptable in the organization. Some firms, such as IBM, promote a version of "contingency theory," which postulates that the appropriate style of leadership depends on the nature of the situation. (This approach is described in Chapter Eleven.) Other organizations promote a single style of leadership. For example, Motorola promotes participative leadership. At Royce Medical the management development program was designed to ensure that as managers began to apply their new skills, they did not lose sight of one of the company's most important values: empowerment. All courses are tailored to help those in management positions apply what they learn in a way that is consistent with using either a participative, consensus, or laissez-faire approach.

Rewarding and Recognizing Managers

Some organizations use participation in management development programs as a reward. Individuals are selected for participation in the program based on their performance. In some cases, organizations may even ask individuals to apply for admission to the program (much like college). A senior management team reviews applications, with participants being selected based on their merit. This approach has been used by Countrywide Financial Corporation, where all applications were reviewed by the COO, Stanford Kurland, who made the final decision about program participants.

In these situations, the program may be held at an off-site location, such as a resort, and the entire event is designed to be a pleasurable experience. At the same time, however, the program participants are expected to develop and use the skills they are learning.

CRITICAL DIMENSIONS OF MANAGEMENT AND LEADERSHIP DEVELOPMENT

Based on our experience in working with managers in a wide variety of organizations, as well as research on the nature and determinants of management success and failure, we believe that there are three critical dimensions that a person must manage effectively in order to be successful at a given level of the organizational hierarchy (described in Chapter Eight). These three dimensions are

1. The person's concept of his or her role
2. The skills demanded by the new role
3. Certain attitudes or psychological factors

We believe that to be successful in a given organizational role, a manager must address each of these critical dimensions in a way that is appropriate for the role and level of the organization at which the individual is operating. In addition, upon being promoted from one level of the organizational hierarchy to the next, the individual must make a transition on all three of these dimensions in order to be successful in the new role. This section examines the specific nature of these three dimensions and the changes that are required for successful career transitions to occur.

Change in Role Concept

The most fundamental dimension of a successful transition to a management role involves changing the concept of one's organizational role from a performing role (doing) to a managerial role (supervising the work of others). This involves understanding and accepting the definition of the new role and learning to behave in new ways. This is an essential prerequisite to becoming an effective manager, but it is not simple.

People do not typically exist independently of their jobs or organizational roles. For most of us, the work we do helps define us to others as well as to ourselves. People ask, "What do you do?" We tend to answer, "I am an accountant (salesperson, engineer, manager, and so on)." They ask what we do, and we describe what we *are,* because our professional roles are fused with our overall identity. It is not surprising, then, that when we change occupational roles we have some difficulty in making the transition from being the kind of person we were in our old role to being a new kind of person as required by our new role.

Part of the difficulty involved in making a successful transition from an old role to a new one involves the very way we think about our job or role. A *role* is a set of expected behaviors. This means that we expect people who have the role of manager, president, or engineer to behave in certain specified ways. Similarly, we expect people who occupy the role of accountant, secretary, or clerk to behave in certain ways. These "role expectations" are grounded in our culturally derived concept of the specific roles with which we are concerned.

To be successful in a given role, a person must master the requirements of the particular role: its responsibilities, skills, and even its psychological requirements. Slowly and subtly, the role fuses with the person. Then, abruptly, the person may be promoted and suddenly face the need to master a new role.

When a person first becomes a manager, he or she will be aware, to some extent, that the new role requires different activities, responsibilities, and even new ways of thinking. Unfortunately, however, few people have a very clear or specific concept of what those new demands are until some time after they have been in the role, and by the time they realize what was required, they may already have failed on the job.

The first challenge facing any person who is making the transition to a managerial role is, then, a change of self-concept to reflect the new role. This, in turn requires

1. Developing a clear understanding of the new role

2. Identifying what the new role's requirements mean in terms of how time should be utilized

3. Creating an action plan for change

Whether people are explicitly aware of it or not, a most fundamental and profound change occurs when we make the transition from performing some technical job to doing the job of a manager. It is analogous to going from a player's role to a coach's role in some sport. The player's role is analogous to the doer's role, while the coach's role is analogous to the first-line supervisor's role. Unfortunately, unlike the coach's role in a sport, the manager's role is much more ambiguous in nature. Many new managers are not entirely sure what they should be doing, that is, they don't understand that this new role is truly different from the technical role previously occupied. They, therefore, continue doing what they have done in the past and hope for the best. The first challenge, then, in helping an individual make the *successful* transition to a management role is to clearly define the new role and communicate expectations of performance to the person who will occupy that role.

A second major aspect of a person's role concept that must be changed in a successful transition to a managerial role involves changing the way time is spent. A manager needs to spend more time supervising the work of others and managing his or her area of responsibility and significantly less time doing technical work. Typically, a manager must spend a considerable amount of time in planning (deciding what to do, when to do it, who should do it, and so on), reading materials and reports, meeting with people, training team members, working with direct reports to set goals, and monitoring performance against goals. These are very different types of activities from the performance activities of jobs such as engineer, accountant, and salesperson.

The new manager must first recognize that more has changed than a job title. The new role demands that there be a shift in the percentage of time spent on various activities: more time will have to be spent in meetings and in reading and planning, and much less time in doing technical work. Although this may seem simple for a person to recognize, in practice it is often difficult to accomplish. For example, a person promoted from a position as engineer to the position of "engineering project manager" may enjoy doing engineering work more than performing the new job requirements. When this is the case, the new project manager may continue to focus more time on engineering duties than on supervising the work of others. When this happens, the productivity of the work unit can decrease, even though the manager may feel that he or she is working much harder than in the past. The person may be working harder but is working on the wrong things. Unlike a coach in sports, it is very easy for a manager to step onto the court and start running with the ball. This leaves team members wondering what they are supposed to do.

When becoming a manager for the first time or being promoted to a new management position, a person should request a copy of the job or role description for the new position, then meet with a superior to review expectations. Next, the new manager should determine how best to invest his or her time on the job in order to meet the role requirements. Typically, this will be very different from the use of time in the former role. Finally, an action plan can help—a plan revolving around time use. The plan might also include steps to help the manager learn to accept the new role—an important part of making the transition on this dimension.

Change in Skills Possessed

The second dimension on which an individual needs to focus in making the successful transition to a managerial role involves developing new skills. In this case, focusing on developing the interpersonal and administrative skills required to manage other people is needed. These are very different skills from those required to be effective in a technical role. Further, most individuals have not been exposed to these types of skills, even if they have received formal management education.

Managerial roles require work-related interpersonal skills such as motivation, communication, and leadership. These skills are required in order to supervise people and handle day-to-day people-management issues. Management roles also require administrative skills such as planning, supervising people, conducting meetings, budgeting, performance evaluation and counseling, and control. Individuals must develop these skills in order to be effective in their new roles.

Based on extensive work with managers and organizations over the last twenty-plus years, we have formulated a framework that helps explain the kinds of skills managers must develop at different stages of the organizational career hierarchy. This framework, titled the Pyramid of Management and Leadership Development, is shown in Figure 9.1. The Pyramid of Management and Leadership Development consists of five different levels of skills that managers must develop over their careers to be effective in their roles. These five levels are (1) core management skills, (2) operational management skills, (3) organizational management skills, (4) organizational development skills, and (5) transition management skills.

The *core management skills* are the skills required of all managers, regardless of the organization they are operating in or the level at which they are

Figure 9.1. Pyramid of Management and Leadership Development

operating. These include time management effectiveness, delegation effectiveness, interpersonal effectiveness, and operational leadership effectiveness (see Chapter Eleven for discussion of the nature of operational leadership). They can be thought of as the foundation skills required of all managers, whether at Apple Computer, Pepsico, or a fifty-person quick-print shop.

At the next level of skills in the Pyramid of Management and Leadership Development are the *operational management skills*. These are skills required to manage day-to-day operations and supervise people. They include recruitment, selection, training and coaching, day-to-day supervision of people, motivation, performance appraisal, and management of meetings. Together with the core management skills, these are the skills needed by first-line supervisors to effectively fulfill their roles.

At the next level are *organizational management skills*. These skills include planning, organizing people, designing and effectively using control or performance management systems, management development, financial management, and team building. These are the skills that effective middle managers need to possess.

Senior managers need to develop and be able to effectively employ *organizational development skills*. These skills include strategic planning (see Chapter Seven), organizational planning, organizational design (see Chapter Eight), strategic leadership (see Chapter Eleven), and corporate culture management (see Chapter Twelve). These are "leadership" versus "management" skills because they focus on the long-term development of people and the organization.

The transition to the ultimate organizational career level—the CEO and COO level—requires the development of the final level of skills in the Pyramid of Management and Leadership Development: *transition management skills*. Developing transition management skills involves understanding how to identify the need for transition and to manage individual and organizational transitions. Basically, these skills involve understanding how to manage change. This, too, is a leadership rather than a management skill.

While role concept relates to an individual's behavior, this second dimension relates to helping individuals develop the ability and knowledge needed to effectively execute their roles. Making the successful transition on this dimension typically involves identifying educational opportunities that will provide the individual with the management and leadership skills needed to perform his or her role effectively. This can involve taking a course, reading a book, completing a self-development module, and using other educational methods. The outcome of these efforts should be that the individual develops a clear understanding of what the skill in question is and knowledge of how to use it effectively.

The Pyramid of Management and Leadership Development framework has been the basis for programs at many of our clients over the years, including

Countrywide Financial Corporation, Bell-Carter Foods, Inc. (described in this chapter), Infogix (whose business is described in Chapter Fourteen), and several Head Start agencies.

Change in Individual Psychology

The third dimension on which individuals need to make a transition involves changing one's attitudes from a performance-oriented to a managerial-oriented psychology. Understanding and learning how to manage this dimension has also been referred to as learning how to play the *Inner Game of Management*.[3]

In making the transition on this dimension, we are not suggesting that a personality change is needed. Instead, we are suggesting that those who become managers for the first time or move to a higher level of management need to understand how to *think* like an effective manager. Actors understand that to effectively play a role (and management is, by definition, a role), they need to learn how to think like the character they will be portraying. Although we are not suggesting that individuals in management roles adopt the role of another person, we are suggesting that by understanding how effective managers think, they can greatly increase their effectiveness, while at the same time infusing the role with their own personality.

Making the transition with respect to one's psychology involves learning how to manage three basic needs in ways that are consistent with the manager's role. These three basic needs are (1) how individuals manage their need for control, (2) the source of the individual's self-esteem, and (3) how the individual manages the need to be liked. Each of these three dimensions of managerial psychology is examined, in turn, next.

With respect to the need for control, an individual must make the psychological transition from a situation in which he or she has relatively direct control over results to one in which the control is indirect because it involves the efforts of other people. In a technical or player's role, control over results is at a maximum. For an accountant, computer programmer, engineer, or salesperson, performance frequently determines the results. However, as soon as the position of first-line supervisor is reached, the relationship between personal effort and control over results becomes more indirect and tenuous. This fact is difficult for many (if not most) people to accept, and yet it must be accepted if they are to make the successful transition to a management role.

When this "decreasing degree of control" phenomenon is not accepted, a manager typically tries to reestablish the feeling, if not the reality, of control. For example, the manager may want to be involved in everything or have all significant decisions checked before they are finally made. The results are typically negative in two respects. First, the manager is bogged down in detail and, in reality, is doing not just his or her own job but the work of other people as well. Second, the procedure can lead to lower productivity on the part of direct reports who are continually checking with the boss, as well as to their reduced motivation and professional development. The manager copes with these problems by working harder and harder.

The desire-for-control syndrome is a fundamental problem for many managers. It gets worse as a person moves higher and higher up in the organizational hierarchy, and there are CEOs of some major corporations who never fully make the psychological transition. There are, for example, CEOs of $100 million-plus companies who feel that they *must* interrupt important meetings to sign all checks (no matter how small) because this is the way they satisfy their need for control.

A second psychological aspect of the management transition process concerns the individual's source of self-esteem. A manager needs to learn to derive a sense of self-worth from being the best manager instead of being the best doer. Because a manager's job is to make use of others to achieve organizational goals, that person must increasingly derive personal satisfaction from the performance of direct reports. This is analogous to a basketball coach who derives self-esteem from the team's ability to win a championship rather than from the personal ability to play offense or defense.

Managers also need to learn how to feel comfortable in managing people who may possess greater technical knowledge or skill. Effective managers do not need to be the "best" technicians on their terms. Even if the manager had greater technical knowledge or skill at one time, as people develop and new people are brought into an organization, the manager may be supervising people with superior skills—even technical skills the manager does not possess at all. For example, a marketing manager may be supervising someone who understands the advertising media better than he does, or a controller may be supervising an accountant who has a greater knowledge of computers. It is a personal challenge to accept and feel comfortable in such a situation. However, the best managers understand that their success does not depend on their own technical ability. Instead, it depends on the abilities of those who work for and with them. Therefore, they seek to surround themselves with star performers who can do the work, while the manager focuses on being the best manager.

People who are unable to effectively manage their source of self-esteem tend to hire only weaker people, and this, in turn, can lead to ultimate failure.

The third aspect of managerial psychology on which individuals need to make a transition is learning how to manage one's need to be liked so that it does not interfere with an individual's capacity to be a manager. Specifically, a person may have to overcome the desire to avoid conflict, increase the ability to provide support to people, and learn to feel comfortable in telling or asking people to do the things required to accomplish goals (even if the manager might be met with resistance).

An individual must develop the ability to deal with conflict and not merely avoid it. Many people in our society not only prefer to avoid conflict but actually cannot or will not confront it, because they fear others will no longer like them if they make waves. Yet by its very nature, a managerial role frequently places a person in a situation in which conflict can only be avoided at considerable cost to the organization. A successful manager must develop the capacity to face and deal with conflict. For example, a manager must frequently face the necessity of providing criticism to direct reports and may find this task distasteful. Unfortunately, it may be essential to provide negative feedback to help employees develop.

In spite of this need, people who possess this ability are relatively rare and are sometimes assigned this as a role to play in an organization. One individual, for example, performed the role of "designated critic" at a CPA firm. It was recognized that he had the ability to face and deal with conflict, while many of his partners did not.

Another problem is that many individuals feel uncomfortable in either asking or telling other people what to do because this may lead to conflict if people do not want to do what they are asked. However, it is a manager's job to direct the efforts of others. Managers must learn to manage their need to be liked so that it does not interfere with this task.

An individual must also develop the ability to provide positive feedback to personnel. Our culture does not reward flattery. Indeed, so strong is the cultural taboo against flattery that there is a bias against praise as well. Yet the human need for self-esteem is fundamental, and praise for work done well is a valued reward. The manager must develop the ability to provide legitimate praise to his or her direct reports, because the absence of praise is functionally equivalent to criticism.

Learning how to effectively manage one's psychology or master the inner game of management first involves having a very clear understanding of one's role. Individuals need to understand that the management role requires not only different ways of behaving but also different ways of thinking. Second, individuals need to learn to accept their new role. This typically involves giving up certain activities that the individual was very skilled at and beginning to focus on new and different (management) activities. Third, there is a need to manage one's time in a way that is consistent with an inner game master. This means that time needs to be devoted to setting goals, providing feedback (both positive feedback and constructive criticism), working with people to develop their skills, and planning for one's area of responsibility. In performing these responsibilities, the individual needs to consider, "How does this feel?" Answering this question can help a person identify the psychological aspects of the role that are most problematic so that they can be dealt with.

In some cases, making the transition with respect to managerial psychology can also be facilitated through developing new skills. For example, an individual may exercise too much control because he or she never learned how to delegate effectively. As a result, previous attempts to delegate tasks to others have been unsuccessful. Hence, individuals hold on to most tasks out of fear that others will not complete them effectively. The problem, in reality, lies with the manager's underdeveloped delegation skills.

It is important in making the transition on this dimension that each individual honestly assess how his or her needs might be interfering with the ability to effectively perform the management role. Next, the individual should develop an action plan for overcoming the problems identified.

MANAGEMENT DEVELOPMENT REQUIRED AT DIFFERENT ORGANIZATIONAL LEVELS

The set of skills and behaviors, as well as the mind-set required to be effective, depend on the level in the organizational hierarchy (described in Chapter Eight) occupied by the manager. Moreover, each of these levels of the organizational hierarchy can be viewed by the manager as a different stage of career growth. Therefore, the content of management development programs should differ, depending on the level of managers involved.

For all levels of management, the first step in any management development program or process is to help individuals understand, specifically, what is expected of them in their roles. This step can be completed by giving individuals written job descriptions that communicate performance expectations, meeting one-on-one with those who have recently been promoted to new positions to help them understand their roles, or through conducting group-based management development programs that focus on developing and implementing effective job descriptions. The outcome of these efforts is to ensure that each manager has a clear picture of performance expectations and, more important, understands how to invest his or her time to maximize results.

The first-line supervisory role will, of course, still involve the performance of technical work, but the individual occupying the role of supervisor must make the transition to a role in which the primary responsibilities involve the management of people rather than the direct performance of technical work per se. This is the first level at which an individual must begin to make a personal and professional transition to a different kind of role—one in which he or she is required to think and act like a manager rather than a technician or doer of specific tasks. This is the key management development task at this level. The focus of management development for these individuals will be on the first two levels of skills in the Pyramid of Management and Leadership Development. This is also the time when individuals should be introduced to the concept of managerial psychology (or the inner game). First-line supervisors should be encouraged to discuss the problems they are having in learning to think like managers. They should then be encouraged to develop action plans that will assist them in making the transition on this dimension.

The next level in the hierarchy—middle management—requires a further change in an individual's concept of his or her role, skills, and attitudes. The key challenge at this level is to learn how to "manage managers." With respect to role concept, this means spending an increasing amount of time (over and above that of first-line supervisors) managing the work of others. In this case, the challenge is to learn how to manage through other managers. Middle managers need to develop the skills in the first three levels of the Pyramid of Management and Leadership Development. With respect to managerial psychology (or the inner game), these individuals now need to feel comfortable working through other managers, learning to derive their sense of self-worth from being a manager of managers, and dealing with conflict among other managers (their direct reports and peers). Further, these managers need to learn how to give feedback based on management (since they are supervising managers) versus technical performance.

Positions at the fourth level of the hierarchy include vice president, senior vice president, and executive vice president. These are leadership positions because those at this level focus not only on day-to-day management but also on the strategic development of the business and their team. Because the primary function of the senior management level is to provide leadership and direction for the overall enterprise, the key management development task is to learn the skills of organizational development and strategic planning, as well as how to manage other senior managers. Senior managers have a unique challenge with respect to role concept: they need to learn when to perform as functional or divisional managers and when they need to operate as general managers of the corporation. Senior managers who have not made this transition create problems for their senior management teams because they push for what is best for their functional area or division, sometimes at the expense of what is good for the company as a whole. Senior managers also have the unique challenge of learning how to derive their sense of self-esteem from not only what they do in their functional areas or divisions but also from how the entire company performs. Finally, senior managers must learn how to deal with conflict at all levels, especially the conflict that arises as they attempt to help the organization transition from one stage of development to the next.

At the final or ultimate level of the organizational hierarchy—CEO or COO (also a leadership position)—the key task is to learn how to guide the organization through the inevitable transitions required during its life cycle. There are at least three dimensions to a CEO's or COO's role concept. First, these individuals need to devote time to managing the company as a whole, including helping senior management identify the need for and then manage organizational transitions. Next, these individuals need to serve as managers of the senior management team. Finally, the CEO (in particular) and to a lesser extent the COO need to spend time as the representative of the company to the outside world. In this context, the CEO might be serving on outside boards or participating in community events. He or she might also be dealing with the firm's advisory board, board of directors, or a parent company (if the firm is part of a larger organization). Failure to recognize this last aspect of this most senior management role can be deadly. In one $75 million organization, for example, the president had ignored his responsibilities with respect to the parent firm that owned his company for too long. The larger company flew him to their corporate offices with no explanation for the trip and promptly fired him for lack of performance.

The CEO and COO need to have developed and be able to effectively use all the skills in the Pyramid of Management and Leadership Development. This means, in a sense, that these individuals should be the most skilled *managers and leaders* in the firm.

Finally, those occupying this most senior level of the organization need to learn to live with very indirect control, to derive their source of self-esteem from the entire company's results (even if the individual in question came out of a specific functional area), and understand that not everyone in the firm will like the changes that will inevitably need to be made as the firm grows and develops.

Table 9.1 schematically summarizes the previous discussion linking the five different levels of management with the three critical dimensions of management success. This table shows that as the individual moves from one level of the organizational hierarchy to the next, the role concept must change from a player's role at the entry-level position of a technician to the role of a kind of head coach, as he or she reaches the level of CEO or COO. It also shows that the skills must move from technical skills directly related to the hands-on performance of the task at the entry level to increasingly higher levels of skills shown in the Pyramid of Management and Leadership Development as the individual moves up the organizational hierarchy. Finally, it shows that the individual must also make a psychological transition from playing the role of a follower or doer to that of a leader as he or she moves to the highest levels of the organizational hierarchy. The primary function of management development is to help people make the transitions required at each level of the organizational hierarchy.

Table 9.1. Critical Aspects of Management Development Transitions

Five Levels of Organizational Career Hierarchy	Role Concept	Skills	Managerial Psychology
5. CEO or COO	"Head Coach"—focused on managing the organization as a whole, being an ambassador to the external environment, and on supervising senior managers.	Transition Management Skills: the ability to identify the need for and manage individual and organizational transitions.	• Comfortable with working through the senior management team to achieve desired results. • Derives self-esteem from the success of the company as a whole and from the results of the senior management team. • Has ability to make tough decisions, to provide needed feedback to the senior management team, and to deal with conflict within and outside of the company (effectively manages the need to be liked).
4. Senior Manager	Manager of a major functional area or division. Understands that being effective in this role involves effectively managing one's area of responsibility, as well as being a member of the corporate management team. Understands when to perform as a functional unit or divisional manager and when to act in the role of corporate leader.	Organizational Development Skills: strategic planning; organizational planning and leadership to position the organization in response to long-range needs identified through strategic planning; management of corporate culture.	• Comfortable working through middle managers to achieve the goals of the functional unit or division. • Derives self-esteem from being both the head of a functional unit and a corporate leader. Understands when to play each role. • Understands the need to make decisions that are in the best interest of the company and knows that this may produce conflict within his or her functional unit or division. Knows how to manage this conflict.

(continued)

229

Table 9.1. (*continued*)

3. Middle Manager	Organizational Management Skills: development of managers; departmental planning, organization, and control to produce a coordinated effort to achieve collective goals. "Manager of Other Managers." Understands the necessity of working through other managers, not directly with technical professionals, to achieve results. Spends more and more time on planning, organizing, and coaching.	• Comfortable letting the managers who report to him or her manage the technical professionals within their area of responsibility. Does not feel the need to directly control technical professionals' efforts. • Derives self-esteem from being a manager of other managers. • Manages the need to be liked in order to deal with conflict and provide feedback to other managers.
2. First-Level Supervisor	Core and Operational Management Skills: delegation, time management, recruiting, training, performance appraisal, and supervision. The focus is on managing the day-to-day activities of technical professionals. "Assistant Coach" or "Player Coach"—understands what it means to make the transition from player to coach. Spends more and more time planning, training, and organizing. May dramatically reduce the amount of time devoted to "doer" activities.	• Must give up direct control of result to technical professionals. Instead, works through them to achieve results. • Derives self-esteem from the results achieved by his or her team of technical professionals and from being the best manager. • Is developing the ability to effectively deal with conflict and provide effective feedback to those who report to him or her.
1. Technician	Technical Skills directly related to hands-on performance of tasks. "Player" (Doer)—100% of the individual's time is devoted to doing work rather than supervising it.	• Has direct control over results. • Self-esteem is based on the person's individual efforts. • Believes that being liked will get him or her ahead (avoids conflict).

BELL-CARTER FOODS, INC.: MANAGEMENT DEVELOPMENT IN THE TRANSITION TO PROFESSIONAL MANAGEMENT

To illustrate the role of management development in making the transition from an entrepreneurship to a professionally managed organization, we examine the way it was and is being used at Bell-Carter Foods, Inc. (Bell-Carter). Tim and Jud Carter—the grandsons of the firm's founders—implemented management development as part of an overall strategy to professionalize the firm.

Corporate Background

What was to become Bell-Carter Foods, Inc. was founded as Bell-Carter Olive Company by brothers Arthur and Henry Bell in 1912. The company began as an olive grower, but in 1930 the firm began packing, distributing, and marketing their own olives under the Bell's brand. The olive market expanded throughout the 1950s and 1960s into grocery stores, delicatessens, and supermarkets.

In the mid-1960s, the third generation of the family joined the business with the entry of Tim (in 1964) and Jud (in 1965) Carter. When Tim and Jud entered the company, sales were only $1 million, but the market was continuing to expand. The company continued with modest growth.

By the time Tim and Jud Carter took over the day-to-day management of the company from their father in 1973 (with Tim managing the sales and administrative side of the business and Jud focusing on production and developing and maintaining grower relationships), the company's sales had grown to $6 million. It was at this time that the olive industry began to experience some problems, along with consolidation. In 1958, there were twenty-seven U.S. olive companies, but by the early 1970s, only a few large players remained. Bell-Carter Olives made a critical decision at this time: to focus on private-label versus branded olives. The Carter brothers determined that the margins in branded olives were so thin that the best they could do was to break even. Private label held greater opportunities.

The company continued to grow on the strength of its dominance in the private-label market. In 1990, the company acquired the operating assets of Olives, Inc., and, in 1992, the firm acquired Lindsay Olive Company, one of the most recognized brands of olives in the United States, when it came up for sale. At the time of the Lindsay acquisition, Bell-Carter's revenues were $53 million. One year later, they had grown to $85 million.

Throughout Tim and Jud's tenure as managers at the firm, they had focused on building the infrastructure needed to support the growing firm. This included developing the day-to-day operating systems needed for a firm that would continue to grow into the future, as well as ensuring that there were adequate resources to support this growth. One of these key resources was management talent. The focus on developing the capabilities of the management team became even more critical as the firm nearly doubled in size in less than a year, and further growth was seen on the horizon.

Growing Pains

A key step in the process of helping Bell-Carter build the infrastructure needed to take it to the future was developing the capabilities of managers at all levels of the firm. Bell-Carter had a number of managers with strong technical skills (for example, in sales, finance, production, information systems). Some of these same people had also been in management positions in other firms. However, Tim and Jud (who had basically grown up in the company) felt that managers at all levels (including themselves) could benefit from a more formal, systematic approach to their development. There were people in management positions who did not yet have the management skills needed to help the firm become more professionally managed.

Managers (especially those at the more senior levels of the company) had become stretched thin by the firm's growth. They were working hard, but many felt that there were never enough hours in the day to get everything done. Fighting fires had become a part of the firm's culture. Managers did not necessarily understand how to manage their time effectively, and the strategic planning process was not as developed as it needed to be.

The management team, especially Tim and Jud, felt under enormous pressure to keep the firm moving ahead. This was leading to tension within the management team as they struggled to take the firm to the next level while at the same time dealing with its continued growth.

Objectives of Bell-Carter's Management Development Program

Although some members of Bell-Carter's management team had received some formal management training (for example, from business schools, professional organizations), others had received little training. Their management skills had been developed on the job. Most members of the senior and middle management teams felt that they were not doing a bad job supervising their teams and helping to manage the company, but most felt that they could be better. First-line supervisors, for the most part, had never been exposed to any type of management development. Therefore, it was felt that they would receive the most benefits. Tim, Jud, and their senior management team believed that developing management talent would be an essential ingredient in helping the firm make the transition to its next stage of development.

The program, then, would be designed to meet the needs of managers at all levels throughout the firm. It would have the following objectives:

- To help participants better understand their roles as managers
- To provide participants with a set of management skills and tools that they could use in effectively supervising their teams and managing their areas of responsibility
- To help participants understand and adopt a managerial mind-set, consistent with their roles
- To develop a language of management development, which would allow individuals throughout the company to provide feedback to one another and help the entire team grow
- To help the firm develop a culture consistent with becoming a professionalized firm

Understand the Management Role. One of the major objectives of Bell-Carter's management development program was to help managers better understand the nature of their roles. Although many individuals occupied managerial positions, they had not yet begun to think or behave like leaders. There was concern that too much of managers' time was being devoted to doing work, and not enough time was being devoted to supervising work and to planning for the company's long-term development. Individuals in management roles needed to understand that their job was no longer to *do* the work but to supervise it.

Develop Managerial Tools and Skills. Another objective was, of course, to help participants develop their skills as managers and to learn about the tools available to managers. Bell-Carter's senior management team felt that because many people in management roles, especially at the first-line supervisor level, had never before participated in formal management training that their program should begin with the most basic skills (at the base of the Pyramid of Management and Leadership Development).

Develop a Managerial Mind-Set. As is true in many firms, managers at Bell-Carter (even those with previous management training) had not been exposed to the concept of needing to manage their own psychology in order to be effective in their roles. Developing a managerial psychology or learning to effectively play the inner game of management, then, became an important part of the company's management development program.

Develop a Language of Management Development. Tim and Jud Carter felt strongly that managers at all levels of the company, from the two owners to first-line supervisors, should complete the same management training program. To maximize the results that might be obtained from the program, it was felt that everyone needed to "speak the same language." For example, if someone was talking about leadership, everyone should understand what leadership meant. Having this same understanding would allow managers at all levels to provide one another with feedback and hold each other accountable for making the necessary changes in their behavior, skills, and mind-set. If managers at different levels participated in different programs, the ability to provide feedback and hold one another accountable would be limited. In essence, people would be speaking different languages. Therefore, it would be very difficult to reinforce and give feedback on management effectiveness because different managers would have different definitions of what this meant.

Develop a Culture Consistent with a Professionalized Firm. Tim and Jud Carter recognized that the culture of their firm (described in more depth in Chapter Sixteen), which had been and continued to be a strength, needed to be somewhat modified to support the continued growth of the firm. In particular, the company could no longer afford to simply react to its environment. Instead, managers needed to develop the ability to plan for and make needed changes in the firm's infrastructure. Although the company wanted to preserve its emphasis on having fun, there was also recognition that certain aspects of the company needed to become more formalized and disciplined. The management development program was intended to help managers develop the skills needed to support these transitions, while at the same time communicating that certain things will need to change.

Nature of the Program

Bell-Carter's management development program was intended to provide managers at all levels with the basic skills needed to be effective in their roles. The four-day program focused on helping participants

- Understand the nature of the management role and how to perform effectively in this role
- Develop the ability to prepare effective role descriptions for themselves and other members of their team, which would support the strategic plan
- Develop and be able to use effective time-management and delegation tools and techniques
- Improve their leadership effectiveness
- Understand how to improve their interpersonal effectiveness
- Develop the ability to create and manage meetings more effectively
- Understand and be able to apply effective decision-making tools and techniques

Each course in the program was designed to build on the previous course. In other words, the program was intended to build an individual's skills over time. Learning was cumulative in nature.

The program was conducted over a period of six to eight months. The first two days of the program occurred back-to-back, with the third day occurring approximately two months later and the final day of the program occurring two months following day three. This schedule provided participants with the opportunity to apply concepts they were learning in the program and then report back on their progress. The intent was to help reinforce concepts and hold people accountable for applying them. Participants were asked to publicly report on their progress at each session; if they had nothing to report, their peers might ask, "Why?" For most people, the thought of having to admit to a lack of progress in front of one's peers could be a very powerful motivator.

As a part of the program, each participant was asked to complete a series of four questionnaires designed to assess their effectiveness in four areas:

- Overall management effectiveness (including role concept, management skills, and managerial psychology)
- Time-management effectiveness
- Delegation effectiveness
- Leadership effectiveness (using the framework that is discussed in Chapter Eleven)

During the relevant session, each participant received his or her own results, and the group's results were discussed in order to identify particular strengths and limitations.

Participants were also given a program binder that contained note-taking outlines, relevant exercises (intended to assist participants in applying concepts to their work experience), appropriate case studies, and readings. When appropriate, films and role plays were also used. Exercises and other program materials were used both during the program and by participants following each session as a way of reinforcing the concepts presented.

The program was designed to be cascaded through all levels of management at Bell-Carter, beginning with those occupying the most senior management roles. A team of two experienced management educators conducted the first two days with Bell-Carter's senior management team in January, 1994. About three weeks following the beginning of the senior manager's program, Bell-Carter's twenty-plus middle managers attended the first two days of the program. Finally, in February of 1994, Bell-Carter's twenty-plus first-line supervisors completed days one and two of the program. By the end of 1994, all managers at Bell-Carter had completed Phase I of the program, consisting of the first four days described here.

It should also be noted that during 1994, Tim and Jud Carter were participating in one-on-one coaching sessions with the two educators who were conducting the group-based management development program. The purpose of this one-on-one program was to help Tim and Jud focus on the issues of most concern to them (with respect to their own development) and to help them address organizational development issues as they arose.

The senior management team also initiated a formal strategic planning process in the fall of 1994. This program included training in the methodology of strategic planning, along with facilitation of plan development (a process similar to the one used by Royce Medical Corporation and described in Chapter Seven). In the spring of 1995, middle managers were trained in the methodology of strategic planning so that they could better support the firm's efforts in this area.

In early 1995, Bell-Carter decided to implement a second phase of the program (for all those who had completed Phase I). This program consisted of two days of training, held approximately four months apart. The first day of this training focused on reinforcing the concepts presented during Phase I (through exercises and case studies), along with presenting tools and techniques for improving communication effectiveness. The second day of this program focused on control systems and corporate culture management (higher-level skills that Bell-Carter felt could be beneficial to all levels of management). Again, all three levels of management participated in the same program.

Also in 1995, Bell-Carter began implementing what they called a make-up program for new managers (those who had not been in management roles when the first round of the program had begun). This make-up program was essentially a condensed version of the Phase I program, which took place over the course of two rather than four days. Again, to maximize learning, the second day of this program was held approximately two to three months following the first.

These make-up programs continued through 1997. In 1997, it was decided that Bell-Carter would develop the capability to conduct what had now become its own management development program using internal trainers. Two internal trainers were selected and participated in a "train-the-trainer" program, conducted by the consulting firm that had originally designed Bell-Carter's management development program. In 1997, the two internal trainers observed as one of the consulting firm's trainers conducted the original four-day program for a new group of managers. The consultant then provided the internal trainers with coaching on how to deliver each segment of the program. Each trainer also received a training guide, which included information on how to present each topic (including a script), slides, and copies of participant materials. In 1998–99, the consultant observed the two trainers in action as they conducted the four-day program for a group of supervisors. Feedback was provided to help the two trainers continue to improve their effectiveness.

Impact of the Program

Anecdotal information collected throughout Bell-Carter's management development program suggested that it had a significant impact on management effectiveness. By the end of the four-day program, even some of the most skeptical managers felt that they had benefited from using what they had learned. Some of the feedback provided by managers in the original program suggested the following:

- Nearly all those in management positions had developed a greater understanding of and the ability to effectively execute their roles as managers.

- Managers at all levels had improved their ability to manage their time effectively. Some members of the supervisory group benefited greatly from learning how to use a time management system. During the last day of the program, one of the more skeptical middle managers said, "I didn't take this too seriously, but I tried using a time management system anyway. I decided that what would work for me was to put all of the pieces of paper that I had written my to-dos on into a binder, along with a calendar. I also organized information in this binder according to the various tasks I needed to perform. I resisted doing this as long as possible, but I am now so much better organized than I ever have been. The stress has also been reduced."

- Managers at all levels, as well as most other employees within the firm, now had written role or job descriptions organized by key result area. There was no longer any question as to who was responsible for what.

- Managers at all levels were delegating more and doing so effectively.

- There was a greater appreciation for and ability to plan. Managers at all levels were setting aside time on a regular basis to plan for their areas of responsibility and to assist the company in implementing its strategic plan.

- The quality of meetings was beginning to improve.

- Formal decision-making tools and techniques were being applied with success throughout the company.

- Managers understood and took greater responsibility for achieving results and worked with their direct reports to establish more performance-based goals.

Although anecdotal information suggested that progress was being made, Bell-Carter was also able to assess its progress using the results of the questionnaires described earlier. Questionnaires were readministered in 1995 to the original groups of managers (who had completed the program in 1994), and the results showed significantly positive changes in the areas already described.

Postscript

Bell-Carter Foods, Inc. is now a $200 million (approximately) specialty foods company, with three divisions: (1) a division focused on packaging, processing, sourcing, and selling olives and related food products (Bell-Carter Olives), (2) a division focused on packaging, processing, and selling pickles (DeGraffenreid), and (3) a division that does contract packaging (Bell-Carter Packaging). Managers in all divisions have participated in the original management development program, and the in-house trainers are continuing their efforts, in partnership with the senior management team, to build the company's management capabilities.

MANAGEMENT DEVELOPMENT AT DIFFERENT STAGES OF ORGANIZATIONAL GROWTH

This section examines the different needs for management development that companies have at the first four stages of organizational growth.

Stage I

At the earliest stage of growth, most organizations do not have formal management development programs for their people. Management development takes place, if at all, through on-the-job training. Although some management development would be desirable for companies in Stage I, the cost of establishing an in-house training program is usually prohibitive at this point.

In spite of this, Stage I is a good time to begin establishing the organization's cultural attitude toward management development. The firm can hold an annual one-day in-house seminar on a management development topic, or it can support attendance at public seminars. It can purchase and distribute management books to its employees or purchase management magazines for circulation. Employees can also be encouraged to participate in continuing education programs or even acquire MBAs. Most significantly, the founding entrepreneur can serve as a role model and can stress, through words and action, that management development is important in his or her firm.

Stage II

During the early part of Stage II, a firm can continue the same approach to management development that was recommended for Stage I. After the firm has reached approximately $5 million in annual revenues, however, it is probably ready for and can afford some form of in-house management development as well.

The principal management development goal for a Stage II company is to ensure that all its managers understand at least the basic skills of management. At this point most people will be first-line supervisors, that is, they will be managing one level of personnel rather than managing other managers. Such people require training in the fundamentals of supervision, including people management skills (motivation, communication, performance appraisal, conflict management), as well as in basic skills in work planning and organization and personal time management. They should understand the fundamentals of delegation and the need to begin to think and act like a manager rather than a doer. Stated differently, they require development of the skills at the first two levels of the Pyramid of Management and Leadership Development as shown in Figure 9.1.

The principal advantage of using an in-house program to provide this training is that the program can be tailored precisely to the firm's people and their needs. A firm may find it useful to have an outside professional management educator help in designing and implementing the program. The firm can typically find such assistance at a local university.

Stage III

By the time a firm has reached Stage III, it ought to be in the process of developing an in-house program of management development. At this stage, the key organizational development issue is professionalizing the firm and its management systems.

To accomplish the transition to professional management, the organization must change the way it thinks about itself and the way it operates. The founder or entrepreneur will no longer be able to fully manage all aspects of operations personally and must use other managers as surrogates. This does not—or should not—mean that the entrepreneur simply uses these managers as extra "arms and legs" to perform specific tasks; rather, there should be real delegation of authority. The entrepreneur must learn to trust the managers to perform their duties and handle their responsibilities well. This, in turn, means that these people will have to think like entrepreneurs or business people rather than simply as functional specialists. To accomplish this change, some form of management development is typically required. The management development program at Metro Realty, described in Chapter Five, is one good example.

Assuming that an organization has already laid the foundation for management development in Stage II by providing a basic supervisory skills program for its people, a major management development goal for a Stage III company will be to reinforce these basic skills. Such skills are not simply learned once and then fully retained. People get into and out of habits, and skills must be reinforced. For example, one function of the five-year driver's license renewal test is simply to motivate people to read the test booklet again and remind themselves of what they ought to be doing. Although most people probably consider it a nuisance to go through the test, it is likely to make them remember long-forgotten parts of the rules of the road. Doing so reinforces the way they ought to be driving.

The primary goal of Stage III management development, however, is to provide the advanced skills of managerial leadership, strategic planning, departmental organization, and control systems required by people who are or will be managing other managers. The skill of strategic planning was described in Chapter Seven, and effective leadership is discussed in Chapter Eleven. These are the skills at the third level of the Pyramid of Management and Leadership Development.

Stage IV

After a firm has reached Stage IV, it will have a greater degree of discretionary resources. Wise senior executives planning for the successful long-term development of their enterprises will then want to invest considerably in building human assets through management development programs. They will realize that their firms are competing not merely in products and technology but in people as well.

A Stage IV company should have an in-house management development program, that is, a management development program that is designed and delivered to meet the company's unique needs and one in which all managers and managers-in-training participate. The description of Bell-Carter's management development program is a model of the type of thinking that should underlie a Stage IV company's program.

A Stage IV company will typically have its own human resources department and training staff. In addition, most firms supplement their in-house staff by using either outside university educators or consultants to help design and deliver management development services.

The primary goal of a Stage IV management development program is to train and develop people with either a general-management or a senior-management perspective. The need for managers at Stage IV relates to the consolidation of the enterprise, as well as to preparation for future growth and development. There is a qualitative difference in the type of managerial skills and capabilities required by managers at this stage. The skills shown at the fourth and fifth levels of the Pyramid of Management and Leadership Development must be developed by these senior executives.

A Stage IV organization is a very significant entity. A great deal of effort is required to manage the internal organization and the business of such a firm.

To accomplish this task, managers require a holistic perspective. They need to think in terms of the Pyramid of Organizational Development both for the care and feeding of the existing enterprise and for the development of new entrepreneurial ventures that will replicate the growth cycle that the parent company has already gone through.

Training people to think strategically and conceptually about the development of an organization requires a more sophisticated type of management development. It requires the use of case histories and exercises designed to broaden the perspectives of people who are accustomed to thinking in narrower terms as functional specialists. Yet it is essential if a firm is to maximize its chances to grow and develop successfully.

INVESTMENT IN MANAGEMENT DEVELOPMENT

Management development is an investment, and all firms need to make such an investment. The owner of an expensive automobile, such as a Mercedes, for example, would or should be prepared to spend 5 percent of the car's value on maintenance to protect the asset. Managers are frequently far more expensive than cars and other machines, yet companies fail to invest in management development, either as "preventive maintenance" to avoid managerial obsolescence or to enhance managers' skills and, in turn, increase the human asset's value.

Although no precise guidelines can be given, we recommend that a company invest between 5 and 10 percent of its annual payroll in management development. If a firm is investing less than 5 percent, it may experience high personnel replacement costs as a result of the Peter Principle (people rising to their levels of incompetence) and related turnover.

Some managers may feel that these are costly investments, and they are, but the alternative is to incur the opportunity cost of lost profit—a loss frequently caused by ineffective management. For example, one medium-sized consumer products manufacturing company that failed to invest $60,000 in a management development program for all its top managers found it cost the firm $1,500,000 in losses from ineffective management by one member of the group.

SUMMARY

This chapter examines the role of management and leadership development in making the transition from an entrepreneurship to a professionally managed firm. Management development is the process of building the present and potential performance capabilities of managers. However, it also serves the functions of helping to shape corporate culture by promoting a desired leadership style, as well as recognizing and rewarding managers.

There are three key dimensions of management development: (1) role concept, (2) skills, and (3) managerial psychology. Each dimension must change as a person moves through the organizational hierarchy.

This chapter presents a case study of how an entrepreneurial company can use management development to help make the transition to a professionally managed firm. The case illustrates the various functions and uses of management development in making this transition. Bell-Carter Foods used and continues to use the management development program, not only to increase people's skills but also to help create the infrastructure (including culture) needed to successfully support a professionalized firm. Although this is not the only model of using management development, it provides a powerful tool for companies in the process of moving from Stage III to Stage IV. The chapter also examines the different levels of management required at different stages of organizational growth.

As we have seen, an organization does not have to be the size of GE or IBM to invest in and benefit from management development. It must, however, make a serious commitment to management development at a level appropriate for its stage of growth.

CHAPTER TEN

Organizational Control and Performance Management Systems

All organizations, no matter what their stage of development, require some form of control or performance management system.[1] When the organization is very small, the entrepreneur can control what is happening through day-to-day involvement and observation alone. The required coordination and information needed for decision making appear almost by osmosis. The owner has a feel for what is happening, what the problems are, and what needs to be done, and this is enough.

As the enterprise increases in size and gains additional people, however, the entrepreneur's ability to maintain control over all aspects of its operations begins to decrease. The organization begins to experience growing pains related to ineffective control systems. For example, people either deny responsibility for tasks or do everything themselves because there are no clearly defined roles and responsibilities. A company can find that its profits are low, even when sales are increasing; it has no way of knowing where it is financially because formal performance monitoring systems are underdeveloped. A firm may experience a high degree of duplication of effort and decreasing productivity because of poor coordination between people and departments. The entrepreneur begins to feel that things are out of control. All these problems suggest that one of the critical challenges facing entrepreneurs in rapidly growing companies is the need to be able to control what is happening.

Companies hire people, give them specific jobs and responsibilities, and expect them to perform well and achieve the enterprise's goals. However, the managers of successful organizations know that this is not enough. They realize that in order to be reasonably certain that the company's objectives will be achieved, they must have some way of influencing or channeling people's behavior. In short, an organizational control system is required.

Organizations use a variety of methods to gain control over people's behavior, including personal supervision, job descriptions, rules, budgets, and performance appraisal systems. These methods are all part of the organizational control system. Although control and performance management systems are essential for organizational survival and growth, the word *control* may have negative connotations for some people. As a result, the term *performance management* is sometimes used as a proxy for *control*; essentially it means the same thing. In this chapter, we use these two terms interchangeably.

As we explained in Chapter Five, a formalized control system is necessary if a firm is to make the successful transition to a professionally managed firm. This chapter describes the use of organizational control as a managerial tool to help in making this transition. First, we present a framework for understanding how to design a control system. Next, two case studies highlight some of the issues facing a firm in designing control systems at the individual and organizational levels to meet its needs as it grows. We also provide a description of how control systems should differ, based on a company's stage of growth.

THE NATURE OF ORGANIZATIONAL CONTROL

The term control has a variety of meanings. For our purposes, it is defined as the process of influencing the behavior of members of an organization to achieve the firm's goals. An organizational control system may be defined as a set of mechanisms designed to increase the probability that people will behave in ways that lead to the attainment of organizational goals. An organizational control system is intended as a mechanism to help manage the performance of people in organizations, and, as a result, it is sometimes also referred to as a performance management system. This notion brings out two important aspects of organizational control: (1) it is intended to motivate people to achieve goals, and (2) it can only influence the probability that people will behave in the desired ways.

Control Motivates People to Focus on Goals

The ultimate objective of organizational control is to try to motivate or influence people to achieve organizational goals, not to control people's behavior in predefined ways but to influence them to make decisions and take actions that are likely to be consistent with the organization's goals.

Ideally, the objective of the control system is to increase the congruence between the goals of the organizational members (individuals and groups) and the organization as a whole. This is important, because individuals are most motivated to work toward the goals of the organization if, by so doing, they are also able to satisfy their own goals. It should be pointed out, however, that although there is usually some degree of correspondence between the goals of organization members and those of the organization as a whole, total congruence is rarely attained.

Control Influences the Probability of Goal Achievement

There can be no guarantee that all people will always behave in ways consistent with organizational objectives all the time. Rather, there is a specified probability or likelihood that such behavior will occur. Control systems are intended to increase the *likelihood* that people will behave in the ways desired by an organization.

TASKS OF PERFORMANCE MANAGEMENT SYSTEMS

In order to motivate people to behave in ways consistent with organizational goals, control systems must perform three tasks. First, they must be able to influence people's decisions and actions in an appropriate direction. As we have seen, without an effective control system people are likely to make decisions and act in ways that fulfill their own personal needs and goals but not necessarily those of the organization. At Tempo Products, for example, employees and departments did their own thing without considering the needs of the company as a whole. This resulted in a number of people and departments that did nothing at all or that, consciously or unconsciously, worked at odds with the goals of the company. It also resulted in duplication of effort between departments, which contributed to increased costs.

Control systems must also coordinate the efforts of diverse parts of an organization. Even when people are trying to act in the best interests of a company, they may find themselves working at cross-purposes. In one $10 million service firm, there were a large number of rush orders because coordination between sales and production was poor. When orders were rushed, many had to be redone because of mistakes in production, which resulted in unanticipated delays for customers and increased costs for the company. Lack of coordination between shipping and production contributed to shipping delays and the resulting customer dissatisfaction.

The third task of control systems is to provide information about the result of operations and people's performance (performance measurement). This information allows the organization to evaluate results and make corrective changes as required. Even if individuals, groups, and the organization have common interests, problems may occur that require correction. At Metro Realty, for example, managers could not be held accountable for failing to meet their budgets because the information necessary to monitor financial goals was not available. When profits began to decline, the company was unable to take corrective action because it did not have adequate information on income and expenses. At Tempo Products, a lack of adequate information contributed to poor performance and ineffective operations. Employees did not know how to improve their performance because managers were reluctant or unable to provide both positive and negative feedback. The result was that, even when individuals were performing poorly, they continued to operate in the same fashion as they had before the evaluation.

DESIGN OF CONTROL SYSTEMS

A performance management system is a system designed to control some sort of organizational activity, such as sales, production, or engineering. More formally, it may be viewed as a set of mechanisms designed to increase the likelihood that people will behave in ways that help to achieve organizational goals in a specified key result area.

We refer to the activities or functions that a performance management system is intended to influence as the operational or behavioral system. This is simply the target or intended focus of the control system. For example, if we want to control sales, then the operational or behavioral system might be (1) a single salesperson, (2) a sales department, or (3) the entire sales of an enterprise.

In brief, a performance management system is intended to help manage the performance of people in an organization at all levels: individuals, teams, departments, divisions, and the organization as a whole.

Key Components of a Performance Management System

The basic components of a formal system of organizational control are (1) key result areas for the company, department, team, or individual, (2) objectives within each specified key result area, (3) goals that define the specific, measurable, time-dated activities that should occur to support the achievement of each objective, (4) a method of measurement for monitoring the performance of members of the organization, (5) a method for providing ongoing feedback on performance against goals, (6) a method for evaluating performance (at the end of the planning period), and (7) a method of administering rewards to motivate and reinforce performance. These seven components constitute what may be termed a company's core control system—a formal mechanism for planning and communicating objectives and goals, measuring, reporting, and evaluating performance, and rewarding performance.[2] The relationships among these seven components are depicted in Figure 10.1. We now describe the components further.

Key Result Areas

As described in Chapter Seven, key result areas can be thought of as critical success factors—the key factors on which achievement of the mission is based. The first step in management control is to identify the key result areas for the organization, department, team, or individual.

For an organization to effectively develop and use performance management systems, key result areas need to be defined at the corporate, strategic business unit, department, and individual levels of the company. As explained in Chapter Seven, at the corporate level of control, key result areas consist of the six key strategic building blocks of the Pyramid of Organizational Development, as well as financial results. For a manufacturing plant, the key result areas might include production volume, quality, scrap, and safety. For an individual salesperson, key result areas might include sales growth, new business development, customer service, sales documentation, and professional development.

It is important to keep in mind that key result areas are *categories* of activities, not the activities themselves. They tend to be stated in one, two, or three words. Further, as suggested in Chapter Seven, there should be between five and nine key result areas for the company as a whole, for individual departments or divisions, and for individual position-holders.

Objectives

As described in Chapter Seven, objectives are broad statements of what needs to be accomplished within each key result area over the course of the planning

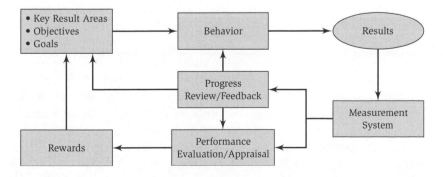

Figure 10.1. Model of Performance Management Systems

period in order to make progress in achieving the mission. Examples of objectives include

- To achieve a satisfactory return on assets
- To grow market share
- To continuously improve management capabilities

Objectives help to direct or channel the efforts of people in an organization to achieve certain results. They are both means to achieve desired ends and a form of ends in themselves.

Goals

Goals are specific, measurable, and time-dated. A goal states what performance ought to be in order to achieve a given objective. The objective of a salesperson may be to generate revenue for the firm, while the goal for the revenue may be last month's (or last year's) sales plus 5 percent. Goals may be based on management judgment, expectations, or historical data.

Goals may be used to establish desired performance levels, to motivate performance, and to serve as a benchmark against which performance can be assessed. For example, "standard costs" can be used in a manufacturing plant as a goal to motivate employees to control production costs and also as a way to evaluate their performance.

Goals are intended to facilitate control both before and after performance. *Pre-performance control* is motivation of performance before the operation or behavioral system is executed. Goals in this area are intended to bring about desired performance levels in people. *Post-performance control* uses goals as standards in evaluating actual performance and as a basis for rewards — the seventh component of organizational control systems.

Measurement System

Measurement is the process of representing the properties or qualities of objects in numerical terms. In organizational performance management systems, measurement has a dual function. One purpose is to provide information that can be used for evaluating performance and making corrections in goal-directed behavior. This is the informational function of measurement. The accounting system, with its measures of financial and managerial performance, is a part of the overall measurement system that contributes to the informational function. That function also draws on nonfinancial measures of performance such as market share, production indexes, and measures of product quality.

Measurement plays another role in control systems. The very act of measuring something has an effect on people's behavior because people tend to pay more attention to the aspects of jobs or goals that are measured. This aspect of measurement may be termed the *process function.* It is related to Marshall McLuhan's notion that the medium is the message.[3] The medium of measurement is itself a stimulus.

An effective control system ought to measure all major goals because of the process function of measurement; otherwise, some goals may be ignored. For example, if a store uses an incentive pay plan that compensates employees on the basis of sales volume as a performance measure, those employees will tend to compete for sales and ignore unmeasured functions such as stock work.

Feedback or Reporting System

The feedback or reporting system is also an important part of a performance management system. A variety of reports, ranging from financial statements to cost reports and performance reports, provide information about the results of operations to management and others. The information contained in these reports is based on the measurements of performance. This information, in whatever form it is presented, needs to fed back to the organization, department, or individual. This feedback loop helps the organization, department, or individual understand the level of performance against goals that is being attained. Regular feedback gives the organization, department, or individual the opportunity to take corrective action in order to increase the probability that goals will be successfully achieved. Even if performance against goals is being measured, if there is no feedback the achievement of goals may only happen by chance.

The results or output of measurement and reporting is to provide a scorecard or scoreboard as a basis for assessing performance. As discussed next, this scoreboard can be used at any level of organizational activity: individuals, teams, divisions, and the organization as a whole.

Performance Evaluation

The sixth component is performance evaluation. While measurement and feedback are occurring on a regular basis, performance evaluation occurs at the end of the planning period (that is, after the due date for the goals that have been established). Performance evaluation is a systematic process by which organizations, departments, and individuals are provided with information on how effective they have been in achieving the goals that have been established for that period of time. Typically, these evaluations include both positive feedback (to reinforce behavior consistent with the successful performance of goals) and constructive criticism (which helps individuals understand what needs to be done to improve their performance).

Evaluative reports generated by the measurement system—containing such items as net income, budgets compared to actual, and return on investment—generally are used in performance evaluation at the organizational and departmental levels. At the end of each fiscal year, senior management should systematically assess overall performance against the goals in the company's strategic plan, using reports generated by the measurement system. In larger companies, the most senior managers of each division and department should complete a similar evaluation. At the individual level, an organization will typically use performance appraisal forms in which individuals are provided with feedback on their performance against their individual goals. The forms should serve as the basis for annual formal performance evaluation meetings between each manager and each of his or her direct reports. Through evaluation, the organization decides how individuals and groups will be rewarded.

The Reward System

Rewards are desirable outcomes of behavior required by organizations. Organizations offer a wide variety of rewards, ranging from monetary items such as compensation or bonuses to recognition and promotion. Rewards can be extrinsic or intrinsic. When people perform tasks because work is interesting or challenging, their rewards are intrinsic. When people perform tasks because of the rewards they expect to receive from others, such as praise or pay, the rewards are extrinsic.

Whatever the nature of rewards, they should reinforce good performance and promote modification of poor performance. For something to be considered a reward, it must be valued by the individual receiving it. For example, if a person values being in charge, he or she might view the opportunity to chair an important committee or a promotion to a management role as a reward. If, however, the person values being part of a team, chairing a committee might not necessarily be viewed as a reward. Further, the rewards that are given must be *seen* as being linked to desired behavior in order to be effective as motivators.

Sometimes organizations fail to offer rewards that motivate people to behave in desired ways, or they offer rewards for one type of behavior while actually trying to motivate another. This has been called "the folly of rewarding A, while hoping for B."[4] For example, a business manager may be rewarded only for not exceeding his budget, even though the firm hopes that he will also pay attention to personnel development. Similarly, an organization that wants to motivate people to be good planners but rewards only "fire fighters" may soon find that some managers have become "arsonists."

Rewards can be useful in motivating employees before behavior occurs because of the expectation of rewards in the future. Once good performance occurs, rewards reinforce the behavior and lead to the greater probability of this behavior happening again. Behavior that is not followed by a reward is less likely to happen in the future.

The System as a Whole

All the components of the performance management system affect the operational or behavioral system for an activity. As shown in Figure 10.1, the first level of control consists of key result areas, objectives, and goals. If a firm, department, or individual does nothing but establish these expectations (and does so in an effective manner), it increases the probability of achieving desired results by about 25 percent. Measurement directs attention toward measured dimensions of goals. It provides information that can be used through the feedback process to help organizations, departments, and individuals take corrective action in order to increase their probability of achieving their goals. If these components are added into the control system (assuming that they are designed well and function effectively), the probability of achieving desired results increases to about 50 percent. If the control system also contains the evaluation and rewards component (assuming that performance evaluations are conducted regularly and effectively and that rewards are valued and linked to desired behavior), the probability of achieving desired results increases to about 80 percent.

THE ORGANIZATIONAL SCOREBOARD

One way of making a performance management system real for people is to convert it into a scoreboard or scorecard. A scoreboard is a device that summarizes all the key results of a game or process, in terms of certain statistical measurements. At a basketball game, the scoreboard shows the points scored by each team, the number of points scored by each player, the total number of fouls by each team and player, and the number of time-outs remaining, as well as the time remaining in the game. In brief, it shows many of the key statistical aspects of the game.

Within business organizations, these scoreboards can be used to provide almost daily feedback to employees about their performance within each key result area and against each goal. These boards, therefore, should contain a list of the key result areas (for the company or department), the goals within each key result area against which performance is being assessed, and the current measurement of performance against each goal.

At an individual level, these scoreboards are most typically contained (or should be contained) in the forms that are used in the performance appraisal process. If an organization relies too heavily on more subjective measures of performance (like judgment, attitude, or leadership) versus more objective measures as reflected in goals that are linked to the individual position-holder's key result areas, the likelihood of achieving desired results (in terms of goals) will be diminished. Further, the evaluation process is much more difficult when individuals need to be assessed on subjective rather than objective criteria.

Illustration of an Organizational Scoreboard

To illustrate the feasibility of applying the scoreboard model of organization control just described, we examine the application of the model in a manufacturing plant. As seen in Exhibit 10.1, the plant has five key result areas: production volume, quality, safety, energy utilization, and scrap.

All these key result areas are different in nature. Production volume is something that can be easily quantified. Energy use and scrap can also be measured but in a different way. Quality and safety require still a different type of measurement.

To use this scoreboard, the company would establish goals for each of these five key result areas and list them in the column titled This Year's Goals. The firm would then show last year's actual performance in the next column. In addition, this year's performance would be tracked on a monthly basis in the adjacent columns.

Virtually any company or any unit of a company can use a format similar to that shown in Exhibit 10.1 to apply the control model to its operations. This approach can be used for the company as a whole, a division, a department, or even an individual such as a salesperson. Indeed, one of the authors observed an example of the application of this framework on a visit to China in 1983 in a chemical plant located in the city of Shanghai. The plant manager was using a blackboard to list the key result areas, current performance goals, prior year's actual performance, and historical best performance, as well as to track the actual performance of the plant to date. Whenever an employee walked past the blackboard, he or she got a quick glimpse at how the plant was performing to date.

Today, some companies provide similar scoreboard information to employees through their intranets. For example, in one Stage III distribution company, employees can view up-to-the-minute information related to orders (including orders shipped, orders backlogged, and so on), sales (including dollar volume, new customers, and size of purchase), and quality (for example, orders returned and defects) on their company scoreboard, which can be accessed from any of the company's PCs. This provides employees with the information they need, on a regular basis, to make adjustments in systems and in their own behavior to better support the achievement of company goals.

Improving the Balanced Scorecard

The organizational scoreboard can be viewed as an improved version of the Balanced Score Card (BSC) that was popularized by Kaplan and Norton and

Exhibit 10.1. Control Model's Application in a Manufacturing Plant

Key Result Areas	This Year's Goals	Last Year's Goals	This Year's Performance											
			Jan.	Feb.	Mar.	Apr.	May	June	July	Aug.	Sept.	Oct.	Nov.	Dec.
1. Production Volume														
2. Quality														
3. Safety														
4. Energy Use														
5. Scrap														

has become widely discussed and used.[5] The basic notion of the BSC is that organizational performance ought to be evaluated from more than simply a financial perspective.

This notion of a BSC was an improvement over the traditional focus on financial performance alone. However, there is a fundamental problem with the original version of the BSC proposed by Kaplan and Norton. Specifically, there is no empirical research to support the factors being proposed in the original version of the BCS to provide balance in performance management. We are implicitly asked to accept them at face value.

The BSC version proposed by Kaplan and Norton is based on the notion that four perspectives ought to be used to evaluate organizational performance: (1) customer, (2) internal business processes, (3) learning and growth, and (4) financial. Although this concept has intuitive appeal, the basic problem is that Kaplan and Norton have not provided any empirical support for these *particular* perspectives. We do not know whether these are the correct perspectives to be used as a basis for assessing organizational performance. This can have serious consequences for organizations. Managers are implicitly being encouraged to focus on these four factors, when others might be more significant.

Instead of the four perspectives proposed by Kaplan and Norton, we believe that the six key variables that make up the Pyramid of Organizational Development ought to be used to provide a truly valid and balanced scorecard. In contrast to the four perspectives of the original version of the BCS, which have not received empirical support, there is empirical evidence to support the six "key strategic building blocks" of successful organizations, as we cite in Chapter One. Specifically, the six key variables making up the pyramid should be used (in addition to financial results) to provide true balance for both performance measurement and strategic management. This should not be viewed as invalidating the original concept of the BSC but, rather, as the next logical generation or iteration of its development.[6] As we know, many products are introduced and then later replaced by improved versions. This is the case with software, where a first release is later replaced with a new and improved version.

DESIGN AND EVALUATION OF CONTROL SYSTEMS' EFFECTIVENESS

For a control system to operate effectively, each of the seven components described must be designed so as to function effectively. This means the following:

- All key result areas must be accurately identified. If one or more key result areas are ignored or not included, the organization will experience problems in achieving desired results. Certain important areas will not receive adequate focus.

- Objectives within each key result area need to reflect what the organization, department, or individual wants to or needs to achieve over the long term. In addition, care needs to be exercised to ensure that objectives within one key result area do not conflict with those in another.

- Goals need to be specific, results-oriented, measurable, and time-dated. In other words they need to be stated in a way that performance against them can be accurately and adequately assessed. Further, all objectives need to have at least one measurable goal.

- A measurement system needs to be in place to assess performance against each goal. If, for example, an organization sets a goal that all of its products need to achieve a certain level of profitability, then the measurement system needs to provide information on product profitability. If the system is unable to do this, the goal is ineffective and either needs to be redefined or a measurement system needs to be created that will allow performance to be tracked against the stated goal.

- Feedback (based on the results of measuring performance) needs to be given on a regular basis. More important, decision makers need to use the information provided by the measurement system to take corrective action to better promote the achievement of the goals. If performance is measured but management does nothing with this information, the control system will break down.

- Performance evaluations need to be conducted at the end of the planning period (which is usually a year) at all levels of the organization. These evaluations need to focus on performance against goals. Further, both positive feedback (which promotes behavior consistent with goals) and constructive criticism (which should result in behavioral change) need to be provided, based on the results achieved against goals. In the absence of performance evaluations, organizations, departments, and individuals will not understand what they can do to continue their effectiveness into the future and to improve their performance.

- Rewards need to be provided, based on the level of goal achievement. It should be clear how rewards are linked to the organization's, department's, or individual's goals. Further, rewards should be established so that they provide something that is valued by those receiving them.

For the control system to function effectively, all parts of this system need to be effectively designed and connected. If any component of the system is poorly designed or is not linked with the other components, the probability that the organization, department, or individual will achieve desired results is decreased.

Increasing Goal Congruence

The effectiveness of a control system is measured by the extent to which it increases the probability that people will behave in ways that lead to the attainment of organizational goals. If a control system sometimes leads to goal congruence and sometimes to goal conflict, it is ineffective, or at least less effective than might be desired.

To be effective, a control system must identify all behaviors or goals that are required to support the organization's continued development and long-term success. If the system does not identify all relevant goals and seek to control them, people may simply channel their efforts toward some desired but uncontrolled behavior. In addition, in order to be effective, the control system must actually lead to the behavior it is intended to (or purports to) produce. For example, a control system may be intended to motivate people toward achieving both a budgeted profit and personnel development. If it produces this effect, it is said to be behaviorally valid. If it leads to behavior that is in conflict with these goals, it is behaviorally invalid. In general, a control system cannot be expected to lead to behavior that is totally consistent with what is desired, but it must have some degree of behavioral validity if it is to be effective.

A control system's effectiveness also depends on the extent to which it repeatedly produces the same behavior, whether this behavior is intended or not. This quality is called the control system's *behavioral reliability.* A control system may have a high degree of behavioral reliability but lead consistently to unintended behavior, or a system may lead to intended behavior but do so irregularly.

Dysfunctional Behavior

When a control system is ineffective, dysfunctional behavior can result. There are two types of dysfunctional behavior: (1) goal displacement and (2) measurementship.

Goal displacement is a lack of goal congruence created by the motivation to achieve some goals sought by the organization at the expense of other intended goals. Goal displacement may be caused by several things, including suboptimization, selective attention to goals, and inversion of means and ends.

Suboptimization occurs when the performance of an organizational subunit is optimized at the expense of the organization as a whole. It is caused by factoring overall organizational goals into subgoals and holding individuals and units responsible for those subgoals. Suboptimization is a common problem and is difficult to avoid in large, complex organizations.

Selective attention to organizational goals is closely related to suboptimization. It occurs when certain goals of the organization are pursued selectively, while other goals receive less attention or are ignored. In this case, a rule or guideline that is part of the control system is followed absolutely, even if it contradicts or prevents achievement of the goal. The original goal is replaced by the goal of following the rules. A third type of goal displacement is caused by the inversion of means and ends. This occurs when a control system tries to motivate attention to certain instrumental goals, which become ends in themselves because of rewards and thereby prevent achievement of other goals.

Measurementship involves a lack of goal congruence created by motivation to "look good" in terms of the measures used in control systems, even though no real benefit is produced for the organization. It involves manipulating the measures used by a control system, that is, playing the numbers game. There are two primary types of measurementship: (1) smoothing and (2) falsifying.

Smoothing is an attempt to time activities in a way that produces the appearance of similar measures in different time periods. For example, a manager may wish to smooth the calculated net income in two adjacent periods. If profit is expected to be unusually high during the first period, this figure can be smoothed by incurring expenditures that otherwise would have been made in the second period in the prior year.

Falsification is the reporting of invalid data about what is occurring in an organization in order to make a person or activity look good in the management system. For example, Enron was charged with manipulating revenues by creating false transactions in order to show good earnings for the stock market. This and similar problems at WorldCom and other companies led to new legislation (Sarbanes-Oxley), described in Chapter Fifteen.

Problems related to dysfunctional behavior point to the importance of designing and implementing effective control systems at each stage of organizational development.

USE OF PERFORMANCE MANAGEMENT SYSTEMS AT THE ORGANIZATIONAL LEVEL: SUPERIOR ALARM SYSTEMS CASE STUDY

This section presents a case study that illustrates the problems that can be created when a company's performance management system is not functioning effectively. It also identifies steps that can be taken to improve specific problems that can exist within these systems, using the framework presented in this chapter.

Superior Alarm Systems is a rapidly growing distributor and installer of electronic alarm systems for automobiles. The firm was originally founded in the early 1990s as an "electronics boutique," where individuals could purchase stereo systems, alarm systems, and other electronic devices for installation in automobiles. With demographic changes, the firm noted a rapid growth in the market for original equipment and replacement alarm systems and by 1995 had totally redirected its focus to just the installation of these electronic systems.

The original location of the firm was a single store in a major metropolitan area in a large western state. The firm had a number of factors that differentiated it from its competition, including the use of original equipment and materials, competitive prices, rapid service, high-quality installation, and field service by means of radio-dispatched trucks. As the firm began to grow, it targeted new geographical markets. By 1996, the firm had organized a franchise operation and had established ten locations throughout the state.

Each of the franchises is organized with a branch manager, a number of installation technicians, and an administrative assistant. The administrative assistant's function is critical to the effectiveness of the operation of the branch because he or she has the primary contact with the customer and is required to relay most of the critical information concerning sales and repairs. The installation and repair technicians are also critical to the effective operation of the firm. Incorrect installation or faulty repair creates significant customer ill will and substantial cost to the company. The so-called branch manager is actually an owner-operator, who has an investment in the franchise. Depending on the size of the branch, the branch manager may also function simultaneously as an installer-technician or even as a salesperson. In some of the larger branches, there may be one or more full-time sales personnel.

By 1999, the firm had grown to approximately $25 million in annual revenue. It was growing at an average rate of 22 percent a year, and because of rapid growth, both in terms of the number of branch operations and in terms of the total volume of sales, there had been relatively little time to develop the infrastructure of the organization.

Development of Control Systems

Certain aspects of the Superior Alarm control systems were more developed than others. The company had developed a relatively sophisticated strategic planning process. The firm had been involved in numerous formal planning exercises over several years since its inception, including planning meetings that involved a considerable amount of discussion concerning problems facing the company, identifying alternatives, assessing their strengths and limitations, searching for information that was relevant, and formulating a broad concept of where the firm wanted to go. These sessions were the basis for the firm's decision to franchise, for example.

One problem with the planning process was, according to the firm's administrative staff as well as the branch managers, that it did not tend to result in a set of specific goals and objectives for the firm or a set of priorities to guide them in carrying out their overall efforts. The frequent complaint was that many of the plans that were made at the beginning of the year tended to be "bumped" by more immediate problems handed down by top management. The introduction of unplanned projects or crises that tended to emerge resulted in shifts in the focus of energy; the result was neglect of many of the projects that had originally been agreed to at the beginning of the year. There was a sense that the firm was making progress but that a great deal of the progress was in an ad hoc or piecemeal manner. The bottom line was that many of the participants in the planning sessions expressed uncertainty about how the content of the meetings would be translated into action.

Although the overall planning process was extensive, there had never been formal consideration of what the company's key result areas ought to be. Accordingly, although the branch managers and, in turn, the installation technicians understood in general what their role was, there was not a specific set of key result areas for which they were held accountable. Similarly, there was not a specific set of goals or objectives for which they were held accountable.

Another problem with the firm's control system related to the nature of its goals: only a few were quantifiable. When goals were measurable, the level of performance expected was frequently unrealistic. For example, the times that were available as "standard times" for installation were thought by all but a few of the most talented and experienced installation technicians to be unrealistic. As a result, many of the employees found the standards to be demoralizing. Moreover, the enforcement of the standards was relatively uneven. Some branch managers tended to stick to standards and to evaluate installation technicians negatively whenever their performance was below standard, which was quite frequently. Other branch managers, who recognized that the standards were not wholly realistic, tended to ignore them.

One strength of the measurement system of the firm was that it was organized on a "responsibility accounting basis." This meant that the firm had good information concerning the profitability of each individual branch. At each branch, the company had institutionalized a monthly financial review of the data. A representative from the home office met with the branch manager and examined the monthly financial report. They also discussed issues involving branch performance on such key factors as market share.

Within each branch, however, the process of performance review was relatively uneven. With the exception of an examination of overall bottom-line profitability, there did not tend to be a review of performance in key result areas that supported that profitability. Discussions of problems would occur as they emerged. There was no systematic attempt to identify the critical success factors of the branch, to measure the branch's performance in each one of those factors, and to examine it in depth.

With respect to performance appraisals of each employee, there was an uneven emphasis by the different branch managers in evaluating their direct reports. Although it was company policy that employees were to be reviewed, based on their performance on a yearly basis, some individuals indicated that over two years had passed since their last review. They also reported that feedback on their performance ranged from some very specific, constructive criticisms to more global assessments of their performance. Many individuals indicated that they were not really sure how they were being evaluated by their managers or whether they were valued or not valued by their managers. One stated, "Well, I'm still here, so I must be doing OK."

At this stage of the firm's development there was not a well-designed compensation program. The administration of compensation increases was on an ad hoc basis. Some individuals had not received a salary increase in more than two years. Further, there were no specific guidelines for salary increases that would be allocated in relation to different levels of performance, such as excellent performance, good performance, or satisfactory performance. Individuals reported that they did not have a clear idea as to how their performance would result in increases in their compensation.

Improvements in the Control System

An analysis of the control system at Superior Alarm indicates a number of problems in the design of that system. There are problems both in the individual components of the control system and in the overall integration of the system. In this section, we examine some of those problems and make suggestions about how they can be solved.

Objectives and Goals. As described in Chapter Seven, objectives and goals are the output of the firm's planning system. A company's strategic planning system should result in a statement of its mission, its key result areas, its objectives, and its goals. In the case of Superior Alarm, the planning system did not provide a foundation for an effective control system in these areas. The basic problem with the planning process at Superior Alarm was that it was not producing a well-defined statement of key result areas. The key result areas are necessary to provide an overall focus for the branch manager and, in turn, for the installation technicians and the administrative assistants. Once the key result areas for each branch are identified and defined, it is necessary to further improve the planning process at Superior Alarm by generating a set of objectives related to each key result area. The next step would be to generate goals related to each objective which, by definition, are specific, measurable, and time-dated. Implementing these steps should help overcome the problems faced by branch managers, installation technicians, and administrative personnel. To help avoid the problem of setting unrealistic goals, the branch manager, installation technicians, and administrative personnel should participate in the process of setting these goals. It is particularly important that great care be devoted to ensuring that the goals are measurable, specific, and time-dated. Otherwise, they will not provide an effective basis for comparison with actual performance.

Measurement Systems. A measurement system permits a company to represent the performance of a branch or individual in quantitative terms. At a company such as Superior Alarm, the measurement system includes the accounting information system, sales management system, and other sources of information. Although there seemed to be ample financial information to assist managers at Superior Alarms, there did not appear to be an adequate source of financial information concerning performance in the branches.

The company should do an analysis of each of its key result areas in order to ensure that measurements are available to assess performance on each of these key factors. The measurements do not all have to be in dollar terms. Some can be in monetary terms; others can be in nonmonetary terms. Some measurements can even be what may be characterized as go–no-go measurements. This means that a manager can do an informal rating of whether something has happened or not happened. For example, customer service might be assessed by the number of written complaints or letters of praise received. Ultimately, the home office might conduct a telephone sample of customers and have the interviewer generate a judgment as to whether the service provided was satisfactory or unsatisfactory. By then tabulating the number of satisfactory versus unsatisfactory responses, we can generate a measurement of branch performance in this key result area.

Rewards. A significant problem with the firm's control system was the lack of linkage between objectives, goals, measurements, and rewards. The firm's compensation system did not appear to be linked to its objectives and goals. Individuals did not perceive that they were rewarded, based on their ability to achieve goals. Because people did not perceive a clear linkage between goal achievement and compensation, there was unlikely to be a great deal of ownership of the goals. People may very well have been motivated, but the firm's reward system was neither enhancing nor channeling their motivation directly toward the goals and objectives that the branch sought to attain.

To improve its control system, the firm should analyze its overall compensation system. To be effective the compensation system should provide incentives for an individual to achieve the objectives and goals that the organization wants to attain. An increasing number of entrepreneurial firms are relying on compensation systems that have a significant component based on incentive compensation. In such circumstances, people are generally provided a base salary that is relatively competitive, as well as opportunities for substantial increases in compensation linked to the achievement of individual and company objectives and goals. Wherever feasible, a company should attempt to tie incentive compensation to measurable factors. However, even where this is not feasible, if management can identify the key factors it wishes people to focus on and indicate how incentive compensation will be based on those factors, it will result in enhanced motivation and performance.

USE OF CONTROL SYSTEMS AT AN INDIVIDUAL LEVEL: THE PERFORMANCE APPRAISAL PROCESS AT SOUTHERN CALIFORNIA PRESBYTERIAN HOMES

The concepts previously presented can be used in the design of employees' performance appraisal process. A sample form that might be used in this process, developed by Southern California Presbyterian Homes (SCPH), a Stage IV nonprofit company that specializes in providing housing and other services for older adults, is presented in Exhibit 10.2. A description of how this form was developed at this company, how it is being used, and the initial response of managers to this process is presented next.

Like many firms, SCPH had traditionally used an employee appraisal form that asked managers to evaluate members of their teams on factors like judgment, leadership, quality of work, and attitude. Each year, managers were asked to provide each member of their team with a score, ranging from 1 to 5 on each of these factors. They were also asked to provide some written comments to support the score they were giving. Even though a score of 3 was considered acceptable performance, as is true in many firms where evaluation is based on more subjective criteria, most employees scored between 4 and 5. In fact, the implicit assumption was that if a person scored below 4, there was something wrong.

Whenever subjective criteria are used to evaluate performance, managers find it difficult to give employees low ratings because, as the criteria are somewhat vague, this can lead to conflict over who is really right.

Exhibit 10.2. Southern California Presbyterian Homes Performance Appraisal Form

Immediate Supervisor: Employee:

For period ended:

Part I: Goals for Each Key Result Area

Note: Performance against the goals listed below will account for 75 percent of the total performance appraisal.

Key Result Area	Goals	Evaluation of Performance
1.	1.	Doesn't Meet/Conditionally Meets/Meets/Exceeds:
	2.	Doesn't Meet/Conditionally Meets/Meets/Exceeds:
	3.	Doesn't Meet/Conditionally Meets/Meets/Exceeds:
2.	1.	Doesn't Meet/Conditionally Meets/Meets/Exceeds:
	2.	Doesn't Meet/Conditionally Meets/Meets/Exceeds:
	3.	Doesn't Meet/Conditionally Meets/Meets/Exceeds:
3.	1.	Doesn't Meet/Conditionally Meets/Meets/Exceeds:
	2.	Doesn't Meet/Conditionally Meets/Meets/Exceeds:
	3.	Doesn't Meet/Conditionally Meets/Meets/Exceeds:
4.	1.	Doesn't Meet/Conditionally Meets/Meets/Exceeds:
	2.	Doesn't Meet/Conditionally Meets/Meets/Exceeds:
	3.	Doesn't Meet/Conditionally Meets/Meets/Exceeds:

(continued)

Exhibit 10.2. (continued)

Part II: Other Criteria

Note: Evaluation of performance against these criteria will account for 25 percent of the total performance appraisal.

Other Criteria	Evaluation of Performance
Job Knowledge and Task Performance: The extent to which I show that I understand the fundamentals, possess the skills, and utilize the methods and procedures required to effectively perform my responsibilities. This includes planning and organizing work to maximize my own and other's performance. *Methods to Measure Performance:*	
Judgment and Decision Making: The extent to which the judgments and decisions I make are made in a timely manner and are appropriate within the context of the situation in which they are made. *Methods to Measure Performance:*	
Leadership and Participative Management: The extent to which I effectively manage or work as a member of my team in accomplishing common objectives. This includes facilitating effective communication and encouraging participation on the part of members of my team. *Methods to Measure Performance:*	
Staff and Employee Morale: The extent to which I respond to staff and employee needs in a timely and consistent manner. The extent to which I promote an environment that encourages people to work individually and as teams to accomplish goals. *Methods to Measure Performance:*	
Willingness to Learn and Improve: The extent to which I display an interest, desire and initiative to learn, attain goals, and grow in job knowledge and skills. *Methods to Measure Performance:*	

Frequently, then, most employees continue to receive favorable performance appraisals, even though they may not be performing at the highest level possible. Further, it is sometimes only by chance that people in these organizations are focused on achieving the organization's goals because their performance appraisal (and typically their compensation) are based on performance against subjective criteria that may or may not relate to goal achievement.

Recognizing that there was a need to develop more objective measures of performance and to focus his team more on the goals of the organization, Gerald (Jerry) Dingivan, president and CEO of SCPH, began a program in 1997 to redesign the firm's performance appraisal process. The first step in this process was to assemble a team of senior managers representing both the home office and the company's facilities, which came to be known as the Performance Management Task Force. The purpose of this task force was to review the current performance appraisal process, including the forms used in this process, and to make recommendations about changes that would make the process more goal-oriented.

Working with a consultant, the task force developed an understanding of what the key components (as described earlier in the chapter) of an effective goal-oriented performance appraisal process should be. Putting this process in place involved several steps, which are outlined next.

Revision of Job Descriptions

Although SCPH had traditionally had fairly detailed job descriptions, the task force determined that an effective performance appraisal process would be best facilitated by using a key result area–based role description format (described in Chapter Eight). Senior and middle managers from throughout the company were provided with training in this methodology and were asked to transform their existing job descriptions into the key result area format. Once each manager had completed a draft of his or her job description, a workshop was held in which each manager was able to obtain feedback from others in order to ensure that the job description accurately reflected the key factors on which that position should be focused. The final step in this process was for each job description to be approved by the manager's immediate superior. Once managers were trained, they worked with the members of their team (supervisors, front-line workers) to help develop key result area–based job descriptions for these positions. In other words, the methodology was cascaded throughout the various levels of the company. The stage was now set to introduce the new performance appraisal forms and process.

Design of the New Performance Appraisal Forms

The Performance Management Task Force met several times to debate what should and should not be included in the new performance appraisal forms the company would use. One thing all task force members could agree on was that the forms should be as simple as possible and that they should include specific goals for which people would be held accountable. The team also felt strongly about the need to move away from numerical scoring of individual performance, at least for a short time. The task force believed that employees throughout the company had come to rely too heavily on using numbers both to just get the performance appraisals done but also as a standard for understanding their performance. The new process should focus both managers and their direct reports on performance against goals, rather than on numbers that represented this performance.

There was also discussion about the need to retain some of the subjective criteria that had been used in the previous evaluation process. The task force felt that some of these criteria were important from a cultural perspective. Five of these factors were, therefore, retained on the performance evaluation form. Although these criteria were retained, the task force also believed that managers should take the time during the goal-setting process to explain or discuss how performance would be measured in these areas. In other words, the goal was to make the evaluation of these subjective criteria somewhat more objective. A decision was made, however, that 75 percent of the individual's evaluation would be based on performance against goals. The remaining 25 percent would be based on performance against the more subjective criteria.

As can be seen in Exhibit 10.2, the form was designed to include the key components of an effective performance management system, plus space for the manager to provide an evaluation. The form provides space to list each position-holder's key result areas (taken from the job description) and space to list up to three goals for which the individual will be held responsible over the course of the coming year. The task force agreed that, at least in the first year of this new process, no individual should be held accountable for more than three goals in any key result area. It was also suggested (when the process was eventually introduced to the firm's entire management team), that managers try to keep the number of goals for any individual to no more than ten. In an effort to keep the form as simple as possible, the task force decided that there was no need to list the individual's objectives on this form (they were included on the job description). Instead, the job description would become an attachment to the form.

Evaluating performance on each goal would consist of circling one of the four statements—exceeds, meets, conditionally meets, or doesn't meet—and then providing comments about why this particular evaluation was given. (Dingivan had added the term *conditionally meets* to the form in an effort to take into account those situations where individuals had given a great effort to achieve a goal but had simply been unable to meet it.) The task force agreed that it was particularly important that comments be included on the form and that they were, in some ways, more important than whatever level of performance had been circled.

Use of the Form

To use the form, managers would meet with each of their direct reports before the beginning of the year to set specific goals. Prior to these goal-setting meetings, key elements of the firm's strategic plan (written in the format described in Chapter Seven) would be shared with each manager. All those in management positions would be asked to establish what they believed their goals should be for the coming year to help the firm achieve its goals. Their immediate supervisor would also prepare a list of goals (organized by key result area) for which they felt that individual should be accountable (in order to support the achievement of the firm's plans). The goal-setting meeting would then take place, and an agreement would be reached between the manager and the direct report (who, in this case, was also a member of the management team) as to what the individual's goals would be for the coming year. For those who occupied technical roles (for example, housekeepers and technicians), it was decided that the "goal" column of this worksheet would contain standards of performance that needed to be met. In other words, goals for these positions would, in a sense, be pre-set. When supervisors reviewed these standards with those holding the positions, the individual in question would also have the opportunity to provide input on these expectations and include additional goals (if appropriate). The idea was to make the performance appraisals of these positions somewhat more programmable.

One concern that the task force had was how to handle a situation in which an individual might not have any goals under a specific key result area for a particular year. It was decided that, in these cases, the manager would simply write in the blank, "see job description." What this meant was that the individual would be held accountable for performance against those objectives that were a part of the key result area–based job description. These objectives would be reviewed as a part of the goal-setting meeting. While the process was being introduced to the management team, it was later decided that managers could choose to include the phase "see job description" within all key result areas if they so desired, even if specific goals were also set. In these cases, the individual in question would be evaluated both on the specific goals and on general performance within each key result area.

As a part of the goal-setting process, managers were also to discuss specifically how they would be evaluating the individual's performance with respect to each of the more subjective criteria. The factors they would be looking at or the behavior they would be looking for were to be recorded in the appropriate space on the performance evaluation form.

At the end of the year, the manager would then complete the last column of the form, thus evaluating the individual's performance against specific goals, relative to the objective listed in the person's job description and against the five subjective performance criteria. Managers would then meet with each direct report and provide their feedback. Space was provided at the end of the form for both the employee and the manager to provide additional comments prior to signing the form. The form would then be submitted to the next level of management for final approval before being sent on to the firm's human resource department.

Training in Conducting Effective Performance Appraisals

It was important that all managers throughout the company adequately understood the new performance appraisal forms and how to use them. To facilitate the effective implementation of this process, the consultant who had been assisting the Performance Management Task Force in the design of the process provided several training sessions on the new performance evaluation process. These sessions took place over the course of eighteen months. Sessions focused on helping managers understand the key components of effective performance appraisal systems, the design of the new form and its advantages over what had been used in the past (from the standpoint of promoting behavior consistent with helping the company achieve its goals), and how to effectively prepare for and conduct effective goal-setting and performance appraisal meetings.

Another important part of these sessions was that they provided managers from throughout the firm with the opportunity to provide feedback on how effectively the new process and forms were working. They were encouraged to make suggestions for changes that might be made so that the forms and the process would better meet their needs. This feedback was collected and reviewed by the Performance Management Task Force. They responded to every idea submitted. Some were used to make minor adjustments in the form or the process that was to be used. Other suggestions for changes were not adopted, but the task force made sure to provide their rationale for not using these ideas.

Results

SCPH fully adopted and is using the new performance appraisal process throughout the company. Although some managers are, at times, still skeptical about the process, most managers feel that this process is much less cumbersome than the one previously used. More important, the new process is helping the firm focus individual efforts on those goals that will be most important to helping achieve its long-term mission.

CONTROL SYSTEMS AT DIFFERENT STAGES OF ORGANIZATIONAL GROWTH

No single control system is ideal for every organization. Each organization is different and requires a different type of system. The major factor that determines the amount of control a given organization requires is the company's stage of growth.

Stage I

Even the smallest organizations need some type of control system, but at Stage I, control typically is relatively informal. Usually, the entrepreneur can exercise control during Stage I simply through day-to-day interaction with people in the organization. By the very fact of constantly being there, the entrepreneur is able to observe what is happening and be on top of almost everything. At this stage, the entrepreneur still knows all the company's employees and is able to observe what most of them are doing and suggest modifications when necessary.

Even in this informal stage, however, the basic functions of control need to be exercised. The organization should have a basic budgetary system and an accounting system. The latter can be a manual system at Stage I, although a computer-based system is preferable. (Several existing software packages are appropriate for Stage I companies.) At Stage I, a company can get by with a relatively informal performance appraisal system, but there ought to be some regular appraisal process.

Stage II

As soon as a firm reaches Stage II, its control needs increase dramatically. The entrepreneur no longer has the time to handle control single-handedly, nor can he or she personally interact with all of the growing number of employees. There is increased need for the kind of coordination that only a formal system can bring. If the entrepreneur fails to recognize the need for a more formal system, the company is likely to experience difficulties.

During Stage II, a company ought to be beginning to develop a formal planning system that includes the basic elements described in Chapter Seven. It also needs a more formal control system to help carry out its plan. It will most likely need to change its basic accounting system to some kind of "responsibility accounting system," which provides information not only on overall financial performance but on product-line profitability and business segment profitability as well.

In Stage II, the evaluation and reward component of the control system must also be developed further. Job descriptions specifying responsibilities are required. Some sort of "management by objectives" approach ought to be introduced, accompanied by a formal performance appraisal system. The firm's compensation program also ought to become more systematic and include an incentive component that is linked to performance. Failure to make these changes during Stage II may lead to the feeling that the organization is out of control.

Stage III

By the time a company has grown to Stage III, it requires more sophisticated and powerful methods of control. This is the stage at which the company must develop a formal control system, along with other components of its management systems.

As we have noted, planning at Stage III needs to be brought down to the level of individual products or profit centers. Similarly, the company's budgeting system needs to be brought down to the level of individual products or profit centers.

The company's accounting information system will typically need to be reconceptualized to provide a greater amount of information for management control. By the time a firm reaches Stage III, it ought to have a well-developed set of management reports dealing with the non-accounting information that is required to monitor the business.

By this stage, performance appraisal linked to management by objectives should be a way of life. A formal performance appraisal system should be in place, and management development programs should have taught the firm's managers how to use it effectively.

If management did not lay the foundation for these systems during Stage II, they will be more difficult and costly to develop during Stage III. If the firm still has not put the systems into place by the time it reaches the later phase of Stage III, it is likely to experience serious growing pains. These may be masked temporarily by continually rising sales if the firm is in a favorable market. Unfortunately, when the market ultimately turns, the company may find itself facing a "scissors effect" of simultaneously reduced revenue and increased costs. This can prove fatal.

Stage IV

By the time a firm reaches Stage IV, its basic performance management system should be in place. Most of the changes to be made at this stage are (or at least ought to be) merely refinements.

The planning system becomes more sophisticated. Moreover, the budget process may be refined to include features such as flexible budgeting (budgeting based on different assumptions about the economy and related level of business). The accounting information system ought to be able to generate accurate, timely, comparative data.

Performance appraisals, oriented toward performance against plan or goals, should be regularly scheduled, and employees should expect that deviations from standard will require factual explanations. An example of the type of performance appraisal process that is appropriate for a Stage IV firm is the one being used by SCPH, described earlier in this chapter.

In short, by the time a company reaches Stage IV, its organizational control system ought to be well developed, functioning smoothly, and in place as an integral part of its overall corporate culture.

SUMMARY

When an organization passes the size at which the entrepreneur can personally function as its control system, the owner will increasingly be stretched thin; with the addition of other employees and managers, the need for coordination will grow. There will also be a need for information about problems being encountered in various aspects of operations, including receivables, inventories (if any), and sales. Thus there will be a growing need for formal controls to supplement the personal involvement of the entrepreneur.

Unfortunately, organizations do not have to be very large before it becomes extremely difficult, if not impossible, for the entrepreneur to perform all functions of the control system. In fact, by the time a company reaches $1 million in annual revenue, it becomes highly unlikely that the entrepreneur alone will be able to exercise effective control. This chapter describes the basic concepts that the entrepreneurial firm can use to develop the type of control systems required at its particular stage of organizational development.

CHAPTER ELEVEN

Effective Leadership

One of the most critical managerial functions in entrepreneurial organizations is leadership. Effective leadership is a prerequisite to successfully making the transition from one stage of a firm's development to another and, for that matter, to operating effectively at any stage. This is true, not only for leadership at the very top of an organization but throughout it as well.

Effective leaders can have many styles. The leadership style of Howard Schultz, chairman and chief global strategist at Starbucks, is very different from that of Orin Smith (now retired), who was initially CFO, then COO and, finally, CEO at Starbucks. Schultz is a classic entrepreneur who is very competitive and focused on creating high performance goals. At the same time, he strikes a balance between having a humanistic approach to management and having the ability to place pressure on his team to achieve great results. Smith was an analytical, mature, professional manager. He shared Schultz's competitive spirit and focus on creating and striving for high performance goals and understood how to motivate members of the Starbucks team to focus on and achieve these goals. But both men were very effective in their roles and contributed greatly to Starbucks' success.

Similarly, the style of Terry Hartshorn, when he was CEO at PacifiCare, was very different from that of Alan Hoops, who was then COO at PacifiCare. Hartshorn was outgoing—very oriented toward the people side of the business and focused on culture and its management. Hoops was also people-focused but more directed to the long-term development of the firm and its day-to-day operations. But both were effective in different ways. In turn, the leadership style of all these individuals is different from that of Jim Stowers Jr. at American Century Investors, who was able to build his company from a new venture to one with many billions of assets under management. Stowers's style was laissez-faire; he set the overall direction for the firm, hired people to help him achieve key goals, and told them to use their own judgment to do the job right.

The key point is that entrepreneurs and members of their organizations must recognize that no one style of leadership is effective and that there are significant differences in leadership style among U.S. organizations.[1] Some leaders, like Angelo Mozilo, founder and chairman of Countrywide Financial Corporation, are incredibly charismatic, while others are quietly effective.[2]

The purpose of this chapter is to provide basic concepts, ideas, and research findings concerning leadership effectiveness, as well as to cite examples of actual leaders who demonstrate effective leadership in organizations. The framework we present is a synthesis of various schools of leadership research. A basic premise underlying our discussion is that the two key factors in effective leadership are (1) the choice of the correct leadership style for a particular situation and (2) the performance of certain key tasks of leadership.

The entrepreneurial manager needs to select a style of leadership appropriate for an organization's current stage of growth. To aid in this selection, we examine the nature of organizational leadership and point out two different types of leadership relevant to entrepreneurial organizations: (1) strategic leadership and (2) operational leadership. We then examine a variety of different leadership styles and the factors that must be considered in selecting a leadership style. We also present some research findings relating to the nature of leadership styles found in entrepreneurial companies. After a brief discussion of leadership theories, we describe the key tasks an effective leader must perform. Next, we present some case studies of leadership in actual organizations. Finally, we consider the nature of effective leadership at different stages of organizational growth.

THE NATURE OF LEADERSHIP

Although many people tend to believe that leadership is an attribute of personality, this has not been confirmed by research, as we discuss later in this chapter. A more fruitful way to think about leadership is that it is a set of behaviors to be performed. In this sense, *leadership* is the process whereby an individual influences the behavior of people in a way that makes them more likely to achieve organizational goals. Under this definition, leadership is an ongoing process, not a set of traits that a person possesses. The process involves understanding, predicting, and controlling others' goal-directed behavior. The leader's ultimate objective is to create a goal-congruent situation—a situation in which employees can satisfy their own needs by seeking to achieve the goals of the organization. Leadership, then, like organizational control, is behaviorally oriented and goal-directed.

As we mentioned, two types of leadership are relevant to the management of entrepreneurial organizations: (1) strategic leadership and (2) operational leadership. *Strategic leadership* is the process of influencing members of an organization to plan for the long-range development of the firm in the six key areas making up the Pyramid of Organizational Development: markets, products and services, resources, operational systems, management systems, and corporate culture. It is oriented toward the development of the organization as a whole and of the organization's ability to function in its environment. Lee Iacocca's performance at Chrysler, Howard Schultz's performance at Starbucks, and Steve Jobs's performance at Apple (after his 1997 return to the company) are examples of strategic leadership. These men created visions for transforming their organizations into "new" types of companies, and all personally embodied this new vision. *Operational leadership,* in contrast, is the process of influencing the behavior of people to achieve operational goals. This dimension of leadership is concerned with the day-to-day functioning of the enterprise.

Both types of leadership are essential for the long-range survival and growth of an entrepreneurship, yet a single individual may not possess the ability to perform both leadership functions. For this reason, some organizations appoint both a CEO, who is responsible for strategic leadership, and a COO, who is responsible for operational leadership. This occurred at Tempo Products, as we explained in Chapter Six. At Countrywide Financial Corporation, Angelo Mozilo (CEO) and Stanford Kurland (COO) had complementary skills, which made for a highly effective duo. Mozilo was extraordinarily charismatic and the source of the company's culture, while Kurland was a true strategic visionary and made development of organizational systems a corporate priority. He was also responsible for assembling many members of the company's senior management team.

STYLES OF LEADERSHIP

More than forty years of research has failed to confirm that there is one style of leadership that is best for all situations. Rather, there are a variety of styles, each of which may be effective or ineffective, depending on the circumstances. This notion has been called *contingency theory* or *situational leadership.*[3]

The following pages describe six basic styles of leadership.[4] These styles constitute a continuum that proceeds from a very directive to a very nondirective leadership style, as summarized in Figure 11.1.

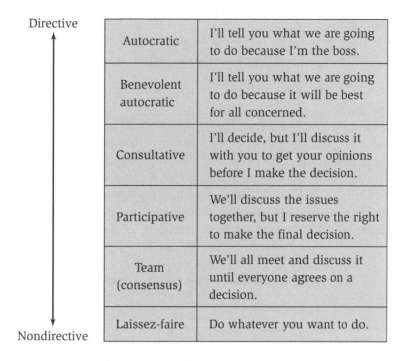

Directive		
Autocratic	I'll tell you what we are going to do because I'm the boss.
Benevolent autocratic	I'll tell you what we are going to do because it will be best for all concerned.
Consultative	I'll decide, but I'll discuss it with you to get your opinions before I make the decision.
Participative	We'll discuss the issues together, but I reserve the right to make the final decision.
Team (consensus)	We'll all meet and discuss it until everyone agrees on a decision.
Laissez-faire	Do whatever you want to do.

Nondirective

Figure 11.1. Continuum of Leadership Styles

It should be pointed out that this is only one of a variety of leadership classification schemes. The major point to draw from it is that in their purest form, these styles are indeed different and may therefore be appropriate for different situations with different personnel.

The Autocratic Style

The autocratic style is a very directive style of leadership. Managers who use this style promote the notion that they have the authority to make all decisions and do not feel the need to explain their rationale to direct reports. This is the "just do it" style of leadership, which can best be characterized by the statement, "I will tell you what we're going to do because I'm the boss," or "Look, I'm head of the department; I'm being held responsible. I will tell you what we're going to do, and that's that." The spirit of autocratic leadership can also be captured in the exchange between a COO of a company and another high-ranking corporate leader in the presence of one of the authors: "When I say jump, you say 'how high?'"

This was the style of leadership used by Sam Walton in the early years of his company and by Steven Jobs, during his early years at Apple Computer and initially upon his 1997 return to the company. It is a style commonly observed in Fortune 500 as well as entrepreneurial organizations. For example, the legendary Jack Welsh, the former CEO at GE, at one time was referred to as Neutron Jack because he was quick to make decisions in a very directive manner, affecting many aspects of the firm and its subsidiaries' operations. However, Welsh made the transition to using a much more participative style in his later years at GE.

The first reaction many people have to this style is negative. Why? Because beginning in the late twentieth century, managers were inundated with information suggesting that the way to maximize results was through maximizing the involvement of team members in decisions that will affect them. Although we agree with this, there are also times when managers *must* use a directive style in order to achieve the best results. For example, if a team is faced with a crisis, there may not be time to involve everyone in the decision. Someone must make it. Another example of a situation that may require a more directive style is when a manager is supervising an inexperienced or unmotivated employee. These types of employees require a more directive approach. In a sense, they *want* to be told what to do.

The Benevolent-Autocratic Style

The benevolent-autocratic style is a "parental" style of leadership: the leader acts on the assumption that he or she knows what is best for the organization and the individuals involved. The degree of direction used in this style is essentially the same as with the autocratic style but is more benign. A manager who uses this style will usually explain the rationale behind decisions, whereas an autocratic leader will not. Instead of simply issuing directives, a person adopting this style might say, "I'll tell you what we're going to do, because that will be best for all concerned." Where an autocratic leader might say, "As a condition of coming to work here, you are obliged to accept what I say," a benevolent autocrat might say, "This is what I want you to do and here's why." This is the classic style found in many entrepreneurships during the initial stages of organizational development.

The Consultative Style

The third style of leadership is qualitatively different, at least to some degree, from the first two. This is the first of two "interactive styles" in which the manager solicits input from direct reports but reserves the right to make the final decision. Managers using the consultative style (as opposed to the other interactive style, discussed next) tend to present their teams with information and ask for their response. To illustrate this, suppose a manager is presenting the organization's goals for the coming year. An individual operating with the autocratic style might say, "This is what we're going to do. These are our goals for next year." A benevolent autocrat might approach the situation with, "This is what the organization needs, and here is how it will affect you." In contrast, a manager using the consultative style might say, "Here is what I think our goals ought to be for the next year. What's your reaction?" Having asked this question, the manager then needs to make it very clear that while input is welcome, the decision is still his or hers to make. If this is not clear, problems can arise as direct reports come to believe that the manager was using a more nondirective style in which "all votes were equal."

The Participative Style

A manager using the participative style also reserves the right to make the final decision. However, managers using this interactive style will tend to ask their teams for even greater input. The basic difference between the participative and consultative styles is the manner in which others' opinions are solicited and used. In the participative style, the group actually helps to develop ideas rather than just give input on the manager's ideas. In the consultative style, the manager might come into a group and say, "Here is what I think we should do. Give me your reaction." The manager using a participative style, on the other hand, may have an idea about what the group should do but basically will say, "Here are the problems. Let's discuss them together and come up with recommendations. Then I'll make the final decision."

An example of the participative leadership style can be seen at Infogix (see Chapter Thirteen). There Madhavan Nayar used a highly participative approach with his leadership team. Most decisions were made and most priorities were set by the team as a whole, but in a critical few areas, Nayar reserved the right to make the final decision.

There are certain challenges inherent in using either one of the interactive styles of leadership. First, a manager must be open to the ideas and opinions of his or her team and willing to change perspective, based on these ideas. If the manager's mind is already made up, everyone on the team will know this and will be extremely frustrated by the fact that the manager is making them go through the motions of providing input, even though this input will not be used.

A second challenge is helping team members understand that, although the manager wants their input, the decision is still the manager's to make. This can be difficult to communicate, especially if none of the team's input is used. Whenever this occurs, the manager should make a practice of explaining a decision to pursue a certain course of action, how the information provided by the team was evaluated, and why (in this case) it wasn't used. This will help the team understand that their input was of value and that the manager wasn't simply creating the impression of soliciting input but really wanted or needed it.

The Team (Consensus) Style

The team or consensus style represents another qualitative shift along the continuum of styles. It is the first of two nondirective styles in which the manager provides team members with a great deal of authority in the decision-making process. A leader adopting this style operates as a member of a team in making the decision. The leader's "vote" counts no more than any other team member's vote. A person using this leadership style might say, "Let's meet, discuss the problem, and reach an agreement on its resolution. I will run the group only as a facilitator because I believe that if you all agree to something, you will be highly motivated to achieve it. I will not, therefore, exercise a high degree of authority." A group with a leader who uses this style is thus given more responsibility than in the other styles. This means that the leadership that is frequently exercised by a single individual under the more directive styles of leadership has been delegated as responsibility to a team of individuals.

There are two versions of the consensus style: (1) true consensus (or the jury) style and (2) majority rules. In the true consensus style, everyone on the team must agree on the direction to be pursued or the decision to be made. If there is even one dissenter, the "jury" must continue its deliberations until a true consensus is reached. This form of the consensus style obviously requires a great deal of time. More important, it requires that all team members be trained in how to use effective decision-making techniques. If team members do not understand the steps that should be followed in making effective decisions, they could meet forever and still not decide anything. Finally, it requires that team members leave their egos at the door. People need to be willing to agree to disagree and not feel that they've lost if a decision runs counter to their original opinion.

The second version of the consensus style is "majority rules." Sometimes a team using this style will agree ahead of time that they will vote on a particular issue. A variation is that the discussion will proceed until a consensus has emerged, with or without a formal vote. Whatever course of action the majority of participants selects (again, the team leader's vote counts no more than that of other team members) is the course of action that will be pursued. It is also important that the team agree ahead of time how ties will be broken if they occur.

Although this version of the consensus leadership style tends to be less time consuming than the consensus version, it is not without problems. First, the majority-rules version of the consensus style creates winners and losers. This can significantly disrupt the ability of a team to work effectively together. Second, the losers can, if not properly managed, undermine the team's ability to effectively implement its decision. We have witnessed more than one case of senior managers who left the room after a majority-rules decision was made and told their direct reports, "That's the worst decision we ever made."

The impact of such statements on the organization can be profound. First, the chances of the decision being implemented are reduced. Second, such statements can significantly undermine the image of the senior management team. The organization may come to believe that there is no true team directing the efforts of the company.

This is not to suggest that the consensus style should never be used. Instead, it is to point out that there are challenges in using this style (as there are in using any of the six key styles). These challenges need to be recognized and managed, if the style is to be used effectively. Although this is a complex style, an increasing number of firms have been experimenting with it for a number of years. These include large, established firms such as Delta Airlines and entrepreneurial firms such as Amgen.

The team style of leadership was also used by Jim Stowers Jr. at American Century Investors—a mutual fund, investment-management company—as he built the company from a new venture to one with more than $65 billion in assets. Stowers had long believed in the value of a team approach to portfolio management, and he extended this philosophy to the management of the company, where an increasing number of decisions were made by the firm's executive committee operating as a team. Stowers believed that teams make better decisions than individuals, and he wanted American Century's executive committee to function as a "team CEO." Nevertheless, he reserved the right to use "his extra vote" to make certain decisions.

The Laissez-Faire Style

The most nondirective style of leadership—laissez-faire—places the responsibility for task accomplishment completely on the direct report. A leader using this style essentially says, "Do whatever you want to do," or "Do the right thing."

As was true of the autocratic style, some people's first reaction to this style is negative. Some even question whether such a style represents management at all. They ask, "How can a manager simply tell someone to 'do what you want to do'?" The laissez-faire style, in fact, is quite a powerful style when used in the right situations. If managers have someone who is highly skilled and highly motivated (that is, understands the requirements of the job and has the skills to effectively perform them), then the manager can just let this person "do it." The manager does not need to devote a great deal of time to overseeing this individual's efforts. Instead, the manager's role becomes one of communicating the goals of the company to team members and letting them determine how they will best support them. The manager is still "managing" the team by ensuring that everyone is moving in a direction that will lead to the overall attainment of the firm's goals. However, the amount of time that the manager needs to spend overseeing individual efforts is greatly reduced. The bottom line: if a manager can use a laissez-faire style in a given situation (if the circumstances are right), this will give the manager a great deal of time while also providing the desired results.

There are two versions of this style, one positive and one negative. A leader operating under the positive version promotes the notion that highly trained individuals do not need a great deal of direction. This type of leader thus gives his or her direct reports considerable independence. Such a leader might say, "You are a professional. You know what your job is. Do whatever you have to do to get it done." This is the version of the style that we include in the continuum of styles presented in Figure 11.1.

The more negative version of the laissez-faire style might be characterized by the statement, "Do whatever you want to do. Just leave me alone." This is an "abdocratic" style—an abdication of authority and responsibility. This version of the laissez-faire style should *never* be used. It will do little to help a manager achieve desired results.

Leadership Styles in Entrepreneurial Organizations

Our research and consulting work has shown a wide variety of leadership styles among CEOs and other managers of entrepreneurial organizations. The most common styles, however, seem to be the consultative and participative styles. The participative style seems to be somewhat more common in high-tech manufacturing and service organizations, while the consultative style is more common in low-tech manufacturing. Perhaps as a reaction to the behavioral literature of the 1960s and 1970s, there seem to be relatively few managers who use autocratic or benevolent-autocratic styles. There are, however, still many entrepreneurs who use these directive styles, especially when their firms are in Stage I or Stage II of their development.

Over the past ten years, our work and research suggests that the most effective leaders of larger companies (Stage III and beyond) tend to use a consensus or team approach to leadership for most decisions. But like Jim Stowers Jr. at American Century Investors, they may reserve the right to cast the deciding vote on other decisions (a participative approach).

FACTORS INFLUENCING CHOICE OF LEADERSHIP STYLE

It is important to understand that a manager does not have to always use (and, in fact, shouldn't always use) the same leadership style. The most effective managers have the ability to use a variety of styles, each suited for a particular situation. Understanding the key factors that need to be considered in choosing an effective style to fit the situation helps managers increase their leadership effectiveness. We have found that consideration of six key factors can help managers in entrepreneurial firms decide which style is best at a given time. The first two factors we discuss are the most important; they probably account for 80 to 90 percent of the influence on leadership effectiveness in a given situation.

Nature of the Task

One of the most important factors to consider in choosing a leadership style is the degree of programmability of the task on which the direct report will be working. A programmable task is one in which the manager can describe, in advance, all of the steps needed to complete it. A nonprogrammable task is a creative task in which it is almost impossible for a manager to define the steps necessary for its successful completion. If a task is highly programmable (that is, the optimal steps for its completion can be specified in advance), then a directive style of leadership is appropriate. If the task is nonprogrammable (that is, the nature of the work necessitates a great deal of variation in individual procedures), a directive style may be difficult or impossible to use, and a more participative or nondirective style will be required. In other words, the greater the degree of programmability of the task, the more appropriate it is for a manager to say, "This is the right way to do this task; we know it's right because we've studied it and worked out the best way to do it." Where the task is less programmable, the manager must use a more interactive or nondirective approach.

Nature of the People Supervised

This factor is really made up of a variety of subfactors, including people's skill and education levels, their degree of motivation, and their desire for independence on the job. This latter subfactor refers to the degree to which people prefer to do their jobs on their own and then return with results, as opposed to wanting more interaction, feedback, and supervision. When examining the nature of the situation, each of these factors should be assessed relative to the task that the individual direct report will be performing. For example, a person can be extremely skilled in one area and very motivated, but the task assigned requires a different set of skills. If a manager in this situation uses a nondirective approach, it can lead to a disaster because the person in question simply did not possess the required skills.

Taken together, all these subfactors can be thought of as a single variable: *potential for job autonomy*. The more highly educated, highly motivated, highly skilled, and in need of independence a person is, the greater is that person's potential for job autonomy. Conversely, a person with low motivation, low task-relevant skills, and low need for independence has a low potential for job autonomy.

People with different potentials for job autonomy require managers with different leadership styles. A nondirective style (consensus or laissez-faire) will be most appropriate with direct reports who have a high potential for job autonomy, while a very directive style is appropriate with people who have low potential for job autonomy. A more intermediate style of leadership is needed when direct reports do not fit one or the other extreme.

As stated previously, these first two factors account for about 80 to 90 percent of what managers need to consider in choosing a leadership style. Figure 11.2 shows the relationship between the two factors we have just described and the six leadership styles described in the previous section.

As can be seen in the figure, a high degree of programmability, combined with a low potential for job autonomy, would ideally require a directive style. At the other extreme—low programmability and high job autonomy—a nondirective approach would be most effective. The other two cells show intermediate conditions where an interactive approach would best fit the situation. For example, a person who is highly motivated and working at a job that requires a high degree of nonprogrammability but is not very skilled may require a leader who adopts a style somewhere in the middle of the continuum, either consultative or participative, at least until the person becomes more experienced.

Supervisor's Style

If a difference exists between a supervisor's preferred leadership style and the style of one or more direct reports, it will be difficult for direct reports to justify their own style unless the supervisor allows the use of it. Direct reports may even feel a need to change their own style to make it closer to that of

		Potential for Job Autonomy	
		High	Low
Programmability of Task	High	**Most effective style** Interactive (consultative, participative)	**Most effective style** Directive (autocratic, benevolent autocratic)
	Low	**Most effective style** Nondirective (consensus, laissez-faire)	**Most effective style** Interactive (consultative, participative)

Figure 11.2. Factors Affecting Choice of Leadership Style

the supervisor. In other words, supervisors have a tendency to consciously or unconsciously evaluate their direct reports on the basis of their own leadership styles. The manager in the superior position in such a situation may need to recognize that people can use different styles and still be effective. Further, when an individual finds that the preferred style (given the evaluation of the first two factors) is different from the supervisor's dominant style, this person may need to find a way to help the supervisor understand *why* it important that this style be used. The bottom line: if a manager uses the wrong style in a given situation, the probability that desired results will be achieved is reduced.

Peers' and Associates' Styles

The dominant style of a peer group can also influence a manager's choice of leadership style. For example, if most managers in a particular group use a consultative style and a few use a benevolent-autocratic style, the latter individuals will feel some pressure to change their style to make it more like that of the majority. Again, however, these individuals can work to educate their peers about the reasons behind their use of a different style and its influence on results. Further, if the individuals using the "nondominant" leadership style begin to achieve superior results, concern about their style will be diminished.

Amount of Available Decision Time

People are much more willing to accept a directive leadership style in crisis situations than in situations where nothing needs to be decided in a hurry. If someone in a room full of people says, "I see smoke," people will not expect to be asked to form groups and discuss alternatives for action. Most individuals will probably be quite comfortable with someone saying, "Stand up and calmly walk out the door, down the hall, and out into the street."

Nature (Culture) of the Organization

Each organization has norms concerning the type or types of leadership style felt to be appropriate for its members. These norms affect all members of the organization and are likely to be influenced by the styles of the organization's founder, CEO, or most successful managers.

Leadership Style Is a Choice

The bottom line is that leadership style is a choice to be made. It is a style to be selected, based on the key factors in the situation. There are six key factors that affect the choice of leadership style. They can be analyzed to determine what kind of style would be most appropriate in a particular situation with particular types of personnel. Again, however, the most important of these factors are the first two.

LEADERSHIP THEORIES

In the study of leadership, the initial emphasis was on attempting to identify the personal characteristics of effective leaders. After more than two decades of research, this approach was abandoned in the mid-1950s because a set of consistently valid and reliable predictive factors could not be identified. This does not mean that such factors absolutely do not exist; it could mean that the statistical tools used were not powerful enough to detect them. In any event, the leadership "trait" theory was abandoned, and a leadership "process" approach was adopted. This new approach proved to have much greater predictive value.

The leadership process approach is based on the premise that leaders can be developed. Instead of being born with certain personalities, as the trait theory suggested, this approach suggests that leaders can learn what to do to be effective. Further research was then conducted to determine what differentiates effective from ineffective leaders. Two key factors—task orientation and people orientation—were identified as being important characteristics of effective leaders.

For a time, these two factors defined two divergent schools of thought about leadership. The "school of neoscientific management" argued that concern for task made a leader most effective, while the "human relations school" argued that concern for people and their needs was the critical variable. However, empirical research showed that neither factor alone was sufficient to explain leadership effectiveness. Both factors appear to be important and independent dimensions of leadership. An effective leader needs to be concerned about both task performance and the nature of the people being supervised. These two dimensions of effective "operational" leadership can be subdivided further, as we discuss later.

TWO SETS OF EFFECTIVE LEADERSHIP TASKS

Two different sets of leadership tasks must be performed in organizations. One of these can be termed the "macro" tasks of leadership. These are tasks of what we can call strategic leadership and include establishing a strategic vision for a firm, monitoring and managing the process of organizational development, and managing the corporate culture. The other set is the "micro" tasks—the tasks of operational leadership, which include all of the day-to-day things that must be performed to influence people to produce the products and services that the organization offers to the marketplace.

Key Tasks of Strategic Leadership

There are three key tasks of strategic leadership: (1) establishment of a strategic vision, (2) organizational development, and (3) management of corporate culture. Each of these tasks is described in turn.

Strategic Vision. The first task of strategic leadership involves formulating and effectively communicating a strategic vision. This is a vision of what the firm is likely to become. Drawing on the concepts of strategic planning, we can think of it as essentially akin to a strategic mission statement. For example, the vision of Angelo Mozilo and David Loeb was to create a nationwide mortgage company, even though their firm—Countrywide—then had only two retail stores. Similarly, Howard Schultz's vision was to create an American version of the classic Italian coffee bar and roll it out on a national basis, even though Starbucks then had only two retail stores in Seattle.

Although the development of a strategic vision is a requirement for effective leadership, the content of the vision does not have to be created by the entrepreneur or CEO per se. Many strategic leaders are effective because they create an environment or process through which the "leadership team" creates a vision for the firm. For example, in 1995 (as discussed in Chapter Seven) the senior leadership team at Starbucks created the strategic mission to establish Starbucks as the leading brand of specialty coffee in the United States by the year 2000.

Organizational Development. A second key dimension of strategic leadership involves organizational development. In this context, the term *organizational development* refers to the whole process of influencing the members of the organization to build the various key aspects of the Pyramid of Organizational Development that have been described throughout this book. This strategic leadership task involves making the ongoing development of the organization a way of life. Once the strategic vision has been articulated, the next challenge is to translate that vision into the organization's choices with respect to its markets, products and services, resources, operational systems, management systems, and corporate culture. For example, Stanford Kurland (formerly COO at Countrywide Financial Corporation) initiated and championed an organizational development program designed to help the company continue the transition from an entrepreneurship to a professionally managed firm. The process involved assessing the company's capabilities (using the Pyramid of Organizational Development as a lens), identifying areas that required further development, and developing the management systems (including strategic planning, performance management, and leadership development) required to help the company continue to grow effectively in the context of the larger enterprise it was becoming. In initiating this program, he was performing the organizational development function of strategic leadership.

Management of Corporate Culture. The third key aspect of strategic leadership concerns the management of the firm's culture. This task ultimately falls to the CEO of an entity, whether it is a corporation as a whole or a division. Initially, the culture of a company is formulated and spread by the company's founder. However, when an organization reaches or exceeds a certain size (Stage IV), it must be formally managed, as explained in Chapter Two. At that point a company needs to establish a formal system for culture management. For example, under Stanford Kurland's leadership at Countrywide, the company began a formal system of culture management in 2001. This included creating a statement of the company's culture and establishing culture management as a "priority objective" in the company's strategic plan. The next chapter examines the nature of organizational culture and how it can be managed.

Key Tasks of Operational Leadership

As discussed earlier, research has suggested that effective leaders need to focus on both tasks and people. Exactly what this means in practice, however, can be difficult to understand: What should a manager do in order to be both task- and people-oriented? To help address this question, research has identified five tasks that further define people and task orientations of operational leadership.[5] To be effective as operational leaders, managers must perform all five key tasks, as described on the pages to follow. These tasks must be performed on a regular basis with each of the individual's direct reports. If any task is not focused on to the extent that it needs to be, the likelihood that desired results will be achieved decreases. Each of these tasks can be effectively performed using any of the leadership styles previously defined. As we have noted, the best style to use depends on the situation.

Goal Emphasis. An effective leader emphasizes the attainment of goals through setting goals, focusing on goals, ensuring the effective communication of goals, and monitoring performance against goals. The late Rensis Likert, an internationally noted behavioral scientist, pointed out that to be effective, a leader has to demonstrate a "contagious enthusiasm for the achievement of organization goals." To be an effective leader, then, an individual needs to understand how to set effective goals and to ensure that those responsible for helping achieve them understand them. The concept of effective goal setting was discussed in both Chapter Seven and Chapter Ten.

Note that in performing this task, the effective leader's style can range from autocratic to laissez-faire. An autocratic leader might simply say, "Here are our goals." At the other extreme, a laissez-faire leader might say, "Let's agree on what our goals are, then you figure out how to achieve them." At the intermediate level, a person with a participative or consultative style might say, "Here's what I think our goals should be. What do you think?"

One of our favorite examples of the succinct application of goal emphasis was observed in an executive committee meeting at Surgitek, then a rapidly growing medical engineering subsidiary of Bristol-Myers. Surgitek's CEO was asked how he might implement the concept of goal emphasis. He turned to the vice president of sales and stated simply, "Sell something."

One of the best leaders we have encountered with respect to goal emphasis is Howard Schultz of Starbucks. In the best sense, Schultz is a demanding leader. He not only wants "guns and butter" but "entertainment" as well. Specifically, Schultz wants growth and profitability. At the same time, he wants people to have fun (a cultural goal). Although these things are sometimes at odds, Starbucks has done a very good job overall at all three. This has been accomplished, in part, because goals have been established to drive results in all three areas.

Interaction Facilitation. To achieve desired results, an effective leader must focus on helping people work together effectively and cooperatively. This is the definition of *interaction facilitation*. A key skill in accomplishing this task, then, is understanding how to create and manage effective meetings. It can also involve developing and being able to use team-building skills. Individuals who effectively perform this task understand that there should be agendas for all meetings (distributed in advance) and that all participants should be prepared for whatever discussion will be taking place during the meeting. These individuals also understand how to manage meetings in a way that desired results (for example, decisions and information sharing) are achieved. Someone using a directive leadership style might accomplish this task by saying, "We're having a meeting. This is our agenda, and this is what we're going to accomplish." A more nondirective way to do the same thing might be to act as a facilitator at a meeting, helping to summarize what people are doing and asking nondirective questions.

Unfortunately, many CEOs or other executives tend to dominate meetings, rather than facilitate the process. Either because of their personalities or because they assume it is their role, they tend to lead (direct) meetings. Where this has become dysfunctional, an outside facilitator can be of great help. The key is getting all issues and opinions on the table and then working to resolve them.

Work Facilitation. Performing this task involves providing or helping personnel obtain what they need to achieve their goals. This can be accomplished in a variety of ways, including helping to schedule a task, making suggestions about how it should be done, providing reference materials, and suggesting knowledgeable sources of information regarding task procedure. A very directive way of facilitating work might be to say, "This is the way you should be doing your job." At the other extreme, a person using a laissez-faire style might simply ask nondirective questions or suggest that people look in certain areas for help.

Supportive Behavior. This fourth task of effective leadership involves providing both positive and negative feedback to direct reports on a regular basis. Positive feedback is important, because it serves to reinforce appropriate goal-oriented behavior and thereby increases the chances that the behavior will continue to be performed. Negative feedback, in the form of expressed dissatisfaction with work and constructive criticism, tends to eliminate dysfunctional behavior.

A directive leader might express supportive behavior with "No, John. Don't do it that way. Do it this way." A person using a more nondirective style might handle a similar situation with, "I'm going to have to evaluate what you do on this project. You do a self-assessment at the same time. Then, let's meet and compare notes, and we'll see where we need to go from there." An extremely nondirective approach might be to say, "You've just completed the project. I want you to review your documentation and critique it. What have you done well? What have you done poorly, and how will you better this in the future?"

Personnel Development. The effective leader helps to develop people. He or she motivates people to be concerned about their future development and to analyze their specific needs for development. One way of performing this task that some managers have found effective is to work with each direct report to set at least one goal on an annual basis that relates to improving the person's skills and performance. As was the case with the other factors, the leadership style used to perform this task can range from directive to nondirective, depending on the personnel and the nature of the work being done. A directive approach might be to say, "I think you should go to a management training program." A nondirective approach might be to say, "What do you see as your developmental needs? I want you to think about them and to decide what you want to do to meet them."

Performance of Key Leadership Tasks in Entrepreneurial Organizations

Our research with entrepreneurial organizations has led to certain general findings. We have noted, first, that there is a consistent underemphasis on the leadership tasks of goal emphasis and work facilitation in such organizations.

Perhaps because entrepreneurs are so goal-oriented themselves and understand what needs to be done to achieve these goals, they may expect their direct reports to be equally goal-oriented and, therefore, may not perceive the need to provide further direction. The problem is that if the people who need to be involved in helping the firm achieve its goals do not understand them or do not have the resources needed to effectively work toward them, the likelihood that the firm will achieve desired results is dramatically decreased.

Second, we have found a consistent tendency for the supportive behavior task to be performed in entrepreneurial firms to a somewhat greater extent than is usual. The larger the firm, the more emphasis it is likely to place on the task, which may reflect the "family feeling" that is so prevalent in entrepreneurial organizations—people feel more comfortable discussing performance and providing feedback when "we are all part of the family." Further, there tends to be almost daily interaction in entrepreneurial firms between senior management and other employees. As the firm increases in size, both this interaction and family feeling tend to decrease.

CASE STUDIES OF LEADERSHIP

The previous sections presented a framework for understanding leadership effectiveness. This section examines some case studies of actual managers facing particular leadership problems in organizations of different sizes.

The George Frazer Case

George Frazer was president of Helix Inc., a rapidly growing company that produced high-tech components for a specialized market. George's partner in the enterprise was its founder, Charlie Bowman. Charlie was the idea man whose designs had led to the development of new products. He had brought George in to manage the business on a day-to-day basis.

Before his exposure to the framework on leadership effectiveness presented in this chapter, George was managing the R&D department and Charlie was managing the manufacturing function. This arrangement seemed logical to both individuals, as Charlie had the detailed background and knowledge of the product, while George had been an engineer himself and was responsible for supervising the other engineers, as well as the administrative aspects of the firm.

Unfortunately, the firm was experiencing a wide variety of difficulties. The problems ranged from unsatisfactory profitability (the firm was actually incurring a loss) to morale problems among the staff.

When George and Charlie reviewed their own styles in light of the continuum of leadership styles presented earlier, George concluded that he could be classified as a classic autocrat, while Charlie could be thought of as a laissez-faire manager. Charlie might even be thought of as an "abdocrat." If we examine the nature of the situation in which George and Charlie were managers, we see that George was supervising highly motivated, highly experienced engineers and scientists who did not want or need a great deal of direction. This conflicted with his style as an autocrat. Charlie was supervising a wide range of people in manufacturing. Some of these were highly experienced operators, but most were relatively new and inexperienced. They required a great deal of direction and training.

One option available to the entrepreneurs was to develop new leadership styles. George would have to develop a more nondirective leadership approach, while Charlie would have to become more directive. Another option available was for them to simply reverse roles, with George assuming responsibility for manufacturing, which required greater direction, and Charlie assuming responsibility for R&D. Given the needs of the firm, they chose the latter alternative.

In less than sixty days after the organizational change took place, there was a fundamental change in the situation at Helix. As George stated, "I'm now running manufacturing and telling everybody what to do and they think I'm training them. Charlie, on the other hand, is sitting in his cubicle reading technical magazines and drinking coffee and ignoring the R&D staff, and they think that's just great." In addition to the change in morale, the company turned its profit situation around in very short order. This case study illustrates the very significant impact of leadership effectiveness on a firm's bottom line.

The Ken Walker Case

With an engineering degree in hand, Ken Walker obtained an MBA degree from a very prestigious institution. He was bright and articulate. After a period of considerable success in a number of organizations, he found himself as the president of a rapidly growing high-tech company. The company, which had been purchased by a Fortune 500 organization, was semi-autonomously managed by its parent. The firm was expected to prepare a strategic plan and to submit it for approval, but day-to-day operations were left to the discretion of the senior management of the entrepreneurial subsidiary. The firm had grown rapidly, to become a classic Stage III firm, with revenues in the range of $50 to $100 million.

In his MBA program, Ken had learned about the benefits of "participative management." He understood that there was a great deal of research indicating that when people participate in making decisions, they are likely to experience a sense of ownership of those decisions and are more motivated to help implement them. Accordingly, throughout his career he had attempted to use participative leadership to the maximum extent feasible.

The situation he faced at Technology Systems Corporation, where he was president, was a bit more complex. He reported to an individual by the name of John Mortenson, who was the group vice president and was responsible for overseeing a number of subsidiary companies, including Technology Systems. As is typical of any large Fortune 500 company, there were certain things that Mortenson found he had to tell Ken to do simply to be consistent with overall corporate policy, procedure, and direction. Still, however, Ken felt it was best if he tried to get people to buy into these decisions. As a result, at the weekly executive committee meeting that the firm conducted, Ken would present problems and ask all of his senior executives to participate in making the decisions. In this case, Ken relied heavily on the majority-rules version of the consensus leadership style. For many of these decisions, this approach worked quite well. However, there were times when decisions that were reached by the executive committee could simply not be implemented because of constraints of meeting the requirements imposed by John Mortenson and the parent company. Instead of addressing this issue directly, Ken would simply bring the issue back up to the group and try to guide the discussion in such a way that the group ultimately reached a decision that would be acceptable to John and the parent company.

Over time, people came to perceive that Ken's style was not really one of true team or consensus leadership. They realized that whenever a decision was reached that Ken felt uncomfortable with, for whatever reason, he would keep bringing the decision back to the executive committee. Finally, as a result of an organizational development and team-building effort, Ken was provided feedback that people were aware of this situation and found it frustrating. They felt that too many hours were wasted in meetings reaching so-called decisions that were not really true decisions.

After considering this problem, Ken decided on a different approach. He announced to the group that henceforth there would be several different categories of decisions. One type would be those in which he had to adopt a benevolent-autocratic style. This meant that he would present to the group what he felt had to be done, given the various constraints that the firm was operating under. He would explain why it had to be done and what the rationale was and what the benefits were for everyone concerned. These were to be known as *benevolent-autocratic decisions.* In turn, he expected the members of the senior executive group to support those decisions to the maximum extent feasible.

The second category of decisions were those he termed *consultative decisions*—those where he had a strong view of what needed to be done but could be convinced to change his view if the discussion presented strong enough arguments. The third category of decisions was *participative decisions*—decisions in which the group could meet and decide as a group, but he had to retain the right to make the final decision. The fourth category was to be *consensus* or *team decisions.* These would be decisions in which the executive committee would meet as a group and reach whatever decision the group felt was appropriate, and his vote would simply be one of the group. Although this system of leadership was not a panacea, it resulted in the elimination of what had become a time-consuming process, as well as a process that had become damaging to morale.

The Richard Ferris Case

A classic leadership case and dilemma is found in the history of Richard Ferris at UAL Corporation. When Ferris was CEO of UAL Corporation, he was known as a forceful leader who held strong opinions. He was not known for his ability to build consensus for his views; rather, he expected people to support the direction he provided.

Ferris was brilliant in one function of strategic leadership but unsuccessful in another at UAL. His basic strategic vision was to have UAL make the transition from an airline company to a diversified travel company.

On the strength of this vision, UAL put together a company that included United Airlines, Hertz, Westin Hotels, and the Hilton International hotel chain. This provided the traveler with transportation as well as lodging. In addition, the company had acquired the company that ran its "frequent flier" program (Mileage Plus) and also had its own travel company, Apollo Travel.

Travelers had an incentive to use all of UAL's components because the Mileage Plus program gave credit for mileage when cars were rented from Hertz or the traveler stayed at Westin or Hilton International hotels.

Unfortunately, the brilliance of the strategic vision articulated by Ferris was not matched by equal skill in managing people at UAL. He did not get the support of the pilots and other key people at the airline company. In fact, he alienated many people. Moreover, he did not "sell" his concept to the Wall Street community, and UAL's stock did not reflect the potential value of his strategic concept.

In the late 1980s, Ferris changed the name of UAL to Allegis to reflect the company's reorientation to a diversified travel company rather than merely an airline. Soon afterward, he was forced out and the company's name was changed back to UAL. Hertz, Westin, and Hilton International were sold. Ferris's strategic vision was completely dismantled, not because it did not work but because of a lack of diplomat-level leadership skills to key internal and external constituencies.

THE LEADER VERSUS THE LEADERSHIP TEAM

Another issue concerning leadership in entrepreneurial organizations is whether a single individual can perform all the functions of leadership described throughout this chapter. Although we have seen successful organizations "led" by a single individual, many of the examples of extraordinary entrepreneurial success were the result of a team rather than a single individual's leadership. These include Starbucks, PacifiCare, American Century Investors, and Countrywide Financial Corporation. For this reason, we now examine how the team leadership process worked in these organizations.

At Starbucks, although the single most influential individual in the firm's development was Howard Schultz, the reality was that a three-person team led the organization. The other two people on this team were Orin Smith (initially CFO, then COO, and later CEO) and Howard Behar (senior vice president of retail operations). Some people termed them H2O—a play not only on the initials of their combined first names with the chemical term for water but also a true allusion to their collective role. Schultz was the visionary, Smith brought analytical skills and a more disciplined organizational approach, and Behar was the leader of retail operations. Schultz pushed the envelope of the Starbucks brand, Smith was concerned about the development of operational infrastructure, and Behar was concerned about the development of the retail system. They were all extremely focused on goals and were concerned about the development of Starbucks as an overall enterprise.

For many years, the three had regular Monday night dinners to informally discuss the business and a variety of operational issues. There was discussion, debate, and conflict but, overall, the three functioned well together.

The top management of PacifiCare was also run by a team: Terry Hartshorn (chairman and CEO), Alan Hoops (COO), Rich Lapellis (who ran the California HMO), and John Siefker, who ran aspects of operations. Together, they were known as "the four Musketeers," which suggests not only how they were perceived but how they operated.

As noted earlier in this chapter, Jim Stowers Jr.—founder and chairman of American Century Investors (formerly Twentieth Century Investors)—believed that teams were better than individuals in making investment decisions, and he wanted to extend this idea to the management of his business as it grew. For a period of about eight years, as the firm grew from approximately $5 billion in assets under management to more than $65 billion, the company functioned with a "team COO" concept. This meant that there was not a COO, and the senior executive team made most of the decisions that would typically be made by a COO. During this period, the size of the team ranged from five to twelve people.

In part, Stowers was trying to help the organization make the transition from an era in which he had made all the decisions to one in which the business was simply too complex to be managed by a single individual. Although the team did the overall planning for the firm and made most of the decisions, there were a few sacred cows—policy decisions where Stowers reserved the right to make the final decision. Stowers was willing to change a sacred cow, if persuaded. For example, he had stated that the company would continue to be a "no load, no minimum" mutual fund business. It was well understood that small account balances were unprofitable for mutual fund companies, but Stowers was willing to incur this cost. This was, in part, based on the belief that the small investor would increase investments in the funds over time. However, after analysis of investment patterns showed that many small accounts did not actually increase their investments, he finally relented and supported a minimum investment requirement for funds.

In 1997, after several years of operating under this team COO concept, Jim Stowers Jr. moved up to chairman, and American Century moved to a more traditional COO concept. However, the team approach had worked quite well for almost a decade.

Another example of an entrepreneurial top management team with complementary skills is Countrywide Financial Corporation (Countrywide). The team included Angelo Mozilo (cofounder, chairman, and CEO), Stanford Kurland (COO), and Dave Sambol, who headed the company's mortgage business. Mozilo, who is the most charismatic leader we have encountered in more than thirty-five years of working with organizations, defined the corporate culture and the initial vision for Countrywide. Kurland, who with training as a CPA was highly analytical and visionary in his own right, helped lead the development of Countrywide from an entrepreneurship to a more professionally managed firm with strong management systems, as well as strong operations.[6] Sambol was a legendary manager of the mortgage division at Countrywide. He was focused on operations and execution but also had a strategic and entrepreneurial perspective. Taken together, this was a very powerful managerial leadership team with overlapping and complementary skills. They, in turn, were supported by a very strong next level of management and leadership. For example, Carlos Garcia, formerly CFO, led the creation of Countrywide Bank, one of the faster-growing banks in the United States.

EFFECTIVE LEADERSHIP AT DIFFERENT STAGES OF ORGANIZATIONAL GROWTH

Previous sections of this chapter have presented the basic concepts and research findings concerning leadership effectiveness that are relevant to managers in entrepreneurial organizations. This section deals with the question of how leadership should differ at various stages of organizational growth.

The task of leadership in rapidly growing organizations needs to be viewed from two different perspectives. First, one of the central problems of an organization is to choose the style of leadership that is appropriate to the situation in which the organization finds itself. During the first two stages of organizational growth, we typically find that an organization requires a great deal of nurturing and an open-ended commitment on the part of senior managers to enable it to survive. This tends to be accompanied by a more directive style of leadership. Typically, we find entrepreneurial organizations in which the autocratic or benevolent-autocratic styles of leadership are used during these stages.

As the organization grows to Stage III and becomes professionalized, it tends to bring in functional specialists and people with greater experience. These people usually have significant ideas of their own about how organizations can be managed, and if the organization is to benefit from their abilities, the style of leadership must be transformed from a more directive style to a more interactive or even a nondirective style. In the latter stages of organizational growth—Stages III through VI—we typically see a range of styles from consultative through laissez-faire.

In Stage VII (to be discussed in Chapter Seventeen), which is concerned with the revitalization of organizations, we may again see the initiation of an autocratic or benevolent-autocratic style of leadership. At this stage, the organization is in crisis, and the situation requires some decisive action. At this point, people are more willing to accept direction; they even expect it. Hence, when Lee Iacocca came into Chrysler he was expected to provide decisive—that is, directive—leadership. He was brought in because he had knowledge of the automobile industry and, presumably, the leadership capabilities to help Chrysler overcome its crisis.

We now take a closer look at the leadership requirements during Stages I through IV.

Stage I

During the first stage of organizational development, it is likely that the entrepreneur, either individually or together with a small team, is responsible for all major decisions in the organization, including both operational and strategic decisions. It is also likely that the entrepreneur is in the best position to make most of those decisions. He or she has an open-ended commitment to the business, and the firm is still small enough for the entrepreneur to be on top of almost everything. Accordingly, it is likely that the benevolent-autocratic or autocratic style of leadership is used and is acceptable to most members of the organization.

At this stage, the entrepreneur is probably concerned more with work facilitation and supportive behavior than with the other key leadership tasks. While the organization is relatively small, goal emphasis occurs almost by osmosis—that is, by day-to-day interaction of employees with the founder. Because relatively few people are involved, formal interaction facilitation is not necessary; people interact in the natural course of their transactions. Similarly, personnel development occurs simply as a by-product of on-the-job training and probably does not require formal training programs.

Stage II

During Stage II, it is likely that the style of leadership used in Stage I is still reasonably effective. However, emphasis must increasingly be placed on the performance of the five key tasks of leadership.

It is surprising how soon the clarity of goals begins to break down as organizations increase in size. An organization does not even have to exceed $1 million in annual revenues before this lack of clarity can arise. Thus there will be an increasing need for goal emphasis. Similarly, even with a relatively small number of people, a growing need for interaction facilitation occurs. Meetings for the purpose of communication rather than for making decisions need to be regularly scheduled. During this stage the entrepreneur's time is increasingly filled, but the need for work facilitation does not diminish. Because the organization is high on its own adrenalin, the need for positive support may not be intense, but the rapid growth of the enterprise can lead to hiring mistakes and, therefore, to an increased need for corrective feedback (a part of supportive behavior). The need for personnel development also increases during this growth stage.

Stage III

The critical factor in leadership effectiveness during Stage III is the need to begin making a transition from a directive style to a more interactive style, such as the consultative or participative style. This means that the entrepreneur must begin to give up some degree of control and learn how to delegate authority rather than merely delegate tasks. Delegation of tasks involves telling people what you want them to do, while delegation of authority means letting people assume responsibility for a task, decision, or functional area—letting them have a say in setting the goals to be achieved, as well as in deciding how those goals are to be accomplished.

The transition in the style of leadership that must be made at this stage is complex, and many entrepreneurs never accomplish it. Their failure in this regard places their companies in jeopardy, because organizations outgrow the entrepreneurs' ability to make all decisions. (Changes in leadership style that a CEO must make during this transition are discussed further in Chapter Seventeen.)

Entrepreneurs during Stage III need to begin developing a trained cadre of managers to whom they can feel comfortable in delegating authority. They need to make sure that these managers know how to perform the five key leadership tasks.

Stage IV

The key leadership need in Stage IV is to articulate and spread the company's culture through the organization. This means that managers must be trained to use a more participative or consultative style with their direct reports. The leader also needs to help create and transmit a shared vision of what the company is to become. When the company was smaller, the concept of its future direction could be communicated more informally. By the time a firm reaches Stage III or Stage IV, however, senior management must exercise the process of strategic leadership to develop and communicate this common vision. This can be done through the strategic planning process described in Chapter Seven.

SUMMARY

This chapter defines leadership as a process and presents information that should help managers make that process more effective. We identify six different leadership styles, ranging from very directive to very nondirective, and note that there is no one most effective style; the most effective leadership style in a particular situation is determined by a variety of factors, including the nature of the task being performed and the nature of the people being supervised.

This chapter also discusses the key tasks that effective leaders perform. Effective leaders are both task-oriented and people-oriented. In performing the function of strategic leadership, effective leaders articulate a vision, focus on organizational development, and manage the corporate culture. In performing the function of operational leadership, they emphasize goals, facilitate interaction and work, are supportive of personnel, and encourage personnel development.

Each manager has the potential ability to choose a leadership style to fit any situation and group of people. This ability can be improved by increased awareness of the factors that influence the choice of an effective leadership style and by increased development of the skills needed to accomplish the tasks that effective leaders perform.

CHAPTER TWELVE

Corporate Culture Management

Chapter Six provided a brief introduction to corporate culture and its management through the use of a case study. In this chapter, we focus on defining corporate culture and providing tools for managing this critical system as a firm grows.

Although the concept of corporate culture is abstract and may seem somewhat elusive, it is nonetheless real and can have a decisive impact on corporate success and profitability. Every organization, from a small entrepreneurship to a multibillion-dollar firm, has a corporate culture whether it knows it or not. The corporate culture is much like a personality, in that it changes over time as a result of a firm's own development or changes in the environment that, at times, may send conflicting messages. As we stated in Chapter Seven, for example, strategic planning can shape the culture through providing a vision. However, if the organization's performance appraisal process (a control system) does not reward individuals for pursuing that vision, individuals will receive conflicting messages about their organization's culture and will be left to select their own meaning.

The basic issue is that unless the cultural change process is adequately managed, a firm may find itself with a culture that does not support the goals it wants to or needs to achieve.

In this chapter, we first describe the elements of corporate culture and how culture is manifested in organizations. Next, we provide a description of how culture changes and how this change process can be managed to maintain an organization's effectiveness as it grows. We then provide case studies of steps that several corporations took to begin effectively managing their corporate cultures. In the final section of this chapter, we describe the nature of corporate culture at different stages of growth.

THE NATURE OF CORPORATE CULTURE

As previously defined, *corporate culture* consists of values, beliefs, and norms. *Values* are what an organization considers most important with respect to its operations, its employees, and its customers—the things an organization holds most dear, strives for, and wants to protect at all costs. *Beliefs* are assumptions that individuals hold about themselves, their customers, and their organization. *Norms* are unwritten rules of behavior that address such issues as how employees dress and interact. The corporate culture is, in essence, a guide to behavior, as well as a mechanism for creating expectations for the future with respect to rewards and action.

Although values, beliefs, and norms are constructed around a range of organizational variables, we believe that how the corporate culture is defined with respect to four areas has the most impact on an organization's success. These areas are (1) customer-client orientation, (2) orientation toward employees, (3) standards of performance, and (4) commitment to change.[1]

Customer-Client Orientation

The importance attached to how the company views its customers or clients, as well as the assumptions employees hold about the nature of their customers and clients, can have a profound impact on how the company operates and thus on its success.

Some companies have been very effective at developing and communicating to their employees their values with respect to customers. Employees at Disneyland, for example, refer to their customers as guests. The word was chosen carefully to send a message to Disneyland employees about the company's customer orientation. It is intended to have an impact on the way employees interact with customers; in fact, employees are trained to make customers feel at home. The goal is customer satisfaction, which Disney hopes will encourage them to return to the park in the future.

Southwest Airlines is another company that has, throughout its history, effectively managed its culture with respect to treatment of customers. The culture promotes having fun and was built on "Luv" (a play on the name of the airfield where the company was born). Customers who travel this airline, which offers no-frills, low-cost travel, experience the caring firsthand, from check-in to baggage claim. Flight attendants have been known to play games in flight (like seeing who has the most pennies) and to sing songs. Since 1988, the company has won the airline industry's *monthly* highest customer satisfaction award (the Triple Crown) over thirty times and has won the *yearly* Triple Crown five times (all the time remaining highly profitable).

People (Employee) Orientation

The second critical cultural area is the view people hold about themselves and others within the organization itself. Again, as was true with customer orientation, there are two components to the value: (1) how people are viewed with respect to their roles within the firm and (2) how important people feel. Some companies devote a great deal of effort to satisfying employee needs and making them feel valued. At the extreme, these organizations develop a strong competitive team spirit that is directed at other companies and even at departments within the same company. At the other end of the spectrum are those companies in which employees are viewed as replaceable. Somewhere in between are companies where some employees are considered valuable assets (by themselves and everyone else) but where other employees are considered second-class citizens.

Southwest Airline's culture also has a tremendous impact on its employees. While other airlines may offer higher salaries, employees remain with Southwest because of the emphasis that the firm places on valuing its employees who are, in fact, referred to as internal customers. This value is attributable to the company's former CEO, Herb Kelleher, who was famous for his antics and desire to promote fun. The company has numerous programs, including its Star of the Month (recipients have their profiles posted on the company's Web site) and its annual awards banquet, held to recognize the contributions that employees make to the company's success.

Similarly, the culture at Starbucks also places an extremely high value on the treatment of people, who are referred to as partners. Starbucks uses a variety of tools to manage its culture, including the formal statement of culture presented in Chapter One. Two of Starbucks' six guiding principles deal with the treatment of people:

1. Provide a great work environment and treat each other with respect and dignity.
2. Embrace diversity as an essential component in the way we do business.

Smaller firms like Bell-Carter Foods (whose management development program was described in Chapter Nine) have also successfully managed this important aspect of culture. Tim and Jud Carter are extremely committed to creating and maintaining an environment in which employees feel valued and in which people can have fun. Jud, Tim, and their entire senior management team have traditionally operated with open-door policies, which allow any employee to bring an issue to them. At their corporate offices, Tim holds a wine meeting once a month in which employees can discuss any issue they would like with him or other members of the senior management team. Finally, the company has traditionally made a practice of celebrating in unusual ways senior executives' birthdays. At their plant in Corning, California, Jud's birthdays have been annual events in which employees try to outdo the previous years. Over the years, these parties have included everything from songs written especially for the occasion to having everyone "dress like Jud" (in khaki pants and a blue work shirt, complete with a red wig). All these events and ways of operating help to communicate the value that the company places on its people.

While it is easy to identify firms like Southwest and Bell-Carter where people are valued, it is equally as easy to identify organizations that have problems with their orientation toward employees, because these firms usually experience very high turnover. Conversely, organizations that are successful at making employees feel valued (by whatever means) tend to experience relatively low turnover. (We do not wish to imply that employee orientation is the *only* cause of turnover, but it is often a significant one.) In one $100 million company, for example, employees expressed much fear about the future and felt that anyone below the senior management level was a second-class citizen. Turnover was rampant, not only among the lower levels of the company but also among members of the executive team.

Performance Standards

Performance standards include things like what and how much employees are held accountable for, the level of quality expected in products, and the expected level of customer satisfaction.

Accountability. In some companies, employees believe that they are held accountable only for coming to work on time. In others, employees are held accountable for achieving goals that will help the organization meet its mission. Sometimes the definition of *accountability* can become distorted, as was the case in one $35 million high-tech manufacturing company that had traditionally placed a high value on "commitment." Over time, employees came to believe that commitment meant spending nine to ten hours a day at work, regardless of what they were doing during that time period. The norm was to come to work early and to never leave the office prior to 5:00 (if possible, staying until 5:30) as a way of showing commitment. Although the company had many employees "working," they were having difficulty meeting their goals because employees were focused on an inappropriate standard of performance.

At other companies, like Royce Medical Corporation (whose planning process was described in Chapter Seven), Johnson & Johnson, and GE, people are held accountable, not only for achieving goals but also for behaving in ways consistent with the company's values.

Quality. With respect to quality, at one extreme quality takes a back seat to increasing the bottom line; at the other, companies find themselves in financial difficulty because they want to offer their customers only "perfect products" (for example, "No product will be released before its time").

Product quality was a significant contributor—along with a willingness to adapt the product to meet the customers' needs—to the success of Japanese automobile companies in the United States. While Ford was advertising that "Quality is Job 1," Toyota, Honda, and Nissan were offering products that were perceived by many customers (and rated by independent agencies like J. D. Powers) to be of higher quality (including reliability and dealer service) than those produced by American automakers. In fact, on J. D. Powers' 2006 Initial Quality Study,[2] Japanese automakers were highest ranked in thirteen out of nineteen segments.

There are also companies that profess to have a focus on quality products and service but do not actually operate in this way. In a small high-tech company, each employee wore a button stating, "Alpha Corporation loves contented customers." Yet when faced with a product problem just prior to its introduction, senior management said, "Ship it. We'll fix it after it's been delivered." The company knowingly released defective products, which sent the message to employees that quality really was not valued. Subsequently, employees smirked whenever there were discussions about quality.

Customer Service. With respect to customer satisfaction, some companies believe that customers will be satisfied with whatever product or service is offered, while others believe that there is a need to achieve a high degree of customer satisfaction and have designed systems to promote this.

In one company, the R&D and manufacturing functions were referred to as Field of Dreams. The belief under which the firm's management operated, employees suggested, was that "if we build it, they will buy it." Even when customers continually requested changes to products, the company's reply was: "This is it. Either buy it or don't." Unfortunately, this company was operating in a highly competitive environment. Competitors began taking away market share.

At the other extreme, the dramatic success of Southwest Airlines has been due, at least in part, to a major emphasis on customer service (as well as the ability to design other systems and processes that support offering low-cost, no-frills airfare). Even though other major airlines (most notably United's now-defunct Shuttle on the West Coast and Jet Blue) have copied Southwest's fare structure, they have been unable to consistently duplicate the caring attitude that Southwest employees have for those who fly with them. On other carriers, passengers sometimes are treated with a philosophy that is something like this: "If you want to go to place X, you will fly us, no matter how we treat you." Nordstrom Department Stores also operate in a highly competitive market, and their emphasis on customer service has played a major role in the company's success. American Express is still another company that focuses on customer service. Typically, a single call is all it takes for a customer to resolve a problem.

Commitment to Change

The fourth major cultural element is how a company views and reacts to change. Growing organizations that embrace change as a way of life tend to experience less difficulty in making the required transitions that have been discussed throughout this book. Those in which change is viewed as threatening tend to experience significant problems. In one $100 million organization, for example, the owner-entrepreneur nominally supported the changes needed to take his company into the future. However, when confronted with the need to make changes in his company's planning process, product line, structure (including delegating more decision-making responsibility to members of his management team), and corporate culture, he resisted. Instead of changing, he held on to the old ways of doing things until his firm began to lose market share. When this occurred, he blamed his senior management team and replaced them for the second time in as many years.

THE IMPACT OF CORPORATE CULTURE ON ORGANIZATIONAL SUCCESS AND FINANCIAL PERFORMANCE

Culture has a critical impact on overall organizational success. As Howard Schultz, founder and chairman of Starbucks Coffee Company, has stated: "When people ask me the reason for Starbucks' success, I tell them not want they expect to hear but what I really believe. People are the key to Starbucks' success." The company's culture is based on the notion that the way Starbucks treats its people affects the way its employees (called partners) treat its customers, and, in turn, its financial performance.

Culture influences every aspect of the Pyramid of Organizational Development, and every level of the pyramid has an impact on culture. This is illustrated by the value one $500 million manufacturing firm placed on relationships. One reason this firm had grown so large and been so successful was that the company had developed and maintained good relationships with its customers. As the firm grew, this became not only an important part of the firm's culture with respect to customers but also with respect to its employees. Rewards and, in fact, the organizational structure reflected the value placed on forming effective relationships. On the company's organization charts, there seemed to be no consistent use of the titles given to positions at each level of the organization. Reporting to the president were vice presidents, executive vice presidents, and senior vice presidents. While the responsibilities of these positions did not vary a great deal, the titles were different. So what explained the variation in titles? In talking with people at the company, it appeared that the individuals at any level who had developed the best relationships with those at the next level were rewarded with the most desirable titles. The cultural belief was, "Success depends on developing good relationships," and the structure reflected this.

In this example, the structure developed out of the culture, but in other cases the culture is influenced by the structure. In another case, the organization's culture nominally promoted "being flexible." At the same time, the culture supported a belief that senior management could use any resource needed to accomplish its goals. As a result, the firm did not have a formal organizational chart or job descriptions, even though its revenues exceeded $100 million. (It should also be noted that these are both examples of ineffective structure design, as discussed in Chapter Eight.) As suggested by this example, because culture supports and is supported by all levels of the Pyramid of Organizational Development, an organization cannot just simply decide to change its corporate culture without making changes in its operations and structure.

Organizations that focus on culture and ignore these other areas are wasting their resources. If, for example, a firm decides it is going to make the transition to a culture that rewards planning but fails to design and implement a strategic planning system in which individuals are rewarded for their performance, the culture will remain unchanged.

Corporate culture not only affects all levels of the Pyramid of Organizational Development; it also has a direct impact on financial performance.[3] Recent empirical research has found that there is a statistically significant relationship between the extent to which corporate culture is embraced (that is, the extent to which employees "live and breathe it") in a company's business units and the overall financial performance of those units, as measured in terms of EBIT (earnings before interest and taxes).[4]

This research supports the notion that corporate culture is a critical factor in an organization's success. It shows that there is a direct relationship between corporate culture and the bottom line of organizational performance.

STRONG AND WEAK CULTURES

Some companies have strong cultures, and others have weak cultures. A *strong culture* is one where people have a very clear sense of what the culture is. They understand it and can explain what it is. A strong culture can be positive or negative. Examples of companies with strong cultures include Amgen, Countrywide Financial Corporation, Disney, Starbucks, and all companies owned by Johnson & Johnson (such as Neutrogena and LifeScan).

A *weak culture* is one where people do not have a very clear sense of what the culture is. They do not understand it and cannot explain it. Falk Corporation (described in Chapter Sixteen) is an example of a company with a weak culture. At this company, the two brothers who served as its most senior executives did not and could not agree about what the culture should be. For example, one brother's behavior suggested that "being reactive and constantly changing course" was important; the other brother's behavior (communicated, in part, by working with the team to develop a formal strategic plan) suggested that "being proactive and planning for changes" was important. Needless to say, managers who reported to them (and, in fact, employees throughout the company) were not sure what the company really valued and how the company wanted them to operate in their roles.

FUNCTIONAL AND DYSFUNCTIONAL CULTURES

There are not only strong and weak cultures but also functional and dysfunctional cultures. A *functional culture* is one that has a positive impact on organizational performance and success. A *dysfunctional culture* is one that has a negative impact on organizational performance. Many companies have both functional and dysfunctional aspects in their culture.

Some examples of companies with positive or functional cultures include Amgen, Bell-Carter Foods, Countrywide Financial Corporation, Southwest, and Starbucks. At Southwest, for example, the company's focus on customer service—both external and internal—greatly contributes to its continued success.

An example of a dysfunctional culture can be seen in the case of Tempo Products, described in Chapter Six. Prior to embarking on the process of formally managing its culture, this company's performance was being undermined, to a certain extent, by aspects of its culture.

REAL VERSUS NOMINAL CORPORATE CULTURE

Many organizations develop "culture" or "philosophy" statements that articulate their values, beliefs, and norms. These may be displayed on walls or in employee handbooks, and if an employee is asked about his or her company's culture, these sheets of paper appear. Examples of culture statements include Starbucks' "Six Guiding Principles," "Johnson & Johnson's Credo," and "Southwest Airlines Mission Statement." Unfortunately for many companies, the information printed on the pieces of paper is, at best, a slight exaggeration of the company's real culture and, at worst, a wish list of what the company would like to be but is not. In the case of U.S. automobile companies in the 1960s, the nominal culture was, "We produce the best automobiles in the world," while the real culture was, "If you can get it to drive out the door, we can sell it." The real culture ultimately led to the irreversible entry of Japanese automobile manufacturers into the U.S. market.[5]

Similarly, after months of working to prepare a formal statement of its values, a medical products firm proudly unveiled the product. When employees walked by the posters that displayed these values, it was all they could do to keep from laughing. While the posters stated that work-life balance for employees was one of the company's most important values, managers (and other employees) felt compelled to work on holidays and weekends as a way of showing their commitment to the company. Many managers had not taken a vacation in more than two years. The real value was, "If you want to be valued here, you need to do whatever it takes, even if it means giving up things in your personal life."

We refer to the statements presented on paper as the *nominal culture* and the culture that people actually operate under as the *real culture*. The difference between the nominal and the real cultures of a rapidly growing $25 million manufacturing firm is illustrated in Table 12.1.

The nominal culture suggests that this firm has some very positive values and beliefs that support its continued success. The problem is, however, that

Table 12.1. Nominal Versus Real Culture: An Example

Nominal Organizational Culture
1. Quality products
2. Ethical dealings with vendors
3. High quality of working life for the employee

Real Organizational Culture
1. The firm is sales-oriented rather than profit-oriented.
2. Current standards of performance seem to be unrealistic.
3. The company appears overly optimistic about its capabilities.
4. There is a lack of accountability.
5. Personnel tend to avoid conflict.

people's behavior is influenced by the real culture. The real culture led people to hide product-related problems rather than solve them (that is, to avoid conflict and responsibility), to blame other people when things went wrong, and to focus their attention on the bottom line because "as long as the product is selling, we must be making money."

At this company, the systems and structure were not in place to support what the company wanted its culture to be—in other words, the culture was not being effectively managed—and the result was that this company could not effectively influence people's behavior to achieve its goals. Among other things, it did not have a well-defined system to reward people for doing what it needed them to do, and no quality-control system was in place. Further, quality-control personnel were viewed as unneeded interruptions rather than as important members of the production team.

As this case illustrates, the real culture does not have to be the antithesis of the nominal culture; rather, it can merely bear no relationship to it. The real culture of any organization can be identified by examining a variety of factors. These manifestations of culture are discussed in the next section.

MANIFESTATIONS OF CORPORATE CULTURE

An organization's culture is manifested in a variety of ways. Aside from people's behavior, an organization's culture is reflected in (1) the language people use, (2) the things that act as symbols and the meaning attached to them, (3) the rituals performed within the company, (4) the rewards provided by the company, as well as the recipients of these rewards (known as heroes), and (5) the company's Web site. Each of these is discussed next.

Language

The words and phrases people use to refer to themselves, events, or the organization are manifestations of the organization's culture. As noted earlier, Starbucks refers to employees as partners. This is intended to suggest an ownership relationship among people employed by the firm. Other companies refer to employees as associates (Wal-Mart), crew members (Chart House), team members (Infogix), and cast members (Disney). This language is intended to have a different connotation than viewing people as employees or staff. For example, the use of the term *cast members* at Disneyland and Disney World is intended to communicate to all employees, even the maintenance people, that they are like actors playing their defined roles in a live stage production.

In many Stage IV (and sometimes smaller organizations), acronyms are used to share and discuss ideas. We have frequently experienced this phenomenon. Although the message behind using acronyms might seem to be that the firm is striving for efficiency and using the minimal amount of time to communicate with one another, a more subtle message is that the firm is creating a language all its own that only insiders will understand.

Culture is also manifested in the language used to talk about the organization itself. With respect to organizational development, perhaps the most feared word is *bureaucracy*. The meaning attached to this word for many employees of entrepreneurships is that of a slow-moving dinosaur that seldom gets anything accomplished. The problem is that "bureaucracy" often becomes equated with "professionalized," even though the latter is a state to be desired and an organizational form that is necessary for continued success. Managing language during the transition process, then, can be critical.

Language can also be a powerful means of communicating a change in culture. For example, employees of one Stage IV consumer products company were expected to behave professionally in every aspect of the firm's operations. People dressed very formally and spoke of and to each other very formally (for example, executives were referred to as Mr. or Ms.). Employees were very businesslike in everything that was done (even though the product produced and sold by this company had the image in its marketplace of being a very friendly and "fun" product). Executives dressed in suits and even in off-site meetings had a difficult time removing their jackets.

The old executive team was eventually replaced by a new, younger team. This team set about changing the firm's culture to one that better reflected the type of product it produced. Casual dress and casual language became a part of everyday life at the firm. Everyone from the president to front-line employees was now referred to by their first names. The president of this company was known to use such phrases as "That's a Big Wow"—something that would never had been used by the former regime. The language, then, reflected a change to a more casual working environment and a focus on the fun that had become somewhat de-emphasized by the former group of executives.

Symbols

Things within an organization to which special meaning are attached are known as *symbols*. Depending on the organization, symbols may include furniture, awards, and dress (uniform). In many companies, the type of furniture or office an individual has symbolizes his or her value to an organization. In one $100 million manufacturing firm, the type of telephone people had was a significant symbol of status. One individual, who occupied an open cubicle, lobbied very strongly for a speakerphone because this symbolized a higher status than the traditional phone that had been provided. Although a speakerphone was somewhat impractical in an open environment, the meaning attached to the phone was so strong that its practicality was secondary in this individual's mind.

If managed properly, symbols can be used to motivate people to achieve the organization's goals. For example, in one $100 million manufacturing company, the field sales operations had created a traveling coffee cup that was given to a sales rep who had done something beyond the call of duty. The individual receiving the coffee cup also received a letter from the divisional manager specifying why the cup was being awarded. The recipient was permitted to keep the cup for a month, and then it was returned to the manager to await being awarded again. A coffee cup seems like something fairly trivial, but at this company it had acquired a great deal of importance. It symbolized that the individual receiving it had provided a valuable contribution to the company.

Rituals

Special events and traditional ways of doing things are what we refer to as *rituals* in companies. Examples of corporate rituals include retirement parties, company picnics, afternoon beer busts, and annual meetings. Generally, rituals are intended to communicate the values and beliefs related to a company's people orientation.

Several years ago, we witnessed the retirement "ritual" at General Ribbon, a manufacturing firm. We were in a meeting with Bob Daggs, the president, and he informed us that we would have to break in about ten minutes because he needed to be at an employee meeting in the company's cafeteria. He explained that one of the company's employees was retiring. When we arrived in the cafeteria, it was already filled with employees sitting and standing along the walls. The retiree was seated at one of the tables nearest the front; the table was otherwise empty. The president asked us to be seated at the table, and he approached a microphone that had been set up in the front of the room. Bob explained why they were there (basically to honor a loyal and long-term employee), mentioned the employee's years of service, and called her up to the microphone. He thanked her for her contribution and presented her with a pen-and-pencil set embellished with the company logo and an envelope containing a monetary gift. He then told the employees that there were doughnuts and coffee for everyone and that they should say good-bye to the retiring employee. It is difficult to capture the spirit of the event, but the goodwill was evident.

Although the entire presentation lasted no more than fifteen minutes, the values and beliefs it communicated and reinforced were much longer-lasting. First, it showed that the company values all of its employees and their service. Second, it reinforced the belief that loyalty and service will be rewarded. Third, it indicated that the company believes its employees are part of a family. The sharing of food (in this case simply coffee and doughnuts) added to the family atmosphere. Finally, it suggested that the leadership of the company is interested in and concerned about its employees.

Celebrations held at companies as diverse as Bell-Carter Foods (birthday parties) and Southwest Airlines (annual awards banquet) are rituals that help communicate to all employees that employees are viewed as a part of the family and that fun is a very real part of the culture.

Like other aspects of culture, however, rituals must be managed, or the values and beliefs they are intended to reinforce can become distorted. Annual meetings can become an excuse to get away at the company's expense instead of as an opportunity to learn from each other and build the team.

Rituals can also be mismanaged when employees no longer understand their intent. Two examples of this mismanagement include (1) the afternoon beer bust—which becomes a time for employees to drown their sorrows at the company's expense rather than a way for employees to informally share ideas and get acquainted—and (2) the meeting that is held each week because "we've always had it," even though attendees agree it's a waste of time.

When, however, a ritual has been effective at communicating its message and employees embrace it, they may choose to maintain it, even at significant cost to themselves. At Hewlett-Packard, for example, during a period when the company's performance was less than expected and significant cuts were being made across various operations, employees voluntarily raised money to sponsor the corporate picnic. The implication of this is that employees clearly understood that the company valued them and that the picnic was only in jeopardy because of the company's performance. Further, the company had effectively communicated the belief that employee loyalty was valued, and employees chose to express their loyalty by sponsoring the picnic themselves.

Rewards and Heroes

There are monetary and nonmonetary things that the company gives employees for behavior consistent with the company's culture and its goals. Examples include bonuses, company-sponsored vacations, employee-of-the-month awards, certificates of appreciation, and items embellished with the company logo and presented in recognition of service of a particular kind. Many firms use certificates to recognize employees who complete a management development program or provide valued service to the firm. These certificates help other employees understand what the company values.

Domino's Pizza is a company that effectively uses rewards to foster its values of teamwork, customer service, and high performance standards. National awards go to winners of annual competitive events and to individuals and stores with the best sales record. Recognition of a different kind is given to poor performers. The slowest delivery times are recognized by inscription of the store's name on a plaque placed near the slowest elevators at corporate headquarters. Finally, founder Thomas Monaghan's impulsive gift of his tie to an especially successful manager has become a tradition, and hundreds of these awards are presented annually.

As is true of the other manifestations of culture, rewards must be managed or they can communicate values and beliefs and promote norms that are at odds with the company's goals. One small $2 million service firm had instituted a "manager-of-the-month" program intended to reward the "best manager." Unfortunately, the program had become a popularity contest rather than a way to recognize behavior consistent with the company's goals. The criteria for determining who should receive this reward were vague, and employees were asked to vote on who they believed to be the best manager. This process was adversely affecting morale because, although the most popular managers won, those who were working hard to meet their goals were sometimes overlooked. Eventually, it might be expected that the good performers who were not rewarded for their behavior would simply give up.

In other cases, firms can overdo it with respect to rewards. In one large company, each time a meeting or event was held, all attendees received some type of memento: a T-shirt, coffee mug, pen, or plaque. Over time, these rewards came to have no meaning to those who received them. Employees complained that they had closets full of T-shirts and cupboards full of mugs. The president of the company, upon hearing this, decided to use rewards more strategically. He did not immediately take away all of these rewards, but he dramatically decreased their use. No one seemed to notice! The hope was that, over time, these types of rewards would again be appreciated.

Those who receive rewards and recognition become a firm's corporate heroes. These people become the role models for the types of behavior that the firm would like to see. Therefore, it is important that those who receive rewards truly exemplify the firm's values, beliefs, and norms. When they don't, the firm may be promoting behavior that is inconsistent with its long-term goals.

It is important to also recognize that corporate heroes can be living or long-deceased, still working in the company or long since departed. These are the people that employees hold up as role models. Herb Kelleher is a living hero in the company he founded—Southwest Airlines. His behavior (which promotes fun) lets all employees know what is acceptable. Similarly, Bill Gates is a living hero at Microsoft, where he represents the values of innovative product development, competition, and other aspects of the company's culture that have helped to support the company's success.

Web Sites

The look and functionality of a company's Web site can suggest a great deal about its culture. For example, the first page of Southwest Airline's Web site typically includes a story about a customer or customer service. Message: "We value customer service." It uses the Southwest colors throughout and has icons like their "Ding" (which brings live updates to customers). Message: "We are fun." The Web site is easy to use. Customers can make and change reservations, check in, and print an entire schedule of flights from one destination to the next. Message: "Doing business with us should be easy." In addition, if a visitor wants to learn more about Southwest, their history, their culture, or their commitment to customers and employees, it's all there and easy to find. Finally, there is a Southwest Airlines blog ("Nuts About Southwest"), where visitors can read about employees, the airline, and customers and post their own comments. Message: "We want you to know what's most important to us, and we want to know what's most important to you."

The Web sites of other airlines (for example, United, American, Delta) communicate very different messages about their culture. The first page on most of these Web sites is all about making the reservation: fill in the departing city, fill in the arriving city, and so on. There are sometimes travel advisory updates and promotion information available with one click. It is difficult to find information on the company's history and culture, with the exception, perhaps, of reading the annual reports, which are typically available. Message: "We're all business."

This comparison is not to suggest that Southwest's culture is better than other airlines. It is, however, intended to show how easy it is to understand the differences in culture simply by reading and using a company's Web site. In brief, Web sites provide a good source of information about a company's culture. Further, as a company works to formally define, redefine, and manage its culture, it will need to also manage the messages it sends to employees and customers through the corporate Web site.

HOW CORPORATE CULTURE CHANGES

Corporate culture should change over time. In fact, culture *does* change over time as the organization grows and as new people are added; we refer to these types of change as uncontrolled change. Culture *should* change over time to support organizational growth; we refer to this type of change as controlled or managed. We discuss these two change processes in the next sections.

Uncontrolled Culture Change

The corporate culture of an entrepreneurship is dictated principally by the founder and the few people he or she initially hires. Everyone understands the culture and buys into it. It is very easy for the entrepreneur to influence and maintain the culture through direct contact with all employees on a daily basis. However, by the time there are four or five generations of employees, it is almost impossible for people at the lower levels of the organization to have any direct contact with those at the top who articulate the culture. Therefore, the culture that those at the bottom of the organization adopt may be very different from the culture the founder and the original group of employees want to promote.

Such different perceptions result from the tendency of individuals to interpret the corporate culture in ways that meet their own needs. In the absence of a well-managed culture, this can lead to the original culture becoming very distorted. This can be a subtle—almost imperceptible—process. We provided examples of such reinterpretations of the culture in the Tempo Products case presented in Chapter Six.

In addition, if the culture is not managed or is not managed effectively, there can be a clash between the old and new cultures that can affect the company's success. In one $500 million service company, the two companies of equal size that merged to create the larger entity had extremely different cultures. One of these companies was very entrepreneurial, while other bordered on being a bureaucracy. In the entrepreneurship, managers were encouraged to do their own thing; in the other, people waited to be told what to do by their managers. In the more "professionalized" company, there were well-developed systems and processes that were consistently used; in the entrepreneurship, if systems and processes existed, they were frequently ignored. After the merger, the senior management team, consisting of the executives from both companies, worked together to develop a strategic plan for taking the new business to the next level. The team tried, unsuccessfully, to blend the two cultures but could seldom see eye-to-eye on what was needed. Over a period of about two years, the new company's performance significantly declined, and the members of executive management were replaced.

Given our previous discussion of the relationship between culture and the organization's infrastructure, any time a change is made in a particular area of the company, there will be an impact on culture, whether or not the organization has planned this change.

Planned Culture Change

As suggested earlier, each time an organization changes any aspect of its operations, there is an impact on culture. If an organization is to be successful as it grows, culture must be managed at each stage so that the values, beliefs, and norms support the other changes taking place. As we discussed in Chapters Two and Six, culture does not become a critical factor until a company reaches $100 million in revenues, but that does not mean that it should or can be ignored. For example, in a $50 million manufacturing company, strategic planning was done, but because the culture and other systems did not support it, it was nothing more than a yearly paper exercise. The company had not found ways to explicitly manage its culture so that it supported planning.

Microsoft, recognized as being one of the most phenomenally successful entrepreneurial ventures of the late twentieth century, went through several periods of cultural change. Microsoft was founded in 1975 by Bill Gates and Paul Allen. At that time, Gates and Allen focused on developing the software for the first personal computer—the Altair (produced by MITS computing in New Mexico). Over the next several years, the company developed software for other computer makers, and by 1980, revenues had reached $8 million. It was in 1980 that Microsoft was selected to produce the IBM-PC operating system (MS-DOS). This system eventually became the industry standard. In these early days of the company (and for obvious reasons), the focus was on the developer, and the culture of the organization reflected this.

As the firm continued to grow, with sales reaching $24 million in 1982, Gates began to realize that the informal manner in which the company had operated in the past would no longer be appropriate for the future. He began to hire professional managers to help take his company to its next stage of development. John Shirley, a twenty-five-year veteran of Tandy, was brought in as COO and began to help develop the infrastructure needed to run the much larger firm that Microsoft was becoming. At the same time, however, the company tried to maintain the feel of a much smaller firm. This was facilitated, in part, by a number of rituals (like the annual holiday party and company picnics), as well as the norm that any employee at any time could e-mail Gates or Shirley directly, if they had a question or concern. Gates and Shirley typically responded quickly and personally to each e-mail received.

The firm continued to promote a family feeling, but its culture also promoted being aggressive and assertive. Conflict was not unusual and in many cases was promoted. Although at times it may have gotten somewhat heated, whenever conflict is dealt with openly, it typically leads to greater innovation and creativity—significant values at Microsoft.

Throughout the 1980s, Gates continued to be in charge of product development and demanded the most from the developers. His "Bill meetings" were opportunities for him to question and critique ideas, as well as to promote his vision for what his firm would become.

As the company entered the 1990s, it faced new challenges.[6] Revenues were now over $1 billion and were derived not just from the firm's sales of its operating system but also from application software. However, the company had not changed certain aspects of its culture to support a firm of this size. There was still a great deal of centralized control. For example, the president of the company still signed all employment requisitions, even for temporary employees. At the same time, however, product developers in different units worked independently on their products. Gates recognized that this needed to change as the environment pushed for software products that worked together. He assumed the role of coordinating the product development efforts. The company began to focus on creating integrated products, and this meant that its product development teams also needed to be integrated.

In 1991, the company began to realize that its primary customer base had shifted from the OEM (original equipment manufacturer, who purchased Microsoft operating software for use in its computers) to the end user (who purchased its application software and who demanded support for its use). Promoting a focus on end-user service and support required not only a shift in the company's infrastructure but also in its culture. Now the company had to promote not only "reverence for the developer" (a value on which the company was founded) but also "reverence for the customer."

In 1991, the company also became more formal with respect to its security. Although it had been viewed as less than positive to wear badges in the mid-1980s, software developers began to realize that they had a great deal of valuable software and ideas in the firm that needed to be protected.

By 1999, the company had grown to over $14 billion in revenues and was continuing to experience great success. However, Bill Gates and the new president, Steve Ballmer, decided that they needed to "reinvent Microsoft," calling their program Vision Version 2.[7] This program was developed to address issues identified through interviews conducted with employees throughout the company. Interviews suggested that people did not necessarily understand the firm's direction and that the company had become too slow to react to market opportunities. The idea, according to Ballmer, was to "reinvigorate the vision," that computing power will be on any device, anywhere.

One key to the new vision was to have programmers continue developing software to support the Windows technology, while at the same time giving programmers the freedom to explore non-Windows-based software that would support the growing Internet business. To minimize the possibility that these different types of software might end up competing for customers, the company redesigned its structure into eight new groups, focused both on technology and customers. Each of the six product development groups targeted a different buyer. The remaining two groups were devoted to basic research and continued product development.

One of the reasons behind the changes made in 1999 at Microsoft was that people had come to feel that the company was becoming too bureaucratic. Decisions were taking too long, and many felt the firm was mired in red tape. Part of the problem was that the company had continued to operate with a culture of centralization. Many decisions were "bumped" to Gates or Ballmer, who were becoming (partly because of the sheer number of decisions to be made) bottlenecks. Before the new Vision Version 2, Gates and Ballmer were involved in every decision. In the new culture, rolled out in 1999, senior managers (those below Gates and Ballmer) were now responsible for running their businesses and managing their budgets as they saw fit (as long as they met their goals). In addition, the company continued to focus its developers on better understanding and meeting the needs of customers.

In September 2005, the company again restructured, this time into three divisions. The reason, according to Steve Ballmer, now CEO, was to "align our Business Groups in a way that will enhance decision-making and speed of execution, as well as help us continue to deliver the types of products and services our customers want most."[8] In other words, this change was intended to continue the process of refining the structure to better fit the company's culture.

HOW TO MANAGE CORPORATE CULTURE

As a result of organizational growth and a lack of time to focus on culture management because other systems have taken precedence, a firm may find itself with a culture that is no longer appropriate for its size. When this occurs, usually by the time a firm reaches $100 million, culture management must become a priority.

For some firms, the problem is simply identifying and finding ways to better manage the existing culture; in others, the dominant culture needs to be changed to support the other changes that are taking place in the organization. In both cases, however, the challenge becomes one of finding a way of managing the culture so that it supports the operations of the larger firm. Using the area of strategic planning, Table 12.2 presents an example of the problem of competing cultures that one firm faced as it began to focus on managing its culture.

The top value, belief, norm, or hero definition is consistent with the culture needed to support an entrepreneurship, while the bottom is consistent with the culture needed to support a more professionalized firm. In the entrepreneurship, the culture emphasizes the ability to simply respond to market opportunities. It is reactionary. This can be a strength for a small firm as it attempts to establish itself in a market. The professionalized firm's culture, however, needs to focus on promoting planning as a way to anticipate and design, in advance, responses to environmental opportunities and threats. This proactive approach is important, because if the changes made are inappropriate, they can be quite costly. Further, firms in a competitive environment that are reactive are usually at a competitive disadvantage because they respond to, rather than are prepared for, threats and opportunities.

The goal of the management process is to create a culture that is consistent with the firm's current stage of growth. As mentioned previously, this top tier

Table 12.2. Example of Entrepreneurial and Professional Cultures

Values:

We value fire fighters.

versus

We value planners.

Beliefs:

Our success is based on our ability to respond

rapidly to changes in our environment.

versus

Our success depends on our ability to anticipate

and plan for changes in our environment.

Norms:

We do not plan; we react.

versus

We know what direction we are going in at all times.

Heroes:

The arsonists and fire fighters.

versus

The planners.

of the Pyramid of Organizational Development does not become critical until a firm reaches $100 million in revenues, but it needs to be managed throughout the development of the organization.

There are four basic steps in the process of culture management: (1) analyzing current culture, (2) determining what the culture should be, given the firm's current stage of growth (the firm's desired culture), (3) identifying gaps between the firm's current and desired cultures, and (4) developing and implementing a culture management plan. Each step is described in turn.

Analysis of Current Culture

The first step in the culture management process is to perform a "cultural audit" to determine what the culture currently is. Because the emphasis is on the real culture, not the nominal culture, we recommend ignoring written culture statements (at least initially) and focusing instead on what people have to say about the culture they live and breathe. As explained earlier, culture is a very fuzzy concept; asking an employee to describe his or her firm's culture usually results in the employee either pulling out the company's philosophy or culture statement and beginning to read it or looking blankly at the interviewer as if he or she is speaking a foreign language. In other words, the direct approach is not effective in gathering information on this subject.

A more indirect approach that has been very effective for researchers and managers alike is to ask employees to write or tell short stories about their experiences in the firm. Employees should be asked to tell a story or two related to critical incidents they have personally experienced or heard about that occurred at the company. Another effective method is to have them construct a story that describes their first day on the job. The construction of these stories can take place on paper, and they can then be read aloud in a group setting or told to interviewers.

The next step is to extract from the stories critical elements of the company's culture. Examples of elements of Tempo Products' culture that were derived from the stories employees told are presented in Chapter Six. The identification of these elements may be done by the employees themselves or by an independent observer. Whatever the case, once the elements have been identified and summarized, they should be circulated to employees for further elaboration or feedback.

An example of two stories that were told by employees at a Stage IV service firm and the elements of the culture that they identify are provided in Table 12.3. As shown in the table, the stories suggest a number of elements of this organization's culture, including concern for quality, the importance of extra effort, concern for people, the importance of first impressions, the concern that people feel valued, and the importance of treating people with respect.

In analyzing stories, it is useful to identify how culture is manifested in the organization. What symbols are important to people? How do they talk about themselves, their customers, and company events (language)? What rituals are important? Who receives rewards (the heroes) and for what? What types of rewards are important to people in this firm? This is important information, not only in terms of identifying the current culture but also in terms of identifying how to manage these manifestations of culture in order to promote a more professionalized culture.

As a result of such analyses, a number of competing subcultures may be identified. For example, each department may adhere to slightly different values. This is important information in the culture management process because the goal of this process will be to blend all of the competing cultures so that they support the overall corporate goals.

In addition to story analysis, a firm may use interviews or culture surveys to collect information on its culture. Through a series of questions that focus on key aspects of corporate culture (for example, treatment of employees and treatment of customers), interviews can collect information on both the firm's current culture and what interviewees believe the culture should be. In most cases,

Table 12.3. Stories and Their Elements

Story 1: Not long after I began working here, I was reviewing some artwork that had been submitted. As usual, I was hoping to be able to approve the work and get the project rolling. The artwork was all right. In fact, it was probably more than just all right. But still it wasn't perfect. It fell into that gray area of being almost what you had in mind.

I showed it to my boss. Like me, she agreed that it was okay, would do the job, and be just fine. We stood a minute looking at the work, each of us wishing it were a bit something more, but recognizing that maybe sometimes okay is good enough. Then my boss turned to me and said, "I want to love this!" And in that moment we both agreed that it was worth it to get that extra something we wanted from the artwork.

Story 2: When I arrived at the company, Allan was working the reception desk, and while I was filling out my application he offered me coffee, decaf, tea, hot chocolate, milk, and water. Every time he offered, I said, "No thank you. I'm fine." When I met with the president, the first thing she asked me was if Mark had offered me coffee or tea, and I said that he had but that I didn't want anything. I was fine. After I interviewed with the president, she took me into the sales department to meet Jerry, the manager. When I met him, he asked me to tell him about myself in two minutes. I started telling him what my experience was and what I had done. He stopped me and said, "No, tell me about yourself." I was very impressed. So far, everyone at this company had been interested in who I was as well as in what I had done.

After I met with Carol, I met another member of the sales team, and the first thing he asked me was if anyone had offered me coffee or tea or something to drink. I said that they had and I was fine, really! Well, I came back for a second interview the next week, and then started work two days later.

Element of Culture Extracted from These Stories

1. We value quality in our products.
2. We take the extra effort to "do it right."
3. We care about our employees.
4. First impressions are important.
5. We want to make everyone who comes in contact with us feel like they are valued.
6. We treat people with respect.

---

it would be very difficult for someone inside the firm to effectively use this method because interviewees may not feel that they can be completely candid.

An alternative is to design and administer a corporate culture survey, which is *not* the same as an attitude survey. Culture surveys should focus only on helping to identify the firm's values, beliefs, and norms, not on things like whether employees are satisfied with their pay and benefits. Typically, these surveys should consist of no more than forty questions, with each question representing a key element of the firm's desired culture. Those completing the survey are then asked to identify the extent to which each element of the firm's desired culture is currently a part of the firm's existing culture.

Whatever method is used to collect information on the firm's current culture, the outcome of the cultural audit will be a list of the elements of the current culture and their meanings. Some managers also find it useful to develop a list of the systems or structures (elements of the company's infrastructure) that promote each of the various cultural elements as a way of identifying possible targets for change.

Identifying of the Firm's Desired Culture

In beginning to explicitly manage an organization's culture, the key question is, What should our culture be, given our current stage of development? In the final section of this chapter, we provide some general guidelines for the elements of corporate culture at different stages of development.

Whatever the stage, however, it is senior management's responsibility to answer this question. In doing so, the focus needs to be on both what the current culture should be today and on what the culture should be in five years. From brainstorming sessions, workshops, or surveys, senior management should construct a set of values and beliefs that it deems will meet the firm's needs. These can be a set of three to five key phrases, each with a paragraph to explain their meaning, or simply a list of the key elements of the culture. If a company chooses to use a list, then senior management should develop its own written definition of each element so that there can be no misinterpretation of its meaning.

We recommend that the culture statement contain no more than five to nine key items so as to help employees remember them. However, these statements might also include brief definitions (no more than a paragraph).

Identifying Gaps Between Current and Desired Cultures

Once a firm's management has identified what it wants or needs its culture to be, it then needs to determine the extent to which the desired culture is currently a reality for employees throughout the firm. The basic question is, To what extent do our employees currently live and breathe the desired values, beliefs, and norms we have articulated?

Addressing this question involves comparing the current culture (as identified through stories, interviews, and surveys) with the firm's desired culture (as articulated by senior management). In some cases, the desired culture will already be a reality. In others, the current culture will be quite different from one that will best support the firm's long-term goals (the firm's desired culture). Closing culture gaps involves developing strategies to better manage the firm's culture.

Developing a Culture Management Plan

A culture management plan focuses on ensuring that those aspects of the firm's desired culture that are already a reality are preserved. More important, however, this plan should focus on developing strategies for closing any gaps that exist between the firm's current and desired cultures.

Developing strategies for effectively managing a firm's culture usually involves focusing on other systems, as culture affects and is affected by everything else in the Pyramid of Organizational Development. This is why it is important to identify those aspects of the infrastructure that are detracting from a firm's ability to realize its desired culture. Similarly, each time a change is made in the infrastructure, senior management needs to consider the cultural implications. To illustrate the impact that other systems can have on culture, Table 12.4 presents excerpts from a culture audit completed for a Stage IV manufacturing firm we call Alpha Manufacturing. As can be seen in this table, a variety of other systems, structures, and processes were supporting the firm's current culture, which wasn't necessarily the culture that the firm needed to support the achievement of its long-term goals.

Sometimes the need for culture change arises because of an acquisition or merger. In this case, senior management must perform an audit of each of the cultures, identify areas of overlap and conflict, and determine the best way to blend the cultures. This may mean that some values of one or both firms will need to be significantly changed or, perhaps, eliminated in order to support the firm's growth. The culture's management is, however, essential in helping the company make a smooth transition because it has such a tremendous impact on employee morale.

When American Century Investors acquired Benham Investors in 1995, they made a special effort to integrate the two company's cultures. In the beginning, there were concerns because Benham's business focused primarily on fixed income rather than equities, whereas American Century was exclusively focused on equities. This could have created a significant cultural conflict. To facilitate the integration of the two companies and their cultures, American Century initiated a number of steps. They assigned a senior executive to devote virtually full time to the integration of the company for a planned period of approximately eighteen months. They engaged the services of a consulting firm that had worked with them for many years to serve as a liaison between the two firms. The consulting firm interviewed a sample of employees from

Table 12.4. Elements of Alpha Manufacturing's Current Culture and Factors That Support Them

Treatment of Customers

Current Culture	Organizational Dimensions That Affect or Are Affected by Culture
Customer and quality orientation are present but not consistent throughout the organization.	There is the perception that Quality Assurance is the "policeman," versus a valued partner in promoting quality. Discrepancies exist between departments as to the extent to which quality goals are effectively set and monitored.
We have a commitment to "doing it right the first time," as long as it doesn't affect the schedule.	This creates stress throughout the company. The product development process is adversely affected.

Treatment of Employees

Current Culture	Organizational Dimensions That Affect or Are Affected by Culture
We pay lip service to balancing work and personal lives, but our actions do not support this.	The company takes on too much in developing plans. Job design may promote some people working excessive hours. Reward-recognition system may promote working long hours.
We are not "confrontational" or "aggressive." We are "polite" and "professional." There is a "kill the messenger" syndrome operating within the company: no one wants to hear bad news; we tell people what they want to hear.	This may contribute to suboptimal decisions being made. This may contribute to communication and meeting-effectiveness problems. The reward system may reinforce beliefs. Managers may not know how to or want to effectively confront poor performers.
We value training and developing our people, if we only had the time!	There is a lack of time to develop human resources. Training varies from department to department. As positions have changed, no formal system has been created to provide training in new skills.

Table 12.4. *(continued)*

Performance Standards and Accountability

Current Culture	Organizational Dimensions That Affect or Are Affected by Culture
We set high goals and will do everything to meet them.	Goal setting is reinforced by and reinforces "people working hard" and feeling that one can't say no.
	Human resources are stretched thin.
	Too many priorities are in the planning process.
People get rewarded for who they know and not necessarily for good performance (against goals).	Managers may not be held accountable for financial resources management.
	People are promoted who are not qualified.
People may not always be held accountable for performing their jobs.	People are not held accountable for following procedures.
	There may be problems in the goal-setting process.
	A lack of up-to-date job descriptions contributes to problems.
We don't take risks.	This attitude affects product and market development processes.
	This attitude affects development of other processes in the organization.
We don't want to become bureaucratic; we are flexible.	Product development and other systems are not adequately defined.
	There are insufficient formal mechanisms to communicate between and within departments.
	There are too many teams and individuals working on the same task.
	There is no formal system to develop effective managers, which contributes to managers not being prepared to assume their roles.
	Planning is not yet integrated throughout the company.

Benham during the first eighteen months to obtain feedback on how the integration was going and whether there were any special concerns. Issues were identified, which were brought to the attention of the executive responsible for the integration, and they were successfully addressed. The consulting firm also facilitated joint sessions for strategic planning and team building between the senior executives of both companies. Meetings were intentionally held in Mountain View, California, at Benham's corporate office, rather than in Kansas City, where American Century was headquartered. The integration was successful—made easier, in part, by the compatible sensibilities of the two CEOs, who had a number of things in common.

Although corporate culture change is a necessary part of the transition process, culture must be managed on a continual basis in order to ensure that it supports the company's goals and operations. The values, beliefs, and norms must be communicated and constantly reinforced because as a company continues to grow, new employees will need to understand what the culture is and what it means.

Senior management is ultimately responsible for the culture management process. Moreover, senior managers actually serve as role models for the rest of the company. It is important, then, that they not only communicate the culture through their words but also through their actions. At one technology company, for example, the founder and CEO decided to decentralize management decision making. Unfortunately, employees continued to complain that the founder still made most of the major decisions. The nominal culture said, ''We believe in providing all of our managers with the authority they need to make decisions.'' But the behavior, for whatever reason, stated, ''The founder will decide.''

A positive example of the role senior management can play in the culture management process is that of a $35 million manufacturing firm. In this firm, employees came to equate commitment with hours worked, regardless of actual productivity. Changing this aspect of the company's culture began with a memo from senior management—sent to all employees—stating clearly that the company wanted people to work smarter, not longer hours. Senior management decided that they would no longer arrive at the office before 7:30 A.M. and would leave the office by 5:30 P.M. Through their behavior, they attempted to show their employees what the new value would be: we value productivity, not just hours worked.

A second way to manage corporate culture is through training programs. Orientation programs can serve as a way to provide new employees with an understanding of the corporate culture, as well as how the infrastructure works to support this culture. Again, however, although the words are important, the other elements of this program—for example, whether the president welcomes them in person or in a video, the first impression left by their immediate supervisor, and the tone of the meeting—can leave a lasting and sometimes distorted perception of the company's values. In the absence of such formalized programs, employees are sometimes left to their own devices to read the handbook and identify what's important in the company.

Management development programs can also serve as a means of conveying the corporate culture, as discussed in Chapter Nine. They help to build a sense of teamwork and, at a minimum, usually communicate to employees that the company values training and professionalized management. Further, management development programs provide managers with the skills they need to support and use the organization's systems in ways that reinforce the corporate culture.

Another way that corporate culture can be managed is through personnel selection. This can be proactive or retroactive. Proactively, the goal is to select personnel who will promote the values, beliefs, and norms of the firm and who are not at odds with the culture. Although this is a very time-consuming process and takes a great deal of planning and execution, it can be very effective. Southwest Airlines uses this mechanism as one way of managing its culture. Their hiring process focuses on identifying attitudes rather than skills.

Retroactive personnel selection usually occurs during culture change. The goal is to eliminate individuals who will not support the new culture or, at a minimum, move them into positions where they can do little to harm the cultural change process. Some companies bring in outsiders, called hired guns, to perform the terminations. Usually, in these cases the entrepreneur realizes that he or she cannot do what needs to be done and either moves up or out of the company.

In other cases, the culture eventually becomes so strong that other employees force the cultural violator out. The person who refuses to adopt the new culture becomes an outsider and leaves of his or her own volition. Individuals who leave under these circumstances sometimes say that the company just wasn't any fun anymore.

Finally, corporate culture can be managed through the administration of rewards. As discussed in Chapter Ten, it is important to ensure that rewards are linked to the behavior needed to achieve organizational goals and objectives, as outlined in the strategic plan. The company should be trying to create corporate heroes out of those individuals who best exemplify this behavior. These individuals can, in turn, act as role models for others. This is why it is not only important for employees to understand what they are being rewarded for but to publicize achievement as a way of motivating others to exhibit the same behavior. In some companies, the best performers are rewarded with bonuses. The reward structure and system must constantly be reevaluated to determine that it is motivating employees to be concerned with the appropriate goals and that these goals have not become distorted.

To illustrate how some of these corporate culture management mechanisms can be used to better manage a firm's culture, Table 12.5 shows the current and desired culture of Alpha Manufacturing. It also provides examples of how this company changed certain systems, structures, and processes in order to help increase the extent to which its desired culture was realized throughout the company.

In brief, Alpha Manufacturing developed a culture management plan that focused on changing other aspects of its infrastructure in order to support its new culture. In addition to developing this plan, the company created a culture management task force, made up of middle managers. Their responsibility was to further analyze the information provided by the culture audit, monitor performance against specific goals that had been set in an effort to better realize the firm's desired culture, and provide feedback to the firm's senior management team.

CORPORATE CULTURE AT DIFFERENT STAGES OF ORGANIZATIONAL DEVELOPMENT

Although the particular elements of a corporate culture will differ, culture should change to meet the demands at each stage of development. This section discusses some of the key dimensions of culture at the various stages of organizational development.

Stage I

The culture of most small organizations emphasizes flexibility, ability to respond quickly to the environment, and the notion that the company is a family, with the entrepreneur serving as the parental figure. The organization seems to be constantly moving and, although there is a certain amount of anxiety about the firm's future, there is also a great deal of excitement. In some Stage I companies, technical wizardry and innovativeness are valued, and often the technicians are the corporate heroes. In others, the focus is on sales and marketing, and those individuals who work in these areas become the heroes.

Culture is communicated through direct interactions with the entrepreneur. Employees, in fact, look to the entrepreneur for direction, so he or she is able to almost daily define and reinforce the corporate culture, as well as to monitor and correct it. Very few entrepreneurs choose to commit their values to paper at this stage of development. Although this is not an absolute necessity, it can serve as a basis for communicating values as the firm grows. Whatever is placed on paper, however, should be supported by the daily operations of the firm.

Table 12.5. Alpha Manufacturing's Current and Desired Cultures and the Tools Used
to Make Its Desired Culture a Reality

Treatment of Customers

Current Culture	Desired Culture
Customer and quality orientation is present but not consistent throughout the organization.	A strong customer and quality orientation is present and consistent throughout all areas of the company.

Strategies for Managing This Dimension

- Continue efforts to improve the company's strategic planning process, including goal-setting regarding quality.
- Set individual quality-based performance goals.
- Continue efforts to provide technical training on customers to employees.

Current Culture	Desired Culture
We have a commitment to "doing it right the first time," as long as it doesn't affect the schedule.	With respect to product and service quality, we are committed to doing it right the first time.

Strategies for Managing This Dimension

- Take steps to make planning a way of life and take it down to departmental and individual levels.
- Establish a process of prioritizing product ideas and managing workloads.
- Formalize a process of better managing interdepartmental policies and procedures.
- Continue efforts to provide effective managerial and technical training.

Treatment of Employees

Current Culture	Desired Culture
We pay lip service to balancing work and personal lives, but our actions do not support this.	Our words and actions support a balance between work and our employees' personal lives.

Strategies for Managing This Dimension

- Continue to improve the company's strategic planning process.
- Develop more effective job descriptions, evaluate current *actual* time allocation by each position's key result areas, and develop recommended percentage time use by key result areas.

(continued)

Table 12.5. *(continued)*

Treatment of Employees (continued)

- Implement a formal structure and staffing plan.
- Develop and implement leadership education, *including a focus on effective time management.*

Current Culture	Desired Culture
We are not "confrontational" or "aggressive." We are "polite" and "professional."	We address conflict and performance problems in a clear, direct, and professional manner.
There is a "kill the messenger" syndrome at the company: no one wants to hear bad news; we tell people what they want to hear.	We encourage people to make suggestions, offer constructive criticism, and constructively challenge the majority as a way of promoting organizational and individual development.

Strategies for Managing This Dimension

- Develop leadership education programs that include training in feedback and conflict management skills.
- Encourage sharing of ideas on teams.
- Practice effective in-process meeting management techniques that promote sharing of ideas.

Current Culture	Desired Culture
We value training and developing our people, if we only had the time!	We make training and developing all of our people a priority.

Strategies for Managing This Dimension

- Make leadership education a requirement for all managers.
- Continue efforts to provide technical training to all employees.

Performance Standards and Accountability

Current Culture	Desired Culture
We set high goals and will do everything to meet them.	We set high but realistic goals and realistically prioritize our work.

Table 12.5. *(continued)*

Strategies for Managing This Dimension

- Continue to improve Alpha Manufacturing's strategic planning process, *including setting realistic priorities and goals.*
- *Establish a process for prioritizing product ideas and managing workloads.*

Current Culture	Desired Culture
People get rewarded for who they know and not necessarily for good performance (against goals). People may not always be held accountable for performing their jobs.	People are rewarded based on their performance, as measured against specific performance goals that are appropriate for their position.

Strategies for Managing This Dimension

- Develop key result area–based job descriptions and clarify roles.
- Use goal-based performance appraisals and provide ongoing feedback to direct reports.
- Train managers in how to provide effective feedback and administer rewards.
- Improve the extent to which policies and procedures are understood and followed.

Current Culture	Desired Culture
We don't take risks.	We promote and reward appropriate innovation and risk taking.

Strategies for Managing This Dimension

- As a part of the strategic planning process, devote time to discussing key strategic issues and finding ways to promote entrepreneurship.
- Train managers and team leaders in how to promote appropriate risk taking.
- Continue efforts to formalize the product development process to enable Alpha Manufacturing to take calculated risks.

Stage II

The corporate culture of the Stage II firm is very similar to that in Stage I. The firm still values responsiveness, but now there is a tendency for this to mean "crisis management." The firm still values flexibility, but now this means something like being flexible and creative enough to operate with less than adequate resources until personnel interviews are completed or until the new facilities are ready. The firm also still values the family, but now there is an extended family living within the same "house," and one's loyalty seems to depend more on which leader (regardless of level) one is most exposed to. Corporate heroes tend to become those people who are the best fire fighters and problem solvers.

It is at this stage of development that the corporate culture of most firms begins to become distorted. Because all employees can no longer have direct contact with the entrepreneur, they are left to develop their own interpretations of the corporate culture, based on what they have heard. Because the entrepreneur cannot be there to monitor behavior, he or she must depend on other managers to do so, but those managers have their own interpretations of the culture. If the company has not yet developed the strategic planning, performance management, management development, and organizational structure consistent with this stage of development, it may be placed at a further disadvantage because, even if it can develop the appropriate culture, there will be no support for it.

At this stage of development, a company should devote at least part of its planning time (as discussed in Chapter Seven) to articulating the culture that will support its efforts and to devising ways to communicate it to employees. Again, if there is an existing culture statement, it may need to be revised to reflect the needs of the current stage of development. In this regard, it should mention a shift toward planning and control in at least an implicit way, as well as an emphasis on meeting responsibilities and goals. Further, as suggested in Chapter Ten, the reward systems should be reviewed and changed, if necessary, in order to support the behavior required to meet the organization's goals.

Stage III

It is at this stage of development that the culture of a firm should make a fundamental shift toward promoting professional management. The culture of a Stage III firm should promote planning as a way of life, accountability for meeting departmental and individual goals, a commitment to training employees to become professional managers, and other behavior consistent with the professionalized firm. However, if the planning, control, management development, and organizational structure systems are inconsistent with the requirements of this stage of development, then the culture will be as well.

At this stage, the culture is, of necessity, still being implicitly managed in most cases. However, senior management can increase the probability that its culture will support its professionalization efforts by at least considering the impact that proposed organizational changes will have on what it believes to be the corporate culture and how that might be managed. In other words, it can build into its change efforts a cultural component that redefines existing elements and clearly articulates new elements. However, the effort required to explicitly manage these elements may need to be postponed until the systems and structure are at least nominally in place.

Stage IV

By the time a firm reaches Stage IV, it needs to develop a formal method for managing its corporate culture. Corporate culture management should become an important part of the planning process, and resources should be devoted to (1) performing a cultural audit to identify potential problem areas, (2) clearly articulating the existing culture and the new culture, if different, (3) identifying gaps between the current and desired cultures, and (4) developing a plan for transforming or maintaining the corporate culture. The latter step should include a process for monitoring the culture on a regular basis to ensure that it is promoting the organization's goals.

SUMMARY

A clear understanding of the meaning and importance of corporate culture remains elusive for many managers. Some managers choose to deny the existence of a culture in their organizations; others are intimidated by the thought of trying to identify anything so fuzzy, let alone of finding ways to manage it.

This chapter addresses these issues. We examine the nature of corporate culture and how culture is manifested in organizations. We also describe methods that can be used to identify an organization's culture and to manage it so as to increase organizational effectiveness. In brief, managers must first determine what their current culture is through performing a culture audit. Next, they must determine what their culture *should* be, given their stage of growth, and, finally, they must design and implement a plan for managing the corporate culture.

Every organization has a culture, and culture can have a profound impact on organizational success because it supports the other changes needed to make the transition from entrepreneurship to professional management. It is, then, important for managers to understand and learn how to manage the culture as their organization grows.

PART FOUR

ADVANCED ASPECTS OF ORGANIZATIONAL TRANSITIONS IN A GROWING AND CHANGING COMPANY

The previous sections of this book have examined the organizational issues that face companies making the transition from an entrepreneurship to a professionally managed firm. But some organizations will have the opportunity to grow beyond Stage IV. This growth will present a new set of problems that are different in nature from those encountered during the first four stages of growth.

Chapter Thirteen presents a more advanced look at strategic planning and organizational development. It shows how the Pyramid of Organizational Development framework can be used as a strategic lens to shape strategy and gain competitive advantage. It also provides a set of advanced strategic concepts and includes a case study of a company—Infogix—that has successfully implemented these concepts.

Chapter Fourteen presents a preview of the future organizational challenges encountered beyond Stage IV. It examines the advanced stages of growth after a firm has become professionally managed. Stage V requires a firm to diversify because it can no longer rely on its initial product line for future growth. During Stage V, a company typically develops new businesses, which leads to the problems faced at Stage VI. Once a firm has diversified, either through internal growth or acquisition, the new businesses must be integrated. This is the developmental focus of Stage VI. Finally, Stage VII requires that an organization deal with the inevitable forces leading to decline, whether they are caused by market saturation, erosion of management's entrepreneurial skills, or the organization's own success. All organizations will ultimately encounter decline and must revitalize. In the revitalization process, management must again give its full attention to the entire Pyramid of Organizational Development.

Chapter Fifteen examines the issues involved in making the decision to go public, as well as the changes that must be made by companies as they transition from private to public companies, including reporting requirements, Sarbanes-Oxley, and boards of directors. This chapter also presents two case studies of companies that have made this transition. One company—99 Cents Only Stores—is a NYSE company focusing on deep-discount merchandise, with more than two hundred stores and more than $1 billion in annual revenues. This company has been public for some time. The other company, PeopleSupport, provides outsourcing for customer support, with operations based in the Philippines; the company only recently became public. Both cases provide insight into the process of going public and operating as a public company.

CHAPTER THIRTEEN

Advanced Strategic Planning

This chapter presents a more advanced look at strategic planning. It builds on the framework for strategic planning and the strategic planning process described in Chapter Seven and examines how the Pyramid of Organizational Development framework can be used to help shape strategy and gain competitive advantage. The concept of *business as a game* is used to further explain the notion of competitive advantage; the concept of *strategic planning* is redefined as *strategic organizational development*. It also presents some advanced strategic concepts as a basis for developing strategy and plans. Finally, it examines how Infogix—an innovative developer of software and pioneer of the "information integrity space"—has used strategic planning to help implement a change in its strategic vision, as well as a tool to transform from entrepreneurship to a professionally managed firm.

BUSINESS AS A GAME

Business can be viewed from several different perspectives. The late, great management theorist Peter Drucker viewed it as a series of problems to be solved.[1] It can be viewed as a process of information flow or as a series of tasks to be performed. All these perspectives have merit and utility. In this chapter, we view business as a game, not in the trivial sense of *game* but in terms of two or more competitors or players who are trying to win.

The Meaning of Winning

Winning can also be viewed from a number of perspectives, and each game has its own concept of victory. For example, the object of the game of chess is to capture the opponent's king and thereby win the game.[2] The object of poker is to win as much money as possible. In both cases, winning is achieved by deploying a combination of strategy and tactics. In poker the array of tools or competitive "weapons" is greater than in chess. At the same time, however, the game of poker includes an element of luck or randomness, which does not exist in the game of chess.

Business as a game is more similar to poker than to chess. It is a game of skill and chance. The object of business is to create value for the owners or shareholders. This is done through a broad array of strategies and tactics, using a wide variety of competitive assets (weapons) intended to increase the probability of a successful outcome. These strategies and tactics are created through the process of strategic planning. Although the probability of achieving a successful outcome can be increased through effective strategic planning, there is always an element of chance in business, just as in poker.

Competitive Strategy

Competitive strategy can be defined in many ways. In a fundamental sense, competitive strategy identifies how the game will be played.[3] It defines how the player will compete—that is, the strategies, tactics, and tools that will be used to play the game and, ultimately, to win. Effectively developing a competitive strategy begins with a competitive analysis—that is, identification of present and potential competitors, their strengths, and their limitations and an analysis of the company's own strengths and limitations. Using this information, the company can then identify how it will use its strengths to maximize the competition's limitations or turn the competition's strengths into limitations. The result of this analysis will be the company's competitive strategy.

Creating Sustainable Advantage

One of the major purposes of strategic planning is to create competitive advantage. The objective is to create as many competitive advantages as possible. Ideally, the competitive advantages will be sustainable—durable and not fleeting. However, even temporary advantages are useful.

In this book, a *sustainable advantage* is operationally defined as anything that serves as a competitive advantage for at least two years. In this sense a *sustainable advantage* is roughly analogous to a *fixed asset*.[4] In many industries, a new product will not meet this criterion. It might give a company about a six-month lead time as the first-mover advantage.

Virtually anything can be a source of competitive advantage. It can be tangible or intangible. A state-of-the-art manufacturing plant, a well-known brand, a great leader, a superior salesforce, technological know-how or a patent, or a high-performance corporate culture—all can be competitive advantages. Great efforts and financial resources are expended to create and protect intellectual property and other sources of competitive advantage. For example, Amgen, a leading biotechnology company, expends a great deal of effort and resources to defend its intellectual property, which is reflected in products like Epogen and Neupogen. As a result, some people describe Amgen as "a law firm that happens to have some pharmaceuticals."

Large established organizations will have developed their infrastructure, and this can give them an advantage. However, large companies tend to become bureaucratic and political and might move slowly. Smaller entrepreneurial organizations can use speed of decision making and unity of purpose and leadership to compete with larger organizations.

Two Major Ways to Win or Lose

There are two fundamental ways to win in business. One way is to have an overwhelming advantage. For example, Microsoft controls the operating systems of most desktop computers to the extent that it has a virtual (if not a legal) monopoly.[5] This overwhelming advantage gives it great competitive power and, in turn, has made it a very successful organization. Similarly, Dell Computer created a direct build-to-order sales model that gave it an overwhelming advantage over Compaq Computer. This ultimately forced Compaq to lose market share and to merge with Hewlett-Packard.

The other way to win is to create enough small advantages that they accumulate to a great advantage. Small but significant advantages can be created at all levels of the Pyramid of Organizational Development: markets, products, resources and resource management, operational systems, management systems, and culture. For example, Wal-Mart has the same products as Kmart, but Wal-Mart has still created an overwhelming advantage over Kmart (and other retailers for that matter) by gradually developing a series of small advantages at all levels of the pyramid. Wal-Mart initially focused on different markets from Kmart. Wal-Mart went to small towns such as Crescent City, California, rather than Los Angeles. It developed its logistics and information systems over a period of many years to the point where they now constitute a formidable competitive advantage. Wal-Mart also developed a unique corporate culture.

In one sense, the second way of winning is even more powerful than the first. If the advantages are not easily visible to competition, they do not know how to counter them. By the time they are visible to a competitor, they will probably have transformed into an overwhelming advantage. This is how Wal-Mart ultimately defeated Kmart.

There are many potential sources of competitive advantage. They can be found at all levels in the Pyramid of Organizational Development.

USING THE PYRAMID OF ORGANIZATIONAL DEVELOPMENT TO DEVELOP STRATEGIC ADVANTAGE

The Pyramid of Organizational Development framework (presented in Chapter One) can be viewed as a model of the "architecture" of a business. As such, it specifies a set of tasks required to build a successful organization. However, the pyramid can also be used as a "strategic template" to create competitive advantage.

The Pyramid of Organizational Development framework can be viewed not only as a model of the architecture of a business, but also as the basis of competition among organizations. Organizations compete with each other on each of the six key dimensions of organizational development: the choice of markets, products, resources, operational systems, management systems, and culture management. This, in turn, suggests that each of these key tasks or building blocks of organizational development are *potential sources of competitive advantage.* We can, therefore, think of these key aspects of organizational development as strategic building blocks. They are not just six key tasks that must be performed to build successful organizations; they are also six key levels of organizational capabilities that serve as the basis for competition among firms.

Viewing the pyramid in this way can assist managers and leaders in both creating competitive advantage and explaining why organizations within the same industries (like Wal-Mart and Kmart) achieve different degrees of success; we develop this dual aspect of the pyramid framework later. It leads to a redefinition of the classic concept of strategic planning and to a broader notion of strategic organizational development, as explained next.

LEVELS OF THE PYRAMID AS SOURCES OF COMPETITIVE ADVANTAGE

We now take another look at the pyramid from the perspective of the potential of each level to be a source of competitive advantage. We show how each building block of the pyramid is a strategic weapon, as well as a task to be completed. This is shown graphically in Exhibit 13.1.

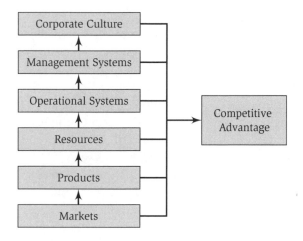

Exhibit 13.1. Six Key Sources of Competitive Advantage

Markets: Identifying a Market Segment and Niche

As discussed in Chapter One, the first task for a new venture to achieve organizational survival or success is to identify a market need for a marketable service or product.

The strategic aspect of this challenge is not merely to identify the market but also, if possible, to capture a market niche—a relatively protected place that would give the company sustainable competitive advantages. Failing to define a niche or mistakenly abandoning the historical niche can cause an organization to experience difficulties and even failure.

The process of identifying the market involves the development of a strategic market plan to identify potential customers and their needs and the creation of a competitive strategy, as discussed in Chapter Seven. Once this task is achieved, the firm has created its position in market space. This, in turn, becomes a source of potential strategic advantage.

The choice of markets to play in can be viewed in a number of ways, including geographical and market segments (both vertical and tiers, as discussed in Chapter Seven). For example, Wal-Mart chose not to compete head-to-head with Sears and Kmart; rather, the company focused its initial choice of locations on rural areas, where its principal competition was mom-and-pop general merchandise stores. Once it achieved critical mass, it began to move into suburban locations and compete more directly with Kmart and Sears. In Southern California (and now in Texas), Robbins Bros., "the World's Biggest Engagement Ring Store," carved out a segment of the jewelry store business by creating a chain of stores focused exclusively on offering engagement rings and wedding bands and on providing a unique buying experience for couples planning to marry (including the opportunity to watch the engagement ring being created and to have their pictures taken to capture the moment). The target customers for Robbins Bros.—couples planning to wed—represent only one segment of the larger jewelry store business.

The second challenge or strategic building block involves the development of products or services. This refers to the process of analyzing the needs of customers in the target market, designing the product, and developing the ability to produce it.

The product or service provided can also be a strategic weapon by differentiating the company from its competition. This is especially true when a company has a proprietary product or one with a clear difference with respect to others. For example, pharmaceutical companies such as Amgen have proprietary products such as Epogen and Neupogen, which are protected by patents. Similarly, Microsoft has a proprietary operating system that enables it to dominate the market for PCs. Usually, the basis for such clear product differentiation is intellectual property.

Often there is no apparent differentiation in the products offered by different competitors, but a difference can still be created by the way in which the product or service is delivered.

In this context, it is also important to distinguish between a nominal product and an effective or real product. A *nominal product* is the goods or the service provided; an *effective* or *real* product consists of the full set of utilities perceived or provided to a customer. For example, Kmart and Wal-Mart sell the same set of nominal products, but the real product that is provided via different shopping experiences in the stores (wide aisles, friendly service) can be quite different. A couple seeking an engagement ring or wedding band can purchase it at a mall jewelry store or a jewelry mart, but the experience of purchasing this product at Robbins Bros. (where the couple can sip a cappuccino while watching their ring being created) differentiates Robbins Bros. from their competitors.

Success during this stage is highly related to the previous critical task—proper definition of a market niche. Unless a firm fully understands the needs of the market, it cannot satisfy those needs in the process of designing the product or service to be delivered.

Resources: Acquiring and Managing Resources

The third task of building an organization is to acquire the resources needed to facilitate growth. However, competitive advantage or success can also occur from the resources an organization already has or from how it uses those resources.

Once an organization has been successful in identifying a market niche and creating a product or service, the organization will require additional physical, financial, and human resources. This is the point at which the quality of the resources and the efficiency of resource utilization will increase in importance and become a potential source of competitive advantage.

In the Disney theme parks, on Southwest Airlines flights, and in Wal-Mart stores, employees are a competitive advantage because of the way they are trained to treat customers. Customers can feel the difference. Human resources are very carefully managed at these companies, beginning with the hiring process (an operational system), continuing through the training process, and following through by providing the best customer experience (corporate culture).

Operational Systems: Developing Day-to-Day Systems to Operate the Firm

The fourth critical task is the development of basic day-to-day operational systems, which include accounting, billing, collection, information systems, advertising, personnel recruiting and training, sales, supply chain operations, production, delivery, and related systems. The development of operational systems is not just a task required to build a company; it is also a potential source of competitive advantage.

Companies compete in their choice and development of operational systems. For example, Wal-Mart ultimately defeated Sears and Kmart with the development of its logistics and information systems. Similarly, Dell Computer defeated Compaq, not with the design of its computer per se but with its innovative systems for online ordering and distribution; Compaq was trapped by its use of a distributor network. Dell's system for online ordering and direct distribution provided it with an approximately 7 percent cost advantage. Royce Medical, described in Chapter Seven, created a competitive advantage through its selling system, with a strong emphasis on telemarketing that was supported by effective customer service and support and product delivery systems.

The development of operational systems is a task that can take several years to accomplish. As such, once these systems are in place, they can constitute a sustainable competitive advantage.

Management Systems: Developing the Systems to Support Long-Term Growth

The fifth task is to develop the management systems, which are essential for the long-term viability of the firm. Management systems include systems for planning, organization, management development, and control. Any or all of these systems can be a source of competitive advantage for a company; having an advantage at this level of the Pyramid of Organizational Development is very sustainable. If a company effectively develops, implements, maintains, and works to continuously improve these systems, it will be difficult for competitors to catch them. These systems take years to build and de-bug, so even if a competitor does decide to embark on developing these or similar systems, assuming that the first to market with these systems continues to focus on them, the second to market will still be operating at a disadvantage.

As discussed in Chapter Nine, Bell-Carter Foods created a competitive advantage through its strategic planning and management development processes. These processes helped them focus on the most important aspects of growing their sales (including beating the competition), building their infrastructure, and developing the management skills needed to support the larger business that they were becoming. End result: there are only two U.S. competitors left in the ripe black olive market and, of the two, Bell-Carter is the more successful, measured in terms of sales and profitability.

Countrywide Financial Corporation was able to move from the number-four mortgage company to a number-one company over a period of about five years. A significant factor contributing to that result was a program of sustained development of its management systems, including a system for strategic planning, management development, and performance management. The strategic planning system was not only developed at the corporate level but was cascaded throughout the company to all of its operating divisions. The system was based on the platform for strategy and the planning methodology presented in this book.[6] However, the company developed proprietary software to support communicating the plan and monitoring ongoing performance. As noted in Chapter Seven, the system was recognized by the 2004 Richard A. Goodman Award for innovative strategic planning from the Association for Strategic Planning. This system constitutes a sustainable competitive advantage.

In addition, Countrywide developed a leadership development program based on the Pyramid of Management and Leadership Development presented in Chapter Nine. Over a period of two years, more than one hundred of the company's top management went through this proprietary leadership development program. This is also a sustainable competitive advantage.

These management systems typically require years to develop, but once developed they constitute a sustainable competitive advantage.

Culture: Developing and Managing Corporate Culture

Just as people have personalities, organizations have cultures, which are composed of shared values, beliefs, and norms. *Shared values* is a term referring to the importance the organization attaches to product quality, customer service, and treatment of employees. *Beliefs* are the ideas that the people in the organization hold about themselves and the firm. Last, *norms* are the unwritten rules that guide interactions and behavior.

Often when all other things are equal, culture can be the critical factor in competitive success. Howard Schultz of Starbucks has stated that when people ask him what is the real source of Starbucks success, he tells them not what they expect to hear but that the key factor is Starbucks' people. Although coffee is made from beans, which are a commodity, Starbucks has created a culture that fosters the motivation, commitment, and development of people, and, in turn, is a key factor in its competitive success.

Southwest's corporate culture is also a source of competitive advantage, which is well recognized and nurtured by its senior management team. The company's culture is frequently the topic of Colleen Barrett's (president of Southwest) monthly column in the company's *Spirit* magazine. For example, her column from the September 2006[7] issue titled, "Internal Customer Care," focuses on the work that the six members of the company's Internal Customer Care (ICC) group do to support the company's culture and "Live the Southwest Way" that includes " . . . exhibition of a Warrior Spirit, a Servant's Heart, and a Fun-LUVing attitude." The focus on culture has created an environment that employees are reluctant to leave, an experience for customers that is unique in the industry, and has contributed to Southwest's continued profitability. In fact, for several years (post-9/11), Southwest was the only profitable airline.

ORGANIZATIONAL INFRASTRUCTURE

The last four of the strategic building blocks (resources, operational systems, management systems, and culture) combine to form what we're calling a firm's infrastructure. In this context, *infrastructure* is defined as the capabilities (both tangible and intangible resources and systems) required to support the growth and development of a firm, as well as its day-to-day operations.

Role of Infrastructure in Competitive Strategy

Recent empirical research has shown that the ultimate sources of long-term competitive success are to be found in infrastructure rather than in markets and products, as conventional wisdom would have it.[8] Although the prevailing paradigm of strategy tends to view markets and products as the principal weapons for strategy, in the longer term they are unlikely to be so. If one firm finds a market, it will attract competitors, and even with the first-mover advantage, history is replete with examples of companies that have lost their position to new entrants. Starbucks, for example, was not the first to establish the coffee café. There were a number of coffee shops in local markets.

Similarly, even though marketing strategy is built around the classic 4 Ps (product, price, promotion, and place), competition typically neutralizes product advantages in a relatively short time. A classic example of this exists in the athletic footwear market. Converse began manufacturing tennis shoes in 1915, followed by basketball shoes in 1917. They were the official shoe of the National Basketball Association for many years and dominated the market until the 1980s. In the early 1980s, new competitors like Nike and Reebok began to market innovative products using new and innovative marketing techniques (including having celebrity spokespeople whose names were attached to the product). Increased competition and the inability of Converse to effectively respond, led to bankruptcy in January 2001. The company was purchased two years later by Nike. Of course, there are exceptions, such as pharmaceutical products with patent protection, but even in these cases, product competition can result in "product equivalency."

Where, then, are the true sources of sustainable competitive advantage? These can be found where there is less potential for imitation, within the "black box"[9] of the business per se. The top four levels of the Pyramid of Organizational Development, which form the infrastructure of the firm, are less susceptible to imitation and, accordingly, provide the basis for long-term sustainable competitive advantage. Thus although competition among firms takes place at all levels of the pyramid, long-term sustainable advantage is primarily found at the top four levels. This is a critical point, and it is counterintuitive. Most people mistakenly believe that the ultimate sources of competitive advantage are products. But products are the result of a system that produces them, including the process of creation of the idea for the product. Products per se are ultimately perishable, but the *system* for generating new product ideas and innovations and then bringing them to market is potentially a sustainable competitive advantage.

Infrastructure as a Source of Competitive Advantage: Examples

Organizations such as Southwest Airlines, Nike, and Wal-Mart became dominant forces in their industries, whereas other comparable organizations in the same industries such as People Express, LA-Gear, and Kmart have experienced difficulties and decline after a period of promising initial growth, even though the core products and markets of these pairs of companies are comparable. This suggests that the source of competitive advantage must be found someplace else.

The ultimate source of competitive success in companies like Wal-Mart, Southwest Airlines, and Starbucks is not in their products but in their infrastructure. There are no products that Wal-Mart sells that Kmart cannot offer. Air transportation is a commodity, and a flight from Los Angeles to Oakland is essentially the same on Southwest Airlines as on United or American Airlines. Starbucks coffee comes from the same beans as Peet's Coffee, and the beans undergo the same dark-roast process.

In all these cases, the source of competitive success can be found, not in the product but in the infrastructure of the company and the way it operates and is managed.

REDEFINING STRATEGIC PLANNING

Chapter Seven defined and treated strategy and strategic planning from a conventional (yet unique) perspective. However, if strategy is viewed from the perspective of the pyramid as described earlier, then it is clear that the conventional notions of strategy and strategic planning are too narrow.

The conventional notion of strategy focuses primarily on markets and products as the primary bases of competition. However, we believe (and this is supported by some empirical evidence and analysis as well) that organizations actually compete at *all levels of the Pyramid of Organizational Development, not just markets and products.*[10]

This suggests the need to redefine and broaden the notion of strategic planning. For this reason we have coined the term *strategic organizational development* as an alternative to describe the advanced concept of strategic planning that we propose in this book.

STRATEGIC ORGANIZATIONAL DEVELOPMENT DEFINED

Strategic organizational development refers to the process of planning and building economic enterprises in terms of all of the six key building blocks of successful organizations, as well as the business foundation. We believe that an effective strategy must deal not only with a company's markets, competition, and products but also with the internal organizational capabilities or infrastructure, which is required not only to facilitate growth but to serve as competitive weapons. In fact, as explained later, we believe that the ultimate source of competitive advantage is found in an organization's infrastructure rather than in its choice and position in markets per se. Accordingly, we believe that strategic organizational development is the next step beyond strategic planning.

A strategic organizational development plan is a written document that details how the organization will take advantage of the market and competitive opportunities and deal with present and potential threats by maximizing the strengths and working to minimize the limitations of its infrastructure. The key difference between classic strategic planning and strategic organizational development is that the latter includes developing specific strategies that define how the company will use its infrastructure as a competitive weapon. This goes beyond the traditional focus on markets, competition, and products. Operationally defined, this means having specific strategies that will help differentiate the company from its competition and support "winning the game," with respect to the company's resources and resource management, operational systems, management systems, and culture.

Developing a resource strategy involves identifying how resources will be acquired, how they will be deployed, and ways they will be managed to promote their effective and efficient use. Developing an operational and management systems strategy involves identifying those systems (for example, logistics, manufacturing, R&D, and marketing) that can provide a sustainable competitive advantage and defining how these systems will be used and continuously developed to maintain this advantage. Developing a corporate culture strategy involves identifying those aspects of the company's culture that provide or can provide a competitive advantage and clearly defining how the culture will be effectively managed to support this advantage. The end result will be strategy statements—typically one to two sentences—that define what these weapons are and how they will be used to win the game.

ADDITIONAL ADVANCED STRATEGIC CONCEPTS

This section examines a number of additional advanced strategic concepts and issues, including the concept of stealth advantages and the strategic aspects of size. Playing for market position and defining or redefining a new market space are also discussed.

The Concept of Stealth Advantages

One of the side benefits of using components of the organization's infrastructure as a source of competitive advantage is that they are relatively hidden or concealed to competition. They can be termed *stealth advantages.*

This is the secret to the ultimate dominance of companies such as Wal-Mart, Countrywide Financial Corporation, and Starbucks. All these companies have essentially commodity products. Yet all three have been able to develop dominant market positions because they have used aspects of their infrastructure, including strategic planning, management and leadership development, and corporate culture, as strategic weapons. Although their competitors could certainly see the results, they were probably not fully aware of how each company used its infrastructure to win the business game.

The use of infrastructure as a stealth advantage is very powerful. It is not only available to large companies like Starbucks and Countrywide Financial Corporation; it is available to much smaller companies as well. For example, Bell-Carter Foods (described in Chapter Nine) has achieved dominance in its space (ripe black olives) through the use of infrastructure.

The Strategic Aspects of Size

Another advanced strategic issue concerns the size or scale of operations of a company in relation to its market position. It deals with the issue of whether a company is attempting to become one of the larger players in its market space or whether it will occupy a position as a "boutique."

Playing for Market Position. All games involve position play, whether in chess, football, or Texas Hold'em. This is true in business as well. One of the key issues that all companies will have to face sooner or later with respect to position involves the question of size or scale of operations. This issue is not just a matter of transitions from one stage of development. It also concerns the competitive space that a company seeks to occupy.

The strategic aspect of size is caused by the nature of competition and markets. It appears that markets evolve until there is a classic oligopoly of a few very large players and a greater number of much smaller players. In this type of situation, midsized companies are at a distinct disadvantage. They neither have the scale nor resources to compete effectively with the largest players, nor the nimbleness and lower cost structures to compete with the smaller, highly specialized players. Accordingly, they need to make a strategic decision about whether to try and become one of the very large market participants or to remain smaller and specialized.

This was the choice facing IndyMac Bank a few years ago. In 2003, the company was the fifteenth-largest mortgage company and was facing competition coming from both ends of the spectrum: giant firms with well-developed infrastructure and greater resources and smaller, more nimble firms with lower cost structures. Under the leadership of Mike Perry, CEO, the company did a strategic analysis of the situation and made the strategic decision to increase the size of the firm in order to ultimately become one of the largest players. During the period from about 2003 to 2006, IndyMac Bank grew from the fifteenth- to the eighth-largest firm in its market space. The company became highly profitable, and its stock price increased over the same period.

Defining or Redefining a New Market Space. Another type of strategic advantage can be created by defining or redefining a new market space. When a company is first to create a market space, there is an opportunity to achieve a variety of strategic advantages, including market position and product (brand) recognition, as well as advantages of scale. These are sometimes referred to as first-mover advantages. For example, this was achieved by PowerBar, Inc. (now owned by Nestlé), which created the "energy bar" category and space. Another example of a company that is in the process of defining a new space is Infogix, discussed later in the chapter.

Similar advantages can be created by companies that do not create a space but succeed in redefining a space. For example, Starbucks did not create either coffee or cafés, but they succeeded in creating a new hybrid category of specialty retail cafés.

The Rule of Three. One theory of industry consolidation suggests that all markets will eventually evolve to an endgame where there are a few very large players and many more boutiques or niche players. Specifically, it is predicted that there will be approximately three major players controlling at least 70 percent of market share, with the remaining 30 percent or less divided among a number of niche players. The top three players controlling the lion's share of the market will have a number-one player with at least 40 percent market share; number two will have 20 percent-plus; and number three will have 10 percent-plus. Number one will be a dominant player by two different measures: (1) it will have twice as much as its nearest competitor and (2) more market share than the other two largest competitors combined.

This concept was a significant factor in motivating a strategic change at Countrywide Financial Corporation. Basically, the firm's management team decided to increase its market share of the mortgage business. Although the initial reaction to this was that it was not possible in the financial services or mortgage business, the senior executive team (led by Angelo Mozilo, CEO, and Stanford Kurland, COO) ultimately embraced this notion and used it as a keystone in formulating the company's strategic mission and core strategy.

Market Duopolies. Although the eventual rule of three is possible, other markets might evolve to where there is a duopoly, with two major players and only much smaller, niche players. Several industries have already evolved to either the troika or a duopoly. For example, in the aircraft industry there is Boeing and Air Bus and a number of smaller boutique players such as Gulf Stream, Bombardier, and Fokker. Similarly, in the home improvement industry there is Home Depot and Lowe's, with no other comparable major player. Another example is the package delivery industry, which is dominated by UPS and FedEx. In principle, there is an opportunity in all of these industries for a number-three player. In the California ripe black olive industry, for example, there are currently only two players — Bell-Carter Foods (described in Chapter Nine and Chapter Sixteen) and Musco Foods.

The key strategy question is whether a company wants to play for one of the top positions or whether it will play for position as a specialist or niche player. Although it is not impossible to dislodge a player from one of the top three positions, it is extremely difficult. For example, Air Bus was able to overcome Boeing's dominance and achieve rough parity in the aircraft industry, but this took many years.

Playing at middle position is very difficult and possibly untenable over the long run. The middle gets unmercifully squeezed by both ends of the competitive spectrum. Usually, a midsized company will have to make a strategic decision to get either much larger (possibly through acquisitions) or much smaller. This was the motivation for the decision to grow IndyMac Bank, as described earlier.

ADVANCED STRATEGIC PLANNING AND ORGANIZATIONAL DEVELOPMENT AT INFOGIX

This section presents a comprehensive case study of a company that has used strategic planning to make the transition from entrepreneurship to professional management, while simultaneously defining a new market space. The company is Infogix (formerly named Unitech Systems).[11] It shows how most if not all the tools described in this book were used at Infogix to help make the transition from entrepreneurship to an entrepreneurially oriented, professionally managed firm.[12]

About Infogix

Infogix, Inc. provides information integrity software solutions that help major corporations ensure the accuracy, consistency, and reliability of their operational, financial, and management information. It is a pioneer of the information integrity space. Today, with nearly two hundred team members and offices in major cities across North America and Europe, Infogix is a world leader in its market space. The organization has both an innovative set of software products and a range of professional services. Its customers include industry-leading organizations such as Citibank, American Express, Verizon, Target, and Wal-Mart. Over four hundred of the Global 2000 use Infogix's products and services. The Excellence in Information Integrity Award, which Infogix has sponsored since 1995, recognizes organizations that have demonstrated exceptional progress toward achieving information integrity. Some of the past winners of this award include Sprint, Bank of Nova Scotia, and TSYS.

Key Events in the Company's History

This section summarizes the key events and phases in the company's history and provides context for understanding the transition that the company made to professional management.

Phase 1: Infogix as a New Venture. The company that today is known as Infogix was founded as Unitech Systems by Madhavan Nayar in 1982. It began as a one-man consulting firm.

Nayar, who holds degrees from universities in India and the Illinois Institute of Technology, pioneered the concept of "information integrity" software solutions at a time when few had realized the need for specifically designed systems that helped customer organizations ensure the validity and accuracy of information.

Nayar has described the need for information integrity as follows: "For us to effectively harness the benefits of the information revolution and avoid the costs of widespread information pollution, we need to recognize and treat information as a shared, universal resource. We need to develop the science, technology, products, and services to measure, monitor, and manage its integrity, much like the environmental science, technology, and industry emerged in the wake of the industrial revolution to answer our need for clean air, pure water, reliable power, and safe food."[13]

In 1982, Infogix developed its first software product—U/ACR—developed for, and in partnership with, the Blue Cross Blue Shield of Illinois. During the next two decades, the company successfully developed a number of other products through similar strategic customer partnerships.

Phase 2: Infogix's Growth and Development. Through 1992, the company grew rapidly, reaching $12 million in revenue and a cumulative annual growth rate of 65 percent for the first ten years.

During this period, the company evolved from a one-person consultancy to approximately eighty people, with a president, executive vice president and COO, and several vice presidents with directors, managers, and employees below them. At the beginning of 1992, the company was reorganized into six operating groups, each headed by a group leader; the position of executive vice president and COO was eliminated. Throughout this stage Unitech adopted a series of conventional business practices for a growing entrepreneurial company. This included the way the company was structured, as well as the way people were compensated.

The company sold its products through sales representatives who were paid a base salary, commissions, and various incentives such as bonuses for selling new products, "salesperson of the month" (and quarter and year) awards, and "100% Club" trips to exotic destinations for those who met their quotas.

Beginning in 1993, the company initiated a series of changes, many of which, seen in retrospect, may have impeded its continued rapid growth but contributed to organizational learning. That year the company decided to decentralize sales management by hiring area sales managers in North America and establishing a separate international sales group. By the end of the year, however, no area sales managers had been hired, and there was no revenue growth. Also in 1993, the senior leaders of the company learned about the management philosophy of W. Edwards Deming and, after several months of study and deliberation, decided to adopt it. The decision was implemented by holding a weekend retreat for influential team members from different groups in the company and then a two-day off-site meeting for everyone. The Deming philosophy was adopted on April 1, 1994.

Phase 3: Impact of the Deming Philosophy. The adoption and implementation of the Deming philosophy is often difficult, if not impossible, in most organizations, particularly in the West. It requires the reorientation and alignment of many of the principles, policies, and practices of running a business. It requires the optimization of the entire organizational system rather than each component; the understanding of the variation and fluctuation of performance across the system and over time; the use of data to understand performance and make decisions; and the recognition that each individual is different from every other. In order to benefit from Deming's philosophy, an organization must be prepared to abandon conventional practices, adopt a holistic approach, and look for long-term results.

The implications of the Deming philosophy were radical and extensive. Quotas and other numerical objectives linked to incentives and compensation were discontinued. Formal performance evaluations and salary adjustments tied to performance evaluation were also eliminated. All processes within the company were to be mapped, defined, and improved.

The reaction of most of the team members of the company was skeptical, if not negative. Many of the star salespeople left the company, and over the next eighteen months, almost 95 percent of the salesforce turned over. Companywide, employee turnover exceeded 50 percent in 1994. An employee survey revealed that employee morale was far below industry average.

In 1994, it was also decided to organize the company into four geographical divisions: three (East, West, and Central) in North America and one international division. The senior executives (group leaders) in charge of sales, marketing, and finance were assigned the responsibility for the three North American divisions. The international group already had a group leader. In addition, each division was organized into business units, which were established in Dallas, San Francisco, Atlanta, Cleveland, Boston, Philadelphia, Chicago, and Paris. Each business unit was headed by a business unit leader and included three sales executives and one application consultant, with each sales executive assigned one hundred accounts in two or three industries.

All the changes during the year resulted in a great deal of uncertainty and anxiety throughout the company, especially among the group leaders. In February 1995, while Nayar was in Europe for a speaking engagement, all the group leaders met to discuss their concerns and decided to present a list of issues and recommendations to Nayar upon his return. The issues concerned primarily Nayar's leadership style. One of the recommendations was for him to play the role of a nonexecutive chairman and for the group leaders to run the company.

The recommendation was not accepted and shortly thereafter, two of the group leaders resigned from the company.

In early 1995, the three divisions in North America were reorganized into two geographic locations: East and West. The product development function was distributed among the three group leaders responsible for East, West, and International divisions. For the third year in a row, there was no revenue growth in 1995.

There were relatively few changes and a modest revenue growth in 1996. At the end of 1996, it was decided to combine the two North American divisions into one and designate a single group leader for North America.

In April 1997, to help revive the company, Project Oxygen was launched. The project consisted of establishing industry-focused customer teams in the business units (now renamed customer units), each customer team consisting of a sales executive, a solution consultant, and an account representative. Each customer team was responsible for a handful of major accounts in a specific industry group (banking and finance, insurance and health care, communications and utilities, distribution and manufacturing). All other existing customer accounts were assigned to the customer teams, based on geographical proximity. Also the business unit leader position was renamed customer unit leader.

Project Oxygen was a significant effort, which required the hiring of over fifty new people in the field and training all of them for three weeks in the home office in Naperville, Illinois. However, some of the customer unit leaders were new, and there was much confusion about how the team concept was to be deployed and practiced. Some teams performed exceptionally well, while others were dysfunctional and had to be rebuilt or disbanded.

In 1998, it was decided to align the customer unit leaders also along industry lines. This meant that all the teams in a given industry group (for example, banking and finance) would be supported by a customer unit leader for that market sector. This was a major change for the teams and the unit leaders. Most teams no longer had a local leader they could go to, and the unit leaders had to travel and oversee the activities of teams based in several locations.

By 1998, Infogix had grown to be a $20 million company, with offices in North America and Western Europe.

Phase 4: The Catalyst for Strategic Change. In March 1999, Nayar attended a Forbes Presidents' Conference, where he heard one of the authors of this book (Eric Flamholtz) make a presentation about a framework for building successful organizations. The approach made sense to Nayar, and in late 1999 he invited Flamholtz and his team to work with the company and apply the approach described in this book.

Organizational Transformation at Infogix

The organizational development process began with a series of interviews with selected group leaders and unit leaders during the summer of 1999 to provide the consulting team with an understanding of the company and its development issues. The next step was a strategic planning retreat, attended by all leaders in early December. The retreat was to introduce all of Infogix's leadership team to the "pyramid framework" described in this book and take the company to the next level of planning capability.

Planning has always been a part of Unitech's culture. The company has always had a well-established strategic planning function, and the leaders of the operating groups have always prided themselves on their strategic capabilities. However, the growth and diversification experienced during the 1990s demanded a new scale of planning altogether. Management needed to address not only new industry segments and larger operating units but increased organizational complexity as well. The strong entrepreneurial spirit and autonomy that had long been part of Unitech's culture now presented a management challenge. Although at one time that spirit had helped to create a vibrant, nimble operating environment, it had also resulted in counterproductive organizational silos that resisted cooperation.

Infogix already had a formal strategy and planning process, but the key was to improve the existing planning system and ensure that it became a way of life. The strategic planning process was intended as a tool for the alignment of the various units of the company.

Role of Strategic Planning in Transformation to Professional Management

At the retreat, a management planning simulation revealed the areas that needed to be strengthened internally. The group discovered that its planning was too grandiose to be feasible and chose to adopt the approach to strategic planning described in this book.

There are two major components to this approach to strategic planning: (1) a conceptual framework that serves as a platform for strategy and (2) the strategic planning method per se.

Platform for Strategy and the Strategic Planning Method

Infogix adopted the pyramid framework as the platform for the development of their strategic plan. This template was used to assess the strengths and areas for further development at Infogix.

Based on this analysis, it was clear that Infogix was relatively strong at the bottom four levels of the pyramid but needed further development at the top two levels, which include management systems and culture management. It also required some redefinition or fine-tuning of the business foundation to fit the founder's (Madhavan Nayar) vision. Although there are many approaches to planning, Infogix chose to adopt the method presented in this book (see Chapter Seven). How the company used this framework to develop its plan is described next.

Developing the Business Foundation. The first step was to develop the new Infogix "business foundation"—a business definition, a strategic vision, and a core strategy. (At Infogix, the term *strategic vision* is used rather than the term *strategic mission*, as used in Chapter Seven.) By the end of the initial planning workshop, the leadership team had defined their business as that of "helping Global 2000 organizations improve the quality of their information through information integrity systems."

This meant that the organization was going to evolve from one that was currently focused on selected tools for automated balancing of accounts and statements to a total information integrity solutions business. This meant, in turn, that Infogix would create a new market space: the "information integrity space." An intermediate step was for Infogix to evolve from its current product portfolio to a business with automated controls, services, and processes for information integrity. This was to happen through three phases:

1. Phase I. Pre-1999: Automated balancing
2. Phase II. 1999: Automated controls, services, and processes
3. Phase III. 2003: Infogix to be true information integrity business

Building on the Business Foundation. Once the new business definition and strategic vision for the organization had been established, there was a need to complete the plan to the level of developing goals and assigning priorities and roles. Another related, key challenge now was to make planning a way of life.

A secret key to this was to hold a series of quarterly planning meetings. At some organizations, planning is episodic. It occurs and then stops. The plan is there, but it is not reviewed on a regular basis or updated. At Infogix, planning was done on an ongoing basis.

Quarterly planning retreats facilitated by Flamholtz and members of his consulting team would become an opportunity for the organization to reflect on progress through the quarter and to set goals for the next quarter.

Developing Priority Objectives. Although there are many objectives in any strategic plan, a well-thought-out set of priority objectives (key objectives that receive the most management focus) is another of the secret ingredients that were important to make planning work at Infogix. These objectives are derived from the strategic vision and related key result areas.

Role of Performance Optimization in Transformation to Professional Management

Another strategic innovation at Infogix was the creation of a unique performance optimization system (see Figure 13.1) that combined with the planning system to create an overall strategic management system. In order to strengthen the levels of accountability and enhance the execution of the strategic plan, a performance optimization process was introduced. *Performance optimization* is a term coined at Infogix to refer to an innovative alternative to the conventional notion of performance management, as discussed next.

The conventional model of performance management typically links the planning system and measurement of results with the evaluation and reward systems within the organization (see Chapter Ten). One thing that is very different about the concept of performance optimization at Infogix, as compared with the conventional concept of performance management, is that the former does *not* link performance directly to rewards. This is for philosophical reasons (examined next) and suggests an important difference in the culture at Infogix from that of many companies.

Madhavan Nayar, Infogix's company leader, believes strongly that rewards ought to be based on *company performance* rather than individual performance. The overall objectives of Infogix's rewards philosophy are to do the following:

1. Attract top industry talent compatible with the unique characteristics of the Infogix environment

2. Retain team members in a long-term developmental relationship

3. Foster an environment that promotes teamwork through collaboration and cooperation

4. Foster an environment for personal and professional development

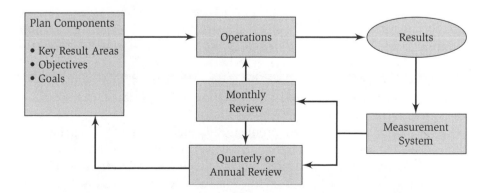

Figure 13.1. The Infogix Performance Optimization System

5. Maintain equity across the company

6. Compensate leadership group members based on overall company performance

7. Manage fixed costs by providing higher variable pay

Thus the term *performance optimization* (used at Infogix) is intentionally different from the more conventional term *performance management.* The latter term would include rewards as a key component of the system, while performance optimization intentionally does not include rewards, for the reasons given.

Use of Measurement in Planning and Performance Optimization

One of the key contributors to the ultimate success of Infogix's strategic innovation with planning and performance optimization was the development of detailed measurements for objectives. As a CPA once said, "What gets measured gets counted!" This means that the things that get measured are the ones that are most important in influencing people's behavior in organizations.

At Infogix a great deal of time and care was put on the development of measurements of goals. In part, this is because Infogix is a highly analytical and process-oriented organization. The company takes great care to be precise with its use of terminology and the need for operational definitions.

The net result is that Infogix has created a detailed set of measurements for every objective and goal. These measurements are critical to making the plan operational and specific. They are a significant strength of its performance optimization system.

Results of the Transformation to Professional Management at Infogix

The transition from entrepreneurship to professional management at Infogix remains a work in progress. The strategic planning–performance optimization system at Infogix also remains a work in progress. Nevertheless, significant benefits (both tangible and intangible) have been realized.

First, there is a clarity and focus to the vision of the company that did not exist to the same extent in the past. People understand that Infogix is in the information integrity business. This broader concept has replaced the more narrow focus on specific information integrity products, such as automated balancing and controls. People now understand that its long-term vision is to help create and, ideally, to dominate the information integrity space. This provides a big-picture context for short-term decisions and actions. One of the company's growing pains was that a relatively large number of people did not understand where the company was headed. This is no longer the case.

Another benefit of the strategic planning–performance optimization process is greater focus on priority objectives. In a business there are countless things to deal with; the Infogix plan provides focus on the priority objectives. People understand what the priorities are and where the emphasis must be for the company to achieve its longer-range vision.

A third benefit concerns the productivity and accountability of people. The specificity of the measurements has increased the extent to which people are accountable for specific results rather than just vague responsibilities. The plan provides a tool that can be used to monitor overall performance of the company, as well as that of specific business units on a systematic basis.

One of the ultimate tests of a company is its financial performance. Venture capital funded firms are generally characterized by emphasis on financial performance, short-term results, and exit strategies that yield the maximum return to the venture capitalists. Infogix has followed a different path. It has been focused on building a strong business for the long term; it has been focused on building the products and the infrastructure for the business, even if this took a great deal of time and investment.

Like other information technology companies, Infogix has had to deal with the collapse of information technology investment since the boom that led up to Y2K. Infogix is a privately held company, and financial information is proprietary. Nevertheless, we can say that the company is strong financially and has gotten stronger over the past five years, in contrast to some of the larger companies in this space like Compaq, Hewlett-Packard, and Sun Microsystems.

A Successful Transition

This case has described how one company—Infogix—made the transition from an entrepreneurship to professional management. It also describes how strategic planning and an innovative system of performance optimization have produced both cultural and tangible results in the business.

Our intention is not to suggest that Infogix is a perfect company. There are no perfect companies. The ultimate criterion for any company is, Are we stronger at the end of a time period than at the beginning? The answer for Infogix is definitely yes.

SUMMARY

This chapter presents a more advanced look at strategic planning. It draws on the Pyramid of Organizational Development framework and shows how it can be used to help shape strategy and gain competitive advantage. It explains that the ultimate sources on long-term competitive success are to be found in infrastructure rather than in markets and products, as conventional wisdom suggests.

The chapter also redefines the notion of strategic planning and introduces the concept of *strategic organizational development,* which refers to the process of planning and building economic enterprises in terms of all of the six key building blocks of successful organizations, as well as the business foundation. This notion implies that an effective strategy must deal not only with a company's markets, competition, and products but also with the internal organizational capabilities or infrastructure, which is required to facilitate growth and to serve as a competitive weapon.

The chapter describes the case of Infogix, which has used strategic planning as a tool to both create a new market space (information integrity) and to make the successful transition from entrepreneurship to professional management.

CHAPTER FOURTEEN

Managing the Advanced Stages
of Growth

T he previous chapters of this book have dealt with the issues encountered
by rapidly growing entrepreneurial organizations as they move through
the first four stages of growth: from a new venture (Stage I) to consolidation of an established firm (Stage IV). If management has accomplished the
developmental tasks described throughout this book, then on completing Stage
IV, the firm will have become a professionally managed organization.

Some firms will have the opportunity to grow in size beyond Stage IV. This
growth will present a new set of organizational development problems that
are quite different from those during Stages I through IV—the transition from
entrepreneurship to professional management.

This chapter is intended to assist the senior managers of such firms in
planning for the future development of their enterprises by examining the
stages of growth that occur beyond Stage IV. It can also help senior managers
of organizations that have already reached those stages of growth and are
either encountering certain developmental problems or wish to avoid the
classic problems at each stage.

We first describe the nature of each of the later stages of growth and then
examine the key problems and challenges that organizations must confront as
they advance to each of them.

NATURE OF PROBLEMS BEYOND STAGE IV

The problems encountered beyond Stage IV are quite different from those of the prior stages of growth. In Stage I, the essential problem is to find a market and develop a product that is appropriate for that market. This involves demonstrating proof of concept. In Stage II, the central problem for the organization is to develop the operational infrastructure. This includes development of both the resources needed to facilitate future growth and the day-to-day operational systems (scale-up) required to run the firm. In Stage III, the central problem is to begin the professionalization of the organization. At this point, the firm needs to focus on developing its management systems—its systems for planning, organization, management development, and control. In Stage IV, the key issue is to "consolidate" the organization by beginning to manage its corporate culture and reinforce the transition to professional management.

In brief, prior to Stage V, the firm's management problems all center around the issues of locating an initial market, developing a product, and building the operational infrastructure, management systems, and corporate culture needed to run a firm that has reached approximately $100 to $500 million in annual revenue (for manufacturing firms) or approximately one-third of this for service firms.

On reaching Stage V, the firm's problems change in nature. The firm must now reestablish itself as a different type of entrepreneurial company—one that is professionalized but still entrepreneurial and able to develop new products and services within the boundaries of the existing organization. Ideally, the firm will have retained its entrepreneurial orientation throughout Stages I through IV. In some cases, however, firms may have lost their entrepreneurial spirit to some degree and must now seek to reestablish it. Once the challenge of developing new products or services has been met, the firm must then focus on developing an infrastructure capable of supporting the now-diversified company it has become.

GROWTH BEYOND STAGE IV

The advanced stages of organizational growth, the critical development areas for each stage, and the approximate size (measured in dollars of sales revenue or budget for nonprofits) at which an organization should pass through each stage are shown in Table 14.1. These are the stages of growth beyond entrepreneurship. They represent the transitions that must be made by all entrepreneurially oriented, professionally managed firms if they are to continue to be successful in their future growth. In this section, we describe, in depth, the stages of growth beyond Stage IV.

Table 14.1. Advanced Stages of Organizational Growth

Stage	Description	Critical Development Area	Approximate Organizational Size (in sales)	
			Manufacturing Firms	*Service Firms*
V	Diversification	New products for existing markets, new markets for existing products, or both	$500 million to $1 billion	$167 to $333 million
IV	Integration	Integration of different business units through developing a new infrastructure to support them (managing resources, developing appropriate operational and management systems, and creating a culture consistent with the needs of the "new company")	$1 billion-plus	$333 million-plus
III	Decline and Revitalization	Revitalization of organization at all levels of the Pyramid of Organizational Development	Varies	Varies

Stage V: Diversification

After an organization has completed the consolidation stage, the next developmental challenge it faces is to diversify. This problem usually arises because the firm's original product or product line has become relatively mature and will not facilitate sufficient future growth to sustain the organization at its current rate of growth, its historical rate of growth, or its immediate future growth expectations. This problem is simply a result of the phenomenon of market saturation.

When a firm initially introduces a product as a new venture, the market is typically unsaturated, and there is relatively little competition. As the firm becomes successful, it typically attracts competitors. A classic example was Apple Computer and the development of PCs. Apple Computer found and developed the market for the personal computer (they were the first to offer a product that required little assembly) but attracted a host of competitors, including IBM. The presence of competition decreases the firm's profit margins and erodes its market share over time.

Sometimes a company can have the market or "playing field" to itself, with limited competition, for a very long time. For example, Mattel dominated the market for dolls for young girls for many years with its icon doll, Barbie. Recently, MGA Entertainment has taken away a significant portion of Mattel's market share with its edgier, multiethnic Bratz dolls.

A related phenomenon is that as the market for the new product becomes increasingly saturated, the new venture's rate of growth cannot be sustained for its given product vehicle. A classic historical example of this phenomenon was the highly successful dBASE II—one of the first software products for database management, marketed by Ashton-Tate, a company that no longer exists. As the potential users of dBASE II were reached, and as new competitors entered the marketplace, it was necessary for Ashton-Tate to identify new products to continue its growth. Ultimately, the company was unsuccessful in accomplishing this task and was, as a result, sold to Borland, which, in turn, was ultimately purchased by another company. In contrast, Oracle Corp, which is itself built on a platform of database management software, has been able to deal successfully with the challenge of product diversification through software applications and has become a multi-billion-dollar company.

One way of thinking about the difference between the issues faced by the firm during Stages I through IV and the issues faced in Stage V is to consider the analogy of a product as an oil field. The central problem in petroleum exploration is to find a new oil field. Once a field has been found, the organization builds up an infrastructure to tap the oil well and convert it into marketable products. As the size of the business increases, the firm has to build its business around that oil well. The central issues here are developing the capability to tap the oil well and marketing its products. From this standpoint, the oil well is essentially a resource that the firm is drawing on. However, this resource has a finite life, which means it will not last forever—only until all of the oil has been pumped out.

Most consumer and industrial markets are very much like oil wells, in that they will not last forever. They may produce a gusher that leads to very rapid growth for an organization, but over time the oil wells inevitably play themselves out. When a firm builds up its organizational and management infrastructure to tap an oil well, it usually does so with the intention of remaining a going concern. This means that if the organization is to continue to exist, it must find other oil fields that it can begin to extract resources from. Accordingly, if the firm is to become more than a one-time venture, it must use some of the resources earned from tapping the oil well to invest in exploration of other oil fields. It should be hiring geologists to search for additional oil fields, spending additional resources in drilling test wells, and so forth.

Companies in totally different businesses from petroleum exploration and refining will find it useful to think of their business in terms of the oil well analogy just described. A company's entrepreneur identifies a new market, which is analogous to a petroleum corporation finding an oil field. The company develops a product that is accepted by consumers, which is, again, analogous to a firm beginning to tap the oil in the field. The firm then builds up the operational management infrastructure necessary to operate the day-to-day business, while simultaneously preparing an infrastructure that is necessary to continue the operation after its first product has been "used up." Thus the challenge of Stage V is essentially analogous to the firm's finding another oil well. If the firm is prudent, it will not wait until its markets are sufficiently dried up to begin locating new markets and building new products. Accordingly, it will be engaged in a process of research and development designed to identify new oil fields and begin their production while its current oil fields are still producing.

Typically, an organization can only expect that a given product vehicle will carry it to the range of $100 to $500 million in annual revenue. As discussed previously, this is simply the normal curve for this phenomenon, and certain companies may not experience the need for a new product vehicle until significantly after $500 million in revenue. A number of firms have reached $1 billion in annual revenue before they experienced the need for a new product vehicle; however, these firms are the exception rather than the general rule. The upper limit for growth through a single product or line of business may be reached well before a firm generates $500 million in annual revenues. For example, Bell-Carter Foods faced this problem at about $100 million, because at that size they had captured about 80 percent of the market for their core product (ripe black olives).

A variation on this problem was experienced by Amazon.com. The cost of developing the infrastructure to operate the business of selling books over the Internet was sufficiently great that the company needed to diversify its product line. Today, Amazon sells a variety of products over the Internet, including magazines, music, DVDs, videos, electronics, computers, software, apparel and accessories, and shoes—as well as books.

When a firm fails to diversify, the result can be stagnation, sale of the company, or even bankruptcy. Even companies with well-established icon brands can ultimately suffer or meet their demise. A classic example is Cuisinarts, Inc.—well known for its upscale food processors that were highly popular in the 1970s. The company filed for bankruptcy under Chapter 11 of the federal Bankruptcy Code in 1989. The food-processing business had become saturated, and though the company still controlled about 45 percent of the food-processing market, it experienced difficulties.

Cuisinarts had not done effective strategic planning and failed to capitalize on its famous name. By the time it filed for Chapter 11, the company had only recently begun branching out to items such as cooking utensils, hand blenders, and other cooking products. Cuisinarts had defined its business as the "food-processing business," rather than more broadly. Unfortunately, its traditional market dried up before Cuisinarts found a new one. Smith Corona, once a leading maker of typewriters, also filed for bankruptcy, in part, because the market for typewriters no longer existed. Typewriters had been replaced by personal computers, and the company had not effectively responded with new products to meet changing customer needs. Schwinn, once a leading brand of bicycles, experienced a similar fate. Although bicycles were still popular, the type of cycle that had become popular was quite different from those offered by Schwinn. The company filed for bankruptcy in the early 1990s.

Thus the central problem of Stage V is to diversify the firm so that it is no longer dependent on its initial product vehicle. The challenge is to establish one or more new product (or service) vehicles that will enable the firm to continue to grow successfully. These may or may not be in the same business as the firm's initial product vehicle. Stated differently, the firm may have to diversify outside its initial business segment. The firm may be developing multiple businesses (typically, but not always through the creation of new divisions). Thus Stage V is a time when the business should be making two transitions: (1) from one product vehicle to the next and (2) from a single business to a set of businesses. This can be accomplished through internal development of new products, identification of new markets, or acquisition of other organizations.

One spectacular example of a company that has taken both internal and external routes to achieve successful diversification is Starbucks. The company has diversified from its original core product (coffee) with the addition of other beverages and products. It has also leveraged the Starbucks brand with other products such as ice cream (a joint venture with Dreyer's) and has made acquisitions in the United States and Europe. Starbucks had the infrastructure to do this.

Another example of a company that was able to diversify successfully is Mövenpick—a company founded by Uli Prager in Switzerland. Prager initially was successful as an entrepreneur with Mövenpick restaurants. Then the company added a wine company, a coffee company, and an ice cream company, all under the Mövenpick brand. In addition, the company developed a series of Mövenpick Hotels.

A third example of a company that was able to successfully build on its core business and diversify is Countrywide Financial Corporation. Country-wide was able to leverage its core mortgage business and diversify (through a combination of internal development and acquisition) into a wide range of financial products and services, including insurance, mortgage securitizations, and banking. By 2006, the company's revenues and profits were relatively balanced from its business mix between mortgages and other related businesses, even though Countrywide was the number-one mortgage originator in the United States.

Stage VI: Integration

In the process of making the transition to Stage V, an organization sets in motion the forces that require it to move to Stage VI—integration. During Stage V, the firm will have made the transition from a single product line (or service line) company to a multiproduct (or multiservice) company. It will also typically have become a multibusiness company. This means that by the time the organization completes the diversification process begun in Stage V, it will consist of a set of (at least partially) related businesses. Developing an infrastructure to support this "new" business becomes the key challenge of Stage VI. The firm now needs to focus on ensuring that it has the appropriate resources, operational systems, management systems, and corporate culture to support the now very different company that it has become. By the time an organization completes Stage V, for example, it will most likely be (or need to be) divisionalized.

The phenomenon of having a number of businesses within a larger entity is not only found in large, established companies such as Countrywide Financial Corporation, Johnson & Johnson, Procter & Gamble (which now owns Gillette), GE, Citicorp, and IBM; it also exists in many smaller organizations. For example, Aerotek—a rapidly growing Stage III company, with $40 million in revenues—has three independent divisions. Similarly, Starbucks had four divisions when it had approximately $350 million in sales.

Another version of the need for integration of different businesses arises from the acquisition of different companies in the same industry. When a company grows by acquiring other firms, there is a potential problem of integration. For example, Maxicare made two major acquisitions that increased its size from $500 million to $1.8 billion in annual revenue. Maxicare then had to deal with the problems of integrating these companies, which had different operational systems (such as payroll and benefits) and different corporate cultures. Unfortunately, Maxicare had overextended itself, and the company had to declare bankruptcy, as we saw in Chapter Two. The company then had to proceed to liquidate many of its operating units.

Some companies such as Johnson & Johnson have developed a core competency in the successful integration of acquisitions. Johnson & Johnson has had a history of successful acquisitions, including companies such as Alza (drug delivery products), Centocor (biotechnology), LifeScan (diabetic monitoring equipment), Neutrogena (personal care and cosmetics), and Scios (biotechnology). The key to Johnson & Johnson's success is that they acquired companies that generally fit their culture and gently brought them into the "J&J way" of doing things. This has contributed not only to successful growth and integration of companies but has led to the consistent recognition of Johnson & Johnson as one of the most admired companies.[1]

Successfully meeting the challenges of this stage involves integrating the operations of the new businesses created or acquired during Stage V, while maintaining the firm's entrepreneurial spirit. During the integration stage, the company has a simultaneous need to have some degree of centralized control over the diverse operating units and to allow divisional managers sufficient freedom to be entrepreneurial in managing their operations. Many companies do not do a good job of striking this delicate balance and lean too heavily toward organizational control. The price is a loss of entrepreneurial instinct and culture and the creation of institutional bureaucracy that is more concerned with form than with substance.

At this stage it may also be the case that certain corporatewide systems will need to be "adjusted" in ways to meet the needs of a new division while at the same time maintaining control. In one $100 million division of a Fortune 500 firm, for example, problems were created because the parent firm mandated that certain operating systems would be used that did not adequately meet the needs of the smaller firm. Further, the parent firm's culture promoted cautiousness, while the subsidiary needed to respond quickly to take advantage of market opportunities. Finally, the compensation system of the parent firm could not reward behavior that contributed to business development; it was structured to maintain the status quo. Without careful management and negotiation with the parent firm, such practices can adversely affect a division or subsidiary's ability to succeed.

The problem of integration is, to a great extent, a function of organizational size, complexity, and geographical dispersion. The greater the revenues (and, in turn, personnel and transactions), the greater the degree of geographical dispersion, and the greater the degree of business variety, then the greater the problems of organizational integration are likely to be.

There is a considerable payoff for successfully meeting the challenges associated with this stage. Once an organization has completed this stage of development, it will typically have achieved more than $1 billion in revenue. Our research data (described in Chapter Three) suggest that the probability of continuing to operate successfully after an organization has reached $1 billion or more in revenues is enhanced. Although some organizations experience difficulty and even fail, organizations are more likely to continue to grow successfully after completing Stage VI. At that point they have become "institutions," with a variety of self-perpetuating capabilities.

Companies that have been successful as institutions of this kind are GE, Nestlé, Procter & Gamble, and Johnson & Johnson. All are companies with self-perpetuating capabilities.

Stage VII: Decline and Revitalization

All organizations, regardless of their greatness or past success, ultimately experience a period of decline. In the late nineteenth century, the railroads were the dominant enterprises, but they failed to use their resources to move into other aspects of transportation. In the early part of the last century, U.S. Steel was the hallmark of the U.S. economy, but it did not retain that position. In the 1950s, General Motors was at its apex, yet it, too, experienced (and continues to experience) decline. Other once-great corporations that have experienced organizational decline include IBM, AT&T, Sears, Kodak, National Lead, International Harvester, Xerox, Levi Strauss, and Ford. This phenomenon occurs, not only in the United States but in other parts of the world as well. Examples of once-great companies in other parts of the world experiencing decline include Reuters, Allied–Domecq, NEC, and Mövenpick. For some companies, decline led the firm to the brink of bankruptcy; for others, it merely led to stunted growth; for still others, it led to their demise.

The phenomenon of decline in organizations has been increasingly recognized by scholars.[2] The same phenomenon that occurs in organizations has also been identified in nations.[3]

Organizational decline is typically a product of many complex factors. Some of the most common factors include increasing competition in a firm's markets, loss of competitive skills from an erosion of leadership, a sense of complacency that inhibits organizational change, and, as described throughout this book, the inability of management to build an organizational infrastructure sufficient to keep pace with the demands of organizational growth.

The most common causes of decline—competition and the related phenomenon of market saturation—tend to increase throughout an organization's life. During the early stages of growth after a new market has been identified, an organization typically grows and prospers, simply as a "reward" for having found the market for that product or service. For example, Apple Computer found the market for personal computers and grew to approximately $1 billion in annual revenues. During this period, IBM—potentially a major competitor for Apple—kept telling its customers that there was no need for personal computers. Once the market was developed to the point where it was large enough to attract IBM's interest, IBM brought out its own version of a PC and took 30 to 35 percent of the total market, squeezing Apple Computer's sales and profitability. Further, the IBM operating system became the industry standard and put additional pressure on Apple. Eventually, a number of other companies entered the market with IBM-compatible PCs. When Apple had the market virtually to itself, it earned premium profitability. Once competition increased, Apple no longer had the profit cushion that would mask its underlying organizational problems. Similarly, although Compaq was successful for more than a decade, competition from Dell Computer ultimately eroded Compaq's position and led to its merger with Hewlett-Packard.

Another major cause of organizational decline is an erosion of leadership and entrepreneurial management skills. Unfortunately, the longer organizations exist and the larger they grow in size, the greater the likelihood that they will outgrow their founder's capabilities. Similarly, as people age, they must inevitably step down from leadership. For example, Herb Kelleher has retired from Southwest Airlines, Phil Knight has retired from Nike, and Sam Walton is deceased and long gone from Wal-Mart. All these companies face the challenge of replacing legendary leaders.

A third contributing cause of organizational decline is an increasing sense of complacency. When an organization is successful, people reasonably expect to be rewarded. Sometimes the rewards are too great for the organization to sustain. Moreover, the very fact that success has persisted over time may lead people to come to expect rewards as an entitlement. This form of managerial hubris can create a self-congratulatory atmosphere that produces a resistance to change and ultimately leads to decline. In many firms, this is reflected in a lack of concern about whether or not there are new products in the pipeline. It may also be reflected in an attitude of, "We know best what the customer wants," without actually listening to customers. Further, and perhaps more dangerous, is the feeling that the company is somehow invincible. This attitude can be disastrous when a firm competes in markets where others have systems in place to both monitor and respond to customer needs. In one $150 million firm, for example, the belief was, "We found the market and we produce the best product. No one can catch us." As the firm basked in the glory of its own success, it watched as competitors slowly took away a significant percentage of its market share.

A final, major contributing factor to organizational decline is the inability of management to develop an organizational infrastructure sufficient for the organization's stage of growth. This problem has been one of the key themes throughout this book. Indeed, the problem is the crucial issue of Stages II through IV, and when management is unsuccessful in meeting these developmental challenges, organizational decline is inevitable.

The key challenge, then, for a Stage VII firm is revitalization.[4] An organization must rebuild itself almost from the ground up. This, in turn, requires that the firm become entrepreneurial in nature once again. Some firms try to achieve revitalization by acquiring other companies that are more entrepreneurial than the purchaser. For example, in a bid to revitalize, Bank of America bought Charles Schwab & Company but later sold the company back to Schwab, who has continued to build it into a brokerage powerhouse. The attempt to "buy" entrepreneurship is unlikely to succeed in most companies. A total revitalization, including a major cultural transformation, is likely to be the only effective strategy.

We should also note that a firm does not have to reach the multi-billion-dollar level before it experiences decline. Decline may occur much sooner. Companies such as Osborne Computer, Ashton-Tate, and Boston Market are all examples of premature corporate decline. By the time a firm has reached the multi-billion-dollar level, however, it is sure to have the seeds of future potential decline within, even though it appears to outsiders to be at the apex of its success and power.

Companies such as American Express, Bank of America, Hewlett-Packard, Simon Properties, and IBM are all examples of successful revitalization efforts. The most entrepreneurial of these is Simon Properties (formerly Melvin Simon & Associates), which underwent a revitalization program in the early 1990s. The company—one of the largest shopping center developers in the United States—developed and manages the Mall of America in Bloomington, Minnesota.

During the early 1990s, the company was experiencing a variety of growing pains, and the size of the company outstripped the managerial capabilities of its founder, Melvin Simon, and his brother, Herbert Simon, who were both primarily real estate developers. The company began a program of revitalization that lasted about five years. This included the introduction of strategic planning, changes in organizational structure, management development, and performance management systems. It also led to the introduction into the company of its current CEO, David Simon (Melvin Simon's son), who had an MBA from Columbia University and was more oriented to being a professional manager than either of the two elder Simons, who were primarily deal-oriented. The company culminated its successful revitalization by going public as Simon Properties. The company's stock price increased from about $24 in 1994 to more than $84 in 2006. Because the company is a REIT, and dividends rather than stock appreciation are the primary measure of performance, this is an impressive return on shareholder investment.

MANAGING TRANSITIONS AT STAGES V THROUGH VII

We have examined the nature of Stages V through VII and the managerial challenges that occur at each of these stages. This section deals with the issues involved in managing the transitions required at each of these stages.

Managing Transitions at Stage V

The transition to Stage V requires a redeployment of entrepreneurial skills. The entrepreneurship that was the basis of founding the firm in Stage I must reemerge and become a dominant force in Stage V. Because the original product vehicle was sufficient to carry the firm along in its chosen market, the managerial problems of Stages II through IV involved building the operational and management infrastructure to support the growing organization. However, the need to diversify translates into the need to be entrepreneurial again.

Unfortunately, it may not be possible for the firm to simply go back to its original entrepreneur and have that person repeat the entire process that began some time ago in Stage I. In some cases, the entrepreneur is no longer with the firm. There are many examples in business where the original entrepreneur has not been available to grow with the firm as it developed from one stage to the next. For example, Steven Jobs and Steven Wozniak both left Apple Computer (Jobs returned in 1997).

Even if the entrepreneur is still with the firm, a significant amount of time usually has elapsed, as the firm passed from Stage I through Stage IV, and at this point the entrepreneur is now burdened by a significant number of organizational activities. This means that the entrepreneur may not have the time or mind-set available for thinking "entrepreneurially" about new products and markets.

It is often, then, extremely difficult for entrepreneurs to repeat their earlier success. There are many examples of firms where there was a brilliant entrepreneurial success but a failure to repeat that success at any significant level. Accordingly, what is needed is to reestablish entrepreneurship in the organization, but it must be done in a different way. Rather than look to a single entrepreneur, firms at Stage V must develop a cadre of so-called entrepreneurial managers.

An entrepreneurial manager is different from a pure entrepreneur. Howard Schultz, Angelo Mozilo, Steven Jobs, and Michael Dell are relatively pure entrepreneurial types—very different from professional managers. An entrepreneur is typically someone who is above average in intelligence and has a very strong sense of the way he or she wants things to be done in the organization—that is, has a high need for control. Some people might even consider the entrepreneur to be a workaholic or to have an obsessive personality. Nevertheless, these are the very personality traits that are both necessary and useful to a firm during its early stages of growth. Although a Stage V firm needs to develop a cadre of entrepreneurial managers, it is not necessary for these managers to have the same personality as an entrepreneur; rather, what is necessary is to train the entrepreneurial manager to mimic or simulate some of the behavioral patterns of the entrepreneur.

During the past few years, a number of organizations have been experimenting with the reintroduction of entrepreneurship and the training of entrepreneurial managers. The term *corporate entrepreneurship* has been used to distinguish this process of reintroducing entrepreneurship through entrepreneurial managers from the entrepreneurs required to start a new company. The entrepreneur is someone who can create a new business where none existed previously. In contrast to the entrepreneur, the corporate entrepreneurial manager is someone who can create a new business venture within an established organization. The challenge, then, is to create development programs that will help people make the transition to being entrepreneurial managers. Further, the firm must develop systems and a way of thinking (a culture) that supports corporate entrepreneurship—the creation of a business within an existing business. 3M is the classic company that has demonstrated this as a core competency. For example, it was the company that developed Post-its and turned it into a multi-million-dollar business.

Managing Transitions at Stage VI

An organization that has completed Stage V has both a multiple product line and a multiple set of businesses to manage. This is typically accomplished through the divisional form of organizational structure, which we described in Chapter Eight.

The central problem facing corporations in Stage VI is how to integrate a set of diverse divisions into one unified business entity. A new kind of operational and management infrastructure must be created and implemented. These new systems at the corporate level must be designed to manage a set of businesses, rather than just one business. Stated differently, from Stages I through V a firm has been developing an organizational infrastructure that is appropriate for a single business entity. By the time it reaches Stage VI, it will have developed a number of these individual business entities and now needs to develop an infrastructure that will support managing each of these individual units as part of an integrated whole.

A variety of issues must be addressed during this stage of organizational growth. One such issue involves questions of managing the corporate culture. Specifically, each of the separate divisions within a company may have somewhat varying cultures. Another such issue involves the process of strategic planning, both at the corporate level and within each division, and the problems involved with integrating both. Similarly, there are issues involving the proper organizational structure of each division and issues involving the specific control systems that need to be developed within each of the business entities. Finally, the firm needs to focus on ensuring that the operational systems at both the corporate and divisional levels of the company effectively support its operations. The systems and culture of each division may need to be, in some cases, blended so as to promote the cooperation needed to achieve goals; in other cases, the company needs to promote the belief that differences in systems and culture between divisions will be maintained in the service of meeting the firm's long-term goals.

A critical issue underlying the design of a management system for a Stage VI organization involves the degree of centralization or decentralization of authority accorded to each division. Companies vary widely in the amount of decentralization that they grant to their operating divisions. This issue can be viewed as points on a continuum. At one end of the continuum are firms that attempt to control virtually everything their operating divisions do. At the other end of the continuum, a corporation essentially operates as a passive investor with a "portfolio" containing various companies. The strategy here is to defer strategic decisions and daily operations to the divisional general managers, while requiring a specified performance in terms of return on investment or amount of profit. This type of managerial philosophy has been used for many years at Johnson & Johnson.

At Johnson & Johnson, for example, divisions may be required to achieve a 15 percent pretax return on investment. The methods of achieving this target return are left to divisional managers. The corporation also requires that various management systems be in place, such as a planning process. In addition, Johnson & Johnson has used its Signature of Quality Award process to motivate the development of operational and management systems at its individual companies. Companies must apply for the Signature of Quality Award and they are evaluated on, for example, business competitiveness, organizational alignment, and information competitiveness. The specific details of these categories are less significant than the process that Johnson & Johnson is using to motivate operating divisions to develop their infrastructure.

The key challenge at this stage, then, involves deciding how best to integrate the systems and corporate culture of the various units created in Stage V into an effective system.

Managing Transitions at Stage VII

The final stage in the organizational life cycle is Stage VII. This stage has been labeled that of organizational decline and revitalization. The key issue facing management at Stage VII involves revitalization of the entire organization.

In contrast to most of the other stages, which constitute a sequential hierarchy as an organization grows in size, an organization can "jump to" Stage VII from almost any other stage. Although it is typically the larger organizations that are most in need of revitalization, there are examples of organizations at $30 million, $100 million, $1 billion, $10 billion, and even $100 billion that have reached Stage VII and are in need of revitalization.

The stage of organizational revitalization seems to be inevitable. The problems that underlie the need for organizational revitalization appear to result from an organization's own success. With organizational success come increases in the organization's size. Increases in an organization's size seem to create a certain degree of resistance to change. This can result from the vested interests of people who control the organization, or it can be that the organization's size has made it very ponderous, creating lengthy delays between the time the organization identifies a trend or problem and the time it takes action. For example, Kodak, which has a distinguished history as a successful company, missed major new markets (such as instant photography, videotape recorders, and 35 mm cameras) because its size, structure, and culture all made it move too slowly. Accordingly, very successful organizations—even those at the apparent height of their success—are already headed toward decline.

Organizational size does not seem to protect against decline; indeed, size itself may be one of the major factors creating the need for revitalization. A wide variety of organizations, including AT&T, Hewlett-Packard, and General Motors, have all faced the need for organizational revitalization, despite their many billions of dollars in assets and revenues. Even such an outstanding organization as IBM has faced the need for a revitalization effort.

In addition, it is becoming increasingly recognized that beyond a certain point size may not be a strategic advantage. For example, T. J. Rodgers, founder of Cypress Semiconductor, once stated: "I would rather see our billion-dollar company of the 1990s be ten $100 million companies, all strong, growing healthy, and aggressive as hell. The alternative is an aging billion-dollar company that spends more time defending its turf than growing."[5]

Although there are a number of issues involved in any example of organizational decline and revitalization, the basic problem that makes revitalization so difficult is that an organization at this stage must focus on all six of the key organizational development areas. The organization must now simultaneously rethink its markets, its products and services, its resources, its operational systems, its management systems, and its corporate culture. Although organizations at every stage must give some attention to all six key areas, Stages I through VI have only required that an organization concentrate on one or two key areas at a time. In Stage VII, it is critical that an organization *simultaneously* concentrate on all six areas, and this makes revitalization so difficult.

THE SPECIAL CHALLENGE OF REVITALIZATION

Stage VII presents the firm with special problems, the most significant being the fact that all six levels of the Pyramid of Organizational Development must be simultaneously focused on and changed. This is the stage where the corporation must reinvent itself. The demands on the leadership and individual members of the organization can be enormous. An organization that has been accustomed to success now faces the real possibility of failure. Moreover, the organization is encumbered by a variety of people with perceived entitlement. The sheer size of the organization requires a great deal of investment in political effort to achieve some kind of a workable consensus among the players, whereas in smaller organizations the decision-making authority may be concentrated in a smaller number of individuals, obviating the need for such politics. Each of these issues is examined next.

Revitalizing Markets

During Stage I the firm is able to establish itself because it has been successful in identifying a single market. In Stage V, diversification efforts lead to the development of new markets. One of the fundamental reasons a Stage VII firm experiences difficulty is that the organization's size has gotten out of sync with its ability to derive revenue from its traditional market segments. Instead of being able to focus its attention on a single market segment, the organization is now typically involved in a number of mature markets, meaning that the rate of growth in these markets is decreasing, with profit margins being squeezed. The firm is trapped in a scissors effect, facing decreasing revenues from its markets on the one hand and rising operating costs caused by its increasing size and related inefficiencies on the other. With both blades of the scissors simultaneously closing in on the organization, management is busy doing its best to hold them apart.

The primary task now facing management is to identify a new set of markets for the organization. These will be markets offering higher potential rates of growth and higher profit margins. There are many examples of the successful search for new markets, including Disney and Nike. Under Michael Eisner's leadership, Disney revitalized from a distressed family-oriented motion picture and theme park company into a global entertainment powerhouse. Similarly, Nike broadened its focus from athletic shoes to athletic wear and built a so-called power brand or super brand. Both companies did this as part of revitalization efforts.

Revitalizing Products

Another typical problem of organizations in decline is the need to develop a whole new set of products and services. A firm that has reached Stage VII has been the beneficiary of a product or set of products that have been well entrenched for a long period of time. Unfortunately, these products have reached the mature stage and may even have been made obsolete by new competition from different companies. The critical problem in this situation is that the moment a firm becomes aware that its products are no longer competitive in the marketplace, it has already lost a sufficient amount of lead time needed to react. Thus the organization is forced into a crisis. At a time when it needs additional revenues to invest in new directions, it finds that its revenues are declining for competitive reasons.

Revitalizing Resources

One of the relative advantages of established organizations is that they should have had the opportunity to accumulate resources over a period of time. These resources need to be invested in both product research and development and in corporate acquisitions for the purpose of acquiring new technologies. Because this is a relatively lengthy process, companies cannot expect a quick fix.

At Stage VII, a company's resource situation will typically be somewhat inconsistent. The firm probably has a significant amount of resources at its disposal, but some of these resources will be redundant. Some of its inventory, its plant and equipment, and even its people will not be appropriate for the new challenges it faces. The firm may also find itself with the need to redeploy some of its assets from one market segment to another. At this stage the firm will have to make major investments to revitalize the organization. Unfortunately, the firm may not be accustomed to making these types of investments and will encounter internal resistance to investing in the resources needed to revitalize itself. When it comes to the issue of resources in organizational revitalization, the process is essentially one of building an almost entirely new organization on the foundation of the existing organization. In a sense, it is analogous to creating a totally new entrepreneurial effort but at a much larger scale. It has been termed a process of "reinventing in the corporation."[6]

Revitalizing Operational Systems

The firm's operational systems are typically quite well established, which can be both a blessing and a burden. It is a blessing because the firm will not have to create some of the basic systems needed to operate a new enterprise. However, if the firm's systems have become too entrenched and are bureaucratic in nature, the firm may well need a scorched-earth policy, requiring it to literally abandon some of its traditional systems. Although abandonment is a drastic option, it may be the only effective catalyst for instituting new operating systems. Unfortunately, until the new systems are instituted, abandonment often has the adverse effect of choking the development of the new enterprise that needs to be created.

An effective strategy is to conduct an organizational assessment to determine which of the firm's systems are in need of revitalization. This assessment can be conducted by external consultants, by convening an internal task force, or a combination of both. If an internal task force is used, care must be taken to prevent members from protecting their vested interests in preserving certain systems, which may be beneficial to that member but hurt the overall organization.

A traditional area for operational system problems involves product development. Organizations needing revitalization usually possess a functional organization structure in which there is divided responsibility for product development. This responsibility is typically divided among production, sales, and engineering, which tends to create a very lengthy product development cycle. The revitalization period requires a unity of purpose within the organization. Accordingly, new products need to be developed with centralized coordination of engineering, manufacturing, and sales. The structure most appropriate for this is a divisional structure. In our judgment, it is not an accident that many of the revitalization efforts occur in organizations that have been using functional organizational structures.

Revitalizing Management Systems

The next area involved in the revitalization process is the firm's management systems. The firm's planning system may be well developed but is probably not as entrepreneurially oriented as needed. There is a need to create and implement an entrepreneurially oriented strategic planning process that focuses on the kinds of questions that we articulated in Chapter Seven.

The firm's organizational structure must be reevaluated. As noted earlier, the structure will probably have to be changed from either a functional or a matrix structure to a divisional structure that allows a considerable degree of autonomy.

Management development may need to be instituted in order to create a cadre of entrepreneurial managers. An entrepreneurial manager is someone who thinks more like an entrepreneur than a professional manager. Professional managers are a valuable asset to the organization and are critically needed during several of the earlier stages of development. However, when an organization reaches Stage VII, it is in serious need of entrepreneurship, and some of the firm's core managers need to rethink their orientation with respect to managing the business. Management development can assist this process, especially by using mind-stretching exercises that are designed to create new patterns of thought and open up lines of creativity.

This is a period of development when the firm faces a paradox in its need for control; it will need both more and less control at the same time. On the one hand, as profit margins decrease, it will be necessary for a firm to control its expenses. On the other hand, there are times when a firm must invest money, regardless of the rate of return, merely to stay in business. This means that some of the traditional accounting measures used in control systems may not be relevant.

One of the critical dimensions of a revitalization effort is, of course, leadership. If existing management is unable to mount a successful turnaround, companies are likely to seek new leadership. For example, Louis Gerstner was recruited from outside to IBM to lead the revitalization effort after an earlier effort led by an insider had failed.[7] Similarly, first Carly Fiorina and later Mark Hurd were recruited by Hewlett-Packard to lead revitalization after an initial effort led by company insiders was unsuccessful. Fiorina was responsible for Hewlett-Packard's merger with Compaq, but she was replaced by Hurd when the company encountered difficulties in making the merger work effectively.

Revitalizing Corporate Culture

Finally, the culture of the firm will have to be modified. All established companies have complex cultures. Sometimes, they may have several subcultures. One of the typical problems of established companies is that, unintentionally, the culture begins to emphasize politics and avoidance of conflict and risk more than performance, quality, customer service, innovation, and profitability. Many people will have well-entrenched positions, and some are likely to resist the required changes, even though they are needed by the organization.

If a revitalization effort is undertaken without attention to the cultural dimensions, it is not likely to be effective. Many of the lessons of Chapter Twelve are appropriate here.

SUCCESSFUL REVITALIZATION: CASE STUDY

One reasonably successful revitalization effort was that accomplished at Navistar (formerly International Harvester). International Harvester had operated in a wide variety of businesses, including agricultural equipment (its historical foundation), diesel engines, and trucks. The company's revitalization strategy was to divest itself of unprofitable operations and focus on trucks and diesel engines, which it sells to other automotive manufacturers, such as Ford. As the focus shifted to trucks, the company focused on refining its product line and establishing the operating systems to support it. The firm also restructured its operations into three major product divisions: heavy truck, medium truck, and bus. Each product division had a general manager who, along with his team, was responsible for developing and implementing a plan for successfully managing the business. Previously, all plans for the company had been developed by a corporate planning department. The firm also embarked on a management development program intended to provide those in leadership positions with the skills needed to assist the company in its revitalization process.

One of the key assets of the business that was retrained and built on during the revitalization process was the firm's network of dealers. Each dealership is a separate business. Many of the dealers are former employees of International Harvester. Navistar has provided a variety of programs to help the dealers become more professionally managed. One resource for dealers was a management development program to help the dealerships make the transition from an entrepreneurship to a professionally managed firm. This program was designed to assist the dealers in developing the skills required to help their firms make the successful transitions required at different growth stages, as well as to develop the skills required by the CEO to lead the firm throughout these transitions. In other words, developing the skills of the dealers was an important component of Navistar's revitalization process.

SUMMARY

Once a firm has completed the development challenges required to take it through Stages I through IV, it has become a professionally managed organization. However, its life cycle is not completed, and the firm must now deal with the problems and challenges posed by the advanced stages of growth—Stages V through VII.

Stage V involves efforts to diversify the firm because it can no longer rely on its initial product for continued profitability. The firm's success has attracted competitors, and its products are now competing in a saturated market. The firm must develop new products or services to "restart" another cycle of success. A prudent firm has not waited until this stage to begin the process of diversification and has been investing a portion of its profits into the development of new products. Because the original entrepreneur is often no longer available, many firms are training managers to mimic the behavior of entrepreneurs, thereby creating "intrapreneurs" who will serve as catalysts for diversification.

Stage VI involves integrating the new businesses that were created around the new products developed in Stage V. These businesses may be only partially related. The challenge is to coordinate these entities while allowing each sufficient independence to derive the benefits of acting in an entrepreneurial manner. Such issues as the amount of centralized control over differing divisions, integrating the separate planning activities, and managing the overall corporate culture must be addressed.

Finally, Stage VII requires that a company overcome the pressures leading to decline, whether they are caused by market saturation, an erosion of management's entrepreneurial skills, the inability to develop an organizational infrastructure to support the growth realized from previous stages, or a feeling of complacency. The organization *must* revitalize itself, but the difficulty in doing so is that management must give its full attention to all six levels of the Pyramid of Organizational Development simultaneously.

CHAPTER FIFTEEN

Making the Transition to a Public Company

A t some point companies might face the decision to go public. This chapter deals with the issues involved in making the transition from a private to a publicly held company. It also describes some of the key issues that publicly held companies must cope with in operating as a public company, including reporting requirements, the Sarbanes-Oxley Act, and boards of directors.

MAKING THE DECISION TO GO PUBLIC

The question of whether to go public can arise as part of an exit strategy for entrepreneurs, or it can be the intent from day one. A major reason for going public is to get access to capital to facilitate company growth. A related reason is to have a vehicle (stock) to use for corporate acquisitions or a related vehicle (stock options) to use to attract and retain talented executives.

Although there are many advantages of being a publicly held company, there are also significant disadvantages, and the decision of whether to remain a private company or go public is a major strategic choice. The rationale for going public might be to benefit the entrepreneur and company employees, but the primary purpose of a public company is to create value for its shareholders. This sets up a potential conflict of interests, and once the company is public, shareholder interests must be the raison d'être of the company.

There are psychological as well as economic aspects to the decision to go public. Entrepreneurs are accustomed to operating in almost total control of their business. Once they are a public company, this will not be possible to the same extent, ever again. This can come as a great shock to people who understand it intellectually but have not embraced it emotionally. Once the event has occurred, the company and the entrepreneur have crossed the Rubicon and passed the point of no return.

Disadvantages of Going Public

For many years, our belief has been that remaining a privately held company offers significant strategic advantages. Operating as a publicly held business is totally different from operating as a private company.

The main advantage of private ownership is that the company is not subjected to the expectations of securities analysts and shareholders (referred to collectively as The Street) for uninterrupted, continuous improvement in earnings per share.[1] The Street is continuously evaluating company performance and prospects. If earnings expectations are not met, the company's share price will reflect it almost instantaneously. This can lead to a short-term focus and overconcern with meeting The Street's expectations.

It is extremely difficult to take a long-term view for development of a business while simultaneously generating earnings that meet the expectations of The Street. In addition, during periods when a company needs to revitalize, it can find it very difficult to maintain—let alone grow—earnings, and its share price can get hammered. The lower the share price and related PE (price-earnings) ratio, the more vulnerable the company will be to an unfriendly acquisition.[2] Because there are great pressures for continuous growth, large companies are always looking to acquire smaller companies with greater organic growth prospects. This means that once a company goes public, it is fair game for larger companies to acquire it. If a company is acquired by a larger company, the game will change even further. Now the company will need to operate as part of a larger entity.

Given all these disadvantages, many companies are either deferring the time of going public until they are larger or deciding not to become a public company at all. Some companies are choosing to remain private, while others are opting for liquidity by selling themselves to larger public companies. For example, PowerBar did not go public. It was purchased by Nestlé.

Some companies (especially troubled companies) are going private after having operated as public companies for many years. In 2006, more than eighty formerly public companies went private. Some very large companies with long histories as public companies were reported to be considering going private. In late 2006, for example, Ford Motor Company was reported to be considering going private. For troubled companies like Ford, the option of going private gives the company time to deal with its problems while not having to be concerned about criticism for its current financial performance.

Advantages of Going Public

There are a number of advantages of being a public company. The greatest is possibly the access to the public capital markets, which can provide the equity and debt capital required to grow a company at a lower cost and with greater accessibility than for private equity.

Going public also provides an opportunity to "monetize" (convert equity into liquidity) the value of the company that has been created for its founders and owners. Many managers receive "warrants" upon joining companies. These are the rough equivalent of stock options, and they can be converted into shares once the company is public.

Once the company has its own stock, it can be used as a vehicle to continue growth and can be used in transactions to acquire other companies. Stock options can also be used to attract talented managers. Stock options, which are used by most, if not all, technology firms in Silicon Valley and by many biotechnology companies, provide a way to keep current compensation relatively low during a company's developmental stages, while offering a long-term payoff to people who join the company.

THE TRANSITION FROM PRIVATE TO PUBLIC[3]

After weighing the advantages against the disadvantages and making the decision to go public, all is not wine and roses. There will probably be a few years of stress and turmoil.

Preparing to Go Public

The process of preparing to go public will undoubtedly be stressful. Safi Qureshey's description of taking AST Research public suggests that the IPO (initial public offering) process is harsh, painful, and sobering.[4] Most entrepreneurs are used to running their own show. They have lavished attention and devotion to their company and think of it as their baby. To the underwriter who will take them public, it is just another product.

The process of selecting an underwriter, the "road show" where the company is put on display to potential investors, and the eleventh-hour decisions about offering price and related matters will all be filled with complexities and pitfalls.

Romancing the Business

In the initial phase, a number of potential underwriters will be romancing the entrepreneur to take the business public. At this point, the entrepreneur will be in control of the process, and everything will be sweetness and light. There will be allusions to, if not outright promises of, absurd valuations. The business will be viewed as the greatest thing since whatever the last greatest thing was: Google, Starbucks, or Krispy Kreme. However, as the process unfolds, the power will subtly shift to the supplier of money.

Creating Competition Among Underwriters

To the extent possible, business owners will want to create competition among the potential underwriters for the IPO. This means preparing a detailed list of specifications—including very specific questions about pricing, underwriting fees, research support terms of the offering, and post-IPO company and market support—in the request for quotation (RFQ) that will be sent to a number of investment banks. This discussion is not intended to be a guide for a do-it-yourself IPO but to indicate the complexity of the process.

Selecting an Underwriter

Once the selection of an underwriter has been completed, the process of the IPO will change dramatically. Now the underwriter will want to determine all of the defects of the company in preparation for the road show for potential investors. A virtual army of investment bankers, lawyers, accountants, and investments analysts will conduct a probing examination of all aspects of the company. They will want to determine all of its blemishes and warts.

This process will include sessions with the entrepreneur and management team in which countless questions are asked. These questions have a dual purpose: to simultaneously prepare the underwriters and management for the questions they will experience in the road show for potential investors. An organizational audit, using the Pyramid of Organizational Development as a lens, can be valuable in preparing for these sessions.

Dealing with Conflicting Objectives

Management should not assume that the underwriter and the potential investors share a common set of objectives for the IPO. The definition of a successful IPO will differ according to their different agendas. Management will want to raise as much money as possible from the IPO, and this will affect their concept of the appropriate IPO price. Some potential investors will not intend to be long-term shareholders. They will be content to "flip" the shares at a profit. The underwriters want to earn their fees and make a profit on the IPO—all of which leads to a potential conflict of business interests.

Meeting the Numbers

Another aspect of preparation for life as a public company is preparing the culture of the organization. Once a company is public, there will be great pressure to "meet the numbers" promised to The Street. If a company has not created the culture of meeting its commitments prior to going public, it is in for a rude awakening. It is critical, therefore, that the company has created the professional management capabilities and systems required to perform as a well-oiled machine, with a management that is disciplined and able to meet its promises.

If this has not been achieved, there can be a variety of problems. For example, one technology company had suggested that its new product would be ready for shipment during the first quarter after going public. In fact, there were quality problems with the product, and the company that had tried to create a culture of customer focus and satisfaction made the decision to ship the product anyway and "fix it in the field." This led to its own employees' cynical view of the company's real commitment to quality products.

OPERATING AS A PUBLIC COMPANY

There are several important issues concerning operations as a public company. These include forming and working with boards of directors, understanding governance issues, fulfilling reporting requirements (including Sarbanes-Oxley), managing the "tyranny of the stock price," and using stock options.

Board of Directors

The purpose of the business enterprise is to increase the value of the enterprise for its shareholders. All public companies must have a board of directors, and good governance practice requires that a majority of the board's members be independent directors.[5] The board of directors has two major functions: (1) oversight (governance) and (2) decision making. The decision-making function concerns the formulation of corporate policy, selection of senior management, review of strategic and business plans, and a variety of other matters. The oversight function involves the ongoing monitoring of corporate business and activities—in particular, compliance with legal obligations and corporate policies. Although one of the functions of the board is to add value to substantive decisions and plans, this needs to be balanced against the board's oversight function, in which it serves as the steward of the shareholders.

There are no firm guidelines for the composition of the board. Based on our experience, however, it ought to include a variety of people with a range of capabilities and experiences. It ought to include people who are experienced with public companies and, ideally, will include former auditors, lawyers, financial advisers, and other professionals.

Functioning as a member of a board of directors is quite different from functioning as a manager or as a consultant. Managers have responsibilities for detailed operations, and board members will not have the detailed information required for effective day-to-day decision making. Similarly, the role of a consultant is to help facilitate decisions and planning or to develop operational and management systems. This is beyond the scope of the responsibilities of members of the board.

There are a number of issues regarding the roles of the board and the company officers. One involves the question of whether the positions of CEO and chairman of the board should be separate. The basic argument for separation is that the duty of the board is to protect the interests of shareholders and that the independence of the board chair from management helps to ensure this. Company practice differs, and there is no clear answer.

A related issue concerns the culture of the board. Again, the duty of the board is to shareholders rather than to management, employees, and even communities. Although these are relevant constituencies or stakeholders, the primary duty of the board is to shareholders.

Reporting Requirements

One of the significant differences between operating as a private company and as a public company concerns Securities and Exchange Commission (SEC) reporting requirements. Federal law requires public companies to file periodic reports with the SEC, including an annual report on Form 10-K and quarterly reports on Form 10-Q. Reports are also required for the disclosure of "significant transactions and events" that occur during a reporting period. These are reported on Form 8-K. This form can also be used for voluntary disclosure of a broad range of other information and events. The criterion is that any material event (broadly defined) occurring during the reporting period must be disclosed on Form 8-K.

There are other regulations of relevance to public companies. For example, Regulation FD deals with "fair disclosure." Its purpose is to prevent selective disclosure of information to the benefit of some investors over others.

The SEC's rules also require an annual meeting for shareholders and an annual report to shareholders. The corporation's annual report on Form 10-K contains the latest year's audited financial statements and mandated management comments on recent financial performance.

These are not trivial requirements. They require substantial effort to report accurate and timely information. This, in turn, means substantial costs for compliance.[6]

Sarbanes-Oxley Act

In the wake of the scandals at Enron and other companies, where shareholders lost many millions of dollars, the U.S. Congress passed the Sarbanes-Oxley Act of 2002.[7] As directed by the act, the SEC adopted rules that require conformance with specific sections. Under the act (which is colloquially referred to as SOX), the CEO and CFO of public companies are required to review and, based on their knowledge, certify that quarterly and annual reports are materially accurate and complete. In addition, quarterly assessments of the disclosure controls and procedures, as well as annual assessments of internal controls over financial reporting, are also required.[8] The company's auditors or CPAs must provide an opinion on the sufficiency of internal controls, as well as the fairness of financial statements.

These requirements under the Sarbanes-Oxley Act have greatly enhanced the power of auditors. The demand for their services has significantly increased, and they are more willing than ever to fire clients. The act has created major change in the operation of public companies.

The cost of compliance with Sarbanes-Oxley can be very substantial and can amount to over $1 million or more per year for even a relatively small publicly held company. One study of the costs of compliance found that the costs among the nation's largest companies "dropped 44% to $4.8 million per year."[9] The biggest reason for the decline in compliance in the second year of the act's passage was the "learning curve" effect. Because it was the second year, there were efficiencies from doing it a second time. However, the study also found that smaller companies were not experiencing as steep a decline in compliance costs. The study cited average total costs of $860,000 for 2005 for companies with market capitalizations of $75 million to $700 million.

The SEC is still studying the impact and effects of the Sarbanes-Oxley Act, especially its impact on smaller companies. Although an SEC advisory panel recommended that smaller companies (defined as those with market capitalizations less than $787 million) be exempt from the requirement of having outside auditors certify their internal controls, the SEC decided not to exempt smaller firms from the requirement that companies file reports on the strength of their financial controls and correct any problems.[10]

These factors have reduced the desire of many companies to go public; if they do go public, some U.S.-based companies are actually looking across the Atlantic to Europe's stock exchanges.[11] For example, one U.S. company—Medafor—which has patented a process for accelerating blood clots during surgery, is seeking capital to market its process in the United States after FDA (U.S. Food and Drug Administration) approval. At the time of the preparation of this book, the company was reportedly considering the London Stock Exchange's AIM market for small and growing companies. According to the company's financial adviser, the reason Medafor is looking to AIM rather than NASDAQ is the high cost of complying with Sarbanes-Oxley accounting and reporting regulations.[12] The company estimated that it would cost $500,000 to $1 million to comply with Sarbanes-Oxley.

Medafor is not unique among firms seeking an IPO. A report by Price-WaterhouseCoopers found that five U.S. companies turned to London's AIM Exchange for their IPOs during the first quarter of 2006.[13] Sarbanes-Oxley has also had an impact on the practice of companies issuing earnings "guidance." Some companies, like Google, have chosen not to issue earnings guidance.

Possible Benefits of Sarbanes-Oxley

Although Sarbanes-Oxley is undoubtedly costly and might tend to inhibit or delay some companies from going public, this is not necessarily all bad. The requirements of Sarbanes-Oxley for accounting and controls make the development of systems and procedures mandatory and not subject to management discretion. Because most entrepreneurs are not interested in organizational infrastructure, the natural tendency would be to under-invest in systems and procedures. Preparing a company to satisfy the requirements of Sarbanes-Oxley can have the side benefit of strengthening the informational and operational aspects of a business. This, in turn, can increase a company's chances of long-term success.

We believe it is possible that the Sarbanes-Oxley Act has already had an effect of this kind. In updating this book, we searched for examples of high-profile entrepreneurial failures to replace examples that were outdated and not likely to be familiar to some readers (for example, People Express, Wang Laboratories, Ashton-Tate). We were surprised that there have been relatively few recent high-profile entrepreneurial failures or victims of what we have termed the Osborne syndrome.

We think Sarbanes-Oxley may be partly responsible, for two reasons: (1) companies are delaying going public until they are better prepared to meet the act's requirements and are therefore better able to operate successfully, and (2) companies that are already public are being forced to do what they should have done voluntarily—beef up their systems and controls.

Tyranny of the Stock Price

Once a company goes public, its stock price will fluctuate daily. For some managers, this is a very useful event because it provides a scorecard to measure organizational success. For others, it can lead to what might be termed the tyranny of the stock price. Some managers, almost literally, live and die every day, according to the fluctuations in their stock price. When the price is increasing, they are happy; when the price declines, they are saddened.

They respond to fluctuations in stock prices in much the way that someone with bipolar disease might respond.

To minimize the impact that this can have on company operations, management needs to operate with both a short-term awareness of its stock price and a longer-term view about building the business. This is easier said than done. If the stock price sinks too low, shareholders will become disgruntled, and this can lead to a cascade of negative events for a company, including the removal of its CEO and other members of the management team.

Use of Stock Options

Once a company is public, it will have a powerful tool to compete for, motivate, and retain talented people: stock options. Options have a dual purpose: (1) they can be used as awards to attract people to join a company, and (2) they can be used as an incentive to align the performance of people with the interests of shareholders. Discussions with the COO of one of our clients suggested he believed that the lack of stock options was a significant handicap in recruiting talented executives to his company. He stated that his company had nothing to compete with options as an incentive. We have also seen cases where the award of options was a significant factor in attracting people to join companies.

The exercise price of options is typically the stock market's final price on the day the option is granted the company's board of directors. At that point, there is no built-in gain for employees who receive the option grants. The intent is to give employees an incentive to increase the value of the company's stock so that they, as well as other shareholders, derive the benefits.

There are complex regulations for accounting associated with the granting of stock options, which are beyond the scope of this book. There are also nontrivial paperwork requirements. Nevertheless, the benefits of stock options seem to outweigh their costs.

TRANSITION FROM A FAMILY BUSINESS TO A PUBLIC COMPANY: THE CASE OF 99 CENTS ONLY STORES[14]

There are many examples of great entrepreneurial success stories from humble beginnings. These include Wal-Mart, Starbucks, Apple Computer, and Hewlett-Packard. Another company that is a great American entrepreneurial success story is 99 Cents Only Stores. Today, 99 Cents Only Stores (99) is listed on the New York Stock Exchange (NYSE).[15] The company is a deep-discount retailer of consumable merchandise, with an emphasis on brand-name products. The company's stores offer an assortment of products that are regularly available to customers in other stores, as well as a variety of closeout merchandise. Deep-discount retail is distinguished from other retail formats in that a substantial portion of the company's purchases are acquired at closeouts and other special-purchase situations. As a result, the product mix changes frequently, due to the availability (or lack thereof) of specific merchandise. As of September 30, 2006, the company operated 241 retail stores, with 173 in California, 36 in Texas, 21 in Arizona, and 11 in Nevada. The story of 99 Cents Only Stores is relevant, not only as a great American success story but because it is a classic example of a company that has made the successful transition from a family-run private company to a successful public company.

Origins of 99 Cents Only Stores

Dave and Sherry Gold's is a classic American entrepreneurial success story. In 1945, Dave's father, an immigrant from Russia, opened a tiny liquor store in downtown Los Angeles.

In 1957, Dave's father received an offer to sell his store for $35,000, but he sold it instead to Dave and his brother-in-law for $2,000 as a down payment, with the rest being paid with no interest over a long period of time.

The New Venture

In 1961, the two entrepreneurs opened another liquor store nearby in Grand Central Market of downtown Los Angeles. As did other, similar stores, they sold beer, wine, and hard liquor for a variety of prices.

As part of the process of doing business, they noticed that items priced at 99 cents were selling so fast that they could not keep them in stock. They decided to experiment with pricing, selling all wines priced between $0.89 and $1.29 at a fixed price of 99 cents. They advertised: "Wines of the world for 99 cents." The experiment was a great success. They found that those items formerly sold at 89 cents sold *more* when priced at 99 cents! Dave Gold had some additional insights from this experiment: (1) Customers preferred the digit "9" in pricing, and (2) customers prefer fewer digits in the price.

Dave Gold has a natural genius for business. He did a number of unorthodox things that worked quite well. For example, he advertised certain products as "the world's worst." He advertised cigarettes as "the world's worst cigarettes for 99 cents." People bought the cigarettes to see how bad they really were! He also advertised certain wines as "the world's worst wine for 99 cents," and people bought those, too, to see just how awful they were.

The Next Phase

In 1972, the two partners divided the business, with each receiving two liquor stores. Now Dave could go his own way. He could buy as much as he wanted and experiment however he wanted.

The Opportunistic Buyer. Dave Gold is an aggressive buyer. He is confident he can sell what he buys, and he is willing to buy in large quantities, including things he has never sold before. In 1973, Dave bought a supermarket that was going out of business at an auction. The purchase included many items that Dave had never sold before. He then purchased a general merchandise store in the Grand Central Market in Los Angeles near his liquor store. This was the beginning of a diversification of his business, and it ultimately led to the development of 99 Cents Only Stores.

Another example of Dave's willingness to buy occurred in 1976. Kimberly Clark, manufacturer of Kotex, had overproduced the product. Dave purchased six truckloads of Kotex. There was, however, one little problem: there was no place to store all of this merchandise. At the time, Dave's father owned an old garage located in Skid Row in Los Angeles. He let Dave use it as a warehouse to store the product, and there was also space for more storage of products.

The Accidental Entrepreneur. After a few months, small retailers began coming to the warehouse to purchase products. This led, in turn, to the creation of a business unit (which still exists today) called Bargain Wholesale, which sells merchandise at below-normal wholesale prices to retailers, distributors, and exporters.

The Genesis and Gestation of 99 Cents Only Stores

It has been said that success is the result of preparation meeting opportunity. One of Dave Gold's greatest strengths as an entrepreneur was his willingness to experiment and take risks. He learned from both successes and difficulties encountered. Since his experimentation with selling wines and cigarettes for a fixed price of 99 cents, Dave Gold had been flirting with the idea of creating a store that would sell everything for 99 cents. His belief that this would be a good idea was enhanced by an experiment that he conducted at trade shows.

It is a common practice at trade shows for exhibited items in a trade show booth to be sold at deeply discounted prices rather than being carted back after the show is over. Dave Gold tried an experiment: instead of selling the products he brought to a trade show at a variety of prices, he separated his products into three tables with three price points: $1, $2, and $5. The experiment had two significant outcomes: (1) total sales exceeded sales of previous years where things were sold at a wide variety of prices, and (2) the "$1 table" sold the most. Dave was still not ready to launch his idea of a "99 Cents Only Stores" concept. The idea would, however, continue to intrigue him.

The Accidental Launch of 99 Cents Only Stores

Dave had been talking about this idea for a very long time with a number of people, including an old friend named Jimmy Wayner. One day in 1982, while driving near the airport, Dave and Jimmy spotted a store for lease. His friend said, "I am sick of you talking about your 99 cents idea. You either rent this building, or you never talk about this with me anymore!"

Dave rented the 3,000-square-foot facility, and 99 Cents Only Stores was born. This first store would be the initial seed of the company that would ultimately become 99 Cents Only Stores. Such was the accidental launch of the 99 Cents Only Stores concept—the first of its kind in the United States.

Growth of 99 Cents Only Stores

Dave and Sherry acquired a warehouse to store merchandise and proceeded to expand the business by opening more stores. Dave and Sherry traveled to trade shows and auctions to find products, which they purchased for 50 cents per unit. They had a van or truck there so they could ship everything back to Los Angeles.

The company was aided in its development of the business by a great deal of free publicity. Because the concept was novel, the media were interested. *The Herald Examiner,* a Los Angeles newspaper, put the company on the front page with a story. The company also received coverage from various local channels, as well as CNN.

In 1984, Dave and Sherry opened their second store. Dave and Sherry raised three children: Howard, Jeff, and Karen. All were involved in the business from an early age. All occupied important positions in the firm.

Going Public

By 1996, 99 Cents Only Stores had a total of thirty-six stores—all in Southern California. In May of 1996, the company did an IPO and became a public company on the NYSE, trading under the symbol NDN. One long-time observer of the company expressed the belief that a major reason Dave Gold took 99 Cents Only Stores public was to give employees a chance to participate in the value created by the growth of the company. The company now has a stock option program in which employees can participate.

Identifying with a Company

Our research has indicated that one of the key factors in organizational success is the extent to which people identify with a company.[16] When people identify with a company and do not merely work there, they tend to make a more open-ended commitment to the company and do whatever needs to be done to help make and continue its success. Additional research and experience has indicated that one of the strengths of a family business is this level of commitment to the business.

Even after going public, the members of the Gold family were committed to the success of NDN. In addition, the family knew a great deal about the business from its many years of involvement. For almost a decade after the IPO, family members continued to be the driving force in the business. By 2004, the company had grown very large and more complex. It now had more than two hundred stores and was operating in four states (California, Nevada, Texas, and Arizona).

Like all companies experiencing rapid growth, NDN was beginning to experience some of the classic growing pains described in Chapter Three. Management focused on dealing with the company's growing pains and preparing to take NDN to the next level of success. The company added new members to its board, added additional depth to its management team, initiated a new process of strategic planning, developed more sophisticated supply chain operations, revised and upgraded its operational systems, and put into effect a number of other initiatives designed to strengthen the company and build on its existing strong foundation. In doing so, the company has applied some of the concepts and tools presented in this book.[17]

Transitioning to the Next Generation of Professional Management

By 2005, under Dave Gold's leadership, 99 Cents Only Stores had grown to 225 stores and almost $1 billion in revenues. The innovative business concept pioneered by Dave Gold had also spawned a number of imitators and, in fact, had created a new business category: the "$1 store concept."

In late 2004, after more than fifty years of involvement in the business and its precursor, Dave Gold made the decision to retire on December 31, 2004. This led to a management succession at the executive levels of the company. Dave Gold continues as chairman of the board. His son-in-law, Eric Schiffer, who holds an MBA from Harvard Business School and joined the company in 1991, became CEO. Dave's son, Jeff Gold, who has been involved in the business for many years, became president and COO and took over responsibility for day-to-day operations. Howard Gold, also involved in the business for many years, became executive vice president (EVP) for special projects. In addition, the company hired a new CFO and created the position of EVP for supply chain operations. It also recruited experienced professionals in several other areas of the company, including human resources.

Prospering After a Decade as a Public Company

In 2006, a decade after its initial listing on the NYSE, the company's business concept is still valid. NDN continues to be a deep-discount retailer of consumable merchandise, with an emphasis on brand-name products. The company also sells merchandise through Bargain Wholesale.

The company's core strategy is to purchase merchandise at deep discounts to their normal price in order to provide significant value to its customers on a wide variety of consumable merchandise. In terms of the framework for strategic planning presented in Chapter Seven, the company is focused on customers in Tier III. The company's supporting strategies are (1) to focus on name-brand consumables (well-recognized brand names), (2) to provide a broad selection of regularly available merchandise, (3) to present attractively merchandised, bright and well-maintained stores, (4) to emphasize strong long-term supplier relationships, (5) to utilize savvy purchasing, (6) to ensure that everything in the store is priced at a good-to-excellent value, and (7) to operate Bargain Wholesale as a complementary unit to the company's retail operations.

Conclusion

The inception and growth of NDN is truly an impressive entrepreneurial success story. The company created its business concept and defined a new business space. The company has successfully made the transition from a family-driven business to a publicly held, professionally managed firm.

THE TRANSFORMATION FROM A SMALL PRIVATELY HELD COMPANY TO A SMALL PUBLIC COMPANY

Another example of a relatively small entrepreneurial company that made a strategic decision to go public is PeopleSupport.[18] This case describes the process and experience of the company in going public. It is a more recent example than the case of 99 Cents Only Stores.

Company Background

PeopleSupport was launched in 1998 during what has become known as the dot-com boom. Beginning with only a business plan, Lance Rosenzweig started the company in a bedroom of his home in Los Angeles, California. By early 1999, the number of servers and people exceeded the capacity of the bedroom, so Rosenzweig moved the company into a small executive suite. PeopleSupport quickly outgrew the executive suite and moved its six employees into the company's first office.

The company's original business model was based on providing outsourced customer service for dot-com companies via Internet chat and e-mail—or, as founder Lance Rosenzweig describes it, "a call center taking no calls." This approach to customer service helped Internet companies serve customers (then 75 percent of American families) who were accessing the Internet from home on their only phone line by way of a dial-up connection. When such customers were in the midst of shopping online, they could not make a phone call without disconnecting from the Internet. Therefore, providing customer service via the Internet offered dot-com businesses a way to avoid having customers abandon a sales transaction prior to completion. PeopleSupport gained over one hundred business customers within its first two years of existence.

The company raised its first round of "angel" funding in late 1998. In July and October 1999, the company closed two rounds of venture capital funding. Another round of venture capital funding was pending in April 2000.

Unfortunately for PeopleSupport, the dot-com bubble burst around that time. Two of PeopleSupport's largest dot-com customers at the time were EToys and Reel.com. EToys went bankrupt and Reel.com's parent, Hollywood Entertainment, laid off employees and sold the e-commerce operations. Other PeopleSupport customers also ran into financial difficulty.

Fortunately for PeopleSupport, the company received its final round of venture capital funding in April 2000, just one day before a steep drop in the NASDAQ composite index prompted many investors to avoid dot-com companies. PeopleSupport management was able to use this cash infusion to sustain the company and avoid the fate of companies that ran out of cash and had to close down. However, the loss of major customers made the PeopleSupport management team aware that they needed to act quickly to save their company.

They adopted a three-pronged approach: (1) seek larger enterprise clients, (2) offer a more comprehensive set of customer support services (including answering phone calls), and (3) significantly reduce costs by moving customer support to an off-shore location. After exploring several options, PeopleSupport decided to establish its off-shore operations in the Philippines, where it could obtain the cost reductions it was seeking, while gaining access to a college-educated, fluent-English-speaking workforce.

This set of strategies enabled PeopleSupport to survive and become profitable. Under the new model, PeopleSupport was able to attract new enterprise customers such as Expedia, EarthLink, and Network Solutions. Also the company began to develop its infrastructure. A new CFO, who started in 2002, strengthened financial disciplines and helped improve the company's bottom line.

Decision to Go Public

Lance Rosenzweig was surprised in late 2003 when a colleague in the investment banking community suggested that PeopleSupport should consider going public. He based his recommendation on PeopleSupport's rapid growth rate, strong financial margins, and positive prospects, which he thought would be attractive to investors. Rosenzweig sought opinions from some of the venture capital firms that had provided early funding to PeopleSupport. These firms agreed that going public was an option. However, they believed the company should not go public solely to enable early funders to realize a return on their investment.

After carefully considering the pros and cons, Rosenzweig and the management team decided that there were three tangible benefits that PeopleSupport could realize in going public: (1) becoming a public company would enhance PeopleSupport's credibility with potential customers that were significantly larger in size; (2) becoming a public company would give PeopleSupport the currency (stock) needed to make acquisitions that could enable the company to offer additional types of outsourced services; and (3) creating a public market for the company's stock would allow venture capital and other early investors to realize a return on their investment.

A Bumpy Road to Going Public

The process of going public initially followed the stages outlined earlier in this chapter. PeopleSupport was courted by potential underwriters who were very positive about the company and optimistic about the valuation. Once a lead underwriter and supporting team of underwriters were selected, the due diligence process and the drafting of a prospectus began with an organizational meeting of roughly thirty people in the offices of the company's law firm, with a video hookup with key management at the company's Philippine operations.

Following the meeting, a drafting team (composed of two sets of attorneys—one representing PeopleSupport and one representing the underwriters, plus auditors and financial staff of PeopleSupport)—spent several weeks gathering data and developing the S-1 Prospectus document that would be filed with the SEC. This process involved many late nights, multiple drafts, and high costs for PeopleSupport. As the prospectus was being completed, drafting sessions took place at the selected financial printer's facility, where break rooms were furnished with snacks and games, meals were available 24/7, and charges kept adding up.

The process took an unexpected turn close to the planned filing date, when the lead underwriter's research department withdrew support and that underwriter could not participate. PeopleSupport then had to interview investment bankers to assume the lead underwriter role. They were pleased when one of the firms from the original underwriting team agreed to become the lead underwriter. This selection helped shorten the timeframe for completing the work necessary to file preliminary documents with the SEC. However, a few steps of the due diligence had to be repeated with the new lead underwriter's team—most notably, a trip to visit PeopleSupport's operations in the Philippines. Finally, this phase of the process ended in May 2004, when PeopleSupport filed a registration statement for a proposed IPO with the SEC.

The next phase of going public—the road show of presentations to potential investors—started in July 2004. Rosenzweig and the CFO recalled a series of days when they would have eight meetings per day (for example, 7:00 A.M., 9:00 A.M., 10:15 A.M., 11:30 A.M., 12:45 P.M., 2:30 P.M., 3:45 P.M., and 5:00 P.M.); they would then catch an evening flight to the next city, check into their hotel after midnight, and get up early to start the whole process all over again. There was very little time to sleep or eat. Investors might eat breakfast or lunch during a meeting, but the presenters only had time to grab a few bites. They maintained their stamina by consuming energy bars in the car between appointments.

Plane travel for the road show also involved challenges. The sequence of cities visited was not based on geographical proximity. For example, one week the team might fly to New York for meetings on Monday, then fly west across the country to Seattle, back east to Boston, west again to Denver, and then east to Philadelphia. Because the schedule was constantly changing, often the team traveled from city to city on one-way tickets. One consequence, in an era of heightened airport security, was that as holders of one-way tickets, team members were often selected for time-consuming special screening.

Rosenzweig recalls trying to explain to his young daughter one weekend what he was doing during these long trips away from home. He told her that he went to a lot of meetings, said the same things at each meeting, and then flew to another city. He said he felt like a broken record. His daughter innocently asked, "Daddy, what is a record?"

Answering questions from prospective investors was the key part of each meeting. The team learned from experience that institutional investors used a range of styles to obtain the information they needed to evaluate the IPO opportunity. For example, at some meetings, the team was able to use the first twenty minutes for a formal slide presentation, followed by thirty minutes of questions and answers. In other meetings, investors made it clear that they did not want to sit through a presentation and began asking questions almost immediately. Meeting audiences were varied. Some of the meetings were with seasoned investors, while other meetings were with relatively young analysts and fund managers.

Unfortunately, the stock market was not acting favorably during the weeks of the road show, as illustrated by the fact that ten other companies with IPOs pending withdrew from the process. Early in August, the lead underwriter suggested that PeopleSupport put the IPO process on ice for a few weeks to see if the stock market would improve.

In September, investing trends seemed more favorable again, so the road show was resumed. On September 30, 2004, the offering "priced" and was announced, and trading began the next day.

Rosenzweig noted that the IPO road show was only the beginning of a process of developing strong relationships with investors. He found that some of the companies he visited during the road show did not invest at the time of the IPO but did invest several quarters later—after following the company's performance and developing a relationship with management. Face-to-face meetings with investors continue on a quarterly basis through mini-road shows to present financial results. It is Rosenzweig's experience that investors who are willing to consider investing in relatively small public companies put special emphasis on getting to know the management team and assessing their ability to implement their business plan and handle tough situations.

Operation as a Public Company

PeopleSupport was able to achieve the three key benefits that management identified as reasons to go public: (1) they gained greater credibility with potential customers; (2) they began to consider acquisitions and completed one, adding transcription and captioning services through the acquisition of Rapidtext early in 2006; and (3) their venture capital investors achieved liquidity on their investment.

CEO Lance Rosenzweig said that the process of financial reporting that is required of a public company has had the positive outcome of pushing management to build a more disciplined company and pay close attention to risk management. However, the cost has been high. He estimates that the consultants and other resources required to meet all legal and regulatory requirements (including those of Sarbanes-Oxley), as well as printing, filing, insurance, audit, and NASDAQ fees and expenses, costs the company about $3 million per year.

Rosenzweig estimates that he devotes roughly 20 percent of his time to tasks and activities related to being a public company, including communicating with investors and keeping current on regulatory requirements. When he travels on business, he tries to set aside time to meet with local investors.

Rosenzweig points out another impact of going public: competitors and customers know virtually everything about PeopleSupport. He says that management has had to adjust to operating in an environment where there are no secrets.

Thus far, shareholders have been supportive. Rosenzweig understands that investors do not like surprises or missed numbers. Therefore, the PeopleSupport management team makes it a priority to make publicly available information about how near-term investments will support planned growth.

Ongoing Success

The company has shown consistent revenue growth in every quarter since going public. In July 2006, PeopleSupport celebrated a milestone when the per-share stock price reached $14.00—double the initial IPO price of $7.00 a share. In addition, in June 2006 PeopleSupport was ranked fourteenth among "Hot Growth Companies" by *BusinessWeek* (out of a universe of 10,000 publicly traded corporations in the Standard & Poor's COMPUSTAT database).[19]

Rosenzweig feels that a critical factor in PeopleSupport's success has been "fostering a culture that makes people want to work with us." For example, in the Philippines, PeopleSupport sponsors sports teams, dances, and other after-hours activities for employees. The company's predominantly young workforce is starving for advancement opportunities, so PeopleSupport invests in leadership development programs and sponsors classes in areas such as public speaking, stress management, and yoga. PeopleSupport gives stock options to *every* employee, which helps each person think like an owner. As a result, the company is a popular employer in the Philippines and is able to select from a high number of qualified applicants. The workforce there has grown from twelve people in 2000 to over seven thousand people in 2006.

PeopleSupport started a call center in Costa Rica in 2006 that will enable the company to provide call support in Spanish to customers who require this service.

Conclusion

In spite of the ups and downs of PeopleSupport's process of going public, the CEO feels that it was the right decision for the company. It helped the company gain credibility and financial capital to support expansion of business-process outsourcing resources and capabilities. Also it helped the management team develop disciplines related to communicating with current and potential investors that continue to be beneficial.

SUMMARY

This chapter examines the issues and process involved in going public and discusses the advantages and limitations of going public versus remaining as a private firm. It also discusses the issues involved in operating as a public company, including reporting requirements and the role of the board of directors. It gives special attention to the effects of Sarbanes-Oxley, from the standpoint of cost and operations of the company.

The chapter also presents two case studies of companies that have gone public and are operating as public companies: 99 Cents Only Stores and PeopleSupport. One is a relatively large company that went public some time ago (99 Cents Only Stores); the other is smaller and only recently went public

(PeopleSupport). Taken together, these cases provide insight into the nature of the decision and process of going public, as well as operating as a public company.

The decision to go public is a key strategic decision, and there is no formula for making it. This chapter is intended as a starting point for entrepreneurs considering this option.

PART FIVE

THE PERSONAL ASPECTS OF ORGANIZATIONAL TRANSITIONS IN A GROWING AND CHANGING COMPANY

The previous sections of this book have examined the organizational issues that face companies making the transition from an entrepreneurship to a professionally managed firm, as well as advanced aspects of organizational transitions. The next two chapters deal with the personal aspects of organizational transitions. Chapter Sixteen examines family business transitions. Chapter Seventeen provides guidance for CEOs, as well as other senior managers, in planning for the future development of their enterprises.

Many entrepreneurial firms begin as a family business or later become one. This can have tremendous benefits, but it also can be the source of very significant problems, both for the family and for the business. Chapter Sixteen deals with the special issues that family businesses face as they work to make the transition to professional management. A "comparative" case study illustrates how family behavior can have a positive or not-so-positive impact on the company's success and identifies specific aspects of the business and the family's behavior that need to be managed to better support organizational transitions. The chapter then describes how family businesses can use the tools of professional management—strategic planning, performance management systems, management development, structure, and corporate culture management—to support not only the transitions that need to be made in their businesses but the personal transitions that may need to be made within the family. Finally, the chapter examines the special issue of the family "albatross."

Although all members of an organization are profoundly affected by its transition, no one is more influenced by the changes involved than the organization's senior management, especially the CEO or founder. The transitions required may lead to a great deal of organizational turmoil and personal trauma, as in the case of Apple Computer, which lost both its founders—Steven Wozniak and Steven Jobs. These men, who were responsible for the founding and developing of a multi-billion-dollar organization and for the technical innovation and entrepreneurial vision that created Apple, were replaced by John Sculley—a professional manager brought in from Pepsico by Jobs himself. Later, Sculley left Apple, and his replacement, Gil Amelio, was himself replaced by Jobs! If it sounds a bit like a Shakespearean play, it is certainly the stuff that organizational nightmares are made of.

Other entrepreneurs face a similar fate unless they are able to change along with their companies. Chapter Seventeen deals with some of the personal, professional, and organizational transitions that the founder or CEO of an entrepreneurial organization must make if the organization is to continue to grow successfully and profitably. The issue here is not whether entrepreneurship or professional management is better. Both are valuable, but each is suitable for a different stage of organizational growth and development.

Chapter Seventeen begins with an examination of the personal issues facing the CEO during organizational transitions and the alternatives available. Next, it considers the organizational issues facing the CEO and the steps the CEO can take when faced with the need for an organizational transition. Chapter Seventeen offers some additional advice to CEOs concerning their role, their organization, and its management during the transition process. The chapter also includes a capstone case involving managing organizational transitions. This case begins with the company's growing pains and outlines the process of planning and making the transition to professional management while developing the organization's capabilities. It discusses changes in corporate culture, as well as in the CEO's mind-set, skills, and behavior. Finally, there are a few concluding words of advice for the CEO and his or her associates.

CHAPTER SIXTEEN

The Special Case of Managing Family Business Transitions

Like other businesses, family businesses often experience the classic symptoms of organizational growing pains. In their efforts to treat these symptoms, family businesses also encounter special challenges from the playing out of family dynamics in the arena of business operations. These companies, then, need to make the transition from the business as an extension of their family (and, in many cases, their homes) to the business as a business. If this special challenge is not addressed, it can greatly undermine the company's ability to move to the next stage of development and, as a result, can adversely affect the company's success.

Although some may think that family businesses are small, many families have created large, successful professionally managed enterprises. These include PowerBar (the Maxwells), Simon Properties (the Simons), and 99 Cents Only Stores (the Golds). The latter two are now public companies (NYSE), and PowerBar, Inc. was purchased by Nestlé.

The purpose of this chapter is to explore the problems family businesses face as they grow and develop. The chapter identifies specific challenges that family businesses face in becoming professionally managed firms and offers recommendations for how the tools of professional management, including strategic planning, performance management systems, structure, management development, and corporate culture management, can be used to address these challenges. Finally, it presents the special issue of the family "albatross."

THE SEPARATION OF BUSINESS AND HOME DILEMMA

Family businesses begin like any other. An entrepreneur finds an unmet or under-met need in the market and begins, through the development of products or services, working to meet this need. In family businesses, however, first hires may include the entrepreneur's spouse, siblings, parents, children, in-laws, cousins, nieces, nephews, or other relatives. At the start of some family businesses, the *only* employees may be family members. Family business owners frequently describe how their spouse and children worked in the living room packaging product to be shipped to customers. Husband and wife, Brian and Jennifer Maxwell worked together in their kitchen to create the formula for the first PowerBar. Dave and Sherry Gold worked together to build 99 Cents Only Stores (see Chapter Fifteen). Fred Wasserman and Pam Anderson were the original architects of Maxicare.

Some family businesses begin with multiple family members. In others, family members join after the business has been started and has begun to grow. For example, after Mel Simon was initially successful as a strip mall (shopping center) developer, he called his brothers—Herb and Fred—to join him in Indianapolis. This ultimately led to the development of Simon Properties (an NYSE company); the developer and property manager of Mall of America.

One advantage of working with family members is that "you know what you're getting" with respect to human resources—at least in terms of how people operate within their family. There is an understanding of each person's strengths and limitations, but more important, there is an unwritten, though real, understanding of each person's role in the family and how family members should behave. When there is little or no separation between work and home, how the family behaves at home—both functionally and dysfunctionally—is probably how the family behaves at work. If the brothers are each other's best friend at home and defend each other to the end, they'll be a team at work. If Dad yells at the kids at home, he'll probably yell at them at work (regardless of who else is there). If a spouse provides constructive feedback *only* in private at home, he or she will probably handle this the same way on the job.

If a company is very small and its employees are *only* family members, the worst that can happen is that a family's dysfunctional behavior leads to the company's demise. The best that can happen is that the family's functional behavior contributes to its success. Assuming that the company continues to grow, the way the family behaves (like the entrepreneur's own personality) will become embedded in the company's culture and will affect how non-family members believe they should behave. In effect, non-family members will become part of the family. If, as the company grows, there continues to be a lack of separation between home and work, each new generation of family members has the potential to bring with them new contributions to this culture.

TWO BROTHERS, TWO COMPANIES, TWO DIFFERENT RESULTS

To illustrate the impact that the family culture can have on the company's operations, culture, and ultimate success, we begin by looking at two different companies in which two brothers played a significant leadership role and in which the results of their efforts were dramatically different.

The Falk and the Carter Brothers

There are a number of similarities between the history of Falk Corporation[1] — a consumer products company — and Bell-Carter Foods, Inc. (whose history was presented in Chapter Nine). Both companies were founded in the early 1900s by the current leaders' grandfathers. Both companies grew along with the market for their products, employed innovative selling or production techniques, and remained very much family-run businesses.

In the mid-1970s, the second generation of the Falk family turned company operations over to the grandsons of the founder — Jim and Tom Falk. At about the same time, Tim and Jud Carter took over day-to-day operations of their grandfather's company. Jim, Tom, Tim, and Jud had all worked in their family businesses, beginning when they were very young, and had been full-time employees for over a decade. They all, therefore, understood their business and their industry. Under the third generation of leadership, both Falk Corporation (Falk) and Bell-Carter Foods, Inc. (Bell-Carter) experienced rapid growth, with both companies growing to over $80 million in revenue by 1993. It is at this point that the story of these two very similar companies begins to diverge.

Jim and Tom and the Falk Family Culture

When Jim and Tom took over the day-to-day management of Falk Corporation from their father in 1978, Jim (the older brother) was made the CEO. Tom was given the title of COO and reported to Jim. This seemed natural — the older brother should be given the more senior role. While Tom and Jim held executive titles, their father, Fred, continued to have a significant role in the company's management, both in his role as a board member and by his presence at the corporate office. Fred came to his office several times a week, and when he was there, it was clear who had ultimate decision-making authority. If there were problems, Fred was there to solve them, just as he would at home.

Over the next decade, Fred spent less and less time at the office. As a result, Jim and Tom needed to find ways to identify and resolve their own and the company's problems (versus taking them to Dad). This is when the tension began to rise.

Each brother had certain strengths that, if effectively deployed, would complement the other and promote the long-term development of the business. Jim was very entrepreneurial—he was literally filled with ideas about what might be done to enter new markets, develop new products and services, and grow the company. Tom, on the other hand, was very skilled at managing day-to-day operations. Tom was a strategic thinker, but his real talent lay in his ability to organize and work effectively with people on the team.

The Battling Brothers. Unfortunately, Tom and Jim were unable to recognize and use each other's strengths. Instead, the competition that naturally exists between brothers was played out in the business.

On the job, Jim was very much the big brother and wanted to be seen as the big brother by all of his employees. He felt that he deserved respect and would require it, if necessary, from anyone who worked for him. When he was in this mode (or mood), people knew to avoid him, because although he seldom raised his voice, he could be condescending and demeaning. Few people complained about Jim because, after all, he was a Falk. Tom, on the other hand, recognized the morale problems that this behavior was causing and did his best to control whatever damage Jim caused when he went into his "big brother mode."

Tom had other problems as well. While Jim had great ideas that he was able to articulate and sell to the management team and the board (that consisted of family members), he seldom stuck with anything long enough to complete it. Tom would try to take over managing projects through to their conclusion, only to be stopped, at times, by Jim. At these times, it was not unusual for Jim to criticize Tom for continuing to invest energy in what seemed to be a losing effort. Needless to say, the management team (Tom's and Jim's direct reports) were confused and began to wonder if the company had any idea which direction it needed to head in.

The Enemy Within. Although Tom wanted to support his brother, it was becoming increasingly difficult to do so. Over a period of about two years, the tension between the two brothers had escalated to the point that the company was about to come to a standstill. The company was growing but not as fast as it should have grown, given opportunities in their market space. Competitors were growing much faster. Needed improvements in products and services and day-to-day operational systems were either stalled (because Tom and Jim could not agree on what to do) or were taking longer and costing more than they should. Although turnover remained low (because of the loyalty of long-term employees to the company they had known before the ascension of Tom and Jim), company morale was at an all-time low. Something had to be done.

Over the three years since Fred had permanently left his office (the one in which Jim was now firmly entrenched), the tension between Tom and Jim was being played out on another stage—in board meetings. As is true of many family businesses, Falk Corporation's board was made up of family members—Jim's and Tom's parents, an aunt, and several cousins. Lucy Falk—Tom and Jim's mother—had never worked directly in the business but had served on the company's board for a number of years. Lucy was a very strong woman who liked to play games. And what better game to play than business!

As the tension mounted between Tom and Jim, Lucy and the rest of the board listened intently to the problems that they were having in working effectively together. The board made suggestions to help improve the situation at the company, and Lucy encouraged her two boys to work it out. Later, both brothers would admit that they thought their mother, at some level, enjoyed their fighting. In the end, the board reached a tough decision: Jim's behavior and inability to effectively manage the company was becoming too detrimental to long-term growth. Jim would remain at the company but would focus totally on new product and service development. Tom would become the company's president, with all senior managers except Jim reporting to him.

Family and Organizational Transitions. One of the first things Tom did when he became president was to work with his senior management team to identify the specific growth-related problems that Falk Corporation was experiencing. In brief, he worked with his team to complete an organizational assessment. Jim reluctantly participated in this process. Tom and his management team discovered that the company had outgrown many of its operational systems and that it needed to begin developing more sophisticated management systems—in particular, a better strategic planning process—to support the company's growth. Not surprisingly, Jim could not understand the need to waste time planning; he had a clear vision of what the company should do, and everyone just needed to get on board. Tom convinced Jim and the board that the company would benefit from implementing a more formal planning process, and Jim reluctantly agreed to participate.

Although it was a struggle, Falk Corporation's management team created and began implementing a formal plan (like the one described in Chapter Seven) in 1994. The planning clearly outlined the company's strategic direction and included specific, time-dated goals for which individual senior managers were responsible. Jim retained responsibility for new product and business development and was given a staff to work with him on this important aspect of the company's development.

The company's strategic plan seemed solid, but there was one nagging issue about which Jim, Tom, and their board could not agree: What business was Falk Corporation really in, and, more important, what business should it be in as management looked to the future?

Over the years, Falk Corporation had experimented with a number of ways to sell their products and services—direct to the consumer, through retail outlets on which a Falk corporate sales representative called, and through independent distributors. The company had retained all these sales channels but had focused over the years less and less on consumer direct. In the early 1990s, a small competitor introduced an innovative way to sell products and services similar to those offered by Falk Corporation direct to consumers. Tom and Jim saw this and recognized that Falk Corporation could, if it devoted the resources, take advantage of this trend.

As this market opportunity emerged and their small competitor began to pursue it, Falk Corporation's planning team and board continued to debate whether they should pursue this business or whether they should focus on other avenues. No one could agree which direction made the most sense, so the company continued to pursue multiple avenues for selling its products and services—at times stretching the sales and marketing team to near capacity as it tried to meet *all* customers' needs. There was clearly a lack of focus.

In addition, Jim was doing all he could (not necessarily consciously) to sabotage his brother's—and ultimately the company's—success. If Tom said, "It should be white," Jim would say, "It should be black." If Tom said, "OK, make it black," Jim would say, "No, white's better." The senior management team continued to pursue their goals, but they were, at times, caught in the middle between Jim and Tom. Even if the senior management team had agreed in a planning meeting to pursue certain goals, Jim might tell someone to do something else. And because he was a Falk, the senior managers would listen. Each time Tom and the senior management team would move forward, Jim would take them back. Unconsciously, it seemed that he wanted to fail. The tension between the brothers made it impossible to create an effective senior leadership team.

The Opportunity Cost. Over a period of three years, as Falk's management team and board continued to debate what business the company should be in, one of their smaller competitors experienced extremely rapid growth—from a start-up company to one with revenues exceeding $300 million (triple that of Falk Corporation). As it became clear that this little competitor—Crystal Corp.—was beginning to dominate the direct-to-consumer market, Falk's management team made the decision to abandon this selling channel and focus on selling to retailers and through distributors. The belief was that Crystal Corp. would leave these channels to Falk and that Falk could dominate them with its products and services.

Finally, Falk Corporation had focus! Unfortunately, the internal conflict created by Jim, Tom, and the board continued to hamper the company's ability to take the steps needed to grow. Although many operational systems problems had been identified and corrected (through the strategic planning process) over the previous three years, problems continued to exist within the product development, sales, and marketing functions. New products were taking much longer than expected to move from concept to launch, in part, because Jim kept changing the specs during the design process or because Jim would sometimes drop an idea midway through the design process to move on to the next. These delays resulted in Falk Corporation missing the opportunity to be first to market with at least two truly innovative products (that were conceived by Jim) that resulted in millions of dollars of revenue for the competitors who released them before Falk. Falk eventually released similar products, which did contribute to their revenues, but they were viewed as copy-cat products versus something created by Falk. Falk was becoming known as a tired old company, as competitors moved quickly to develop and launch products aimed at meeting changing customer needs.

New competitors were springing up every day, and Falk's sales team was having difficulty, not only gaining new customers but also retaining the customers that the company already had. One problem was the lack of product innovation—the time it took to bring a new product to market. Another problem was that customers wanted lower prices, which Falk's management team felt it could not provide. A final problem was that Falk's approach to marketing (unlike its competition) had changed little in over ten years. The sales team frequently complained that marketing materials simply missed the mark. The fact was that Jim, Tom, and the board were not willing to invest in marketing because they remained convinced that they knew what was best for their customers.

Even with all of the internal problems and conflict, Falk Corporation continued to grow over the next several years. Revenues grew from $80 million in 1993 to $120 million in 1998. The board believed that this growth was acceptable. (In that same time, Crystal Corp. had gone from $50 to $500 million, continuing to focus on the direct-to-consumer business.) Tom, Jim, and the board also believed that Crystal Corp. would never make significant inroads into its business—that is, that Crystal Corp. would remain in the direct-to-consumer business and not sell its products through distributors or retailers. Crystal Corp. was, therefore, not considered a competitor because they were, in effect, in a different business. Unbeknownst to Falk Corporation, Crystal Corp. was already making plans to enter "their market" with a major focus on selling through two new channels—retail and distributors.

New Focus. The game was not over, but it was clear that Falk Corporation had missed significant opportunities and that it would now be faced with ever-increasing challenges in its market. The good news was that Crystal Corp. became the enemy on which all Falk managers and family members would now focus. Rather than focusing their energy on fighting with each other, Tom, Jim, the board, and the management team focused on how they could defeat Crystal Corp. (or at least minimize the damage that could result from their entrance into Falk Corporation's market). Tom and Jim, with the support of the board, became co-captains in this effort. They worked with an executive coach to clearly define their roles, identify and understand how to use each other's strengths, and develop strategies for working effectively with their management team. Their company retained its place in the market and developed and reinforced its reputation for providing a high level of customer service. Unfortunately, the damage caused by the previous ten years of infighting was already done. Falk Corporation would continue to exist but would never become what it might have been. The battle between the brothers had caused them to ignore the real opponent. As a result, they missed an opportunity to become a major player in their market.

Tim and Jud and the Bell-Carter Family Culture

Tim and Jud Carter took over their family's business from their father in 1973. Focusing on the strengths and likes of each brother, Tim (the older brother) became CEO, with responsibility for managing the sales and administrative sides of the business (including finance). Jud became president, with responsibility for managing production and developing and managing grower relationships.

To listen to the Carter brothers' stories about their childhood, it is obvious that they grew up very much as partners and best friends. Their stories also suggest that there is a high level of trust, respect, humbleness, and willingness to learn—all wrapped in a sense of humor—among not only Tim and Jud but also within their extended family. Tim and Jud carried with them all these elements of their family culture into their roles as leaders of their company.

True Partners. From the very beginning the two brothers managed their company as true partners. All strategic decisions about the business were made jointly by Jud and Tim, with input from and, as needed, approval of their board (which, like Falk Corporation's board, was composed of family members). Day-to-day decisions were made by each brother, given his respective area of responsibility. This was important because Tim's part of the business (administration, finance, sales, and marketing) relocated in 1979 to Lafayette, California, with Jud's part of the business (production and grower relations) located in Corning, California—200 miles apart.

Each brother trusted that the other would do what was best for the company. This is not to suggest, however, that the brothers operated in isolation. They talked almost daily on the phone about both day-to-day and long-term issues. The partnership worked. The strong relationship between the brothers provided a basis for a cohesive leadership team at Bell-Carter.

The company went through several transitions from the mid-1970s to the mid-1990s, moving first from a branded company to a private-label company and then to a private-label *and* branded company. As discussed in Chapter Nine, perhaps the most dramatic transition occurred with the acquisition of the Lindsay brand in 1992; within a year, sales went from $53 million to $85 million.

Tim, Jud, and their senior management team weathered each transition, in part, because the brothers' partnership and teamwork became very much ingrained in the company's culture and was embraced by its management team. The acquisition of the Lindsay brand and the inventory from the now-bankrupt Lindsay put enormous stress on not only the Carter brothers but on the company as a whole. Tim, in particular, grew increasingly frustrated with his management team's inability to effectively plan for and execute on key initiatives that would help the company win in an environment that now contained only three other significant competitors.

Professional Management. In 1994, Tim and Jud decided to contract with an outside firm to assist them, not only with taking their strategic planning process to the next level but with helping each of them understand what they could do differently in order to be an effective leader of the now much larger company that Bell-Carter had become.

The strategic planning process focused on where the company was—one of four major competitors in the ripe black olive business—and where the company needed to be to continue its success into the future. In developing the strategic plan, Tim and Jud were only two members of the company's ten-person planning team. Although their votes could count more than other team members, that's not how they approached most decisions that the team made. Instead, they worked as a part of the team to decide where the company would go and how it would get there.

There was, however, a key point in the first (1994) strategic planning retreat in which Tim chose to use his "extra" vote (and for good reason). The team had decided that Bell-Carter should be in the business of "processing and selling ripe, green olive and olive-related products to our customers." After a half-day of debate, Tim arrived the next morning and said, in effect, "We can't do everything and be everything to everyone. We need to focus. I am recommending that we limit our business definition to 'ripe and green olives'." The entire team was given the opportunity to challenge the concept, but in the end, they all agreed that this was the right way to go.

With the business concept finalized, the team worked together to establish the company's strategic mission, which included quickly (within three years) becoming a $100 million company, becoming a leader in the ripe olive category, and establishing a presence in the green olive business. The team identified key ingredients to successfully achieving this mission and assigned responsibility for managing each to a team member. For example, the plant manager, working with Jud, was in charge of working toward becoming the "best cost producer." The vice president of sales and marketing was given responsibility for profitability—increasing sales and growing market share. The CFO was responsible for tracking financial performance. Each team member had a role, and the team trusted, much as Jud and Tim trusted each other, that the job would be done. All team members also knew, however, that they could go to anyone for help when needed.

The team established quarterly review meetings to discuss progress against the plan. Each team member was asked to report on the progress made against his or her goals. If problems were identified, the entire team provided help in solving them. The plan was *their* plan, not just Tim and Jud's. There was no question among the team about who Bell-Carter was, where it was headed, how it was going to get there, and who was responsible for what. Unlike the Falk brothers, Tim, Jud, and their management team were on the same page, and when potential problems arose, the team worked them out together.

A Cohesive Leadership Team. In addition to the work that took place during the planning meetings, the Carter brothers built in some fun. Most of the team golfed together—even those who weren't golfers were asked to come along if they wanted to. Some members of the team even learned how to play over the years that followed. Certainly, every annual meeting included one or more dinners and social events. At these events, everyone learned that they could be themselves because they were, in a sense, all family. There was a great deal of joking and laughter—a sense of true camaraderie. This spilled over into the larger organization, where there was—and still is—a true sense of being a team among not only the managers but the entire employee base of the company.

At about the same time that the company was developing its 1997 strategic plan (in 1994), Tim and Jud began an executive coaching program. Unlike the Falk brothers, however, the program was not started because of a crisis or because of problems between them or between them and their management team. Instead, the brothers believed that they could benefit personally from working with an adviser on specific development issues—personal and organizational—that they faced. This was very consistent with the family culture that, "we can always be better than we already are."

This program began with the coaching team soliciting feedback from Tim's and Jud's direct reports about what they could do to improve their effectiveness as the leaders of a company that would soon have revenues of $100 million. Those providing feedback were very candid (there was little fear of reprisals), with some people saying, "You can put my name on that if you want." It was clear that the partnership and trust that Tim and Jud had had between them throughout their lives had been embraced by those with whom they worked.

Using the information provided by the members of their team, Tim and Jud worked with their respective coaches to create their own personal development plans. These plans identified what each needed to focus on in the coaching process. In addition, each coaching session included not only one-on-one work but also a segment in which the two brothers worked together with their coaches on identifying and developing strategies for resolving organizational development issues (which they would then take back to the larger team).

Over the next several years, other members of Bell-Carter's management team would participate in the coaching process and, as described in Chapter Nine, all managers would participate in a management development program that was intended to help them take their skills to the next level. Tim and Jud participated in the first management development program, along with their direct reports. Not only did the sessions help managers take their skills to the next level, but they also helped teams of managers from throughout the company identify organizational development issues that the planning team needed to address. These were taken, without fear of reprisal, to one of the planning team members (sometimes directly to Jud or Tim) for resolution. The culture emphasized that the company, Tim, and Jud were always looking at ways to improve.

Although Bell-Carter did not have a formal culture or values statement, everyone—those inside and those outside of the company—understood the culture. During the company's 2006 strategic planning meeting, Tim and Jud were asked to define (on paper) the elements of the culture. Among other things, they identified the following:

- "Work hard, but have fun." Tim said that when he and Jud first joined the company, things were tough and they both agreed that if they weren't having fun, they should find something else to do.
- "B's or better." Bell-Carter doesn't need everyone to be an "A" player. Tim and Jud jokingly said that they would have been gone a long time ago

if this were the case. But Bell-Carter does need people who are "above average" and who are willing to work to improve.

- "Common sense and good judgment." The implicit message in this statement was, "We trust you to base your decisions and actions on what will be best for you and the team."

Managers throughout the company were empowered to make their own decisions, in the context of the company's overall goals. This contributed to the company's ability to grow because not every decision and action was pushed up to the top.

There is a sense of fun and playfulness at Bell-Carter, which leads to a competitive but not hostile environment. Tim's and Jud's sense of humor is the basis for this, and it spills over into the company's culture. For example, when we told the Carters that we were going to write two books—one about successful and the other about unsuccessful companies—and that we wanted to include Bell-Carter as a case study, Jud asked, "Which book will we be in?"

Tim and Jud would be the first to admit that mistakes were made during their tenure as leaders of the company—by them and by others. As long as the person or team making the mistake did so based on their best judgment and in the context of the company's goals, there were seldom repercussions. Instead, people used this as an opportunity to learn what to do differently in the future. In the few cases where a manager exercised extremely poor judgment or blamed others for mistakes, action was taken, and that manager was soon no longer a member of the Bell-Carter team. These terminations were not done in a harsh manner; in all cases, everyone on the team, including those at lower levels of management and sometimes on the front line, knew full well why the decision was made and respected it.

The Payoff. By 2000, there were only two ripe black olive companies remaining in the United States (down from four in 1993), and Bell-Carter was one of these companies. Bell-Carter had achieved and then surpassed its target of $100 million in sales and was now looking for opportunities outside the olive business. In 2002, the company purchased DeGraffenreid Pickle Company in Springfield, Missouri, and transformed its business once again. Although certainly not the only factor, the way that Jud and Tim were able to use (not necessarily consciously) the positive aspects of their family culture in their business certainly contributed to the company's success.

The Next Generation. In 2002, Tim and Jud decided that it was time for them to begin scaling back. They had put systems in place, including a well-developed planning process, to support the company's continued development. In addition, they had a management team who was empowered to manage day-to-day operations and had the skills to do so. They still, however, needed to deal with the issue of their successor.

They had been thinking for some time about their successors, as had other key members of their executive team. It was not a given, during any point in their tenure, that the next leader or leaders of the company would be family members. Tim, Jud, and the rest of their family-run board wanted to be sure that whomever they selected had the skills to continue the company's success. But this wasn't the only criterion on which their decision would be based. The person or people who would take the company into the next century also had to fit with and embrace Bell-Carter's culture.

One possibility was to look to one of the other members of the executive team—Ken Wienholz (who had been vice president of sales and marketing and became COO) and Mike Hoversen (CFO). The problem was that both Ken and Mike, like Tim and Jud, were looking to scale back within the next several years, so this basically wasn't an option.

There were family members working in the business. Tim's son (Tim Jr.) had worked with the company off and on as he was growing up. After college, he had worked for a couple of years in various positions at other companies. When he returned to Bell-Carter, he first worked in production, then sales and marketing, eventually becoming the head of Bell-Carter's Import and Specialty Foods business unit. Bill Floyd, Tim and Jud's nephew, was general manager of Bell-Carter Packaging Company in Modesto. Tim's son-in-law, Mike McLaughlin, had been hired in 1999 as the company's plant manager and over the next several years had been promoted to vice president of operations. Mike had worked for The Quaker Oats Company in a number of positions over a period of thirteen years and, during that time, had earned his MBA from the Kellogg School. Of the three, Mike had the most experience as a manager, and he was in his early forties. Age and experience, however, were not the only things that mattered. He also had to fit with the company, and he had to learn the business.

Mike's fit with the company had, in fact, been assessed with his initial hiring. In 1999, Bell-Carter was just about to complete the recruiting of its new plant manager. According to Tim, the final candidates were "OK." At an executive team meeting, Jud said, "Too bad we can't find someone like Mike." Tim said, "Maybe we can." They contacted the recruiter and told her that they had another candidate they wanted her to speak with—never telling her that Mike was a relative. She spoke with him, liked what she heard, and wanted to continue the recruiting process. Mike became one of the final three candidates and was interviewed by Bell-Carter personnel, with no one but the executive team knowing who he was. When he was hired, based on everyone's recommendations, people were shocked to find that he was married to Tim's daughter!

Over the next few years, Mike focused on learning the olive business and on understanding what it meant to be a part of the Bell-Carter executive team. Being an executive at Bell-Carter meant embracing the "work hard and play hard" part of the culture. Serious discussions among the executive team, made up of Jud, Tim, Mike (as head of operations), Ken Wienholz (as head of sales and marketing), and Mike Hoversen (CFO), were frequently punctuated with humor, as team members made fun of themselves and each other.

In 2006, Mike moved from the olive side of the business to become president of DeGraffenreid Pickle Company. Ken became president of the Olive Company. Mike and the executive team believed that this move would help him better understand the other side of the business and get to know the people who worked in pickles. It was in early 2006 that Tim, Jud, and their board decided that Mike was now the heir apparent. The transition to his role as the head of Bell-Carter Foods was beginning.

SPECIAL CHALLENGES OF MANAGING FAMILY BUSINESS TRANSITIONS

What happened at Falk Corporation and at Bell-Carter Foods are not isolated cases of the challenges that family businesses have in making the successful transition to a professional firm. Although these two cases compare what happened in businesses where the leaders were brothers, similar scenarios (both positive and not-so-positive) are being played out in businesses that are managed by husband-and-wife teams, mother-father and son-daughter teams, aunts-uncles and nephews-nieces teams, and teams representing a cross-section of all family members. Some of the challenges that family businesses face in making the transition to professional management are identified and discussed next.

The Impact of How Family Members Work Together and Interact on the Job

Conflict can be positive. It can lead to new and innovative ideas as people challenge each other to think differently. However, when family members use the workplace as a battleground, they can actually stall the company's growth and development.

A company in which there are battles between family members is less likely to recognize growing pains and take steps to overcome them. And if an effort is made to implement new systems or take existing systems to the next level, success may be undermined because not all family members have bought into these needed changes. In other cases, as was true at Falk Corporation, the focus on fighting within the family can contribute to missing significant market opportunities, to declining performance, and even to failure. In another company owned and managed by two brothers, there was frequently open warfare, including swearing, yelling, and name-calling. The company was experiencing a very high level of turnover because, as one person put it, "We were never sure when their anger at each other might turn on us." For every step forward that the company made, it seemed to take two steps back, as the brothers continued to fight over just about everything. In the face of higher competition and declining results, the business was sold.

In addition, the interactions of family members on the job can facilitate or inhibit the development of an effective, cohesive leadership team. If people are "caught in the middle," they will be less inclined to speak their mind because of the danger of being caught in a crossfire. This, in turn, can adversely affect creativity, motivation, and, ultimately, growth.

How the Company Identifies and Selects Its Leaders

In some family businesses, it is a given that a family member will always be in the most senior leadership position. At Falk Corporation, for example, there was little debate that Jim would assume the most senior leadership role because he was the older brother. In this family, succession was based on tenure rather than qualification for the position. Non-family members were not even considered for the job; it would have been, at some level, a violation of the (unwritten) rules to give Tom (the younger brother) the most senior leadership position. Tom, in fact, was supposed to follow Jim's lead.

At Bell-Carter, the hope was (and still is) that a family member would become the next leader of the company. This, however, was not and is not a given. The Carter brothers not only had the option of leaving the company, but if they had not been qualified for the positions, they would not have been given leadership roles. On paper, Tim was the CEO and Jud was the president and COO, but titles meant little in terms of how things really worked. They felt, and their board agreed, that the best way to run the company (and one that would be the most fun) would for them to share the leadership role. This structure built on and allowed them both to benefit from the individual strengths that each had developed over the years.

The Role the Workplace Plays in Family Life

For successful entrepreneurs, work is and needs to be a critical focus of attention. When, however, the workplace becomes everything to a family, problems can start to arise. This is particularly the case when entrepreneurs use the workplace as the arena for pitting family members against each other.

A specific type of battle can arise when the entrepreneur has yet to name his or her successor or has told more than one family member that he or she *will* be the successor. Family members, especially children, may be pitted against each other to capture the ultimate prize. The family suffers, as does the company.

Integration of Non-Family Members on the Executive Team

When the business grows beyond the capabilities of family members to manage it, non-family members will be needed for key management positions. This means that senior managers, who bring different skills, experience, and perspectives but who are *not* family members, will need to be integrated into the management team and given the authority they need to effectively fulfill their roles.

If family dynamics have created a dysfunctional corporate culture (as was the case at Falk Corporation), the culture will undermine these managers' ability to be effective. Their participation as decision makers on the executive team may be marginalized; they may feel caught in between competing family members; and they may not be given the authority needed to effectively manage their areas of responsibility. They may, in fact, come to feel that they are not really needed.

If the family dynamics have created a functional culture (as was the case at Bell-Carter), the integration of non-family members will still be challenging. Family members will need to manage their desire to make decisions on their own and will need to ensure that non-family members have the authority they need to effectively fulfill their responsibilities and achieve their goals. However, if the culture of the company promotes teamwork, trust, respect, and openness of communication, these issues can be quickly identified and addressed.

TOOLS FOR SUCCESSFULLY MANAGING TRANSITIONS IN FAMILY BUSINESSES

As is true of any company, making the successful transition from one stage to the next in family business involves using the tools of professional management (discussed in Part Three). In a family business, however, one of the biggest questions the founder needs to face early on is how to deal with conflict—specifically, how to deal with family members who resist the changes needed if they are to move to professional management. One option, of course, is to ask the family member to leave the business entirely. This can be a particularly difficult option to implement when one is dealing with a spouse, child, or sibling. It can be made somewhat less painful if there is a buy-out of the family member and a message sent to the company that this person has made the decision to move on to something else.

Another option is to put the family member in a position, somewhat isolated from the rest of the business, where he or she can do no harm to the business. The person can be assigned "special projects" that at least nominally contribute to the growth of the business. The downside of this option is that everyone in the company will probably understand why this move has been made, and unless the projects are truly value-added, the family member may continue to cause problems for the entrepreneur because he or she no longer feels valued.

A third option is to seek outside advice or coaching for the individual family member or all family members about what might be done to help the individual grow and help the family work more effectively as a team. This is the option pursued by Falk Corporation and it was, even though somewhat late, successful in helping the two brothers find a way to work effectively together and continue growing their business. This solution will *only* work if all parties are willing to change their behavior and hold each other accountable for doing so. If there is no true commitment to change, any resources invested in this process (including family members' time) will be wasted.

There are certainly other options beyond these three. The key, however, is that the founder of a family business needs to establish, very early on, norms of behavior for family members on the job. These norms may call for behavior that is different from behavior at home. In particular, how conflict and resistance to change will be dealt with among the family needs to be clear to all. Certainly, family members may need to take time periodically to provide feedback on how things are working and what can be done differently to work more effectively with each other.

It is important to keep this issue in mind as the family business implements the tools of professional management, as described next.

Strategic Planning

One of the most important ingredients in successful strategic planning in family businesses is that *all* family members are in agreement about who the company is (business concept), where it is going and what it wants to become (strategic mission), and how it will get there. Even when a company is very small, all family members need to be on the same page with respect to the company's plan. When there is disagreement between family members about the business foundation, as was the case at Falk Corporation, it can lead to wasted resources and an inability to focus on what is really important to the company's success. The company may come to a standstill and cease to grow.

Regardless of the leadership style used, the entrepreneur needs to find ways to ensure that those family members involved in the business are supporting the company's plan. In many cases, this will mean involving family members, at a very early stage in the company's development, in the creation of the strategic plan. Family members should be encouraged to share their thoughts and express their concerns, and the entrepreneur will need to decide how this information will be used and how strategic decisions will be made. For example, in one $10 million family business, the entrepreneur worked with her two brothers, husband, and three non-family members to develop her company's strategic plan. Although most decisions were made using a team approach, she made it very clear that because she owned the business, there were some decisions that she would make and would expect her team to embrace them.

It is also important that the entrepreneur discuss with family members how he or she (and the rest of the family) will deal with situations, if they arise, of family members implicitly or explicitly *not* supporting the plan. Agreeing up-front about the steps that will be taken can minimize problems continuing over the longer term, as they did at Falk Corporation. The most effective way to do this is to ensure that there are quarterly meetings during which family members can share and discuss concerns that they have about progress being made against goals. Again, however, there needs to be a process in place that defines how decisions will be made.

Not only is it important for family members to agree on the company's plan, but it is also important that they agree on the *process* that will be used to develop the plan. In one successful company, the brother of the entrepreneur encouraged him to implement a more formal strategic planning process. The owner agreed that this would be great, but he decided not to participate in the process. The process worked, for a while, but the owner, Ken, continued to do whatever he wanted to do, regardless of what was included in the plan. The company did not fail, but managers became increasingly frustrated and questioned why they were wasting their time on a process that Ken didn't think was worthwhile. Ken eventually sold the company.

Finally, there needs to be agreement about how the company's vision fits with the family's vision. Specific questions to be addressed include

- Is the business something that the family wants to retain control of indefinitely?
- How will family members' roles change over time? For example, is the expectation that a family member will always occupy the most senior position within the company?
- Will the business be required to support nonproductive family members just because they are family?

Organizational Structure

From the very beginning of the business, family members need to clearly define their individual roles, responsibilities, reporting relationships, and decision-making authority. In brief, they should define how they are going to work together. In identifying these roles, a family business has a unique advantage—there is at least some understanding of what each person's strengths are. Roles, then, can be designed to take advantage of these strengths and qualifications (as was the case when the Carter brothers assumed their leadership roles). Although this violates a basic rule of creating an effective structure (that the structure should be designed to fit the company's strategy and not be built around people), it can work very well in start-up family businesses. As the company grows, however, it will want to use a more sophisticated approach to this process.

By the time the company enters Stage II, there should be written role descriptions that clearly define not only family members' roles, responsibilities, reporting relationships, and decision-making authority but also those of other team members. These role descriptions help to communicate basic expectations of each team member's performance—that is, they identify how each person should be spending his or her time. They help to remove the ambiguity that can sometimes lead to non-family members wondering who's really in charge or who's in charge of what. In the absence of this information, non-family members may feel that anyone and everyone who is a family member can tell them what to do and that they need to get busy doing it.

As the company grows, there will be a need to continually revisit and refine the organizational structure so that it fits with the company's size and strategy. New management positions will be created, and the level of expertise needed to successfully fulfill the responsibilities of all management positions will change. The CEO of a $100 million business needs to have a different level of skills from that of the CEO of a $10 million business.

Family businesses face a challenge in filling these positions as they grow. In some companies, like Falk Corporation, it is a given that a family member will always be in the most senior position in the company. Unfortunately, in some of these companies, this philosophy can negatively affect not only the company's success but the overall caliber of other managers that the company is able to attract. It is frequently a mistake to give family members senior management positions simply because they are family members. It is more effective to identify the skill set required to be successful in each role, let family members know what they need to possess to be a candidate for that role, and then help those identified acquire the skills needed to be ready to accept that position when it is created or vacated.

In many family businesses, there is conflict over job titles. This is actually a battle over self-esteem and family dominance. This issue, while trivial at one level, can lead to dysfunctional consequences, as at Falk. At Bell-Carter, titles were not the important thing; the success of the company was.

Management and Leadership Development

As is true of any company, in family business there needs to be a focus on individual development from the very beginning. This is especially important if the plan is for family members to always be in leadership positions within the company. An ongoing focus on this development process needs to be not only the individual skills that family members need to develop, but how the family will work effectively together in taking the business to the next level. When there is conflict between family members, it may be helpful for the family to seek outside assistance in identifying and overcoming specific issues (as was true at Falk Corporation).

As the company grows, family members can participate, along with other team members, in more formal management development programs, both in-house and in outside programs (like the family business programs offered at universities like Harvard and Stanford). In addition, personal coaching can be effective for individual family members or small teams of family members. The goal of this educational effort is to develop the talent—before it's needed—to take the company to the future.

In some family businesses, the founder may actually make the desire to have an effective manager as a successor explicit by telling children or other potential successors basically, "If you don't have or can't develop the skills needed to effectively manage the business, you won't be given that position."

A special issue for family businesses is how to grow family members. Specifically, is it effective to have those family members who will become the senior leaders of the future *only* work within the family business? There does not appear to be a single correct answer to this question. Some senior executives, like the Carter brothers and Peter and Steven Lowy at Westfield's (see Chapter Four), who spend the majority of their careers in the family business, become excellent leaders. Others, like the Falk brothers, struggle.

There appear to be a couple of keys to success if personal growth is going to happen within the business. First, the "executives in training" need to be exposed during their tenure within the company to every aspect of the business—sales, marketing, production, fulfillment, administration, finance, and so on. They need to understand the business and how it works. Second, they need to be open to learning best practices from outside their business and then bringing these practices into their business. This learning can take place in university-based programs, through industry associations, through using a personal coach, and through other associations like Vistage International and YPO (Young President's Organization). Executives in training need to help their organizations grow by continuing to grow their skills. In some cases, as was true of Tim Carter Jr., a family member may decide that he or she can benefit from spending time in another company before making the decision about returning to the family business. Again, either can work ... But the key is to create early on a culture of continuous learning.

Control and Performance Management Systems

With respect to control and performance management systems, the basic issue facing the entrepreneur and his or her family is how to hold family members accountable.

In the early years of the business, this can be accomplished by creating basic goals for the business, identifying what each family member's role is in helping to achieve these goals (as discussed earlier), and holding regular meetings, during which progress against goals can be shared and problems discussed. These meetings should focus on the business and business goals rather than family-specific issues. The intent is to train family members to separate the business and the roles they play in the business from what they do at home. Establishing a system early on will also provide the foundation for the evolution of this system as the company continues to grow.

Another issue that a family business needs to deal with early is rewards. In brief, how will family members be rewarded for their participation in the business? As discussed in Chapter Ten, rewards should not become an entitlement. What this means in a family business is that family members should not expect to be rewarded simply because they are family. Early on, the entrepreneur needs to create a culture of performance-based rewards. When rewards for family become based on something other than performance, family members (like anyone else) may come to resent the fact that there is little or no differentiation between those who are high, medium, and low performers.

This is not to say that the family cannot earn and is not entitled to special incentives, like profit sharing. This is up to the entrepreneur and his or her family to decide. If, for example, the company's board is made up of family members, the board may share in the company's profit, which is, in part, a recognition of the assistance they provide to the entrepreneur in growing the business. Whatever the case, the reward system needs to be clear.

As the company grows, the company's and family's performance management system needs to continue evolving. Like all employees, family members should have responsibility for working to achieve goals and should participate in providing and receiving feedback on performance. Their rewards (with the exception of special incentives that have been created for family members) should continue to be based on performance.

Leadership Effectiveness

A unique challenge that family businesses face is that the style of leadership used in the business will tend to reflect the family's style, whether it fits or not. At Falk Corporation, it was a given that the CEO or president would be the ultimate decision maker. This worked when the company was small. As the company grew, however, pushing all decisions to the top became ineffective. At Bell-Carter, Tim and Jud made corporatewide decisions jointly, managed their areas of responsibility, and sought each other's advice when making major decisions in their areas of responsibility. They worked as a team rather than having one person preside over the other or over the entire company. They recognized that they could not and should not make all decisions themselves if they were to continue to grow the business.

The entrepreneur needs to ensure that he or she and all family members understand and practice effective leadership (as discussed in Chapter Eleven). What this means is that over time, the family's natural style may need to be replaced or adjusted to fit the now-larger company that their business has become.

Culture

As stated throughout this chapter, the culture of a family business reflects the culture of the family, not just the entrepreneur. This means that the way family members operate at home will be how they tend to behave in the business. The key to successfully managing the culture of a family business, then, is to take the best of ''who we are at home'' to the business and leave the rest in the hall closet.

As discussed in Chapter Twelve, being a family (whether the company actually includes family members or not) is very much a part of the culture of most Stage I and Stage II firms. It is interesting to note, however, that the challenge for those who are part of the real family is to view the business as a business (versus a family). This will be difficult to do, but when there is little separation between home and work, problems can arise that can adversely affect the company culture, and in turn, the company's overall results.

As stated previously, one strategy to help the family make this transition—from how we behave at home to how we should behave at work—is to establish norms for working together. Once norms are established, *all* family members need to be held accountable for operating in ways consistent with these norms, and all family members should be encouraged to provide feedback to one another when a norm has been violated. This discussion can take place very early in a company's history and should be revisited periodically to ensure that it still fits with what the company has become.

A specific aspect of the culture that family businesses need to manage is the perception that non-family members have of them. It is natural for non-family members to feel that family members receive special treatment. When carried to an extreme, this can cause resentment among the employee base, declining morale, and even turmoil. In one company, the brother of the entrepreneur, who was also the head of sales, was described by his direct reports as abrasive, abusive, and controlling. Employees also suggested that he didn't have the skills to be effective and was only in his role because he was the owner's brother. No one, however, was willing to share this directly with the owner because they thought he wouldn't do anything about it anyway. Over a period of two years, the company lost some good salespeople and was unable to meet its sales goals. The head of sales repeatedly suggested that it was because he didn't have the right people. As the company continued to grow, a new manager of HR was hired. He quickly identified the problem and shared the issue with the owner. The owner was not totally surprised; he had suspected for some time that his brother was the problem but hadn't wanted to hurt his feelings. With information from the manager of HR, however, the owner confronted his brother, told him that he needed to change his behavior, offered him a coach, and stated very clearly that if the situation didn't improve, he would need to put his brother in a position other than management. Unfortunately, the situation did not improve, in part, because the sales team was unable to believe that their manager could change, and the brother was given a new position.

This example suggests several things that family members need to consider and manage. First, family members' behavior will be continually scrutinized by the general employee base. If a family member uses his or her relationship with the entrepreneur as a source of power, employees will resent it. The bottom line: family members need to be acutely aware of their actions. Second, when a family member behaves (or is allowed to behave) in a way that damages relationships with employees, the damage will be difficult to overcome. Employees will have a hard time believing that the person has really changed. Overcoming this damage will take time and a concerted effort. Third, in addition to managing the culture of the entire company, the entrepreneur needs to be acutely aware of how the actions of those family members who are also employees are supporting or detracting from these efforts. To the extent that the entrepreneur feels comfortable, he or she may want to solicit input from non-family members about this issue as a part of the performance appraisal process.

A SPECIAL ISSUE: THE FAMILY ALBATROSS

Some family business owners use their businesses as a way to take care of one or more family members who they believe can't make it in another business. These family members might be thought of as the family albatrosses. *Albatross,* in fact, is defined as "a constant, worrisome burden," and a "barrier to success."

The family albatross is given a position that may nominally make a contribution to the company, but the real reason for the person's involvement in the business is to provide a means of support and a source of self-esteem. In some cases, the albatross will evolve into a valued member of the company's team. In one family business, for example, the son (a college graduate) of the entrepreneur became the head of facilities management, which in the early years was really the head of janitorial services. The family and other employees believed that this person would never really make a contribution. Over the years, however, he learned the business and eventually became a member of the senior management team, respected for his in-depth knowledge and understanding of how the business worked.

In other cases, especially those in which working in the family business is viewed as an entitlement, the albatross may not grow but may expect to be promoted or receive other perks (regardless of the contribution being made). If no real contribution is being made to the company, everyone—both family and non-family members—will know it. If this situation is not carefully managed, it may become a source of resentment which, in turn, can affect overall company morale. So the challenge for the owner is to find ways to maximize the contribution this person makes and try to turn someone who is perceived as an albatross into a real contributor.

This is not to suggest that having an albatross in the business should be avoided. This is a decision that needs to be made by each owner and his or her family. If, however, the decision is made to bring in a potential albatross, several steps can be taken to maximize the contribution this person will make to the business.

First, the albatross can be given a position that builds on his or her skills, expertise, and experience and that will provide some value to the company. If, for example, the albatross studied psychology in college, he or she might work on things like employee satisfaction surveys or partner with the head of HR on special projects. The title of the position should reflect the role that the person will actually be performing.

Second, the albatross can be given a position that is at least somewhat removed from the main business operations. In other words, the position might not be integrated with the rest of the company's operations and may report directly to the owner or entrepreneur.

Third, the albatross (like all other employees) needs to be given specific performance goals. It should be clear that the individual is expected to work hard to achieve these goals and will be recognized and rewarded based on performance. The owner cannot relax these standards, because when this happens, the albatross will cease moving forward.

Fourth, the owner needs to find ways to help the albatross understand the business and develop new skills that will be helpful in becoming a productive member of the team. This training or coaching can be provided by other employees; it doesn't have to be provided by the owner. Having clear standards of performance with respect to personal development is also important.

If the albatross takes advantage of the position given (for example, not coming to work, not completing work, or disrupting the work of other employees), the owner may need to find another solution to the problem. The problems associated with having an albatross in the company suggest that it can sometimes make more sense to keep the person out of the business and deal with the family responsibilities to this individual in a different way.

SUMMARY

This chapter examines the special issues that family businesses face in making the transition to professional management. Family businesses are not necessarily small, although they typically begin small, as do all entrepreneurships. Some families have created successful professionally managed, publicly held companies. These include Simon Properties, 99 Cents Only Stores, and Westfield's.

As they grow, family businesses face similar challenges, including finding ways to effectively manage family interactions on the job, developing strategies for identifying future leaders (which may or may not be family members), finding ways to effectively integrate non-family members into the executive team, and dealing with family members who are adversely affecting the company's ability to develop the infrastructure needed to support continued growth and success. The key is recognizing these challenges and developing functional ways of addressing them. In addition, family businesses (like all businesses) need to effectively develop and use the tools of professional management, including strategic planning, performance management systems, organizational structure, management and leadership development, and corporate culture management. This chapter identifies how these tools can be used to support successful transitions in family businesses.

CHAPTER SEVENTEEN

The Transition CEOs Must Make to Survive Beyond the Entrepreneurial Stage

Most of this book has dealt with the organizational and managerial issues that arise when entrepreneurial firms make the transition from one stage of growth to another. This chapter, in contrast, is more personal. It is directed primarily to the CEO of an entrepreneurial company, because this person will have the major responsibility to direct and guide the transition process of the entire organization. However, the ideas included here should also be of interest to senior managers, corporate advisers, venture capitalists, and others who are concerned about the welfare of business enterprises.

The chapter focuses on two kinds of issues facing the CEO: (1) personal issues, such as the nature of the CEO's role, behavioral and attitudinal changes required, and changes required in managerial style during organizational transitions, and (2) strategic issues involved in designing and implementing the changes required for healthy organizational development.

PERSONAL ISSUES

To understand transitions that CEOs must make as their firms grow, it is useful to first consider who they are as people and how they got to be CEOs. Unlike the CEOs of large, Fortune 500–type organizations, who are typically promoted through the ranks over a period of many years, the CEO of an entrepreneurial company is typically someone who either founded the company, was part of a founding group, or is the spouse or child of the founder.

Characteristics of Entrepreneurs

Although there are no precise demographic and psychological profiles available, our experience has shown that CEOs of entrepreneurial companies tend to have certain things in common. About 90 percent of these people have one of three types of background: (1) a marketing background, (2) a background in some technical area, such as engineering or computers, or (3) a background in a particular industry. For example, an individual may have sold computers for a large company before deciding to start his or her own company. Alternatively, a person may have been an engineer or other technical specialist and become skilled at product development before deciding to establish a new business. Finally, someone may have worked in a particular industry such as travel, executive search, construction, real estate, or garment manufacturing.

Most CEOs of entrepreneurial firms are enthusiastic about markets and products but are not very interested in management or the nuts and bolts of day-to-day operations. Many find accounting boring. They have no more interest in their own accounting system than the typical homeowner has in the household's plumbing—they want it to work, but they do not care to understand how it works. Many tend to look at financial statements only to determine the bottom line.

Entrepreneurs are typically above average in intelligence, willing to take risks, uncomfortable in environments in which they are told what to do, want things done quickly, and are fond of seeing things done their way. Most, but not all, do not have good listening skills. They are accustomed to being the dominant person in business situations. Most of these CEOs have made open-ended commitments to their business, which means that business does not merely consume a great deal of their life; in most instances, their business *is* their life. The pejorative term *workaholic,* however, would be a misleading description of such people; rather, they view the business as a complex game and a source of profound personal pleasure. Above all, entrepreneurs possess a strong desire to be independent of others' ability to control their behavior. They like to feel they are in control.

The Personal Control Bind

The most important of all these characteristics, from the standpoint of making organizational transitions, is the entrepreneurial CEO's desire for things to be done his or her way—the desire for control. The typical CEO of an entrepreneurial company either consciously or unconsciously values control, both as an end in itself and as a means to other ends. This personal preference has most likely been reinforced in a variety of ways for a relatively long time.

During the first two stages of organizational growth, the typical attributes of an entrepreneurial CEO are beneficial and necessary for the company.

Fledgling enterprises need strong direction and open-ended commitment to make everything work properly. At this time, a compulsive CEO who knows about everything that is going on and pays attention to the smallest detail will have a tremendous positive impact on operations.

Many consequences of an entrepreneurial CEO's desire for control, however, are less favorable during the later stages of a company's development. Specifically, both the CEO and the organization's staff may have become used to the idea that almost every issue, whether major or not, will be brought to the CEO's attention for decisions or final approval. More insidiously, if the CEO has not been extremely careful, an entire organization inadvertently may have been built on people weaker than the CEO. In other words, the CEO may have become an unwitting bottleneck in the organization. Even though the firm has grown in size and added many managers and professional specialists, the CEO may remain the most skilled person in the company in most, if not all, areas. This means that the CEO has not been able to increase the company's capabilities beyond his or her own admittedly considerable personal skills. Such a situation puts limits on the organization's capacity to grow and develop.

The CEO's desire for personal control over everything done in the organization, which was a considerable strength during Stages I and II, thus becomes a limitation or bind on the company during Stage III. Some CEOs consciously want to retain control and therefore do not want to hire people who are better than they are at any particular task. Others are afraid that if they hire someone to perform a task that they cannot do themselves, they will become too dependent on that person. For example, the CEO of one service firm with $5 million in annual revenues was doing most of the company's computer programming work himself. When asked why he was spending his time in this way, he replied, "If I had someone else do it, I would be vulnerable if he left me."

Some CEOs are able to recognize their own limitations relative to their companies' changing needs. As one founder and CEO of an entrepreneurial firm stated, "I'm an entrepreneur. I'm very good at controlling things—making a decision and seeing it accomplished by sheer willpower alone, if necessary. But our company has grown beyond that style. I'm not uncomfortable with the company, but I'm not as effective." Such CEOs realize that, for the good of the firm, they need to make the transition from a manager who is used to controlling everything and being the center of all that happens to someone who is still important but is not an omnipresent, omnipotent figure.

Even when the need for it is recognized, however, this type of change can be stressful. For some CEOs, whose identities are closely bound up with their companies, it represents a threat—a potential loss of potency. Many CEOs are simply not able to give up control to any significant degree and end up strangling their organizations.

Some CEOs go through the motions of giving up some degree of control because intellectually they know that this is essential but emotionally they cannot bring themselves to do it. For example, one entrepreneur built an organization that achieved $1 billion in revenues in less than one decade. Recognizing that the size of the enterprise now made it impossible for him to manage in the old way, he brought in two presumed heavyweights in the business—experienced, professional managers he had to pay high salaries to attract. One was a marketing manager, and the other was a finance-oriented manager who would be responsible for day-to-day operations. The entrepreneur himself moved up to chairperson. Unfortunately, he then proceeded to turn the professional managers into managerial eunuchs. When the organization began to do poorly, he announced that he had experimented with professional managers but, reluctantly, he had to reassume control himself.

Alternatives for the CEO

Four basic alternatives are available to the CEO of an entrepreneurial organization who recognizes that the organization can no longer be run in the old way. They are (1) do nothing, (2) sell the business and start over, (3) move up to chairperson and bring in a professional manager to run the organization, or (4) make a systematic effort to change personal behavior to fit the needs of the company at its new stage of development. Let us look more closely at each of these alternatives.

First, the CEO can do nothing—that is, can continue business as usual—and hope for the best. This could be called the ostrich strategy. The strongest argument for this course of action is that the company has been successful with its current style to date, and, to use an old cliché, if the company's not broken, there's no need to fix it. Unfortunately, corporate graveyards are littered with companies that had promising starts but, because of this strategy, did not continue to develop.

The second strategy is for the CEO to become chairperson and bring in a professional manager to run the business. This is the approach Steven Jobs tried at Apple Computer. After Apple reached $1 billion in revenue, Jobs recruited John Sculley of Pepsico, who had the track record of a successful professional manager. The pitfall is that if the strategy is to be effective, the founder must give up considerable control to the new manager. And the strategy may not work out politically. It certainly did not for Jobs, who left Apple Computer in 1985 and returned more than a decade later after the company continued to struggle. A variation on this theme is for the entrepreneur to turn over the CEO position to another individual in the firm who is better suited to handle the CEO position. This was done by Howard Schultz at Starbucks and Bill Gates at Microsoft.

A third strategy is for the entrepreneurial CEO to sell the company when it gets too big to continue with an entrepreneurial style, then set about building a new company. A variation on this theme is merging with another company to bring in new senior managers. This was the strategy of Steven Jobs, who began to develop a new company—NEXT Software, Inc. (now defunct)—after leaving Apple.

Finally, a CEO may choose to make the personal and managerial style changes necessary to be able to take the organization to its next growth stage successfully. A critical ingredient in the success of such an attempt is the CEO's willingness to live with less control over the organization and its activities.

The CEO as Organizational Glue

The CEO who elects to stay with the company and delegate authority to managers now faces another problem. As more than one such person has asked us, "What do I do now? What is my role?" It is likely to be more than a little unsettling for a person who has been hyperactive and involved in virtually all phases of an organization's activities to find that all tangible roles have been delegated and the only thing left is to be a catalyst—a kind of organizational glue.

The entrepreneurial CEO has become accustomed to being the most versatile person in the orchestra: the individual who could play violin, bass, trombone, drums, or harp. He or she could even be a one-person band. Now, however, the CEO's job is more like that of an orchestra leader. The CEO may not be at all sure that he or she likes or values this new and unfamiliar role. It does not seem to be productive in a concrete way.

In fact, this role is indispensable, yet the CEO may not be equipped to handle it because he or she does not adequately understand this new role or have the skills required to effectively perform it, or both. Moreover, many CEOs cannot admit weakness by letting anyone guess that they know neither what to do next nor how to do it. Some try to bluff their way through by acting like an executive and issuing peremptory edicts. Others try to cope by becoming hyperactive, burying themselves in their work. Often, however, this is merely make-work or busy work—an attempt to fool themselves into believing that they are still doing something valuable. A CEO who does not know what to do next but is afraid to admit it and seek help is setting the stage for future organizational crises.

At this stage of the company's development, the CEO's proper role is to be concerned with the future direction of the enterprise and its long-term objectives. It is to be a strategic leader and a role model for others. Finally, it is to focus on the culture of the enterprise. Each of these aspects of the CEO's new role requires the ability to think abstractly or conceptually about the business rather than merely in terms of concrete products. Unfortunately, many entrepreneurial CEOs either do not have the ability to think conceptually or do not feel comfortable thinking this way.

ORGANIZATIONAL ISSUES

In addition to making personal changes, CEOs and other senior managers of entrepreneurial firms must face the challenge of helping their organizations make the transition to professionally managed firms. This section describes some steps they can take to meet that challenge. It recapitulates several themes we have developed throughout this book. There are two broad areas that the CEO must focus on: (1) understanding the target of change for the organizational development process, and (2) managing the steps in the organization development process.

The Target of Organizational Development

To help his or her firm make the transition from an entrepreneurship to a professionally managed firm, the CEO must understand how to manage the key aspects of the management systems component of the Pyramid of Organizational Development at each stage of growth. This has been the subject of this book, with Chapters Four through Six focusing on Stages I through IV individually. Table 17.1 presents a summary of how the four management systems should look at each stage of growth.

Table 17.2 shows what management's overall focus or target should be during each of the first four stages of growth. It also summarizes what each of the key aspects of the Pyramid of Organizational Development will look like at each stage of growth. In brief, management's overall focus should be to make and sell the basic product and service in Stage I, to expand resources and develop operational systems during Stage II, to build the management infrastructure during Stage III, and to develop strategies for effectively managing the corporate culture in Stage IV.

In Stage I, the key challenge for management is to identify a market and, if possible, to establish a market niche. During Stage I, the firm must also develop its core products and services. During this stage of development its resources will be stretched thin, and its operational systems will be relatively basic. Management systems will be relatively informal, and its corporate culture will also be informal but will be understood. The culture will be transmitted primarily through the day-to-day interactions with various people.

By the time the firm reaches Stage II, its markets and its products and services should be relatively well established. It will now be going through a period of rapid growth, with its resources being stretched thin. The firm will be in the process of developing its operational systems, but there will probably

Table 17.1. Management Systems at Different Stages of Growth

Growth Stages	Strategic Planning	Organizational Structure	Management Development	Control Systems
I	Very informal "In entrepreneur's head"	Prefunctional structure	On-the-job training	Control through "personal observation"
II	Basic corporate strategic plan Annual retreat	Functional structure	Basic management development program: first-line supervisors; fundamentals of management	Personal management control system Responsibility accounting Basic reporting and meeting system
III (A)	Corporate strategic planning	Functional structure	Basic management development program for all levels	Basic "MBO" System
(B)	Departmental strategic plans	Divisionalizing	Advanced management development	Cost and profit center control system Performance appraisal system
(C)	Strategic planning is "a way of life" Divisional strategic plan	Divisional structure	Leadership development	Comprehensive control systems
IV	Same as above	COO Complex structures	Same as above	Control systems for decentralized management

433

Table 17.2. Organizational Characteristics During Each Stage of Growth

Key Organizational Development Areas	Stages of Organizational Growth			
	I	II	III	IV
Overall management focus during each stage	Make and sell	Expand resources and products	Build the management infrastructure	Spread the culture
Corporate culture	Informal but understood	Attenuating	Tenuous	Explicitly defined
Management systems	Informal	Informal	Formalizing	Formal
Operational systems	Basic	Developing	Well developed	Well developed
Resources	Thin	Stretched thin	Increasing surplus	Strong
Products	Develop core products	New products	Established products	Established products
Markets	Define markets and niche	Market defined	Well-defined market	Well-defined market

434

be many problems in this area. Its management systems will still be relatively informal, and its corporate culture will begin to be attenuated as increasing numbers of people enter the organization. Management's overall focus should be on expanding its resources and developing the operational systems needed to support further growth.

By the time the firm reaches Stage III, it has a well-defined market and perhaps even a niche. It will also have relatively established products. During Stage III, as the firm is professionalizing, it may well be developing an increasing surplus of resources. Its operational systems should be relatively well developed. The key issue during Stage III is to develop and begin formalizing the firm's management systems. Corporate culture, however, will become more tenuous as increased numbers of people join the firm but have not yet adopted all of its values. The overall focus of management during this stage will be to build the overall management infrastructure.

By the time the firm is in Stage IV, its markets and products will still be the same as Stage III, which are relatively well developed and established. Its resources will be relatively strong, and its operational systems should be developed. By this time, the firm's management systems should also be well developed, and the key issue will be to work on management of the corporate culture. At this point, the firm will have at least five hundred people, and the people who have joined the firm will have entered in various waves. The critical issue will be to help all the people who have joined the firm develop and support the same set of values, beliefs, and norms that constitute core aspects of corporate culture.

Steps in the Organizational Development Process

There are four key steps in the process of making the transition from an entrepreneurship to a professionally managed organization: (1) conduct an organizational audit, (2) formulate an organizational development plan, (3) implement the plan, and (4) periodically monitor progress. Although the steps are relatively straightforward to explain, in practice they can be quite complex to perform, as illustrated by the case studies in Chapters Four through Six.

Step 1: Organizational Audit. The first step in making the transition from an entrepreneurship to a professionally managed organization is to do an organizational audit—a systematic assessment of the strengths, limitations, and developmental needs of an organization's performance in six areas: markets, products and services, resources, operational systems, management systems, and corporate culture. The purpose of the audit is to gather data about the organization and its functioning and to use this information in making judgments about the organization's effectiveness and requirements for future development.

One component of an audit, and a good place to begin, is to use the Survey of Organizational Growing Pains, presented in Chapter Three, to assess the degree of the organization's distress. This survey should be given to a sample of people in the firm. The results of the firm's Growing Pains scores can be interpreted in terms of the scoring shown in Table 3.1. They can also be compared with the scores of comparable firms (both in terms of company size and industry) by reference to the database shown in Tables 3.2 and 3.3.

Another method of data collection that can be used in an organizational audit is the focus interview—an interview that involves meetings between a trained interviewer and selected members of the organization. The interviewer asks a variety of questions dealing with critical aspects of organizational performance. The process of the interview and the sequence of the questions is often as important as their content. (Exhibit 17.1 gives an illustrative sample of types of questions used in an organizational audit.) A number of interviewers may be used, and the information they derive may be pooled in an analysis session.

An organization can do its organizational audit internally. If an organization chooses to complete the process in this manner, an employee trained in organizational development, with a degree from a reputable university and several years of experience, ought to be given responsibility for completing this process. However, the basic problem is that many people are uncomfortable in discussing organizational issues with someone who is inside the firm's political system for reasons of confidentiality. Alternatively, the organization may have an independent consultant perform the audit. Such a person may have a greater degree of objectivity and more experience in conducting such audits than any organization employee, and, equally important, is outside the political system of the firm.

An organizational audit often includes a special study of the firm's management capabilities and developmental needs. This sub-audit may be termed a management development audit.

Step 2: Organizational Development Plan. Once the organizational audit has been completed, the next step is to prepare an organizational development plan—a plan for the systematic development of an organization in each of the six key areas: markets, products, and so forth. The plan must list the specific objectives and goals that the organization wants to achieve in each key area.

Step 3 and Step 4: Implementing the Plan and Monitoring Progress. The third step in making the transition is to implement the organizational development plan, and the fourth step is to monitor and revise the plan. Many organizations use an organizational development task force to serve as a planning and advisory group in this area.

Exhibit 17.1. Sample Questions for an Organizational Audit

---

1. Market and Market Niche

  1.1 What are the firm's present market segments?

   a. Have the market segments been clearly identified and defined?

   b. Has a strategic market analysis been conducted to answer the following questions:

   (1) Who are our customers?

   (2) What are their needs?

   (3) Through what channels do they buy?

   (4) What is value for them?

   c. What are the key factors that will determine success in satisfying customers' needs?

   d. What is the firm's strategy for competing in the markets it has selected?

   (1) Who are the firm's major competitors?

   (2) What are their strengths and limitations?

   (3) What are their comparative advantages?

   (4) What are our comparative advantages?

   e. Is there a good (satisfactory, better than satisfactory, optimal) fit between the market's needs and the firm's strategy?

  1.2 Does the firm have a present or potential market niche (a place where it possesses sustainable competitive advantages)?

   a. If it has a niche, is that niche relatively permanent or perishable?

   b. If it does not have a niche, can one be developed?

2. Products and "Productization"

  2.1 Have the firm's present products been adequately geared (productized) to meet the needs of its present markets?

   a. If not, why not?

   b. If so, what can be done to improve the fit?

  2.2 Are there any present or potential market segments for which existing products (ours or competitors') are unsatisfactory?

   a. In what respects?

   b. Can we develop products to capture such markets?

  2.3 How effective is the firm's process (skills) at "productization" (tailoring products to meet market needs)?

3. Resources

  3.1 How adequate are the firm's present resources to implement its strategy?

  3.2 What additional resources are required to implement the firm's market strategy and productization plans?

   a. People

   b. Financial resources

   c. Facilities

   d. Equipment

   e. Technology

   f. Other

Chapters Four through Six describe how specific organizations underwent the transitions from one growth stage to the next. As we noted there, organizational development is a lengthy process and may require time ranging from several months to many years. During this period it is often useful to repeat the audit process to assess what progress, if any, has been made. This should include the readministration of the Survey of Organizational Growing Pains.

MANAGING ORGANIZATIONAL TRANSITIONS: A CAPSTONE CASE

To help tie together the concepts and approaches presented in this book and to illustrate how one CEO faced the transitions discussed in this chapter, we examine the case of Bob Mason. We discuss both the personal and organizational transitions that had to be made by Mason's company, Medco.

Medco's Early History

Bob Mason, the founder of Medco, began his career as a salesman for a major medical products manufacturing and marketing firm. Bob worked hard to learn all he could about the industry and discovered that the company for which he was working was not adequately meeting all of its customers' needs and that there was an untapped market for medical products. So in 1988, he decided to start his own company. Apparently, Bob's belief about the demand for his products was accurate, because within a few years his firm began to experience rapid growth.

By the beginning of 1995, the company had reached more than $20 million in annual revenues, and it was estimated that by 1999 it would achieve $50 million in yearly sales. Medco's personnel increased from twenty-five in 1988 to two hundred in 1996.

Growing Pains

As early as 1993, Medco was beginning to experience certain organizational problems—symptoms of growing pains. Some symptoms were more serious than others, but they all signaled that there were deeper problems that eventually could lead to Medco's failure. These symptoms are described next.

- *Many people were not aware of what others were doing.* A significant number of people did not understand what their jobs were, what others' jobs were, or what the relationships were between their jobs and the jobs of others. This problem resulted, in part, from a tendency to add personnel without developing formal descriptions of roles and responsibilities. Because employees were added on an ad hoc basis whenever a staff shortage seemed imminent, there was often little time to orient them to the organization's operations or to train them adequately in what their own responsibilities would be. Indeed, there was no formal training program.

Some people were given job descriptions but did not adhere to their specified roles. Others were given a title but no explicit responsibilities. Surprisingly, many individuals often did not know to whom they were to report, and managers did not know for which employees and activities they would be held accountable. People learned what they were supposed to do on a daily basis; long-range planning was nonexistent.

- *Interactions between departments was a problem.* Managers often did not understand what their responsibilities were and how what they were doing fit in with the firm's overall operations. New departments were created to meet Medco's product and marketing needs, but many managers were not aware of how these departments fit in with the rest of the organization. One manager complained, "People sit outside my door, but I don't even know what they do." Another new manager described his introduction to Medco as follows: "I was walked to an area and was told: 'It's your department. Run it.'"

  This lack of formal roles and responsibilities made it easy for personnel to avoid responsibility whenever a task was not completed or was completed unsatisfactorily. This also led to duplication of effort between departments. Because no one knew precisely whose responsibility a particular task was, two or more departments or people often would complete a task, only to find that it had already been accomplished by someone else.

- *People felt that there were not enough hours in the day.* Most employees felt overloaded. They commonly stayed after-hours to complete their work. Department managers, in particular, felt that their workload was too great and that deadlines were unrealistic.

  This situation resulted, in part, from the lack of adequately developed operational systems to support Medco employees' work. The accounting, operational planning, and communication systems were adequate for a small company but quite inadequate for one as large as Medco had become. Systems for purchasing, inventory control, and even distribution were either poorly developed or nonexistent.

- *People spent too much time "putting out fires."* Perhaps the best indication that Medco was beginning to choke on its own growth was that employees spent an increasing amount of time dealing with short-term problems resulting from the lack of long-range planning. This was particularly evident in the constant lack of space within the company's headquarters. It appeared to most employees that as soon as the company increased its office space, that space was already filled, and it was time to begin planning for another move. It seemed that there was never enough space or equipment to support the company's staff adequately. When they worked at the firm's headquarters, salespeople usually arrived early to ensure they would be able to find a vacant desk from which to make their calls. Employees who did not go out into the field attempted to handle the cramped space by creating schedules for using phones, computers, and even desks.

- *Employees began to feel that Medco never planned; it simply reacted.* (An informal joke around the company was: "At Medco, long-range planning means what I am going to do after lunch.") This was caused partly by the changes in the marketplace and the new demands placed on the company. It also resulted from the tendency of entrepreneurial companies like Medco to spend most of their time simply staying afloat, without keeping an eye on the future.

    Employees began to think that, simply because crisis was the norm at the company, that is the way they should operate. They began to call themselves fire fighters and even took pride in their ability to deal with crises.

- *There were not enough good managers.* Most managers at Medco were promoted to their positions in recognition of service. Some were good managers, but most were described by their direct reports as good technicians who lack people skills. Further, they were seen as clones: many employees believed that management had one and only one way of doing things and that to deviate from the norm would result in adverse consequences.

    Plenty of people had the title "manager," but relatively few really behaved as managers. After promotion, many people simply kept doing the things they had done in their former roles. They were poor delegators, often doing the work themselves rather than assigning it to others. As a result, employees came to believe that their managers did not trust them. Bob Mason was a strong individual who wanted things done his way, and he wanted to control almost everything. Bob recognized this, referring to himself as "someone who sticks his nose into everything." Few decisions were made without Bob's approval or review. As a consequence, one of two things tended to happen concerning managers: (1) the stronger managers tended to butt heads with Bob and ultimately left, and (2) the remaining managers were slowly marginalized. Those managers who decided not to leave Medco tended not to take Bob on, at least directly, and they had little real authority and certainly no power. Inadvertently, Bob had created an organization of what might be called managerial pygmies. In effect, Bob was a victim of his own need for control. This phenomenon is part of what has been termed the *entrepreneur's syndrome.*[1]

- *When business plans were made, there was very little follow-up and things often did not get done.* As is true of many small and growing firms, Medco had traditionally operated on an ad hoc basis. No formal strategic planning system was needed; Bob had provided all of the firm's direction. Further, the informal structure had allowed Medco's employees the freedom to generate new product and marketing ideas.

  As the company grew, however, Bob and his senior management team began to realize that the firm needed to monitor its operations. Unfortunately, Medco had not developed the systems necessary to have accountability.

- *There was a lack of understanding about where the firm was going.* Many Medco employees complained that not only did they not know what was expected of them; they could not understand where the company was headed in the long term. This resulted from the inability of Medco's management to communicate its vision for the future to the company's personnel. Employees were aware that changes were being made but were not always sure how these changes would affect them or their departments. Consequently, employees experienced high levels of anxiety. When this anxiety became too great, many left the firm.

- *Most people felt meetings were a waste of time.* Employees complained that too many meetings were held among top managers and not enough among the lower levels of the organization. In addition, those meetings that were held were often inefficient and did not result in resolutions to problems. Few meetings had written agendas or minutes, many of those attending described them as free-for-alls. They were at best discussions, and at worst fights between departments or individuals. Worst of all, they went on interminably.

  Moreover, people complained that most meetings were called on an ad hoc basis. Because these meetings were unscheduled, people typically came to them without any sense of their purpose and certainly with no preparation. Thus they tended to have the atmosphere of bull sessions in which people shot from the hip. In addition, people felt that they could not plan their work because they were constantly interrupted for "crisis" meetings.

- *Some people began to feel insecure about their place in the firm.* This problem grew out of the many changes taking place and the large number of problems the firm was encountering as it grew. Some original members were terminated and replaced. This caused people to wonder who was next. Although many recognized that some employees had not grown as the company grew, they worried about their jobs and their places within the firm. This, in turn, led people to spend an increasing amount of their time covering their own interests.

- *The company grew in sales but not in profits.* Medco, like many entrepreneurial firms, traditionally had been most concerned with increasing sales. It adopted the philosophy of many growing firms: "If we're selling more, we must be making more profits." Unfortunately, this is not often the case. The other side of the profit equation—costs—often increases along with sales, and if costs are not contained, the firm soon may find itself in a position of losing, rather than making, money. Thus, although Medco sales were increasing at a rapid rate, profits were remaining relatively constant.

Medco's problems certainly are not unique. Indeed, they are the classic symptoms of organizational growing pains. It should be noted that while these symptoms represent problems in and of themselves, they also suggest a deeper, more systemic organizational problem. Specifically, they signal that the organization is coming precariously close to choking on its own growth. This, in turn, indicates that the organization must change its very nature; it must make a transition to a different kind of organization—a more professionally managed firm.

The Need for a Transition

During 1994, Bob Mason recognized that his firm was experiencing problems. He began a program to help his company successfully make the transition from an entrepreneurship to a more professionally managed firm and, in turn, overcome the problems associated with growth. The four steps in the program were as follows:

Step 1: Perform an organizational audit.

Step 2: Formulate an organizational development plan.

Step 3: Implement the organizational development plan.

Step 4: Monitor progress.

Step 1: Perform an Organizational Audit

An organizational audit was performed to assess Medco's current state of development and future needs. The audit involved collecting information from employees about their perceptions of Medco and its operations. One tool used in this process was the Survey of Organizational Growing Pains. This survey measures the extent to which an organization is experiencing the ten classic symptoms of growing pains and is in danger of choking on its own growth.

Medco's scores on the survey ranged from 30 to 34, with an average score of 32. This indicated that the company was experiencing some very significant problems, which required immediate attention. Specifically, the audit revealed that the company needed to

- Better define organizational roles and responsibilities and linkages between roles.
- Help employees plan and budget their time.
- Develop a long-range business plan and a system for monitoring it.
- Increase the number of qualified present and potential managers.
- Identify the direction the company should take in the future.
- Reduce employee and departmental feelings that they always need to do things themselves if a job is to get done correctly.
- Make meetings more efficient by developing written agendas and taking and distributing meeting minutes.
- Become profit-oriented rather than strictly sales-oriented.

Steps 2, 3, and 4: Formulate and Implement an Organizational Development Plan and Monitor Progress

Having identified its organizational problems and developmental needs, Medco proceeded to the next step: designing and implementing a program that would resolve problems and help the company develop the infrastructure necessary to accommodate its rapid growth.

Management met at a retreat to design a plan for the firm. The plan included specific action steps to overcome its problems.

Some of these steps were (1) acquisition of human resources and development of operational systems needed to make the transition to professional management; (2) implementation of a strategic plan that defined the company's business, mission, strategy, key result areas, objectives, goals, and action plans; (3) implementation of control systems to motivate people to achieve the company's goals; (4) design of a management and leadership development program to help people become better managers and overcome the "doer syndrome"; and (5) development of a system to explicitly manage the corporate culture. In addition, Bob began to focus on making some important changes in his own role, behavior, and attitudes.

Acquisition of Resources and Development of Operational Systems. As the company grew, so did its need for greater skills and sophistication in certain functional areas. A controller was recruited to replace the firm's bookkeeper. A national sales manager was appointed. Medco also hired a personnel director and a marketing manager. Moreover, the firm engaged a consultant to serve as its "adjunct" management and organizational development adviser. In brief, the firm made a significant investment in its human resources. These people, in turn, were responsible for developing the operational systems required to manage growth in various areas. The most significant of these were systems for job descriptions and performance appraisals.

Implementing Strategic Planning. One of the first steps Medco took to manage its growth was to begin developing a strategic plan. The major goal of this process was to motivate the company's managers to begin to take a longer-range view than "what's happening after lunch." A related goal was to affect the corporate culture at Medco and make planning a way of life.

The process began with a two-day strategic planning retreat that focused on some fundamental issues necessary to guide the future development of the company, including

1. What business is Medco in?
2. What are our competitive strengths and limitations?
3. Do we have a market niche?
4. What do we want to become in the long term?
5. What are the key factors responsible for our past success, and to what extent will they contribute to our future success?
6. What should our objectives and goals be for developing Medco as an organization?
7. What should our action plans be, and who is responsible for each action plan?

In addition to these generic strategic planning issues, which are relevant to all organizations, the company also examined certain company-specific strategic issues.

After the strategic planning retreat, a draft of a corporate strategic plan was prepared. This plan specified the firm's business definition, strategic mission, competitive strategy, key result areas, objectives and goals, and action plans. The plan was circulated among the firm's senior managers for their comments and input. It was revised and approved by Bob and then distributed to all senior managers. The plan provided a blueprint for future development, including specific goals focused on eliminating the problems leading to the company's growing pains.

The firm then held quarterly meetings to review the company's results, compare them with the plan, and make required adjustments. This signaled that the plan was more than merely a plan on paper. It was a real management tool.

A key decision made by management during this retreat was to be more selective in accepting new business until the firm had digested its present growth by building the required infrastructure.

Control and Performance Management Systems. As part of Medco's effort to develop its overall management systems, a performance management system was put into place. As an output of the firm's strategic planning, Medco had identified specific goals in each of its key result areas.

The next step was to develop measurements that could be used to monitor performance against each goal within the specific key result area. These measurements were developed as part of an organizational development team meeting in which all of Medco's senior management participated. Once the measurements that were to be used to monitor performance in each key result area had been decided upon, the next step was for Medco to revise its information system so that the data required could be obtained. Some of the data came directly from the firm's accounting information system. For example, information about sales, gross margins, and net profitability came from this source. Other information had to be obtained separately. The firm's management team felt that one of the vital aspects of the business concerned the percentage of merchandise that was being shipped to dealers, as opposed to end users. This information began to be monitored on a regular basis.

Management and Leadership Development. Bob and Medco's other senior managers realized that people were Medco's true asset. The firm's technology, products, and equipment were really not proprietary; the true differentiating factor was the motivation and skills of its people.

Recognizing this, Medco believed the company had to make an investment in building its management and leadership capabilities for two reasons. First, there simply were not enough effective managers. Although many people had managerial titles and could recite the right buzzwords, relatively few were really behaving as managers. They were spending too much time as doers rather than managers. There was little true delegation, and insufficient effort was given to planning, organizing people, and appraising performance.

Another need for management development was more symbolic. Bob recognized that some of the people who had helped build Medco to its current size were in jeopardy of becoming victims of the Peter Principle—they had been promoted to their level of incompetence. Bob felt that the company owed its people a chance to grow with it, and he saw management development as a chance to provide them that opportunity. Quite frankly, he felt that if people had this opportunity and failed to grow, the firm could feel it had met its responsibilities to them.

To deal with these issues, Medco asked a consultant to design a management development program for its personnel. Two programs were developed: one for top managers and one for middle managers.

Corporate Culture. Although Bob Mason had been aware that his firm had a culture, he had never taken any serious steps to manage it. He had always wanted the firm to be sales-oriented, aggressive, and profit-oriented. He hadn't realized that there were also a great many other facets to the firm's culture that had been embedded since the earliest days of its operation.

As the firm began to change, Bob became increasingly aware that he needed to manage the firm's corporate culture in order to reinforce the change. One of the unintended aspects of the firm's culture that had developed was that people felt that if they worked hard they should be rewarded, regardless of the results. Bob felt that people needed to learn that hard work was simply not enough and that they had to be oriented toward bottom-line results.

A second aspect of the firm's culture had been that decisions would be pushed up to Bob. Because Bob was acknowledged to be an entrepreneurial genius and because his personality had tended to lead to nuclear explosions whenever someone made a mistake, people naturally pushed decisions to his desk. Bob now wanted to reverse the culture and push the decisions down to the lowest level of responsibility in the firm where they could be meaningfully made. The firm also tried to emphasize that under the new culture, mistakes would be examined and corrected, but that people would not feel the brunt of a nuclear explosion if a mistake was made.

A third aspect of the Medco culture had been that "we're good crisis managers." This meant that Medco managers had to learn to turn on a dime and solve whatever crises came up. Mason now wanted Medco to revise its culture to emphasize the importance of long-range planning. He wanted the culture to become one of "planning is a way of life at Medco."

A fourth aspect of the Medco culture had been "we're hands-on managers." This needed to be revised so that managers stayed in touch with operations but delegated responsibility to the lowest level capable of performing the required tasks.

One of the most important aspects of this change was that Bob, together with the senior managers, now realized that the management of the corporate culture was an important part of the strategic leadership function that they had to perform.

Changes in the CEO. Bob Mason realized that just as Medco had to change, so did he. Bob realized that his basic skills were as a salesman and as an entrepreneur. He had worked hard, and he had built a successful company. He had the title of president, but he realized he was not acting like a president.

In spite of the fact that he was the CEO of the company, Bob continued to spend too much time dealing with the technical and marketing aspects of the business. This is what he knew how to do, and this is what he enjoyed. He knew he was not devoting a sufficient amount of time to the broader aspects of organizational development.

Bob also understood that there were certain other problems with his management style and capabilities. In spite of the fact that his organization had grown substantially, he still wanted to control too many details of the business. He knew he still poked his nose into too many areas of the business. He began to understand that this was not only a problem that he was facing but that his behavior was seen as a role model by other managers in the organization who, in turn, were doing the same things at their level of responsibility.

The first change Bob made was to decide to change. He then proceeded to redefine his concept of his role. He decided to spend more time on the planning and organizational development aspects of the business and less time in many of the technical areas. He made a decision to give up control over the marketing area by delegating more responsibility than he had in the past. He decided to change his leadership style from one where most of the decisions were benevolent-autocratic to one in which there was a great deal more participation. There were always going to be decisions where he would, in effect, have to decide what was best for the company and then announce it to the organization. However, he decided to get his senior managers more involved in planning, not only the overall organizational changes but in making day-to-day operational decisions.

Another aspect of Bob's behavior that needed to be changed was the way he was dealing with stress. Bob, like most entrepreneurs, was constantly under a great deal of pressure. Periodically, he would explode—or as one of his managers put it, "go nuclear." When Bob went nuclear everybody headed for the hills. If something went wrong, Bob might "nuke 'em" in a meeting. This had led, over time, to people avoiding giving Bob bad news. In turn, this had created serious problems for the business because Bob was, at times, simply not in touch with information he and other senior managers needed to have to make effective decisions. As people began to see Bob dealing with conflict but not exploding, they became more open in discussing problems—even disagreeing with the direction that Bob was proposing. His management team began to be a team in the true sense of the word.

Bob sent another signal to the organization about his willingness to change by participating in the organization's new management development program. As he stated, "If I want people to change, I've got to lead by example as well as by word."

Program Results

For eighteen months, Medco implemented its new program of organizational development. After this period, the organizational growing pains score decreased from an average score of 32, which put the company in a "red flag" danger zone, to a score of 21, which indicated some problems but nothing of major concern. This improvement occurred, despite the fact that the firm continued to grow. Moreover, the firm's profitability increased significantly during this period, as a wide variety of operational inefficiencies were eliminated.

In brief, Medco had made a fundamental transformation. It had gone from a firm about to choke on its own growth to one that was able to absorb growth and operate profitably and effectively. Medco had made the transition from an entrepreneurship to a professionally managed firm, and Bob Mason had made the transition from an entrepreneur to a true CEO.

SOME FINAL THOUGHTS FOR THE CEO

In this section, we would like to offer some final thoughts to present and potential CEOs of entrepreneurial organizations. These ideas are distilled from our research and consulting work with CEOs who have worked to manage their company's and their own transitions.

- *Understand your role.* First, it is important to remember that, regardless of the number of people working for you, the final responsibility for the development of your organization is not merely yours in the formal sense; it is yours emotionally as well. Your people will look to you as "the Rock." They will expect you to provide support to them, but they will not acknowledge your own needs. There is nothing personal in this. You are simply an object to them. You have all the power, and they perceive you as having the greatest skill. They may even think of you as Superman or Superwoman.

- *Think out loud—carefully.* You will also find that anything you say has enormous impact on the people around you. You may make an offhand comment and find that people have scurried around to do what they thought you sent them a signal to do, even though you were merely thinking out loud. If you do think out loud, you may be viewed as indecisive because people feel that you change your mind too often. Similarly, a hint of a negative comment about one of your employees is likely to echo through the grapevine and reverberate to a much greater extent than you ever intended or believed possible. Consequently, you may not have anyone to talk to about your own problems in the organization. You may not be able to think out loud. Many CEOs take on confidential advisers for this reason. Doing so is not a sign of weakness or an indication that you can't perform your job; it is simply a functional necessity. You will probably find that you do need to talk things out, and it helps to have someone you trust serving as a sounding board.

- *Do not forget the organizational plumbing.* One of the key tasks in making the successful transition from an entrepreneurial to a professionally managed firm is not to forget the organizational plumbing—the unglamorous day-to-day systems that are necessary for your organization to operate efficiently and effectively. The organizational plumbing includes the accounting system, the information system, the personnel recruitment and training system, credit and collection, advertising, manufacturing, shipping, and operations planning and control. One CEO of a major company going through a rapid growth spurt ignored the company's organizational plumbing and later found that there was a mess in the firm's accounting system that required more than a year to fix. Bank reconciliations had not been done for more than a year, even though the firm's revenues exceeded $300 million.

- *View your organization as a fine machine.* You should view your company as a machine. It has a variety of parts, and all these parts must be properly connected if the machine is to function. Your managers are key connecting rods in your organizational machine. A major part of their role is to serve as a mechanism of transmission between different parts of the organization.

- *View your people as assets.* Your people are, in fact, valuable assets.[2] They are just as costly as your furnishings, computers, or other equipment. If you would purchase a Mercedes for more than $60,000, you would undoubtedly be willing to spend the necessary $500 to $1,500 per year on maintenance. Many of your employees cost you many thousands of dollars. You are more likely to derive a positive return on your investment in them if you provide training and development for your human assets.

- *Overcome the poverty syndrome.* Even if your business did not begin in a garage, you may still be bringing a poverty mentality to the way you operate. One area in which you can no longer afford the poverty syndrome is the area of employees and advisers. Hire only the best and expect to compensate accordingly. Hire fewer people, if necessary, and motivate them to do the work of more. A few highly motivated, well-trained people can often outperform a large number of less-qualified people, thus exerting more real force.

- *Remember the omelette.* Every chef knows that if you want to make an omelette, you must break some eggs. If you are aware of your firm's growing pains and understand the need for change, you must be prepared to face the negative side of change as well. You will not be able to continue to operate exactly as you have in the past. Both things and people will have to change. Some people will resist change because it is uncomfortable or because change is not in their personal interests. Others will be unable to change. Some people will leave the organization, voluntarily or not. Thus our final word of advice for CEOs is, "Remember the omelette."

SOME THOUGHTS FOR THE ASSOCIATES OF A CEO

Throughout this chapter we have examined the issues facing the CEO during organizational changes and transitions. This section offers some guidance to the associates of a CEO who is confronting the need for personal, professional, and organizational transitions. Specifically, it is intended for senior and middle managers, as well as others who may be in the position of needing to motivate a CEO to make some changes or to assist the CEO in the change process.

In our experience, not all CEOs are aware of the need to make the personal and professional changes that have been described throughout this book. Especially if the CEO has been the founding entrepreneur of a business, he or she may simply feel that because the company has been able to operate for a very long time without changes, changes may not be needed. This attitude reminds us of an individual who jumped off a thirty-story building in the downtown area of a major metropolitan city. He got down to the fifteenth floor, looked around, and said, "No problem yet." Unfortunately, he was in for a very unpleasant surprise.

The "no problem yet" phenomenon is often found in successful entrepreneurial businesses. A business may have experienced relatively uninterrupted success for a very long time, sometimes in excess of twenty years, before a wide variety of problems finally accumulate and push it into a crisis. Others around the CEO may be quicker to see the emergence of difficulties yet may be unable to convince the CEO to pay attention to the warning signs.

The central challenge facing the associates of a CEO who finds himself or herself in this situation is to get that person's attention. In our experience one of the best ways to get the individual's attention is to provide information about the growing pains facing the business, together with the framework that has been described throughout this book, so that the CEO can understand the significance of those growing pains. To accomplish this, the Survey of Organizational Growing Pains can be administered to a number of members in the firm. Ideally, this should be done on a confidential basis so that the CEO cannot ask people to justify their scores. The scores on the survey will indicate the degree of seriousness of the problems facing the organization. In the case of many CEOs, this may be enough to get their attention. In certain other cases, it may be necessary to obtain the assistance of an independent consultant to perform an organizational audit and provide confidential feedback to the CEO in order to get his or her attention. The consultant is in a better position to confront the CEO with issues that require behavioral change, as well as overall organizational change.

Once management has the attention of the CEO and an acknowledgment that there are developmental problems facing the company, the next step is to formulate an organizational development plan. Because one of the problems typically facing entrepreneurial companies in need of transition is the need for the CEO to give up some measure of control, we strongly recommend that the organizational development process be a participative process that includes all of senior management. To assist in this process, it is important that all members of the organizational development team share a common framework and perspective as to what needs to be done. For example, most of the firms we are familiar with that have accomplished this have shared the framework and perspective that has been presented throughout this book, so that each individual had a common language and common frame of reference for dealing with the organization's problems.

The next step will be a series of organizational development meetings. These meetings can be conducted over a period of time and are designed to focus in a systematic manner on all of the key issues facing the organization at its current stage of growth. By using the framework presented in the Pyramid of Organizational Development, the organization can examine its markets, products, resources, operational systems, management systems, and corporate culture in order to identify the changes that are required to help the firm move to the next stage of growth successfully. Our experience in working as advisers with organizations suggests that the best way to accomplish this is to hold these meetings on a regularly scheduled monthly basis. During this period of time, the management team can expect to devote a day to a day and a half per month to the organizational development effort. In some cases, depending on its specific situation, a greater amount of effort will be required.

If the associates of the CEO have been successful in getting that individual's attention prior to the emergence of a crisis, then the organizational development process will have the advantage of being able to proceed in a thoughtful way without undue stress. If a CEO should wait for a crisis to precipitate an organizational development effort, then the management team will be faced with the dilemma of simultaneously trying to run the business on a day-to-day basis while finding time to engage in the total restructuring of the organization's infrastructure.

We would advise the associates of a CEO who are trying to convince that individual of the need for change that a great deal of patience will be required.

Most CEOs of entrepreneurial companies have relatively strong opinions about the way their firm should be managed. Accordingly, one behavioral trait may well be a frequent use of the word *no,* regardless of the idea that is brought to their attention. If the CEO's associates are timid, they may feel frequently rebuffed by this initial reaction. The strategy that has to be undertaken here is to present the concepts and ideas to the CEO, let the initial reaction occur, and then re-present the ideas, perhaps even in a different form. Over time, the CEO will begin to become more comfortable with the thought that perhaps the organization requires some change.

It is important to remember that most of the organizations that will require the kinds of transitions we have been talking about in this book are very *successful* organizations. These organizations are not failures. Instead, their very success has caused them to outgrow their infrastructure and, in turn, created the need for change. Many CEOs will perceive the criticism of growing pains as somehow being a criticism of what they have accomplished. Nothing could be further from the truth. It is, therefore, important for the associates of the CEO to present the need for change in the context of the organization's success and their desire to help this success continue. Otherwise, the CEO is likely to resist change, simply because it is interpreted as a criticism.

Although nothing can guarantee the motivation of any individual to change, we have become increasingly optimistic that an awareness of the need for organizational transitions can be created in entrepreneurial CEOs if it is done in a skillful manner. Indeed, we have described a number of examples of successful transitions throughout this book.

SUMMARY

This chapter examines the personal issues facing the CEO during organizational transitions. It focuses on the changes that the CEO needs to make as an organization grows and examines the alternatives available to CEOs who face such transitions. The chapter presents some steps that may be taken by a CEO whose organization is in transition from one stage of growth to the next and examines a case study of how Bob Mason—CEO of Medco—made these changes. The chapter also presents some final advice for CEOs of entrepreneurial organizations, as well as the associates of those CEOs, to assist them in making the required transitions.

There is no one way to make a successful transition from an entrepreneurship to a professionally managed organization. However, the key to making this change is for the entrepreneur to recognize that the company's former mode of operation will no longer be effective.

All change is accompanied by risk, and many of us feel uncomfortable during the process of change. Unfortunately, the need for organizational transitions and their accompanying personal changes is inevitable. Those who do not believe this are likely to increase the risk that their organizations will experience significant difficulties. However, if knowledge is truly power, then entrepreneurs who understand the need for the kind of transition described in this book will be set up for the possibility of continuing success. We wish them well!

NOTES

Chapter One

1. See Eric Flamholtz, "Towards an Integrative Theory of Organizational Success and Failure: Previous Research and Future Issues," *International Journal of Entrepreneurial Education*, 2002–03, *1*(3), 297–320; Yvonne Randle, "Toward an Ecological Life Cycle Model of Organizational Success and Failure," unpublished doctoral dissertation, Anderson School of Management, UCLA, 1990.

2. See Eric Flamholtz and Stanford Kurland, "Strategic Organizational Development, Infrastructure, and Financial Performance: An Empirical Investigation," *International Journal of Entrepreneurial Education*, 2005, *3*(32), 117–142; Eric Flamholtz and Wei Hua, "Strategic Organizational Development and the Bottom Line: Further Empirical Evidence," *European Management Journal*, 2002, *21*(1), 72–81.

3. See Flamholtz and Hua, "Strategic Organizational Development and the Bottom Line: Further Empirical Evidence," 72–81.

4. See Eric Flamholtz and Zeynep Akeshirili, "Organizational Success and Failure: Empirical Test of a Holistic Model," *European Management Journal*, 2000, *21*(1), 488–498.

5. The material in this example is based on an interview with Howard Schultz, Santa Monica, California, April 26, 1995. All direct quotations are from this interview.

6. Il Giornale Coffee Company to Fund Starbucks Acquisition Corporation, Private Placement Memorandum, July, 24, 1987, pp. 36–38.

7. Howard Schultz and Dori Jones Yang, *Pour Your Heart into It: How Starbucks Built a Company One Cup at a Time*, New York: Hyperion, 1997, p. 140.

8. Schultz and Yang, *Pour Your Heart into It*, 201–202.

Chapter Two

1. "Starting Small and Growing Big: The Essentials of Managing Growth," *Dividend*, Winter 1983, p. 8.

2. Steve Coll, "The Rise and Fall of Adam Osborne," *California Magazine*, November 1983, p. 92.

3. Tom Peters, *Thriving on Chaos: Handbook for a Management Revolution*, New York: Knopf, 1987.

4. Our research has shown that there is a statistically significant relationship between corporate culture and financial performance. See Eric G. Flamholtz, "Corporate Culture and the Bottom Line," *European Management Journal*, 2002, *19*(3), 268–275.

5. Jack Welch and Lee Iacocca are exceptions, which indicates that the lack of charismatic leaders does not have to characterize professionally managed companies.

6. Jill Andresky, "The Mess at Maxicare," *Forbes*, June 27, 1988, p. 64.

7. *Los Angeles Times*, August 12, 1988, Part IV, p. 2.

Chapter Three

1. Although the primary focus of this book is profit organizations, not-for-profit organizations can and do experience the same types of problems.

2. See, for example, Gary McWilliams, "Pulling It All Together," *Datamation*, March 1, 1987, p. 24.

3. For a discussion of how to quantify these costs, see Eric Flamholtz, *Human Resource Accounting: Advances in Concepts, Methods, and Applications* (3rd ed.), Norwell, Mass.: Kluwer, 1999.

4. This survey has been validated. See Rangapriya Kannan-Narasimhan and Eric G. Flamholtz, "Growing Pains: A Barrier to Successful Corporate Entrepreneurship," *Silicon Valley Review for Global Entrepreneurship Research* (*SVRGER*), 2006, *2*(1), 4–24.

5. Rensis Likert developed the so-called Likert Scale, described earlier. It is validated as an "interval level" measurement instrument.

6. Grange, Inc. is a real company. Its name, the names of its managers, and other facts have been changed to preserve the company's anonymity. The Growing Pains scores presented in this chapter and the actions the firm took to manage them are, however, real.

7. See, for example, Adam Osborne and John Dvorak, *Hypergrowth: The Rise and Fall of Osborne Computer*, Berkeley, Calif.: Idthekkethan, 1984.

8. See Eric Flamholtz and Wei Hua, "Strategic Organizational Development, Growing Pains and Corporate Financial Performance: An Empirical Test," *European Management Journal*, 527–536.

Chapter Four

1. Yahoo! Inc., Form 10-K, December 31, 2004.

2. "Starting Small and Growing Big: The Essentials of Managing Growth," *Dividend* (Winter 1983), p. 8.

3. Evelyn Iritani, "Flaunting Its Fibers," *Los Angeles Times Business*, Sunday, May 28, 2006, p. C1.

4. Iritani, "Flaunting Its Fibers," p. C2.

5. For further discussion of how Lowy built Westfield, see Jill Margo, *Frank Lowy: Pushing the Limits*, New York: HarperCollins, 2000.

6. Westfield Group Annual Report 2005, p. 1.

7. For further discussion of Branson and Virgin, see Robert Dick, M. Kets de Vries, and R. V. D'Avaucoun, *The House that Branson Built: Virgin's Entry into the New Millennium*, Fontainebleau, France: Insead, 2000.

8. Robert A. Mamis, "'Face to Face' with Adam Osborne." *Inc.*, November 1983, p. 21.

9. Mamis, "'Face to Face' with Adam Osborne," p. 22.

10. For Osborne's own account of his company's rise and fall, see Osborne and Dvorak, *Hypergrowth: The Rise and Fall of Osborne Computer*.

11. This is not just a figure of speech. The Survey of Organizational Growing Pains presented in Chapter Three was administered at Maxicare as part of an organizational assessment, and the scores placed the company in the purple zone. This was reported to management along with recommendations for changes, which were not followed.

12. Compaq Computer merged with Hewlett-Packard in 2002. Although this was called a merger, it was a de facto acquisition, with Hewlett-Packard in complete control of the new entity.

13. Simon Caulkin, "Compaq's Compact Fortunes," *Management Today*, May 1985, p. 92.

14. "Sam Zell: Portrait of the Entrepreneur as a Young Man," *Dividend*, Spring 2006, p. 17.

Chapter Five

1. A "transformation" involves a metamorphosis from one state to another, for example, as a caterpillar undergoes a transformation to a butterfly.

2. John Merwin, "Anticipating the Evolution," *Forbes*, November 4, 1984, p. 166.

3. Henry Altman, "A Business Visionary Who Really Delivered," *Nation's Business*, November 1981, p. 54.

4. Altman, "A Business Visionary Who Really Delivered," 55.

Chapter Six

1. The actual numbers and certain other facts have been changed to preserve the company's confidentiality.

2. Flamholtz, "Corporate Culture and the Bottom Line," 268–275.

Chapter Seven

1. Small and subtle differences can be very significant. For example, humans and chimpanzees have 99 percent of their DNA in common, but the small difference of 1 percent is *very* significant.

2. See Flamholtz, "Towards an Integrative Theory of Organizational Success and Failure," 297–319.

3. Please note that this mission statement was finalized in July 1996. The firm had initially developed a much longer mission statement, which the management team felt was not inspirational enough and far too detailed.

4. "Ossur Acquires U.S. Orthotic Company Royce Medical," Press Release, July 28, 2005.

5. See Master Plan for Universal Preschool in Los Angeles County, February 12, 2004 (see www.laup.net/downloads/Proj_UPK_MasterPlanFinalDraft.pdf) and First 5 Santa Clara County Commission Preschool for All Master Plan, August 2005 (www.santaclaracares.org/rfq/pop_mp_overview2.pdf).

6. For another example of the use of strategic planning in making the transition to professional management, see Stanford Kurland and Eric Flamholtz, "The Transformation from Entrepreneurship to Professional Management at Countrywide Financial Corporation," *International Journal of Entrepreneurial Education*, 2005, *3*(1), 81–98.

Chapter Eight

1. Alfred P. Sloan, *My Years with General Motors*, New York: McFadden-Bartell, 1964.

2. "Microsoft in 2004," Harvard Business School Case Study #704-508, 2004.

3. "Microsoft Realigns for Next Wave of Innovation and Growth," Press Release, September 20, 2005.

4. See G. A. Miller, "The Magical Number Seven, Plus or Minus Two," *Psychological Review*, 1956, *65*, 81–97.

5. For a detailed description of the process Pardee Homes used to successfully manage its structure, see Michael McGee, Eric Flamholtz, and Kathryn Schreiner, "The

Transformation to Professional Management at Pardee Homes," *International Journal of Entrepreneurial Education*, 2005, *3*(2), 185–204.

Chapter Nine

1. See Flamholtz, *Human Resource Accounting*.

2. Westfield Group Annual Report, December 31, 2005, p. 21 (see the annual report archive at www.westfield.com).

3. For further discussion, see Eric G. Flamholtz and Yvonne Randle, *The Inner Game of Management*, New York: AMACOM, 1987.

Chapter Ten

1. Although these concepts are primarily focused on entrepreneurial transition, the discussion here applies to large, established companies and not-for-profit organizations as well.

2. For a more in-depth discussion of control-performance management systems, see Eric G. Flamholtz, *Effective Management Control: Theory and Practice*, Norwell, Mass.: Kluwer, 1996.

3. Marshall McLuhan, *Understanding Media: The Extensions of Man*, New York: McGraw-Hill, 1964.

4. S. Kerr, "On the Folly of Rewarding A, While Hoping for B," *Academy of Management Journal*, 1975, *18*, 769–783.

5. See R. S. Kaplan and D. P. Norton, "The Balanced Scorecard: Measures that Drive Performance," *Harvard Business Review*, January-February 1992, 71–79.

6. For a more detailed discussion of the problems of the version of the balanced scorecard proposed by Kaplan and Norton, see Eric G. Flamholtz, "Putting Validity and Balance into the Balanced Scorecard," *Journal of Human Resource Costing and Accounting*, Autumn, 2003, 15–26.

Chapter Eleven

1. See, for example, the discussion of the difference management style can make in successful organizations in T. H. Peters and R. H. Waterman, *In Search of Excellence*, New York: HarperCollins, 1982.

2. Joseph L. Badaracco Jr., *Leading Quietly*, Boston: Harvard Business School Press, 2002.

3. For discussions of a contingency theory, see, for example, F. E. Fiedler, *A Theory of Leadership Effectiveness*, New York: McGraw-Hill, 1967. For a discussion of situational leadership, see P. Hersey and K. H. Blanchard, *Managing Organizational Behavior*, Prentice Hall, 1977, pp. 159–186.

4. The late Rensis Likert developed a classic typology of four basic leadership styles (autocratic, benevolent-autocratic, consultative, and participative) in his book, *New Patterns of Management*, New York: McGraw-Hill, 1961, pp. 222–236. This typology was subsequently retitled as Systems I-IV in Likert's *Human Business Review* (March-April 1958), p. 36. The conceptualization in this chapter is related to both of these prior efforts. The labels for our first four styles of leadership are identical to Likert's, but the definition of behavior that we use for each style differs to some degree. The other two styles we list—consensus and laissez-faire—represent somewhat different patterns from those previously conceptualized by others.

5. This conceptualization is a slight modification of the four-factor theory of leadership proposed by D. Bowers and S. Seashore in "Predicting Organizational Effectiveness with a Four-Factor Theory of Leadership," *Administrative Science Quarterly*, 1966, *11*, 238–263. The four factors that Bowers and Seashore identified are goal emphasis, work facilitation, interaction facilitation, and support. In this chapter we have subdivided the factor originally labeled "support" into two dimensions: supportive behavior and personnel development.

6. Sambol replaced Kurland as president and COO in 2006.

Chapter Twelve

1. There is empirical research support for these factors. See Eric Flamholtz and Rangapriya Kannan-Narasimhan, "Differential Impact of Cultural Elements on Financial Performance," *European Management Journal*, February 2005, *23*(1), 50–64.

2. "J. D. Powers and Associates Reports: Redesigned Initial Quality Study Shows That Vehicle Design Plays as Critical a Role in Consumer Perceptions of Quality as Defects and Malfunctions," Press Release, June 7, 2006.

3. Flamholtz, "Corporate Culture and the Bottom Line," 268–275.

4. Flamholtz, "Corporate Culture and the Bottom Line, 272.

5. See David Halberstam, *The Reckoning*, New York: Morrow, 1986.

6. See "Remaking Microsoft," *BusinessWeek*, May 17, 1999, pp. 106–116.

7. See "Remaking Microsoft," 112.

8. "Microsoft Realigns for Next Wave of Innovation and Growth," Press Release, September 20, 2005.

Chapter Thirteen

1. See Peter Drucker, *Management: Tasks, Responsibilities, and Practices*, New York: Harper & Row, 1973.

2. Chess is a metaphor for warfare or combat. Even the language of chess refers to aspects of medieval warfare: castles, knights, bishops, queens, kings, and pawns (or serfs).

3. All strategy is, by definition, competitive strategy.

4. In accounting, fixed assets must have an expected useful life greater than one year. A current asset has a useful life of one year.

5. A *legal monopoly* means that the monopoly is conferred by governmental statute. We are *not* inferring that what Microsoft has achieved is illegal.

6. See Eric Flamholtz, "Managing Organizational Transitions: Implications for Corporate and Human Resource Management," *European Management Journal*, 1995, *13*(1), 39–51.

7. "Colleen's Corner — Internal Customer Care," *Southwest Airlines Spirit*, September, 2006.

8. For a summary of this research, see Flamholtz, "Towards an Integrative Theory of Organizational Success and Failure," 297–320.

9. See Eric Flamholtz and Wei Hua, "Searching for Competitive Advantage Inside the Black Box," *European Management Journal*, 2003, *21*(2), 222–236.

10. Flamholtz and Hua, "Searching for Competitive Advantage Inside the Black Box," 222–236.

11. This case was coauthored by Madhavan Nayar, Company Leader, Infogix.

12. In 2005, Infogix changed its name from Unitech Systems to Infogix.

13. Madhavan Nayar and Eric Flamholtz, "Making the Transformation from Entrepreneurship to Professional Management: The Case of Unitech Systems," *International Journal of Entrepreneurial Education*, 2005, *3*(2), 170–171.

Chapter Fourteen

1. Vito J. Rancanelli, "The World's Most Respected Companies," *Barron's*, September 11, 2006, pp. 29–34.

2. The phenomenon of decline in organizations has been increasingly recognized by scholars. See K. S. Cameron, R. Sutton, and D. Whetton (eds.), *Readings in Organizational Decline*, Cambridge, Mass.: Ballinger, 1988. This same phenomenon that occurs in organizations has also been identified in nations. See Paul Kennedy, *The Rise and Fall of the Great Powers*, New York: Random House, 1987.

3. Paul Kennedy, *Economic Change and Military Conflict from 1500 to 2000*, New York: Random House, 1987.

4. For a discussion of the issues involved in organizational revitalizations, see Eric G. Flamholtz and Yvonne Randle, *Changing the Game: Managing Organizational Transformations of the First, Second and Third Kinds*, New York: Oxford University Press, 1998 (esp. Chapters 4 and 6).

5. Brian Dumaina, "What the Leaders of Tomorrow See," *Fortune*, July 3, 1989, p. 58.

6. See, for example, Joel Dreyfuss, "Reinventing IBM," *Fortune*, August 14, 1989, pp. 29–30.

7. See Louis V. Gerstner Jr., *Who Says Elephants Can't Dance?* New York: Harper Business, 2002.

Chapter Fifteen

1. The term *The Street* refers to Wall Street metaphorically, not just literally to Wall Street but to investors, analysts, and others who evaluate a company's earnings and prospects.

2. The term *PE* refers to the "price earnings ratio" of a company, which is the ratio of the company's share price divided by its earnings. It is a commonly used construct to evaluate a company as a potential investment.

3. This section is intended as a big-picture overview of the IPO process. It is not intended as a handbook for going public. The actual process should be guided by experienced legal, financial, and other professionals.

4. Safi Qureshey, "How I Learned to Live with Wall Street," *Harvard Business Review*, May-June 1991, pp. 4–9.

5. For a good overview on the role of the board of directors, see *Corporate Director's Guidebook* (4th ed.), Committee on Corporate Laws, American Bar Association, 2004.

6. The intent of this section is *not* to provide detailed guidance about SEC reporting requirements but to suggest the increased complexity and requirements once a company goes public.

7. A detailed discussion of the requirements of SOX is beyond the scope of this chapter. For further information, go to www.Sarbanes-Oxley.com.

8. This is the famous (some would say infamous) section 404 of SOX.

9. Wall Street Roundup, "Compliance Costs Fall, Study Finds," *Los Angeles Times*, April 19, 2006, p. C4.

10. Wall Street Roundup, "Compliance Costs Fall, Study Finds," p. C4; "SEC Won't Exempt Smaller Firms From Anti-Fraud Law Requirements," *Los Angeles Times*, May 18, 2006, p. C4.

11. Jeffrey Stinson, "Europe Widens the Playing Field: Financial Markets Get Bigger Role Amid Tougher U.S. Regulations," *USA Today*, May 10, 2004, pp. 6A–7A.

12. Stinson, "Europe Widens the Playing Field," p. 7A.

13. Stinson, "Europe Widens the Playing Field," p. 7A.

14. This case is based on a combination of interview discussions with various individuals affiliated with 99 Cents Only Stores, including several members of the board of directors, as well as an article titled "It all Started with a Dream," published in the company's newsletter "The 99'er," Summer 2005, pp. A2–A3.

15. The company's stock symbol is NDN.

16. Eric G. Flamholtz and Rangapriya Narasimhan-Kannan, ''Differential Impact of Cultural Elements on Financial Performance, ''*European Management Journal*, February 2005, *23*(1), 50–64.

17. Eric Flamholtz, one of this book's authors, joined the board of directors of NDN in May of 2004.

18. This case was prepared by Kathryn Schreiner, under the direction of Eric Flamholtz. It is based on interviews conducted with Lance Rosenzweig—PeopleSupport's founder and CEO.

19. See *BusinessWeek*, June 5, 2006.

Chapter Sixteen

1. Falk Corporation is a fictitious name for a real company. The nature of the company and certain aspects of its operations have been disguised.

Chapter Seventeen

1. See Flamholtz and Randle, *The Inner Game of Management*.

2. For a discussion of how to measure and account for people as assets, see Flamholtz, *Human Resource Accounting* (3rd ed.).

INDEX

A

Accountability, 301–302
Action plan, 169
Aerotek, 365
AIM Exchange (London), 385, 386
Air Bus, 348
Allegis, 292
Allen, P., 314
Allied Lyons, 193
Allied-Domecq, 367
Alpha Manufacturing, 321–323, 326–329
Altair computer, 314
Alza, 365
Amazon.com, 11, 30, 76, 363
America Online, 74, 76
American Airlines, 312, 344
American Century Investors, 93, 116–117,
    215, 273, 279, 293, 294, 321, 324;
    professionalization at, 114–115
American Express, 303, 349, 369
Amgen, 10, 11, 20, 279, 305, 337
Anderson, P., 45, 46, 402
Anderson School of Management (UCLA),
    215–216
Apollo Travel, 292
Apple Computer, 3, 11, 20, 36, 45, 56, 75, 82,
    159, 166, 222, 274, 275, 361–362, 367,
    370, 387, 430

Apria Healthcare, 45
Arrow Electronics, 86
Ashton-Tate, 362, 369, 386
Association for Strategic Planning, 342
AST Research, 381
AT&T, 367, 373
Audit, organizational, 44, 435–436; sample
    questions for, 437
Australia, 79, 215–216
Australian Graduate School of Management,
    215–216

B

Balanced Score Card (BSC; Kaplan and
    Norton), 252–253
Ballmer, S., 192, 315, 316
Bangalore, India, 74
Bank of America, 368–369
Bank of Nova Scotia, 349
Barbie dolls, 362
Bargain Wholesale, 391
Barnes & Noble, Inc., 210
Barrett, C., 343
Behar, H., 209, 210, 293
Behavioral reliability, 256
Beliefs, 17, 299, 342
Bell, A., 231
Bell, H., 231

Bell-Carter Foods, Inc., 222–223, 242, 300, 301, 310, 342, 346, 348, 363, 414–416, 419, 420, 422; corporate background of, 231–232; family culture at, 408–414; growing pains at, 232–234; impact of program at, 237–238; management development at different stages of organizational growth, 238–241; management development program objectives, 232–234; nature of management development program at, 234–237

Bell-Carter Olive Company, 231, 238
Bell-Carter Packaging, 238
Benesch, F., 184
Benham Investors, 321, 324
Bentonville, Arkansas, 15–16
Berkshire-Hathaway, 193
Bezos, J., 76
Bhatia, S., 74
Blacktown Delicatessen (Sydney, Australia), 80
Blue Cross Blue Shield of Illinois, 350
Board of directors, 383–384
Boeing, 41, 348
Bombardier, 348
Booth, M., 191
Borland, 362
Boston Chicken (Boston Market), 24
Boston Market, 22, 35, 369; versus Starbucks, 24
Bowman, C., 289
Branson, R., 79, 81
Bratz dolls, 362
Bristol-Myers Squibb, 193
Brown, D., 95
Brown, H., 95
BSC. See Balanced Score Card
Budgeting result area, 41, 97–98, 109–110, 169
Bureaucracy, 308
Business: concept, 149–150, 163–164; core strategy, 9; definition or concept, 8; foundation of, 8–9; strategic mission, 9
Business Week, 397
Butterfield & Butterfield, 77

C
Cadillac, 154
Caltech, 74
Canion, R., 89
Capacity building, 13
Carter, J., 231, 233, 234, 236, 300, 301, 403, 408–414

Carter, T., 231, 233, 234, 236, 300, 301, 403, 408–414
Cashmere House, 79–80
CBS, 156
Cendant Mortgage, 158
Centocor, 365–366
CEOs: alternatives for, 430–431; and case study for managing organizational transitions, 438–448; and characteristics of entrepreneurs, 428; as organizational glue, 431–432; and organizational issues, 432–438; and personal control bind, 428–430; and personal issues, 427–432
Change: assessing need for, 48–70; commitment to, 303; resistance to, 106
Chapter 11, 24, 46, 84, 363, 364
Charles Schwab & Company, 368–369
Chart House, 307
Chevrolet, 153, 154
Chih-Yuan Yang, J., 76
Chrysler, 274, 295
Citibank, 349
Citicorp, 365
Clairborne, Liz, 77–79, 82
Coca-Cola, 8, 158
Columbia University, 369
Communication, 99, 111
Compaq Computer Corporation, 61–62, 70, 75, 82, 159, 166, 337, 341, 357, 377; versus Osborne Computer, 89–91
Compensation, 100, 111–112
Competitive advantage, 338–343; infrastructure as source of, 344–345; six key sources of, 339 Exhibit 13.1
Competitive analysis, 151 Fig. 7.1
Competitive strategy, 343–345
Consolidation stage (IV), 37–38; developing successful organizations in, 119–121; developmental emphasis in, 38 Fig.2.4; keys to successful firm in, 139–140; managing corporate culture in, 119–141
Consultants, 186–187
Contingency theory, 274
Control, 244–245
Control result area, 39–40, 98, 110
Converse, 344
Copyspot, 215
Core management skills, 221–222
Corning, California, 301, 409
Corporate culture, 22; change in, 312–316; at different stages of organizational development, 326–331; and identification of firm's desired culture, 320; and identification of gaps between current and desired cultures, 320–321; managing,

17–18, 119–141, 286; manifestations of, 307–312; and planned culture change, 313–316; real *versus* nominal, 305–307, 306 *Table* 12.1; shaping, 217

Corporate culture management: and customer-client orientation, 299–300; developing plan for, 321–326; and functional and dysfunctional cultures, 305; impact of, on success and financial performance, 303–304; and nature of corporate culture, 299–303; and people (employee) orientation, 300–301; and performance standards, 301–303; and strong and weak cultures, 305

Corporate entrepreneurship, 371

Costa Rica, 397

Countrywide Financial Corporation, 8, 9, 17, 41–42, 63, 93, 187, 215, 222–223, 273, 274, 285, 286, 293, 294, 305, 342, 346, 348, 364–365

CPM system (Digital Research), 75

Crescent City, California, 337

Crystal Corporation, 406–408

Cuisinart, Inc., 363

Culture management, 133–134, 342–343

Culture result area, 42, 96–97, 106–109

Curtis, C., 156

Curtis Publishing Company, 156

Customer service, 302–303

Customer-Client orientation, 299–300

Cypress Semiconductor, 373

D

Daggs, B., 309

David's Cookies, 78, 82

dBase II, 362

DEC (Digital Equipment Corporation), 91

Decision-making, 98, 110

Decline, 367–369

DeGraffenreid Pickle Company, 238, 412, 414

Dell Computer, 76, 91, 159, 167, 337, 341, 368

Dell, M., 12, 76, 91, 166, 370

Delta Airlines, 279, 312

Demmings, W. E., 350

Design Corporation, 204–206

Development result area, 41

DFP. *See* Diversified Financial Products, Inc.

Digital Research, 75

Dingivan, G., 265

Disney, 17, 156, 305, 307, 341, 374

Disneyland, 299–300

Diversification, 361–365

Diversified Financial Products, Inc. (DFP), 112

Divisional organizational structure, 192–194; M-type, 193

Domino's Pizza, 12, 17, 30, 77–78, 116, 184, 217, 310

Dreyers, 11, 210

Drucker, P., 335

Dysfunctional behavior, 256–257

E

EarthLink Network, 76, 393

eBay, 11, 30, 76, 77, 79

E-commerce, 76–77

Economy, declining, 105–106

Eisner, M., 374

Energy bars, 12

Enron, 257, 385

Entrepreneurial management, *versus* professional management, 38–42; comparison, 40 *Table* 2.2

Environmental scan: and competitive analysis, 151; and identifying firm's market segment, 152–154; market analysis in, 150–151

Epogen (Amgen), 10, 337, 340

Equity Office Properties, 91

Equity Residential Properties, 91

EToys, 393

E*Trade, 76

Evaluation, organizational, 44

Expansion stage (Stage II), 31–33; developing successful organizations at, 83–87; developmental emphasis in, 32 *Fig.*2.2

Expansion stages, 73–92

Expedia, 393

F

Fair disclosure, 384

Falk Corporation, 52, 403–408, 414–420, 422

Falk, J., 403–408

Falk, T., 403–408

Family atmosphere, 106, 122–123

Family business transitions: control and performance management systems for, 421; and culture, 422–423; and family albatross, 423–425; and leadership effectiveness, 421–422; management and leadership development in, 420–421; managing, 401–426; organizational structure in, 418–419; and separation of business and home dilemma, 402–403; special challenges of managing, 414–416;

Family business transitions: control and performance management systems for, *(continued)*
  strategic planning for, 417–418; tools for successfully managing, 416–423
Family-style management system, 95
Federal Express, 8, 77–78, 88, 116; professionalization at, 112–113
FedEx, 348
Ferris, R., 292
Fields, D., 78, 82
Filo, D., 76
Fiorina, C., 377
Flamholtz, E., 22, 352, 354
Floyd, B., 413
Fokker, 348
Ford Motor Company, 302, 367, 377, 381
Frazer, G., 289, 290
Fritzi of California, 184
Functional organizational structure, 190–192

G

Game, business as, 335
Garcia, C., 294
Gates, B., 75, 76, 311, 314–316, 430
Gel Cast Ankle Support, 171
General Electric (GE), 193, 242, 302, 365, 367
General Magic, 76–77
General Motors, 154, 192, 367, 373
General Ribbon, 309
Gerstner, L., 377
Gillette, 158, 365
Goal congruence, 256
Goal displacement, 256
Gold, D., 78, 388–391, 401, 402
Gold, J., 391
Gold, S., 78, 388, 390, 401, 402
Google, 76, 382, 386
Grange, Inc., 48, 54; growing pains scores at, 64 *Table* 3.4; management of growing pains scores at, 43–68
Gribi, J., 91
Grim, T., 171
Grocery Outlets, 158
Growing pains. *See* Organizational growing pains
Growing Pains Survey: using measurements of, for making transition, 62–63
Growth rates, 68–69
Gulf Stream, 348

H

Haagen-Dazs, 11
Haines, D., 170–172

Haines, J., 170–172, 182
Haloid Process, 157
Harrison, C. F., 133, 134
Harrison, R., 121–129, 132, 133, 139
Hartshorn, T., 272, 293
Harvard Business School, 391
Harvest Bar (PowerBar), 79
Hawthorne Community Medical Group (HCMG), 45
HCMG. *See* Hawthorne Community Medical Group
Head Start, 8, 12–13, 215, 216, 222–223
Health Maintenance Organization Act (1973), 45
Helix, Inc., 289
Herald Examiner (Los Angeles), 390
Heroes, 310–311
Hertz, 292
Hewlett-Packard, 17, 75, 91, 166, 167, 310, 337, 357, 368, 369, 377, 387
Hilton International, 292
Hollywood Entertainment, 393
Home Depot, 348
Honda, 302
Hong Kong, 80
Hoops, A., 272, 293
Hotmail, 74–75
Hoversen, M., 413, 414
Hughes Aircraft, 153
Hurd, M., 377
Hyundai, 153

I

Iacocca, L., 274, 295
IBM, 17, 36, 41, 75, 76, 82, 90, 91, 159, 166, 217, 242, 365, 367, 369, 377
Il Giornale, 21
Illinois Institute of Technology, 350
Industrial Abrasives, Inc., 165
IndyMac Bank, 63, 347
InfoEnterprise, 193 Fig. 8.3
Infogix, 63, 187, 223; advanced strategic planning and organizational development at, 349–357; growth and development at, 350–351; impact of Demming philosophy on, 351–352; key events in history of, 349–352; organizational transformation at, 353; performance optimization system, 355 *Fig.*13.1; result of transformation to professional management at, 356–357
Infrastructure, 68–69, 343–345
Inner Game of Management, 223
Innovation result area, 41

Integration, 365–367
Intel, 156
International firms, 79–81
International Harvester, 367, 378
Internet firms, 76–77
Italian culture, 21

J

Jacoby & Meyers, 153
Jaguar, 152
Jamba Juice, 36, 45, 77–79, 82
Japan, 13, 157
Japanese automobile industry, 302
JCPenney, 153
J.D. Powers agency, 302
Jobs, S., 3, 75, 274, 275, 370, 430, 431
Johnson & Johnson, 158, 193, 216, 302, 305,
   365–367, 372
J.P. Morgan, 115
Juice Club (Jamba Juice), 79

K

Kelleher, H., 31, 300, 311, 368
Kellogg School, 413
Key result areas, 167–168
Kildall, G., 75
Kimberly Clark, 389
Kmart, 15, 16, 18, 19, 153, 167, 337, 339,
   341, 344
Knight, P., 3, 368
Kodak, 192, 373
Koo Koo Roo, 22
Kotex, 389
Krispy Kreme, 382
Kurland, S., 274, 285, 286, 294

L

Ladies' Home Journal, 156
Lafayette, California, 409
LA-Gear, 344
Language, 307–308
Lapellis, R., 293
Leadership: autocratic style of, 275–276;
   benevolent-autocratic style of, 276; case
   studies, 289–294; consultative style of,
   276–277; continuum of, styles, 275
   Fig.11.1; effective, 272–297; effective, at
   different stages of organizational growth,
   294–297; factors influencing style of,
   280–283; and George Frazer, 289–290; and
   Ken Walker, 290–292; laissez-faire style of,
   279–280; and leader versus, team,
   292–294; nature of, 273–274; participative
   style of, 277; and Richard Ferris, 292;

strategic, 285–286; styles of, 274; styles of,
   in entrepreneurial organizations, 280; team
   style of (consensus style), 278–279;
   theories, 284; and two sets of effective
   tasks for, 284–289
Leadership development, 116–117; and
   change in role concept, 218–220; and
   change in skills possessed, 220–223;
   critical dimensions of, 218–226;
   management development versus, 215;
   nature of, 214–216; and promoting
   leadership style, 217; Pyramid of
   Management, 221, 222
Leadership result area, 41–42, 98–99,
   110
Level One Communications, 156
Levi Strauss, 367
Liederman, D., 78, 82
LifeScan, 305, 365–366
Likert, R., 286
Lincoln, 153
Lindsay Olive Company, 231
Loeb, D., 285
Loro Piana (Italy), 80
Los Angeles, California, 29, 80, 153,
   388, 392
Lowe's, 348
Lowry, P., 420
Lowry, S., 420
Lowy, F., 79, 80
Lufthansa, 87
Lurian, I., 31

M

Macintosh (Apple Computer), 82, 367
Macro structure, 189–190
Macy's, 153
Mall of America (Minneapolis, Minnesota),
   369, 402
Management: development, 116–117,
   131–132, 214–242; difference between
   entrepreneurial and professional, 38–42;
   review, 169–170; transformation to
   professional, 117
Management development: and case of
   Bell-Carter Foods, Inc., 231–238; and
   change in individual's psychology,
   223–224; and change in role concept,
   218–220; and change in skills possessed,
   220–223; and critical aspects of
   management development transitions,
   229–230; critical dimensions of, 218–226;
   and enhancing management skills,
   216–217; functions of, 216–218; *versus*

Management development: and case of Bell-Carter Foods, Inc., *(continued)* leadership development, 215; nature of, 214–216; pyramid of, 221 *Fig.* 9.1, 222; required at different organizational levels, 226–230

Management systems, 145 *Fig.* III.1; developing, 16–17, 22, 341–342; at different stages of growth, 433–434

Managers: rewarding and recognizing, 217–218

Market, defining, 9–12, 21, 82, 89–91; and market analysis, 151–152; and market niche, 157–160, 339–340; and market segment, 152–154

Market duopolies, 348

Mason, B., 438–448

Massachusetts Institute of Technology (MIT), 192

Mattel, 362

Maxicare, 36, 50–51, 56, 61–62, 86, 88, 365, 402; Pacificare *versus,* 45–46

Maxwell, B., 12, 79, 82, 402

Maxwell, J., 12, 79, 82, 402

MCA Entertainment, 31

McDonald's, 17, 160

McLaughlin, M., 413

Medafor, 385, 386

Medco Enterprises, 197, 438–448

Melvin Simon & Associates, 215, 369

Mercedes, 152, 154, 241

Metro Realty, 50, 51, 54, 94–112, 116, 120, 246; and declining economy, 105–106; growing pains at, 96–99; loss of personnel at, 104–105; making transition at, 100–104; old *versus* new, 107–108; organizational development program, 101–102; problems encountered at, 104–106; program outcomes at, 106–112; and resistance to change, 106

MGA Entertainment, 362

Micro structure, 189–190

Microsoft, 10, 11, 20, 45, 74, 75, 156, 159, 192, 311, 314, 337, 340, 430; divisions, 192; Vision Version 2, 315. *See also* MS-DOS operating system

Milan, Italy, 20, 21

Mileage Plus, 292

Mission, 165

Mitchell, B., 95–96

MITS Computing, 314

Monaghan, T. S., 30, 78, 82, 184, 311

Mortenson, J., 290–291

Motorola, 217

Mountain View, California, 324

Mövenpick, 364, 367

Mozilo, A., 41–42, 273, 274, 285, 348, 370

Mrs. Fields' Cookies, 77–78, 82, 88

MS-DOS operating system (Microsoft), 76, 314

M-type divisional structure, 193

Musco Foods, 348

N

Cents Only Stores, 77–78, 153, 387–392, 397, 401, 402; genesis and gestation of, 389; growth of, 390; origins of,D 388

Naperville, Illinois, 352

NASDAQ, 393, 396

National Basketball Association, 344

National Lead, 367

Navistar, 378

Nayar, M., 277, 349–351, 353, 355

NBC, 156

NEC, 367

Neiman-Marcus, 153

Nestlé, 11, 79, 160, 347, 367, 380, 401

Neupogen (Amgen), 337, 340

Neutrogena, 305, 365–366

New venture stage (Stage I), 29–31; developing successful organizations at, 73; developmental emphasis in, 30*Fig.*2.1; key issues at, 73–81

New York Stock Exchange (NYSE), 387, 390, 401

NEXT Software, Inc., 431

Niche, *versus* segment, 157

Nike, 3, 20, 91, 156, 344, 368, 374

Nissan, 302

Noah's Bagels, 30, 36, 77–78

Nordstrom Department Stores, 303

Norms, 17, 299, 342

O

Objectives and goals, 168–169

O'Melveny & Meyers, 153

Omidyar, P., 76, 77, 79, 82

Operational leadership, 130, 274; and, 287; in entrepreneurial organizations, 288–289; goal emphasis of, 286–287; and interaction facilitation, 287; key tasks of, 286–289; and personnel development, 288; and supportive behavior, 288; work facilitation, 287–288; and work facilitation, 287–288

Operational management skills, 222

Operational systems, developing, 21–22, 88–91, 341

Oracle Corporation, 362

Organization result area, 39

Organizational control systems, 243–271; and case of Southern California Presbyterian Homes, 262–269; design and evaluation of effectiveness of, 254–257; design of, 246–251; at different stages of organizational growth, 269–271; and dysfunctional behavior, 256–257; and increased goal congruence, 256; nature of, 244–245; and organizational scoreboard, 251–254

Organizational development: discrepancies between growth and, 42–43; formulating plan for, 44; and foundation of business, 8–9; implementing and monitoring plan for, 44–45; nature of, 8–18; plan, 436; pyramid of, 10 *Fig.* 1.1, 18–25; six key organizational development tasks, 9–18; skills, 10*Fig.* 1.1; strategic, defined, 345–346

Organizational development, pyramid of, 18–25; focus on, as whole, 23–24; implications of, 18–19; as lens to build and evaluate organizations, 20; research support for, 19–20; six key drivers of, 19; and Starbucks, 20–24

Organizational evaluation, 44

Organizational growing pains: causes of, 43*Fig.* 2.5; by company size, 60*Table* 3.2; in different industries, 61*Table* 3.3; and financial performance, 69; growth rates, infrastructure and, 68–69; interpretation of survey scores for, 59*Table* 3.1; measuring, 57–68; minimizing, 69–70; nature of, 48–49; questionnaire, 58; recognizing, 48–70; ten most common, 49–57

Organizational growth: advanced stages of, 361*Table* 14.1; beyond stage IV, 360–361; consolidation stage of (IV), 37–38; discrepancies between, and organizational development, 42–43; expansion stage of (II), 31–33; identifying and surviving first four stages of, 26–46; managing transition between stages of, 43–47; new venture stage of, 29–31; new venture stage of (I), 29–31; professionalization stage of (III), 33–37; stages of, 26–43, 27*Fig.*2.1

Organizational hierarchy, 201–202

Organizational infrastructure, 343–345

Organizational scoreboard, 251–254, 252; illustration of, 252; as improved version of Balanced Score Card (BSC), 252–254

Organizational structure, 188–213; alternative forms of, 190–195; case studies of, 204–210; and controls, 116; criteria for evaluation and design of, 195–204; of Design Corporation, 204–206; at different stages of growth, 210–212; divisional, 192–194; of GoodEats, Inc., 207–208; of Hitek Manufacturing, 206; matrix, 194–1954; nature of, 189; of Pardee Homes, 208–209; of Starbucks Coffee, 209–210; three levels of, 189–190

Osborne, A., 33, 75, 82, 84, 85

Osborne Computer, 33, 35, 42, 45, 56, 62, 75, 369; *versus* Compaq, 89–91; and Osborne syndrome, 84–87, 118

Ossur, 183

P

PacifiCare Health Systems, 46, 70, 187, 272, 293; *versus* Maxicare, 45–46

Page, S., 130–133

Pardee, G., 208

Pardee Homes, 63, 187, 192

PC-DOS operating system, 76

Peet's Coffee, 344

People Express, 45, 56, 62, 87, 88, 344, 386

PeopleSupport: background, 392–393; decision to go public, 393–394; going public, 394–396; success of, 396–397

PepsiCo, 210, 222, 430

Performance appraisal, 98, 110

Performance management systems, 245–246; and case of Superior Alarm Systems, 246–250; and feedback or reporting system, 249; goals, 248; key components of, 246–250; key result areas, 247; and measurement, 248–249; model of, 247*Fig.* 10.1; objectives, 247–248; and performance evaluation, 249–250; and rewards, 250

Performance optimization, 355–356

Perron, K., 79, 82

Perry, D., 104, 105

Perry, M., 347

Personal computers, 75–76

Personnel development, 288

Personnel, loss of, 104–105

Peter Principle, 41

Pez dispensers, 76–77

PHH Mortgage, 158
Philippines, 393, 394, 397
Pike Place Market (Seattle, Washington), 20
Planning result area, 39, 97, 109
Plastic Molding Corporation, 191
PowerBar, 11, 30, 36, 63, 77–79, 187, 347, 380, 401, 402
Prager, U., 364
Prefunctional organizational structure, 191
Price Institute for Entrepreneurial Studies, 216
PricewaterhouseCoopers, 386
Pringles (Scotland), 80
Procter & Gamble, 365, 367
Productization, 12, 13
Products, developing, 12–13, 21, 82–83, 89–91; and ability to develop organization to provide, 83
Professional management: comparison, 40*Table* 2.2; *versus* entrepreneurial, 38–42; mastering tools of, 143–146; willingness to transform to, 117
Professionalization stage (III), 33–37, 93–118; at American Century Investors, 114–115; and case of Metro Realty, 95–112; developing successful organization at, 94–95; developmental emphasis in, 35*Fig.*2.3; at Federal Express, 112–113; keys to success in, 115–117; at Starbucks, 113–114
Profit result area, 39
Project Oxygen (Infogix), 352
Proof of concept, 73–74
Public company: advantages of becoming, 381; disadvantages of becoming, 380–381; and making decision to go public, 379–381; making transition to, 379–398; operating as, 383–387; transition from family business to, 387–392; and transition from private to public, 381–383; and transition from small privately held company to small, 392–397
Pyramid of Management and Leadership Development, 221–222, 227, 228
Pyramid of Organizational Development, 18–25, 274, 285, 303, 304, 321, 432

Q
Quaker Oats Company, 413
Quality, 302
Qureshey, S., 381

R
Radican, P., 46
Recruiting, 99, 111
Reebok, 344
Reel.com, 393
Reporting requirements, 384
Resources, acquiring, 13–14, 21–22, 87–88, 340–341
Responsibilities, management, 97, 109, 189
Result areas, key, 167–168
Reuters, 367
Revitalization: case study, 377–378; and corporate culture, 377; decline and, 367–369; and management systems, 376–377; and markets, 374; and operational systems, 375–376; and products, 374–375; and resources, 375; special challenge of, 373–377
Reward system, 250
Rewards, 310–311
Richard A. Goodman Strategic Planning Award, 187, 342
Rituals, 309–310
Robbins Bros., 339, 340
Roddick, A., 79
Rodgers, T. J., 373
Roles, management, 97, 109, 189, 218–220; change in, concept, 218–220, 233
Rolls-Royce, 153, 154
Rosenzweig, L., 392–397
Royce Medical Corporation, 148, 187, 215, 217, 236, 302, 341; addressing key strategic issues at, 175–178; background, 170–172; budgeting process at, 178–180; departmental and individual planning at, 182; development of strategic plan at, 170–183; environmental scan and organizational assessment, 172–175; quarterly management review and implementing, 181; results of planning effort at, 182; retreat, 174–175; strategic statement of, 177; written strategic business plan of, 178, 179–180
Rule of Three, 348
Ryan, M., 133

S
Saks Fifth Avenue, 153
Sambol, D., 294
Sarbanes-Oxley Act, 91, 257, 379, 383, 385–386
Saturday Evening Post, 156
Saunders, J., 80
Scaling-up, 83

Scheib, E., 29

Schiffer, E., 390

Schultz, H., 3, 14, 20–22, 36, 113, 209, 272, 274, 285, 287, 293, 303, 343, 370, 430

Schwinn, 364

Scios, 365–366

SCPH. *See* Southern California Presbyterian Homes

Sculley, J., 430

Sears, 15, 16, 367

Seattle, Washington, 20, 285

Security and Exchange Commission (SEC), 384, 385, 394

Segment, niche *versus,* 157

Separate islands syndrome, 123

Services, developing, 12–13, 82–83; and ability to develop organization to provide, 83

Shirley, J., 314

Siefker, J., 293

Simon, F., 369, 401, 402

Simon, H., 369, 401, 402

Simon, M., 369, 401, 402

Simon Properties, 215, 369, 401, 402

Situational analysis, 163

Situational leadership, 274

Size, strategic aspects of, 347–349

Sloan, A. P., 192

Smith Corona, 364

Smith, F. W., 78, 82, 112, 113, 116

Smith, O., 22, 36, 210, 272, 293

Southern California Presbyterian Homes (SCPH), 8, 262–269; design of new performance appraisal forms at, 265–267; revision of job descriptions at, 265; training in conducting effective performance appraisals at, 268; use of new performance appraisal form at, 267–268

Southwest Airlines, 17, 31, 77–78, 120, 159, 161, 299–300, 301, 302–303, 310–312, 341, 343, 344–345, 368

Spirit magazine, 343

Springfield, Missouri, 412

Sprint, 349

Stage I firm. *See* New venture stage

Stanford University, 76, 348

Starbucks, 3, 12, 14, 17, 20–25, 35, 36, 45, 70, 93, 116–117, 159–161, 164, 187, 210, 272, 285, 287, 293, 300, 303, 305, 343, 344, 346, 348, 365, 382, 387, 430; professionalization at, 113–114; six guiding principles of, 23

Stealth advantages, 346

Stock options, 387

Stowers, J. Jr., 273, 279, 293, 294

Strategic board, 152

Strategic business plan, 162–169

Strategic leadership, 129, 274, 285–286

Strategic Mission Statement, 159, 164–165

Strategic planning, 116, 131, 147–187; and analysis and resolution of key strategic issues, 155–162; at different stages of organizational growth, 183–186; and environmental scan, 150–154; and management review, 169–170; nature of, 148–149; and organizational assessment, 154–155; process, 150–170, 151*Fig. 7.1;* redefining, 345; and strategic business plan, 162–169

Strategic planning, advanced, 335–358; and business as game, 335; and concept of stealth advantages, 346; and creating sustainable advantage, 336–337; and Infogix, 349–357; and meaning of winning, 336; and strategic aspects of size, 347–349; and using Pyramid of Organizational Development as source of competitive advantage, 338–343

Strategy: competitive, 336; definition of, 148, 166–167; issues, 149–150; supporting, 161, 162; three levels of, 160*Fig.7.3*

Student magazine (Branson), 81

Sun Microsystems, 357

Superior Alarm Systems: development of control systems at, 258–260; and performance management systems at organizational level, 257–262

Supporting systems, 190

Supportive behavior, 288

Sustainable advantage, 337–338

Switzerland, 364

Symbols, 308–309

T

3M, 171

Tandy Corporation, 314

Tang Hsiang Chien, 80

Target, 349

Tata family, 79

Technology Systems Corporation, 290–292

Teledyne, 193

Tempo Products, 50–54, 56, 245, 246, 274, 313, 318; background of, 121; culture management at, 133–134; decision makers at, 123–125, 135–136; elements of culture at, and attenuation, 121–129; family atmosphere at, 122–123; management development at, 131–132; new products culture and implementation at, 134–140;

Tempo Products, *(continued)*
  organizational design, 129–134; playing by
  ear at, 126–127, 137; redefining culture at,
  129–134; spirit of fun at, 127; strategic
  planning at, 131; uniqueness of, 125–126
Texas, 161
Texas Instruments, 75
The Body Shop, 79–80
The Simon Institute (Simon Properties), 215
Toyota, 302
Training and development, 99, 111
Transition management skills, 222
Transitions: managing, at Stage V, 370–371;
  managing, at Stage VI, 371–372;
  managing, at Stage VII, 372–373
Tse, A., 79–80, 83
Tse Cashmere, 77–78
TSYS, 349
Twentieth Century Investors, 293

U
UAL Corporation, 210, 292
Ultraspace Corporation, 194
Underwriters, 382
Unitech Systems, 349, 353
United Airlines, 210, 292, 312, 344
United Health Care, 46
United Kingdom, 89
United States automobile manufacturers, 13
United States Bankruptcy Code, 46
United States television manufacturers, 13
Universal Pre-School Initiative (California),
  187
University of California, Los Angeles, 184,
  216
University of Texas, 12, 76
University of Washington, 20
UPS, 348
Urumqi, China, 80
U.S. Department of Defense, 153
U.S. Food and Drug Administration (FDS),
  385
U.S. Steel, 13, 367

V
Values, 17, 299, 342
Vaughn, B., 79

Verizon, 349
Virgin Group of Companies, 79, 81
Visage International, 420
Vision, strategic, 285–286
Volvo, 153

W
Wager, D., 210
Walker, K., 290–292
Wal-Mart, 15, 16, 18, 19, 153, 161, 167, 307,
  337–339, 341, 344, 349, 368, 387; sample
  operations strategies for, 163*Table. 7.2*
Walton, S., 16, 275, 368
Wang Laboratories, 386
Wasserman, F., 45, 46, 402
Wayner, J., 389, 390
Web sites, 311–312
Web Van, 12
Webster, K., 178
Welsh, J., 276
Westfield Group, 79–81, 215–216,
  420
Westin Hotels, 292
Weyerhauser Company, 208
Weyerhauser Real Estate Company,
  208
Whitman, M., 77
Whole Food Markets, 79
Wienholz, K., 413, 414
Windham Hill Productions,
  215
Wooden, J., 184
WorldCom, 257
Wozniak, S., 75, 370

X
Xerox, 13, 157, 367
Xinjiang province (China), 80

Y
Yahoo!, 76
YPO (Young President's Organization),
  420

Z
Zell, S., 91